Mike Walsh

Sams **Teach Yourself**

SharePoint® Foundation 2010

in **24 Hours**

SAMS 800 East 96th Street, Indianapolis, Indiana, 46240 USA

Sams Teach Yourself SharePoint Foundation 2010 in 24 Hours

ISBN-13: 978-0-672-33316-3

ISBN-10: 0-672-33316-3

This material may be distributed only subject to the terms and conditions set forth in the Open Publication License, v1.0 or later (the latest version is presently available at http://www.opencontent.org/openpub/).

Library of Congress Cataloging-in-Publication Data:

Walsh, Mike, 1947-
  Sams teach yourself SharePoint foundation 2010 in 24 hours / Mike Walsh.
      p. cm.
  ISBN 978-0-672-33316-3
  1. Intranets (Computer networks) 2. Microsoft SharePoint (Electronic resource) 3. Web servers. I. Title.
  TK5105.875.I6W353 2010
  004.67'8—dc22
                                    2010018993

Printed in the United States on America

Trademarks

All terms mentioned in this book that are known to be trademarks or service marks have been appropriately capitalized. Sams Publishing cannot attest to the accuracy of this information. Use of a term in this book should not be regarded as affecting the validity of any trademark or service mark.

Warning and Disclaimer

Every effort has been made to make this book as complete and as accurate as possible, but no warranty or fitness is implied. The information provided is on an "as is" basis. The author and the publisher shall have neither liability nor responsibility to any person or entity with respect to any loss or damages arising from the information contained in this book.

Bulk Sales

Sams Publishing offers excellent discounts on this book when ordered in quantity for bulk purchases or special sales. For more information, please contact

U.S. Corporate and Government Sales
1-800-382-3419
corpsales@pearsontechgroup.com

For sales outside of the U.S., please contact

International Sales

international@pearsoned.com

Editor-in-Chief
Karen Gettman

Executive Editor
Neil Rowe

Acquisitions Editor
Brook Farling

Development Editors
Sheri Cain
Mark Renfrow

Managing Editor
Kristy Hart

Project Editor
Anne Goebel

Copy Editor
Apostrophe Editing Services

Indexer
WordWise Publishing Services LLC

Proofreader
Language Logistics

Technical Editor
Steve Mann

Publishing Coordinator
Cindy Teeters

Book Designer
Gary Adair

Composition
Jake McFarland
Nonie Ratcliff

Contents at a Glance

Table of Contents

About the Author

Mike Walsh has been a SharePoint MVP since October 2002. He works as a technology consultant for Logica in Finland, having spent all but 1 year of his working life living and working in various European countries outside his native Britain.

Mike became an MVP for the SharePoint Team Services (STS) product through actively sharing his STS knowledge in the newsgroup for that product. He has continued to be active in SharePoint newsgroups and (now) forums, mainly for Windows SharePoint Services for both versions 2.0 and 3.0. He has worked on the Ask the Experts stand at several Microsoft European conferences over the years. He was an early beta tester for Office 2003, including WSS 2.0; Office 2007, including WSS 3.0; and Office 2010 including SPF 2010.

Mike wrote *Sams Teach Yourself SharePoint 2007: Using Windows SharePoint Services 3.0* and has contributed a chapter to each of the SharePoint MVP books, *Real World SharePoint 2007* and *Real World SharePoint 2010*.

We Want to Hear from You

As the reader of this book, you are our most important critic and commentator. We value your opinion and want to know what we're doing right, what we could do better, what areas you'd like to see us publish in, and any other words of wisdom you're willing to pass our way.

You can email or write me directly to let me know what you did or didn't like about this book—as well as what we can do to make our books stronger.

Please note that I cannot help you with technical problems related to the topic of this book, and that due to the high volume of mail I receive, I might not be able to reply to every message.

When you write, please be sure to include this book's title and author, as well as your name and contact information. I will carefully review your comments and share them with the author and editors who worked on the book.

Email: neil.rowe@pearsoned.com
Mail: Neil Rowe
         Executive Editor
         201 West 103rd Street
         Indianapolis, IN 46290 USA

Introduction

I've concentrated in this Introduction on just four things.

First, on the target audience for the book because I think that it is important that people don't read this book with the wrong impression about who it will be useful for.

Second, I've tried to make it completely clear that this is a book about SharePoint Foundation 2010 the product. Yes, people about to use SharePoint Server 2010 should find it useful, but it's not a book about SharePoint Server 2010.

Third, I wanted to give you a quick reference here to what is covered in the hours. Hour titles are one thing, but a bit more meat was necessary and needed to be in a single place for easy reference.

Fourth, in saying what a cheap machine I used for this book, I wanted you to be aware that despite the official Microsoft line that you need really powerful machines with fast expensive processors, lots of internal memory, and fast SSD drives, it's possible to take a portable computer from a rack in a department store and use that for running SharePoint Foundation 2010. So don't let those official Microsoft guidelines put you off working through this book on a personal machine.

Target Audience for This Book

This book has been written as a training guide for three main groups of people:

▶ Users and administrators who need to learn the basics of SharePoint 2010

▶ Programmers who are now required to write SharePoint 2010 programs and need a basic introduction to what SharePoint 2010 supplies out-of-the-box before they do so

▶ Users of Office 2003, 2007, and 2010 who can make use of the options in those products in connecting to SharePoint sites

The book's main focus is to provide basic information on SharePoint 2010 for users and administrators with the Teach Yourself approach. Users can find the administration sections interesting, whereas administrators need to know that because this is a general book rather than a specialist administration book, it covers the basic issues well but only dips into those administration options required to follow the other hours of the book. Programmers can gain knowledge of unique situations and features, and Office users can appreciate hours on the interaction of Office products with SharePoint systems, which most books fail to cover; SharePoint Foundation 2010 is entirely sufficient as the SharePoint end of the combination. Because users often work in environments with back versions of Office, the differences in Office 2007 and Office 2003 are often indicated.

What This Book Covers and What It Doesn't

The book is almost entirely about SharePoint Foundation 2010 (SPF 2010), with some comments on additional functionality available only with SharePoint Server 2010 (SPS 2010).

Reading this book can be advantageous for the target audience if they have (or will have) SPS 2010 because that product is SPF 2010 with additional (and usually complicated) functionality.

By the Way

> Programmers without any SharePoint knowledge can find this book useful as a source for the background information they need about SharePoint before they read a SharePoint Programming book.

It is easier to acquire the basics of SharePoint Server 2010 by initially excluding all the additional complications that SPS 2010 offers. In addition, using a SharePoint Foundation 2010 installation makes it much easier for people without their own SharePoint test environments to create them without needing to spend a fortune on hardware.

This book looks at some of the things that you can do with SharePoint Designer 2010, such as creating workflows that provide more than the basic workflow included in SPF 2010. This book does not go into many details of how to use SharePoint Designer 2010 to customize a SPF 2010 site. In other words, if you are looking for a book on "branding" SPF 2010 sites, you should look elsewhere.

Another area of improvement to the built-in SPF 2010 website that is not covered here is the use of Visual Studio 2010 to create completely new functionality. SharePoint experts are usually divided between the Development experts who know a lot about SharePoint programming (typically using Visual Studio 2010) and the administration experts who know a lot about installing and using SharePoint (and typically little about development). There are (many) specialist books on Share-Point Development more suitable for SharePoint programmers, and adding a mini section on Visual Studio here would serve little useful purpose.

Organization of This Book

This isn't a reference book with every list type and parameter described, focusing on a few more commonly used elements in some detail.

The chapters in each section of the book were written in order. Because this book was written with a working SharePoint test system, some sites or lists in a few places might not match what you actually see on your computer. Don't bother about this because everything you need *will* be visible.

Hour 11, "Using What We've Learned So Far in a Site," considers a universally understood solution area and how the things you have learned up to this hour can be applied to that one solution area. The idea is to provide an example of the thinking that goes behind the creation of a site. Apart from this one example (and it is just an example, nothing more), the book offers building blocks you can use in any kind of SharePoint site that you need to create. Learning what sort of things to use for that sample solution area should help you in creating sites for your real-world scenarios.

This book is divided into five sections:

▶ **Part I, "The Basics,"** (Hours 1–12) covers the basics.

▶ **Part II, "Search,"** (Hours 13–14) covers the built-in search function and how to enhance that with Search Server 2010 Express.

▶ **Part III, "Working with Office Products,"** (Hours 15–20) covers the combination of Microsoft Office products and SPF 2010.

▶ **Part IV, "Workflow and SPD 2010,"** (Hours 21–23) deals with adding workflows (in general and with SPD 2010) and some other nonbranding functions available when using SPD 2010.

▶ **Part V, "Other Available Functions and Methods,"** (Hour 24) reviews the other functions and methods available to enhance your sites and includes some useful book references for further reading.

The hours include the following:

▶ **Hour 1, "Introducing SharePoint Foundation 2010,"** introduces SharePoint Foundation 2010.

▶ Hour 2, "**Installing SharePoint Foundation 2010**," gives details of how to install the standalone (basic) installation of SPF 2010 on a single server running Windows Server 2008 R2.

▶ Hour 3, "**Adding Users and Giving Them Rights**" discusses the various types of users, creates users required later, and then gives them rights to access the SPF 2010 site.

▶ Hour 4, "**Using the Administration Site**," looks at the (Central) Administration site and looks at some common actions using it.

▶ Hour 5, "**Planning a Site's Structure**," describes the different types of sites and how (and when) to create them.

▶ Hour 6, "**Using Libraries and Lists**," is an introduction to libraries and lists and to the relationship between a list and the web part of a list (List View Web Part).

▶ Hour 7, "**Creating and Using Libraries**" looks at the different types of libraries and at how to add files to Picture Libraries and Document Libraries.

▶ Hour 8, "**Creating and Using Views and Folders**," describes how to create and use views and why you shouldn't use folders.

▶ Hour 9, "**Looking at List Types and the Included Web Parts**," continues looking at lists and then looks at the web parts that come with the product that aren't directly related to Lists.

▶ Hour 10, "**Learning About Authentication and Access Rights**," includes more information about authentication and shows how you can change the user being used to access a site or a web page.

▶ Hour 11, "**Using What We've Learned So Far in a Site**," takes a practical working case in which SPF 2010 is used and shows how data is collected and then used to build a suitable site structure.

▶ Hour 12, "**Using Wikis and Blogs**," looks at the standard Wiki and Blog functions provided by SPF 2010.

▶ Hour 13, "**Using SPF 2010 Search and Installing Search Server 2010 Express**," covers the standard SPF 2010 search function and then installs the free Search Server 2010 Express product to (in Hour 14) improve the search function.

▶ Hour 14, "**Improving Searches**," shows the additional possibilities for search offered when Search Server 2010 Express has been installed on top of SPF 2010.

▶ **Hour 15, "Using Different Versions of the Main Office Products with SPF 2010,"** looks at how various versions of the main Office products work with SPF 2010.

▶ **Hour 16, "Using Outlook 2010 with SPF 2010,"** describes what functionality is available when Outlook 2010 is used with SPF 2010. Brief mention is made of the differences when using the earlier versions of Outlook.

▶ **Hour 17, "Sharing OneNote 2010 or OneNote 2007 Notebooks with SPF 2010,"** describes how you can store OneNote 2010 and 2007 notebooks in a SPF 2010 site.

▶ **Hour 18, "Sharing Access 2010 Tables with SPF 2010,"** describes the various methods available of combining Access tables with SPF 2010.

▶ **Hour 19, "Producing a Report from a Single SPF 2010 List,"** describes how to use the Report Wizard in Access 2010 to create reports from a single SPF 2010 list.

▶ **Hour 20, "Creating a Report from Several SPF 2010 Lists,"** shows how you can produce reports that combine the data from two or more SharePoint lists.

▶ **Hour 21, "Creating Workflows in SPF 2010,"** gives a general overview to workflows with SPF 2010 and shows how to create the built-in three-stage workflow.

▶ **Hour 22, "Using SharePoint Designer 2010 to Create Workflows,"** shows how to use SharePoint Designer 2010 to produce more complicated workflows than those described in Hour 21.

▶ **Hour 23, "Using SharePoint Designer 2010 to Solve Common User Requests,"** looks further into some standard SharePoint Designer 2010 possibilities.

▶ **Hour 24, "Learning to Add Even More Functionality to Your SPF 2010 System,"** looks at several additional possibilities for enhancing SPF 2010 sites and also at additional functionality available only by upgrading to SPS 2010.

Hardware and Software Used in This Book

▶ A cheap, commercial HP portable with a middle-of-the-road AMD processor, 4GB, and 500GB hard disk was bought and used for both the usual client (Office 2010) software and for the VM (running SPF 2010) because my existing portables had 2GB memory that led to slow (but not impossible) usage.

▶ The 32-bit operating system that came with the machine was replaced with 64-bit Windows 7 (to make all the 4GB memory usable).

- ▶ VM Workstation 7.0 was used for the virtual machines.

- ▶ 64-bit Office 2010 installed in Windows 7.

- ▶ Windows Server 2008 R2 installed in the Virtual Machine (VM).

- ▶ SharePoint Foundation 2010 was installed in that VM.

- ▶ Screenshots were created using SnagIt! from TechSmith (installed in Windows 7; http://www.techsmith.com/screen-capture.asp).

- ▶ A 3-year-old portable running Vista and (only) Office 2007 was used for the Office 2007 tests in the Office + SharePoint hours.

- ▶ A 6-year-old portable running XP Pro and (only) Office 2003, both updated to the latest possible level, was used for the Office 2003 tests.

PART I

The Basics

HOUR 1

Introducing SharePoint Foundation 2010

What You'll Learn in This Hour

- ▶ The main SharePoint 2010 products
- ▶ A brief history of the product range
- ▶ Why study SPF 2010 and not SPS 2010?
- ▶ The interaction between Office and SPF 2010
- ▶ Why do we spend time here installing SPF 2010?

This hour gives you an idea of what SharePoint products can be used for. It also includes some information about the different SharePoint products that became available in 2010 and how we got here from the start in 2001.

Getting Familiar with the SharePoint 2010 Products

Since the beginning in 2001, SharePoint products have been used to quickly and easily create a website that is useful out-of-the-box.

The product that this book deals with is SharePoint Foundation 2010 (SPF 2010). Throughout the life of the SharePoint products, there have always been two different main products at different price points and at different levels of complexity. Share-Point Foundation 2010 is the fourth product in the "virtually free" line, with Share-Point Server 2010 (SPS 2010) the fourth product in the line of expensive (and complicated) products.

Unlike previous versions of SharePoint that initially were available in only 32-bit versions and later in both 32-bit and 64-bit versions, the present 2010 versions are 64-bit only. They can however still be used with 32- or 64-bit versions of Office and can still be amended using both 32- and 64-bit versions of SharePoint Designer 2010 (SPD 2010). (See Hour 22, "Using SharePoint Designer 2010 to Create Workflows," and Hour 23, "Using SharePoint Designer 2010 to Solve Common User Requests.") Note, however, that the use of SPD 2010 for branding sites is not covered in this book.

Brief Comparison of SharePoint Products

Table 1.1 simplifies the two main subranges and how their relationship has developed over time.

TABLE 1.1   Overview of the Two SharePoint Lines

Year	Services Line	Portal Line
2001	SharePoint Team Services	SharePoint Portal Server 2001
2003	Windows SharePoint Services 2.0	SharePoint Portal Server 2003
2007	Windows SharePoint Services 3.0	Microsoft Office SharePoint Server 2007
2010	SharePoint Foundation 2010	SharePoint Server 2010

SharePoint Team Services (STS) and SharePoint Portal Server 2001 (SPS 2001) were two completely different products that had nothing much in common except the name and that both were used to create websites.

An installation of SPS 2003 first started by installing a full copy of WSS 2.0 before seamlessly going on to install additional SPS 2003 items on top of it.

Moving on to the 2007 products, a lot of functionality was added to the server before either product was installed. That functionality was (unfortunately, because it led to confusion) known as the WSS 3.0 "Technology." When the technology was in place, there were two completely different installation routines for WSS 3.0 (the application) and for MOSS 2007.

Whereas a WSS 3.0 (application) installation used the WSS 3.0 technology to create a fairly standard website, a MOSS 2007 installation used the WSS 3.0 technology but added a lot of its own functionality to it and thus created a much more powerful and multiwebsite system.

Because both products used WSS 3.0 technology, WSS 3.0 fixes and service packs and so on applied to both WSS 3.0 (application) and to MOSS 2007 installations. MOSS 2007 fixes and service packs however applied only to MOSS 2007. There were no fixes and service packs that were only for the WSS 3.0 application, showing that the WSS 3.0 application added no additional functionality to that provided in the WSS 3.0 technology.

The situation is the same as with the 2010 products. There is a technology that is still confusingly called by the same name as the "series" product SPF 2010. Again there are different installations for the two products with SPF 2010 (application) creating a website based entirely on using the functionality in the SPF 2010 technology and with SPS 2010 creating a set of websites that use the same functionality but which also add many additional functions to the SPF 2010 technology.

The SharePoint 2010 products can be installed only on 64-bit hardware running 64-bit operating systems and are themselves 64-bit only.

The one main exception is SharePoint Designer 2010, which is available in both 32-bit and 64-bit versions. You can use either version with an SP 2010 product. SPD 2010 is, however, an Office client product.

By the way

Why Study SPF 2010 Rather Than SPS 2010?

This book is about installing and using the free product called SharePoint Foundation 2010. Because, however, this product was created using the functions provided by the SPF 2010 technology and because SPS 2010 also uses that technology (and creates sites based on it), the book can also be used to gain knowledge of the basic fundamentals of SPS 2010, while avoiding all the additional complications that product's additional functions bring.

For people completely new to the SharePoint products, starting with SPF 2010 is what I recommend because otherwise you might well be learning about the additional functions provided by SPS 2010 while not being aware of the basics of that product.

Both SPF 2010 and SPS 2010 are designed to be usable out-of-the-box. As you see in Hour 2, "Installing SharePoint Foundation 2010," the final installation phase of SPF 2010 actually opens a ready-made website that you can tweak and customize as you see fit.

Most changes are possible through using ready-made functions and require no additional software. Some of the changes are possible with the use of the SharePoint Designer 2010 free tool; its sole function is to work with SharePoint 2010 sites.

Because SPD 2010 can work only with SharePoint 2010 sites, if you also have WSS 3.0 or MOSS 2007 (or even WSS 2.0 or SPS 2003) sites to administrate, you should keep a copy of SPD 2007 handy for them. I recommend that it should be on a different client machine. If you must have both products on the same client machine, use the 32-bit versions of both of them.

By the *Way*

Office 2010 client applications and client applications of another Office release level (typically Office 2007 but possibly Office 2003) should not be used on the same client system. Earlier SharePoint releases have been badly affected by such "mixed" systems, and it's probable that similar problems might be experienced with the SharePoint 2010 products.

Did you *Know?*

Microsoft does not charge for SPF 2010. However, to run it, you need to have a suitable operating system (a suitable version of 64-bit Windows Server 2008 or—for testing and perhaps development only—a copy of 64-bit Windows 7), and you need to pay full product and licensing costs for that.

If you also want to use a full copy of SQL Server 2008 instead of the free copy of SQL Server 2008 Express included in a Basic Installation (or in the Advanced Installation + Single-Server option), you need to pay full product and licensing costs for that.

Typically, you will start using SPF 2010 on a single server installation using the built-in database system, and when you run out of power and database space, you will move up to a two-server system in which the first server runs SPF 2010 and the second server runs SQL Server 2008 (full). Adding the extra server adds both to your server costs and your database system costs. The resulting system is however still considerably cheaper than an SPS 2010 system of any size.

The Interaction Between Office and SPF 2010

The interaction between the Office 2010 range and SPF 2010 is not identical to that between the Office 2007 range and WSS 3.0. Thus the various sections on the cooperation between Office and SharePoint will now look—as far as space and logic permits—at the differences in what can be achieved through Office 2003/Office 2007/Office 2010, respectively, and SPF 2010.

If the client system runs Office 2007, the functions available for the SPF 2010/Office combination are equivalent to those provided for a WSS 3.0/Office 2007 combination. Similarly if the client system is running Office 2003, the functions available for the

SPF 2010/Office combination are equivalent to those provided for a WSS 2.0/Office 2003 combination.

There is little point in rushing an upgrade to SPF 2010 from (say) WSS 3.0 if all you are interested in is Office/SharePoint interaction; if you are forced to keep your client systems at Office 2007 level; and if you are prepared to sacrifice the administration improvements in SPF 2010. It should be noted that there are a lot of "ifs" there, though.

Did you Know?

Another thing that is relevant in connection with the combination of Office and SharePoint is that in most cases this combination works identically whether the SharePoint system in use is the full SharePoint (SPS 2010) or the free SharePoint (SPF 2010). If you are, for instance, storing your Outlook attachments in a SharePoint site so that readers of your email always see the latest copy of the attached document (and not simply the version that was current at the time you sent the email), it makes no difference whether the SharePoint system you store it in is SPF 2010 or SPS 2010. It does however make a difference if you use Outlook 2010 or Outlook 2007 because inexplicably this function is no longer present in Outlook 2010.

It's always been the case that the best interaction between Office and the latest version of SharePoint is through the use on the client of Office products of the latest generation. Development of SPF 2010 and Office 2010 has been parallel and on the same time scale, thus any new features in the SPF 2010/ office combination are available only if the Office on the client system is Office 2010.

Did you Know?

On the other hand, if you attend presentations of SharePoint 2010 at Microsoft or some other software vendors, you are often shown functionality that is only in the most expensive version (Enterprise Edition) of the SharePoint Server 2010 product. Usually there is no mention of any such restriction, so you should be wary of making a decision on which SharePoint product is the right one for you based on such a presentation. Often there is only one "nice-to-have" function that is the sole "reason" for you paying double CAL charges (charges per user) than if you had selected SPS 2010 Standard Edition, and you need to be fully aware of this before making a decision.

A cost/benefit study might also show that most of the functionality you need is available in the "free" SPF 2010 version and that a good part of the additional functionality you need could be added with SharePoint Designer 2010 or maybe even with Visual Studio 2010. There is no point in paying for bundled software (and SPS 2010 is in effect SPF 2010 plus bundled software) if you don't really need it.

By concentrating on SPF 2010, this book gives you a good idea of to what extent that product alone (with, if necessary, some customization) can solve your problems.

Why Does the Book Include Installing SPF 2010?

Finally, a word on why the book includes an hour on Installing SharePoint Foundation 2010 (Hour 2).

> Search Server 2010 Express is installed as an addition to SPF 2010 in Part II, "Search."

You might already have a SharePoint 2010 site (either SPS 2010 or SPF 2010) that you can use. This can enable you to follow most of the book and discover some of the functions of SPF 2010 (and SPS 2010). However, what the company site will not, in most cases, let you do is to administrate the site—if you already have administrator rights on a SPS 2010 system, it's a bit late for you to be reading this book. Yet only by administrating the site and having full rights to create and change things using SPD 2010, for instance, can you get a proper feel for what is possible.

Once I decided that installation needed to be included, I also needed to decide just how much time should be spent on it. The decision I made was that as this is a Share-Point book, the assumption will be made that a suitable operating system has been installed already. I will make a few comments on what changes might be made after installation of the operating system and prior to the installation of SPF 2010, but the installation of SPF 2010 is the essential part of Hour 2, not the operating system on which it is installed.

I also decided that although it is possible to install SPF 2010 directly onto Windows 7, I would not do so for the book as it is not the kind of environment that anyone other than a low-level developer is likely to use in real life. So instead I assume that a suitable form of Windows Server 2008 has been installed.

The recommendation is to do this installation in a Virtual Machine (VM) system both because then you can still run Windows 7 as your main operating system (with the VM system running "under" it), but also because using a VM system means that you can make copies (typically snapshots) as you go along so that you have a place to go back to if you find yourself experiencing problems.

These days, even reasonably priced notebooks come with 4GB of main memory, which is more than you need to run both your Windows 7 environment and SPF 2010 in a virtual machine.

The "By The Way" sections that follow are the result of my personal experiences—now and over the years.

At the time of this writing, only HP notebooks among the cheaper notebook models have the possibility to have a maximum of 8GB others are already at the maximum 4GB. At the moment replacing the 2x2GB chips in such a portable is expensive, but at some time in the future systems might require more than 4GB, so it's useful if the option is there.

Make sure that the Virtual Software you use can support 64-bit operating systems. At the of time writing, the latest version of Virtual PC did not do so. What did was VM Workstation, and if that is too pricey for you, Parallels (the "for Windows" or the Mac versions) also supports 64-bit operating systems and costs less that $100. Look too for trial versions of the operating system that are typically for 6 months for server operating systems as compared to the 30-days limit for the trial version of VM Workstation that might well be a stretch for working through this book. As for the VM Fusion versus Parallels for the Mac question, I've found my SPF 2010 VMs in Parallels to be snappier on my 2GB-memory MacBook, and this outweighs the advantage given by using the same environment copy in VM Fusion that I use in VM Workstation. With 4GB main memory and thus a more modern MacBook, things might be different. Finally you may see a "requirement" that the SP 2010 require four-core systems. This is totally untrue. Two-core systems work well enough, and they don't even need to be the fastest processors. When creating this book, I used a two-core middle-of-the-road processor with no problems.

Summary

This hour briefly outlined the two different SharePoint lines and an equally brief introduction to the names that were used for them since version 1. A section covered some of the products that you can use to add functionality to SPF 2010 or to amend the built-in functionality. Finally, there was a section on why the book includes an hour on installing SPF 2010.

Q&A

Q. *I saw something at a Microsoft presentation that I can't see in the copy of SPF 2010 that I installed. Where is it?*

A. Several different versions of SharePoint 2010 exist. The Wow! functions that Microsoft often demos are found only in the most expensive version. Visio Services, for instance, is available only if SPS 2010 Enterprise version is installed.

Q. *I have some WSS 3.0/MOSS 2007 sites I need to maintain. Why can't I use SharePoint Designer 2010 to maintain them?*

A. Until this version, it has always been possible to use the new version of SPD (or FrontPage) to maintain the back version of SharePoint, even though some of the new functions then weren't available for use. With the 2010 version of SharePoint, SPD 2010 supports only SP 2010 sites.

Officially this was so Microsoft could concentrate on producing quality software. In my view, doing so is inconsiderate of valid customer needs.

Q. *What do I do if I want to use SharePoint Designer to support WSS 3.0 and SPF 2010 for the same client?*

A. Microsoft recommends the installation on your client of the 32-bit version of SPD 2007 and the 32-bit client version of SPD 2010 (but not the 64-bit version). I—because of previous bad experience of mixing Office versions on client systems when used with SharePoint systems—suggest that you use two different client systems. An old spare machine can run SPD 2007, and the new one can run 64-bit SPD 2010 along with all your other Office 2010 applications.

If you support users, you can find it useful to have a second client system that runs only Office 2007 level applications—and maybe even a third running only Office 2003-level applications!

Workshop

Quiz

1. Which is the free version of SharePoint 2010?

2. What is not free when using the free version of SharePoint 2010?

3. What is the main requirement for a VM system to run an SP 2010 product?

Answers

1. SharePoint Foundation 2010 (SPF 2010).

2. The operating system, and if a full copy of SQL Server is used, the SQL Server system.

3. It needs to support a 64-bit operating system.

Installing SharePoint Foundation 2010

What You'll Learn in This Hour

▶ Making some amendments to the operating system

▶ Installing SPF 2010 in the simplest possible way

For those of you without access to SharePoint Foundation 2010 (or SharePoint Server 2010) systems to work through this book, this hour shows how to install SharePoint Foundation 2010 (SPF 2010).

You can, for instance, use a regular portable running Windows 7 if you have one that preferably has 4GB of main memory. You can install in that VM Workstation to keep the SPF 2010 system completely separate from your normal usage of that portable.

Those of you with access to SPF 2010/SPS 2010 might still prefer to set up your own machine because that will ensure that you can follow the sections that require Administrator permissions, which some of you won't have in your company systems.

Knowing Which Computer Type You Need to Install SharePoint Foundation 2010

As explained in Hour 1, "Introducing SharePoint Foundation 2010," SPF 2010 installs only in a 64-bit machine running a 64-bit operating system. That operating system can either be a 64-bit version of Windows 7 (any version including Home Premium) or a particular 64-bit version of Windows Server 2008. (The choices are Windows Server 2008 including Service Pack 1 or Windows Server 2008 R2.)

More memory tends to speed up the installation phase, so always amend your virtual machine's (VM) memory so that from the start it uses the memory you intend to finally use instead of waiting until after the installation of the software.

The operating system can either be run native or in a VM. If run in a VM, the VM software must support the installation of a 64-bit operating system.

SPF 2010 requires much less memory than SPS 2010. It can easily install in 1GB and can run reasonably in that amount of memory. If running in a VM on a portable that has 2GB memory, don't assign much more than 1GB to the VM. If running in a VM on a portable with 4GB memory, you can assign 2GB to SPF 2010. Much more memory than 2GB probably won't have much effect on the basic test installation created in this hour.

Client systems can, within reason, be anything. Most Windows operating systems from XPPro upward (Vista and Windows 7 at the time of this writing) work fine. Intel Macs also work, but you cannot apply any of the chapters on the interaction between Office and SPF 2010 (or the hours on SPD 2010 and SPF 2010) unless you have a second VM running under the Mac alongside the VM running SPF 2010 (or unless you add all the client software to that single SPF 2010 VM, which isn't a good idea).

Amendments to Windows Server 2008 R2

Because this book is about a SharePoint product, I won't spend time on actually installing Windows Server 2008 R2. I assume that you can do that and, if you use a VM system, you know how to create a virtual machine and install an operating system in it.

Here are a few notes on what you should do after you install Windows Server 2008 R2. After installation, you see a screen similar to Figure 2.1.

By the Way

If you are not in the United States using a U.S. keyboard, avoid using special characters in your password for the server that are not located in the same place in your keyboard as in a U.S. keyboard. After a cold restart, you need to enter the character as if you were using a U.S. keyboard, but after a warm restart you need to enter the characters where they are located on your keyboard. For most special characters, this is annoying, but there are keyboards with keys located where no key is located in a U.S. keyboard; therefore, that key has no U.S. equivalent.

The screen in Figure 2.1 is the result of making the following amendments to the operating system as installed:

▶ Activating the operating system (line one)

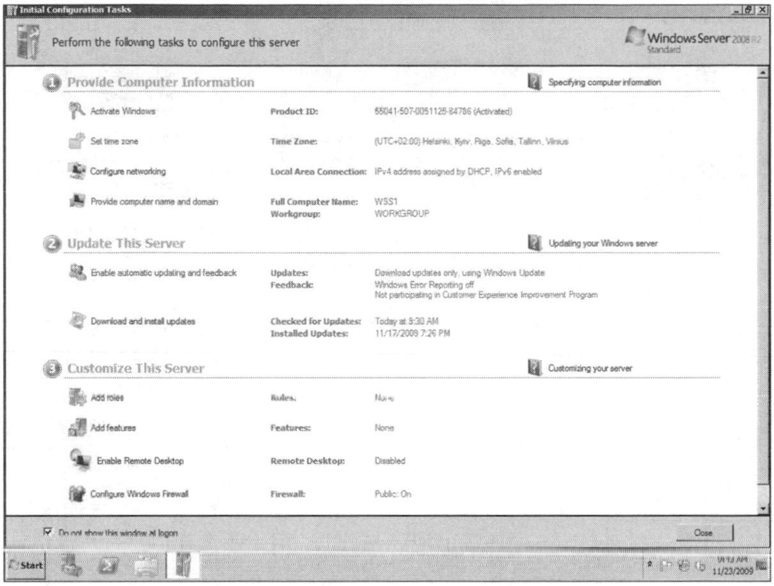

FIGURE 2.1
Initial configura-
tion tasks

If you don't see this screen, go to Start > Run. In the Run box, type **oobe**.

▶ Giving the computer a short name (here, "SPF1") and making it part of a
workgroup

▶ Specifying that updates are downloaded but not automatically installed

At the moment, the Internet Enhanced Security Configuration is enabled (see
Figure 2.2). This is a nuisance for a test installation, so you need to turn it off. Do so
by going to Administrator Tools > Server Manager. The Server Manager function
starts (see Figure 2.3).

Select Configure IE ESC, which appears in the Security Information section on the
right side, and turn it off for administrators and users.

Make sure to note the password for Administrator. Now, it's time to install SharePoint
Foundation 2010.

Installing SharePoint Foundation 2010

To install SharePoint Foundation 2010 (SPF 2010), you must first download a copy of
the latest version of SPF 2010 from the Microsoft site. Because the application is free
to use, it is available to everyone as a free full version; there's no need to select either
a trial version or get a nontrial version from MSDN or TechNet.

FIGURE 2.2
Internet Explorer
Enhanced Secu-
rity Configura-
tion dialog

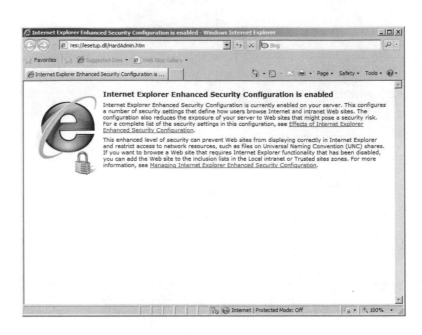

FIGURE 2.2
Internet Explorer
Enhanced Secu-
rity Configura-
tion dialog

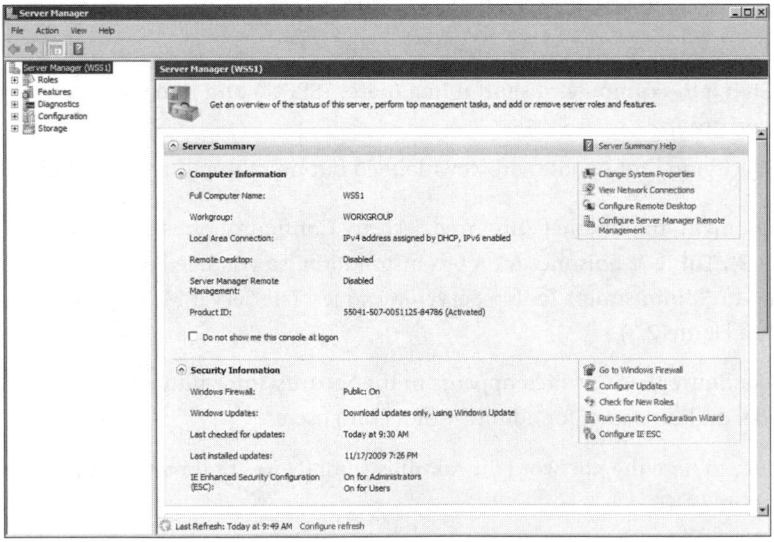

FIGURE 2.3
Security Man-
ager dialog

To ensure that you get the most recent version (which might, by the time you read this book, include Service Pack 1 or 2), go to the Microsoft Downloads page (http://www.microsoft.com/downloads) and search for "SharePoint Foundation 2010." This search yields the page shown in Figure 2.4 (at the time of writing).

FIGURE 2.4
Download Page
for SharePoint
Foundation 2010

Because SPF 2010 is a free product, you do not have to note or acquire a Product Key. You just need to download the product (when in the VM) and run it when you are prompted to run or save the install. (Use Save if you want to keep a copy of the .exe file and then double-click the file).

The first SPF 2010 installation screen is a greatly improved version of the equivalent 2007 installation screen (see Figure 2.5).

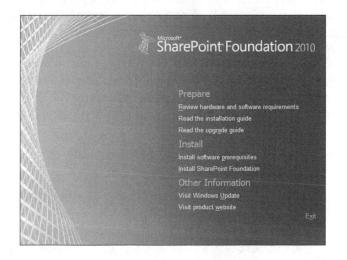

FIGURE 2.5
Installation
screen for SPF
2010

Note that the software prerequisites are the first option in the Install section. You no longer need to hunt for documentation that tells you what you need to install before you install SPF 2010.

At this point, follow these steps to install SPF 2010:

1. Select Install Software Prerequisites, which starts a routine that first tells you what will install and then installs them (see Figure 2.6).

FIGURE 2.6
The Prerequisites Screen

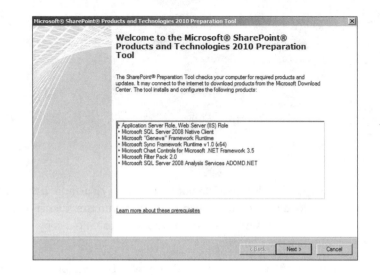

It's never bad to read an installation guide, so if you are a patient person, by all means, read all three sections in the Prepare section. Here, I don't bother.

2. At the end of the prerequisites phase, select Finish. Figure 2.7 appears, a key page for most Installations. Rather than just jumping into the Basic Installation (the Standalone option), which is what you will use (the simplest installation), here are the main differences between the two installation types:

   ▶ Standalone installs everything on a single server, which includes the installation of a copy of SQL Server 2008 Express.

   ▶ Server Farm gives you more options:

      ▶ **Standalone** enables you to specify the location of the search index files, but otherwise the installation is the same as a Standalone Installation and also like that installs SQL Server 2008 Express. (SPF 2010, unlike WSS 3.0, actually says so on the page-progress!)

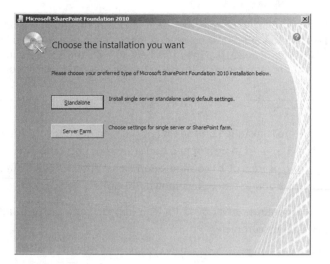

FIGURE 2.7
Choosing the
Installation type

> ▶ **Complete** installs the full SPF 2010 product on the server, but it
> does not install SQL Server 2008 Express. Also, it enables you to say
> on which server your database system is. (Because of this, your
> database system should already be installed if you use this option.)

Here in the original screen (Figure 2.7), select Standalone.

3. After the files have been copied to the server by the installation routine, the
Run Configuration Wizard screen appears (see Figure 2.8). When you get here,
select Close. Doing so starts a lengthy process of installing the software on the
server, so go grab a cup of coffee.

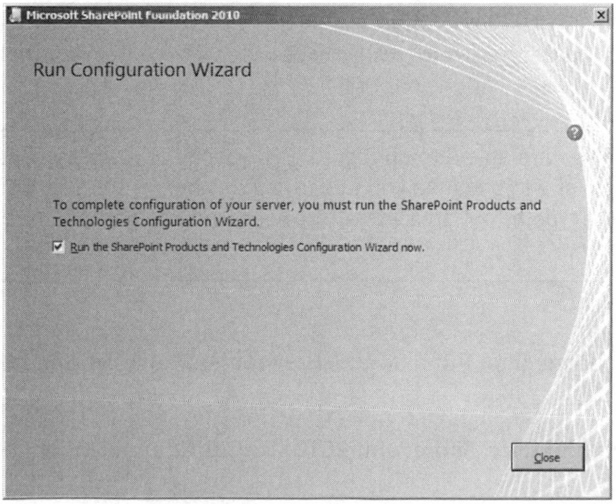

FIGURE 2.8
Run Configura-
tion Wizard

You have the opportunity to unselect the Run the ...Configuration Wizard in case you might be installing SPF 2010 on several machines in a farm. (This is, however, more likely with SPS 2010.) Then it is best to have the software installed on all the servers in the farm first and then run the Configuration Wizard on all servers.

As the software is installed on the server, a screen advises you that several services (such as IIS) need to be stopped and started as part of the process. Then, there is a long process of 10 configuration steps; patience is required particularly on steps 2 and 8. Progress is shown, though.

4. Finally, a Configuration Successful screen appears, and the installation and configuration are complete.

Before the default website can be opened, the user needs to log in (see Figure 2.9).

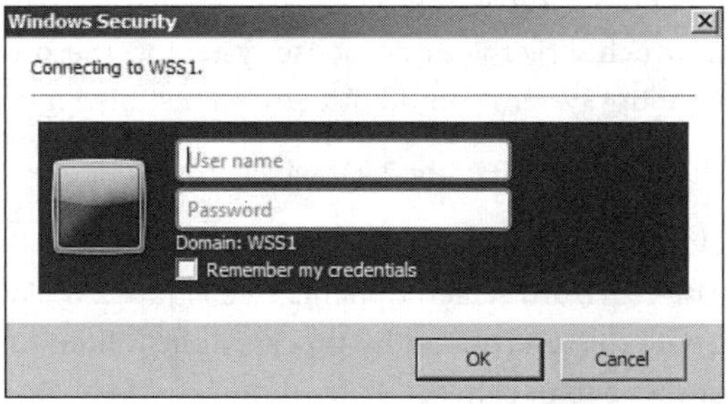

FIGURE 2.9
Connecting to
SPF1

Windows Security	✕
Connecting to WSS1.	
	User name
	Password
	Domain: WSS1
	■ Remember my credentials
	OK Cancel

The only user we have available at the moment is the Administrator. Enter both **Administrator** and the password, and you see the website (see Figure 2.10).

If at this stage you are asked to configure IE8, specify as little as possible. (This is a server, after all.) If, because you specifying IE8 before the site appears, you get an error, just type **http://spf1** in the browser, and you get the correct screen (see Figure 2.10).

You need to check one final thing: Make sure that you have an Administration Site. To do this, follow these steps:

1. Go to Start and select SharePoint 2010 Central Administration (see Figure 2.11).

FIGURE 2.10
The SPF 2010
default site

Those new to SharePoint won't know this, but this look (Figure 2.10) is closer to the earlier "portal" versions than to the earlier plain "Services" versions of SharePoint.

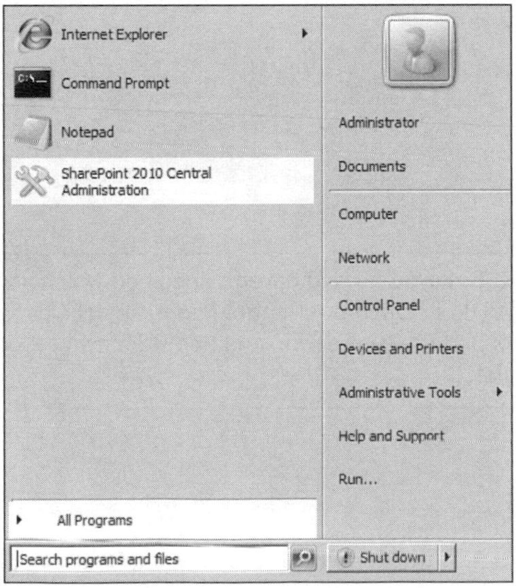

Did you Know?

FIGURE 2.11
SharePoint 2010
Central Adminis-
tration in Start

2. After the inevitable request for you to sign in with Administrator and Password, you see Figure 2.12.

3. You can now visually verify that you have a Central Administration site.

With that, installation is complete.

Note, however, the port used by Central Administration (in this case, 41170) because you can't always access the server's Start button (or Administration Tools) and access it from there. Also add this address (http://SPF1:41170 for this example, but for you, the address you see in your system!) to your Favorites list in your browser.

FIGURE 2.12
SharePoint 2010
Central Adminis-
tration

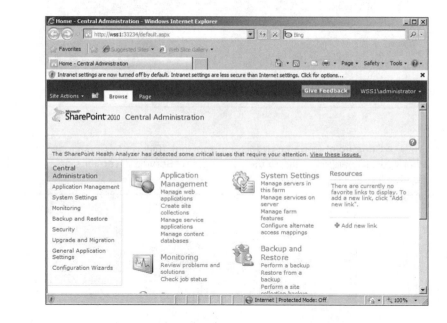

If you don't have a U.S. keyboard and haven't specified which keyboard you have, this is a good time to do it. Open the Control Panel, select Change Languages or Other Input Methods and the Keyboards, and add the new keyboard. Then select it in the drop-down list.

Summary

This hour suggested a few amendments after you installed the operating system and then showed you how to install a basic installation of SharePoint Foundation 2010.

Q&A

Q. *How do I install SPF 2010 so that I can use an existing copy of SQL Server 2008?*

A. Do not select the initial Standalone option. When you then select the Server farm option, do not select the Standalone option.

(Even if you already have a full copy of SQL Server 2008 installed on the single server, it will still not be used for the SPF 2010 databases).

Q. *The 2007 products contained differences between the (basic installation) database system installed by WSS 3.0 and by MOSS 2007. Is that still the case?*

A. In the 2007 products, the database systems installed by Basic Installations were different versions of SQL Server 2005 Express. The main difference was that the WSS 3.0 version had no database size limit, whereas the MOSS 2007 version had a 4GB size limit. In the 2010 products, both SPF 2010 and SPS 2010 use the same version of SQL Server 2008 Express, and both have a 4GB database size limit.

Workshop

Quiz

1. Why should you change the VM default selection of memory before the installation phase?

2. Which part of the entire installation process of SPF 2010 takes the longest time?

Answers

1. More memory means that the installation phase is noticeably quicker (provided you don't grab too much memory from the VM's host system).

2. The Configuration Wizard phase.

HOUR 3

Adding Users and Giving Them Rights

What You'll Learn in This Hour

▶ Different default accounts used to access a SPF 2010 site

▶ Creating local users (on the server)

▶ Creating SharePoint groups and the benefits of having them

▶ Creating a new SharePoint group with additional permissions

▶ Using an AD group: advantages and disadvantages

At the moment, the only way to access the site created in Hour 2, "Installing Share-Point Foundation 2010," is to use the administrator name and the password specified for it when the operating system was installed.

The (server) Administrator account is used throughout this book unless specified otherwise; however, you need to be aware of the rights that other (nonadministrator) users can have in SPF 2010 websites. In this hour, you create more users and give them different rights to access sites.

Getting to Know the Different Account Types

Normally, an SPF 2010 server in a company is part of an Active Directory (AD) setup, and each prospective internal user of the SPF 2010 site would already have a name in the form of domain\<username> and password.

In Hour 2, you created the simplest standalone server installation—one that when following most of this book you will never perhaps connect to a network—so you need to create users on the server, because these users can then always be available. You then give those users rights to access the site.

Normally, this method would be used only by the administrator of a company system to give him the ability to simulate users with different rights than his normal domain\username gives him so that he can support users with (typically) less rights than himself.

Did you Know?

> Over the years, the options for authorization to SharePoint systems have widened. The most common other method (after the use of domain names) is Forms-Based Authorization, which is beyond the scope of this book.

Creating a Single User

To create a single user to your SPF 2010 website, follow these steps to create a user called MyAdmin. These steps will be repeated for several other users. The list of those users is below the steps needed to create one user.

1. Go to Start > Administrative Tools > Computer Management. Figure 3.1 shows the Computer Management page.

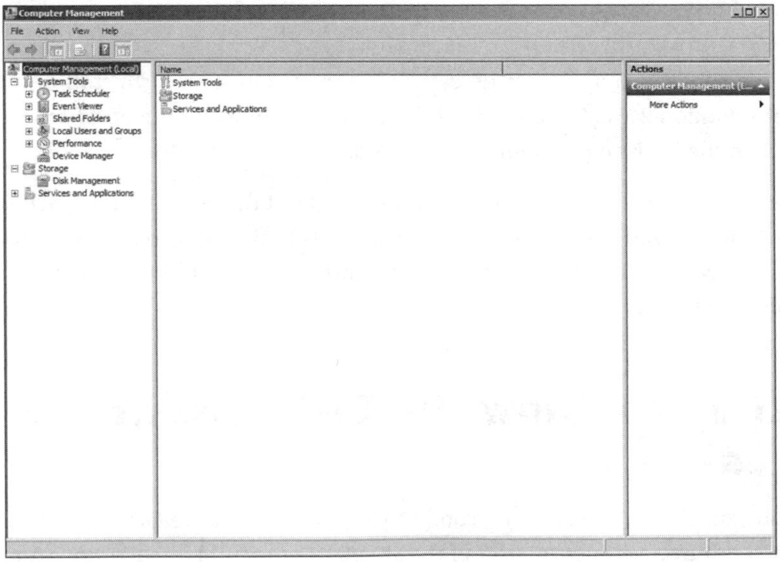

Computer Management
File Action View Help
Computer Management (Local)
System Tools
Task Scheduler
Event Viewer
Shared Folders
Local Users and Groups
Performance
Device Manager
Storage
Disk Management
Services and Applications
Name
System Tools
Storage
Services and Applications
Actions
More Actions

FIGURE 3.1 The Computer Management page

2. Select Local Users and Groups, and then select Users (see Figure 3.2).

FIGURE 3.2
A list of users on the Computer Management page

3. Under Actions, select User > New User. Figure 3.3 shows the completed New User dialog with the text required to add the MyAdmin user. To select User Cannot

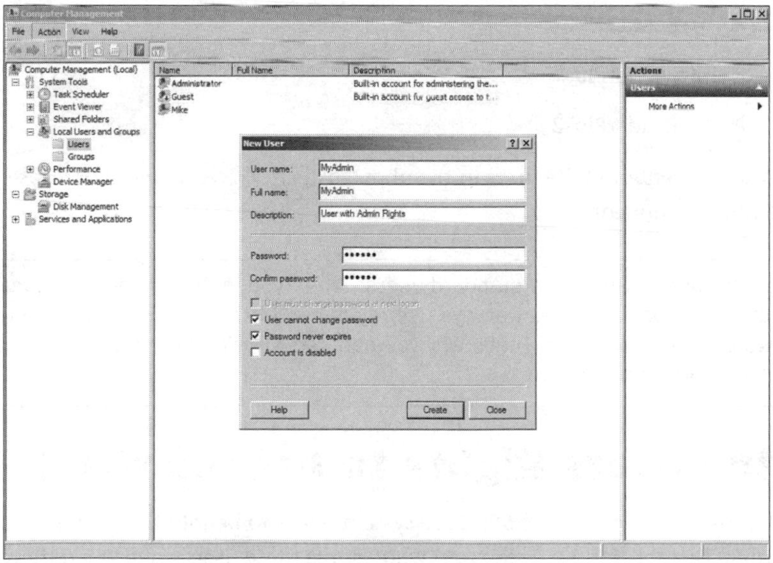

FIGURE 3.3
Creating a new user

Change Password and Password Never Expires, you first need to deselect "User must change password at next login."

By the Way

For test systems, I always give each user account the same password. To make sure I can work it out even if I can't remember it, I use the same password for the server (and thus, the Administrator account) with both lowercase letters and at least one number; I change the final (odd) character to another odd character. This way, because I use the Administrator account all the time, I'll remember that password and can quickly guess the other one.

By the Way

You need to make the changes in step 3 because this will be a test system, and you don't want bother with the expiration of passwords. It's also what you should probably do if you ever have a single SPF 2010 system connected to the Internet and you want to use local server names/passwords for access, even though this isn't the safest option possible.

   4. Click Create to return to the empty version of Figure 3.3. From here, you can directly enter the next user from the list below.

   Repeat the above steps for the following users:

   ▶ MyContrib

   ▶ MyDocLib

   ▶ MyReader

   ▶ MyReaderPlus1

   ▶ MyReaderPlus2

   5. After you enter all the users in the above list, click Create and then Close. Figure 3.4 appears.

By the Way

Administrator and Guest are standard users. When you install Windows Server R2, you must specify a user. I always use my name, Mike, and give it the same password as Administrator. That's why you can see Mike in the above list along with the MyAdmin etc. users.

Giving Users Rights to Access the Site

After the users are created, the SPF 2010 system needs to be told that these particular users can access the SPF 2010 sites and what rights these users have when they access them. To achieve this, follow these steps:

   1. While still in the virtual machine (VM) or on the server, open Internet Explorer and enter **http://SPF1**. After a brief delay (and perhaps the need to sign in as Administrator again), you see the default site. (Refer to Figure 2.10 in Hour 2.)

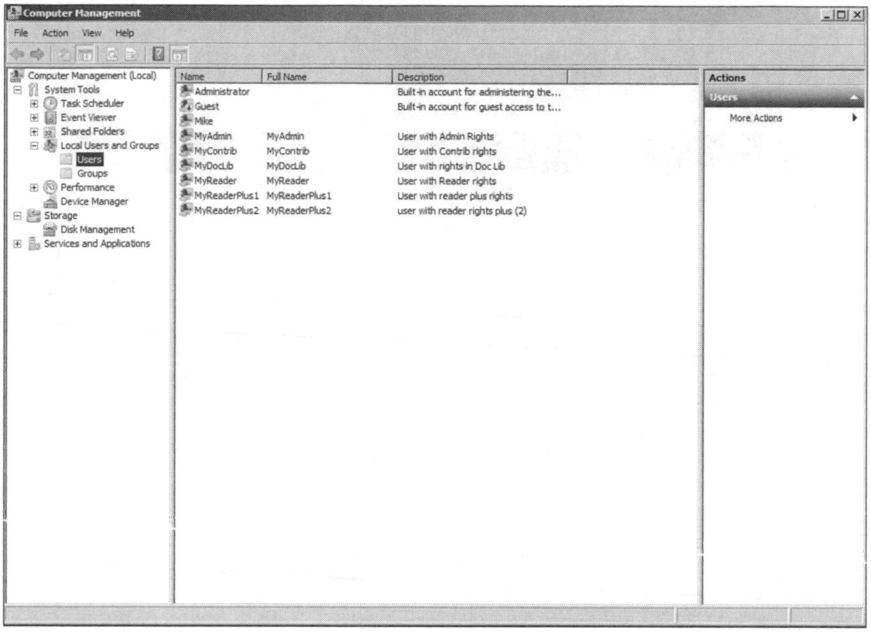

FIGURE 3.4
List of users
after adding sev-
eral new ones

2. From the Site Actions drop-down menu, select Site Settings (see Figure 3.5). The Site Settings page appears (see Figure 3.6).

FIGURE 3.5
Site Actions and
Site Settings

FIGURE 3.6
Site Settings

3. Select People and Groups from the section Users and Permissions. The People and Groups page appears (see Figure 3.7).

FIGURE 3.7
The People and Groups default page

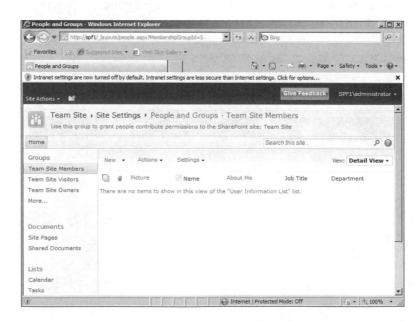

4. In the New drop-down menu, select Add Users. An empty Grant Permissions window appears (see Figure 3.8).

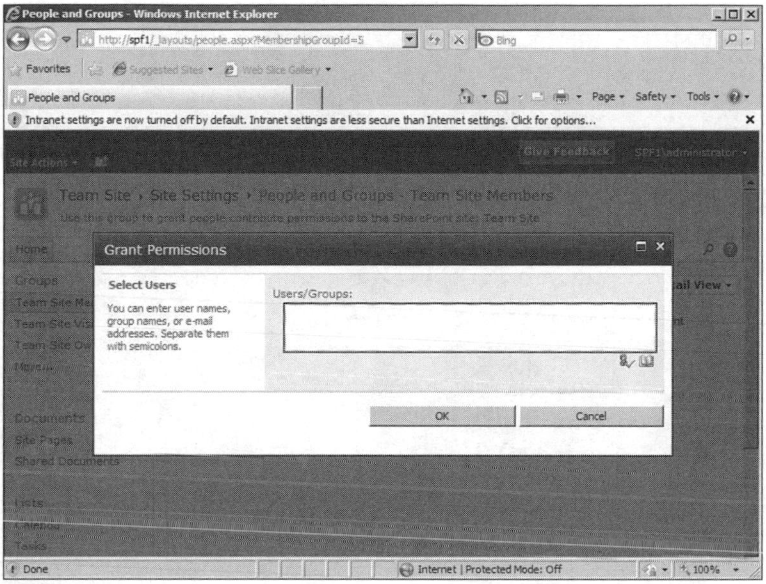

FIGURE 3.8
The Grant Permissions window

This group of Team Site Members is described as being able to Grant People Contribute Permissions (refer to Figure 3.7). This is where we add the MyContrib and MyDocLib users.

5. Write **MyContrib; MyDocLib** in the User/Groups box shown in Figure 3.8 and click OK.

   Figure 3.9 (on the following page) shows what happens: Users MyContrib and MyDocLib are now listed as the members of the Team Site Members list.

The next actions are to go to Team Site Visitors and add MyReader, and to go to Team Site Owners and add MyAdmin. You do this in exactly the same way described above for the Team Site Members group.

Getting Familiar with SharePoint Groups

SharePoint groups are made available to solve the administration problem of not wanting to enter every single users' name every time access to something (a Site or a List, for instance) is granted to that user. (Another solution to the same problem is grouping users by the use of an Active Directory group; for more on this, see the end of this hour.)

Imagine if we could not group users. At first, for a small company, everything would be okay. Say that 50 users are given the rights to access a SPF 2010 site by entering

FIGURE 3.9
The list of Team
Site Members

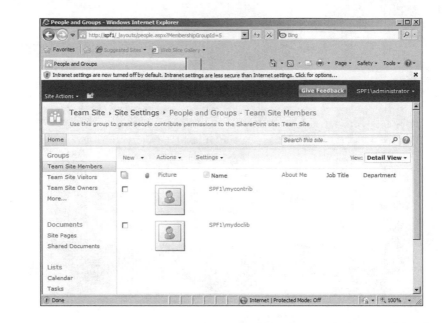

the username of each user. But what happens if, one month later, another site is created? And, during this time, two users have left and three new users have arrived in
the meantime. We would need to give all 51 users rights to the new site again by
entering the names of all 51 users. Add more sites and the manual effort increases.

You might be thinking, that's only manual effort and adding a new site doesn't happen that often. That's true, but when you add 50 users are you going to make a manual error and miss one of them, and if you do, what will be the result? Probably several weeks later, a user will call the hotline saying that she can access sites 1, 2 and 3,
but not 4. The other problem is that, when a new user arrives at the company, you
need to know which sites to add him to, and you need to go into each site to do so.

Wouldn't it be much easier if you had just one list of users no matter how many sites
you have?

That is the main reason for a SharePoint group: It's a place to put users who share the
same access rights to one or more SPF 2010 sites. (This is not restricted to sites only, as
you will see later.) Now whenever a new site is created, the appropriate SharePoint
groups are given access rights to it and not a list of tens (or hundreds) of users individually. If a new user arrives, he is added to the appropriate SharePoint group(s) for
her job description.

I sneaked it past you earlier, but you already added users to SharePoint groups when
creating users in the "Giving Users Access Rights to the Site" section. Team Site

Members, Team Site Visitors, and Team Site Owners are three SharePoint groups created automatically as part of the installation process.

Only Team Site Owners was initially given a member (Administrator) as part of the installation, but all three of these groups were also given (different) access rights to the default site created in the SPF 2010 installation.

In the next section, you will create an additional SharePoint group similar to the Team Site Visitors SharePoint group but with slightly amended rights. When that SharePoint group has been created and given access rights to a particular site, you can add to it the two users we haven't so far added: MyReaderPlus1 and MyReaderPlus2.

Creating a New SharePoint Group

In this section, you create a SharePoint group called ReadPlus. To do so, follow these steps:

1. In the Team Site Members page (refer to Figure 3.9), click the Groups heading All the current groups are listed, including a brief description of their rights (see Figure 3.10).

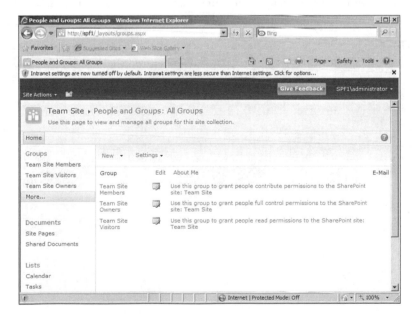

FIGURE 3.10
Listing of All Groups

2. Click New and, in an empty version of the Create Group page (see Figure 3.11), you can fill out the details for the new SharePoint group called ReadPlus. (We are creating a new SharePoint group because we don't want to use one of the

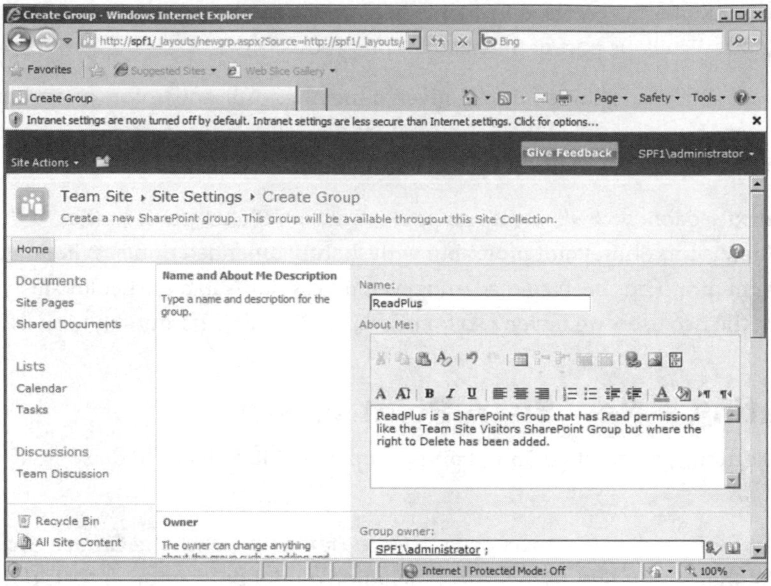

FIGURE 3.11
The top half of the Add Share-Point Groups page

standard SharePoint groups–Team Site Members, Team Site Visitors, and Team Site Owners–for one of our users.)

3. For our purposes, leave the default values as they are in the second half of the screen and click Create. The group ReadPlus is now listed with the previously created groups (see Figure 3.12). Success!

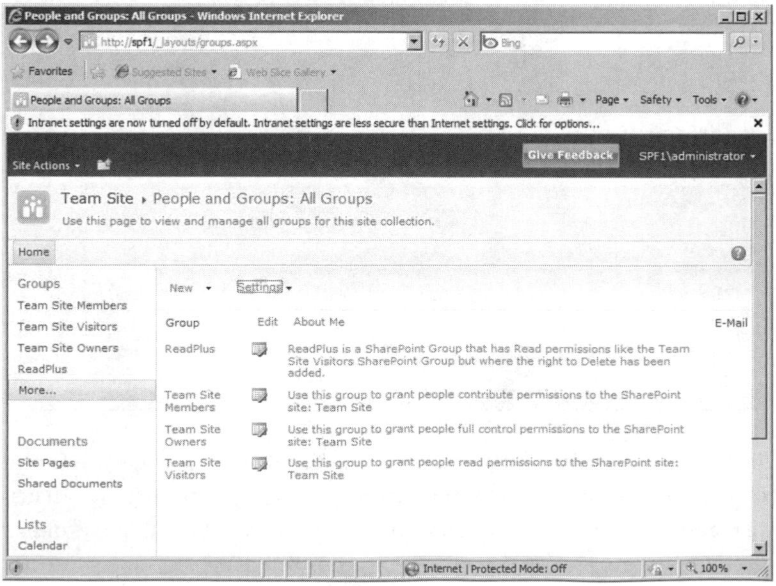

FIGURE 3.12
A List of All Groups including ReadPlus

Did you Know?

If you click ReadPlus in Figure 3.12, you see that Administrator has automatically become a member of this new SharePoint Group.

Specifying the Permissions of a SharePoint Group

Currently, you haven't chosen the access rights for the members of this new Reader-Plus SharePoint group. Here's how to do that:

1. At the Team Site Start page, click the Site Actions drop-down menus (near the top-left) and select Site Permissions. The Permissions: Team Site page appears (see Figure 3.13).

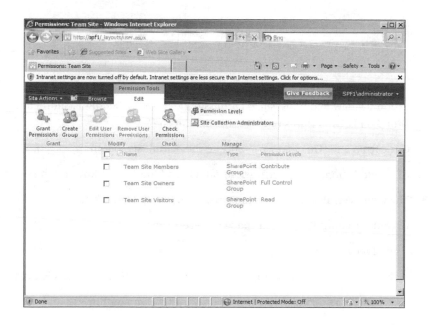

FIGURE 3.13
The Site Permissions screen

2. Select Permission Levels. This shows a list of the present (default) Permissions Levels: Full Control, Design, Collaborate; Read and Limited Access.

3. Select Read. At the bottom of the page that appears, select Copy Permission Level. The Copy Permission Level page appears (see Figure 3.14).

4. Fill out the Copy Permission Level "Read" screen, as shown in Figure 3.14.

5. Scroll down the page and select a Delete option (Delete Items or Delete Versions). Then, scroll to the bottom of the page and click Create.

FIGURE 3.14
Copying the Read
Permission Level

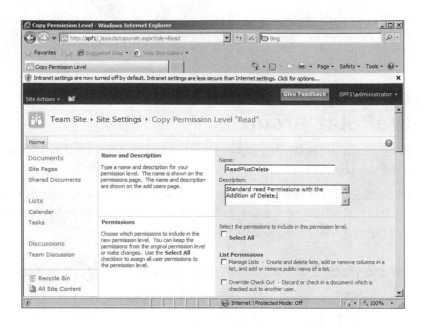

Now there is a screen listing six different Permission Levels. The final step is to assign the new ReadPlusDelete permission level to the ReadPlus SharePoint Group and give it rights to access the default site.

6. Click Team Site. This takes you back to the default site again.

7. Click Site Actions > Site Permissions again, and then click Grant Permissions.

8. The Grant Permissions screen appears, as shown in Figure 3.15.

Fill out the Grant Permissions page as necessary:

   ▶ Type **ReadPlus** in the box.

   ▶ Click the arrow next to the person image. (ReadPlus becomes ReadPlus ;)

   ▶ Select the Grant Users Permission Directly radio button.

   ▶ Select ReadPlusDelete.

9. Scroll down and click OK.

There's now a new list of those SharePoint groups that can access the Team Site. In addition to those listed in Figure 3.13, there's also the ReadPlus SharePoint group listed with the information that it has the ReadPlusDelete Permission Level.

There's one final thing to do and that is to add the two users MyReaderPlus1 and MyReaderPlus2 to the ReadPlus SharePoint group. I'll leave you alone to do that

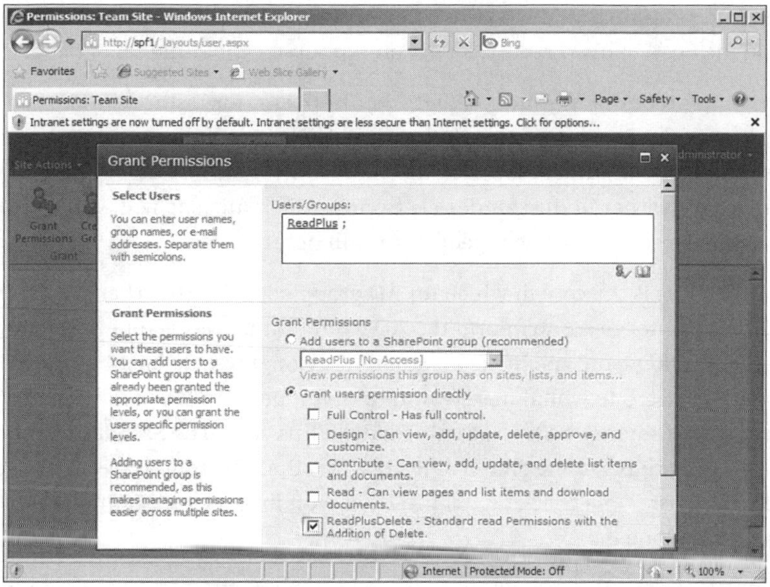

FIGURE 3.15
Grant Permissions

because Grant Permissions followed by adding the two users and selecting the correct SharePoint group is close to what we previously did earlier in this hour.

What About Active Directory Groups?

You can use Active Directory (AD) groups instead of SharePoint groups to provide a way of assigning rights to a number of users at one time. At first glance, their use seems to be the obvious choice for a company environment where AD groups are already in use, and deciding whether to use an AD group or a SharePoint group often depends on how the AD support people operate and their relationship with the SharePoint administrator.

> Companies typically use Active Directory for their network. Users in the company can then be split up for administration purposes into Active Directory groups which have different access rights to resources in the network. For instance, the AD group for the Personnel Department members would be the only one able to access the part of the file structure that contains salary information.

By the Way

The best example of using an AD group is when a suitable AD group already exists. Let's say that there already is an AD group for the members of the Personnel department. In that case, you can use that AD group to restrict access to a SharePoint site (or something else such as a List) to members of the Personnel department thus avoiding the need to also create a SharePoint group for the same set of people.

Usually, that is a clear-cut situation, but what happens, for instance, if the AD team put the boss of the Personnel group in her own AD group (because she has more powers than her staff) and doesn't tell the SharePoint Administrator? Then, unless they have also left her in the standard Personnel AD group, she will no longer have access to the SharePoint sites her people can still access.

A worse example is the case in which an AD group doesn't exist. Then the Share-Point Administrator needs to inform the AD team that he wants a new AD group to be created. The AD team might create groups only on a weekly basis, so the SP Administrator needs to wait patiently until that happens, in the meantime, no doubt receiving emails saying, "Why haven't you done this yet?" The SP Administrator can only give access rights to the SharePoint site when the AD group is available, so he either has to waste time checking if it's there or wait for an email from the AD team saying they've done it.

A similar situation is if a user needs to be given rights to the site. The SP administrator knows which group or groups to add the user to but the AD team might not. Again the process goes from the user's boss to the SP administrator who needs to contact the AD team, and so on.

Faced with this kind of time delays and additional bureaucracy, it's often the case that the SharePoint Administrator will create a SharePoint group to solve the problem.

Rather than having a mixture of SharePoint groups and AD groups used for the same SharePoint site, it might well be advisable to always use SharePoint groups for all SharePoint access rights and let the AD team take care of access rights to network systems. However, a final decision on this needs to be based on the internal routines of a company (and also invariably on how well the SP administrator and the AD people work together). Here, we use only SharePoint groups.

Summary

This hour looked at the rights users have when they access sites and how these rights can be specified. We created users local to the server, assigned these to existing SharePoint groups, and then created a new SharePoint group with a different set of permissions.

Q&A

Q. *Can you specify two (or more) permissions for the same SharePoint group?*

A. You wouldn't normally because you would have SharePoint groups that overlap permissions with other SharePoint groups. That is, one set of permissions includes all the individual permissions of another set of permissions.

However, there is nothing to stop you from having a set of permissions that covers only most of the permissions in another set of permissions, yet also includes one additional permission. In that case, some of the users might need to belong to the sum of those permissions, and the SharePoint group those users are in would need both sets of permissions.

Q. *Is it possible to create a new set of permissions (called DeleteOnly) in which only the Delete permission is selected? Then it would be possible to specify the normal Read set of permissions and the DeleteOnly set and have the same effect as the method you used.*

A. Yes, in SharePoint, you can often obtain the same result in many different ways. In this case, I prefer the approach I took, but it's really just up to your preference.

Workshop

Quiz

1. What are the four main users to whom you can give access rights to a site?

2. What is the principal advantage in giving a SharePoint group access rights to a site compared to giving such rights directly to a user?

Answers

1. Local users on the server, individual domain users, SharePoint groups, and AD groups.

2. The main advantage is that it's common for the same set of users to be given access rights to the same sites. By using SharePoint groups, this becomes less of an administrative nightmare.

Using the Administration Site

What You'll Learn in This Hour

▶ Ensuring access to the SPF 2010 site

▶ Working with the Administration site

This hour is about working with a site that the installation of SPF 2010 has created for the use of Administrators. Before we start working with that Administration site, the following section discusses how to make sure you can access any site in the SPF 2010 system.

Ensuring Access to the SPF 2010 Site

So far we've accessed the site from a browser running in the server. (From now on, I'll assume that you are running the server in a VM.) Then it was perfectly fine to access the site using http://SPF1 because the server knew what SPF1 was—it was its own server name.

The next step is to access the VM from the host machine of the VM software. That host machine—probably running Windows 7—is where our client software (Office 2010; SharePoint Designer 2010 and maybe other client programs) has been installed, so mostly we will access the site from there.

The problem is that the host machine doesn't know what http://SPF1 means.

What happens if we try it anyway will vary depending on what search routine we have connected to the browser. If we have a search product (such as Bing or Google) connected, there will be a results page from that search product giving the results of an Internet Search for http://SPF1. If there isn't and you are using Internet Explorer as your browser, you will see the page shown in Figure 4.1.

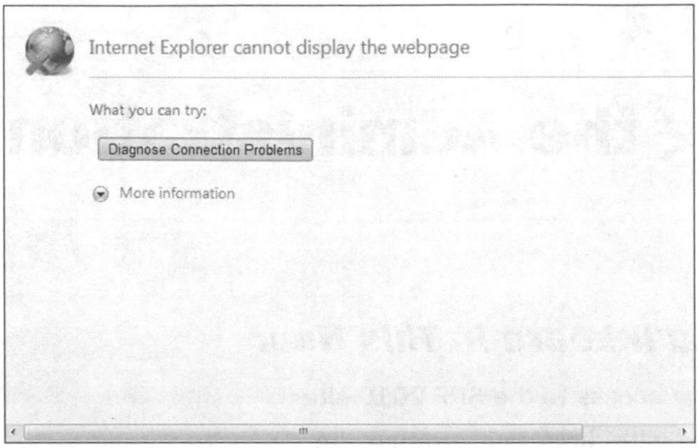

FIGURE 4.1
Internet Explorer
cannot display
the web page

We need an alternative to using http://SPF1, which is to use the TCP/IP address of the site rather than the server name. To use the TCP/IP address, follow these steps:

By the Way

I find it useful to amend the Hosts file of the host machine (if this is running a Windows version) so that the Host knows the TCP/IP address to use if http://SPF1 is used from the host machine. (Hosts is in C:\Windows\ system32\drivers\etc and the file already includes an example of what to write.) For most of the book, however, I used the TCP/IP address when accessing the server from the host machine, so amending the Hosts file isn't necessary. Try working without it for at least the next few hours to get full benefit from them.

We need an alternative to using http://SPF1, which is to use the TCP/IP address of the site rather than the server name. To use the TCP/IP address, follow these steps:

1. Open the command prompt and enter **ipconfig /all**. Figure 4.2 shows the output of this command.

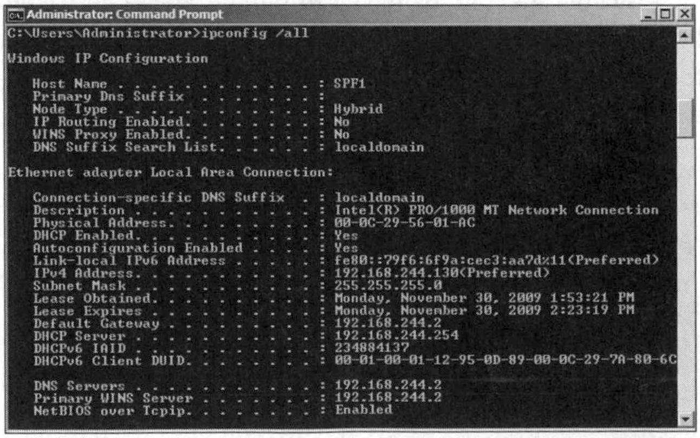

FIGURE 4.2
The result of
ipconfig /all

By the Way

If your VM and the host system are both part of an AD domain, the rules for that domain might automatically give your server a domain name such as spf1. domainname.com, and in such a case, access from the host system might work.

You have to find the correct section, but here the TCP/IP address we want is 192.168.244.130.

2. Note the TCP/IP address.

At this stage, trying http://192.168.244.130 from the host system gives you Figure 4.1 again, so you must get rid of the Windows Firewall in the server. At the moment, it is blocking our access from the host system.

3. Go to Start > Administrative Tools > Services and scroll to Windows Firewall (see Figure 4.3).

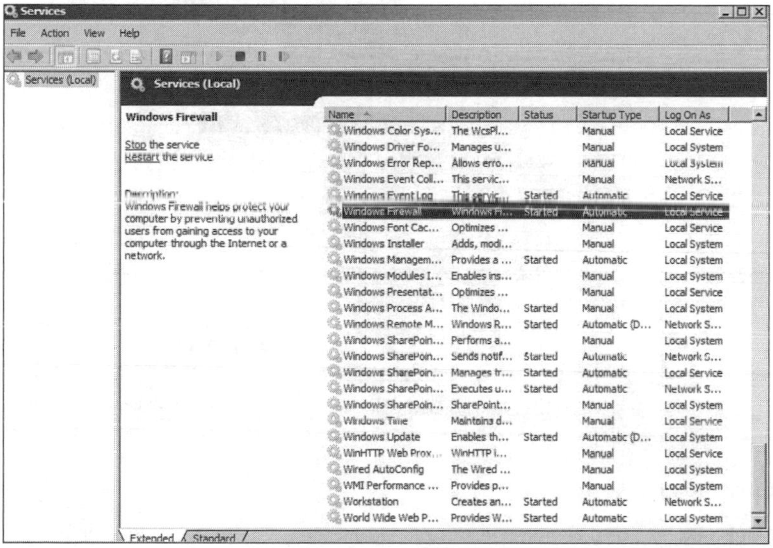

FIGURE 4.3
Finding Windows Firewall in Services

Because this is a test system, we use the brute force method and simply disable it completely. For production systems, fine-tuning is possible via Start > Administrator Tools > Windows Firewall with Advanced Security (which will run only if the Windows Firewall is not disabled.

Did you Know?

Make sure that you use the Command Prompt from the VM. Otherwise you get the wrong TCP/IP address and, try as you will, you won't be able to connect to the host system's TCP/IP address. (Don't think that's obvious. It is, but I wasted almost an hour wondering why I couldn't connect after I had too quickly noted the wrong TCP/IP address!)

By the Way

If you don't see such an address, check your VM's definition of which network adapter is in use. With some VM systems, including VM Workstation, networking is not available at all if the "Tools" for that product (here "VMWare Tools") have

By the Way

> not been installed. Disabling and then Enabling Network connections is another thing to try before re-doing ipconfig /all.

4. Double-click Windows Firewall. Set it to Disabled (see Figure 4.4).

5. Click Stop.

6. Click OK.

At this stage, if you try to access the site using http://192.168.244.130 from anywhere other than the server, it still won't work. You must carry out Step 7 first.

7. Reboot the server.

After the reboot, you can access http://192.168.244.130 from the host system.

By the Way

> When you get the authentication box, make sure that you now write the name as **SPF1\Administrator**. If you write only **Administrator**, the "domain" will be automatically set to the name of the host system (in this case Win7), and the username won't be valid.

When this has been successfully done, the next step is to try to access the server from a different client machine. This can be anything with a browser, so in my case, I tested it with a MacBook running the Snow Leopard version of the Mac operating system and using Safari as the browser. (If that works, anything will!)

This final check is useful if you want to work with your site as if it were a real production server. Then you would naturally not want to restrict yourself to working with the host machine of the VM. You would want the server to be accessible from a number of different client systems, possibly running different operating systems and browsers. (In my case my test from the Mac didn't work.)

In such cases, look at the Networking definitions of the VM system. Figure 4.5 shows the Networking settings that were required in VM Workstation 7.0.

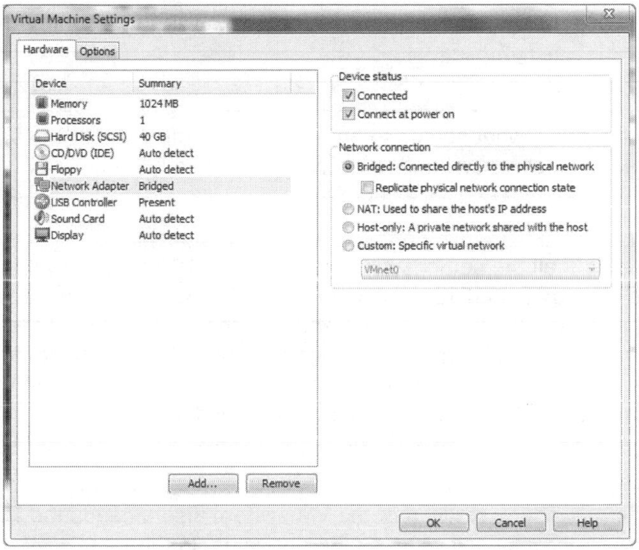

FIGURE 4.5
Specifying the fully correct VM networking settings

> I use VMWare Workstation throughout and there is a 30-day free test version of it, but if you don't like being restricted to 30 days free use, you should try instead the totally free VMWare Player from the same company.

Did you Know?

> In a normal household network, PCs might be switched on or off. The TCP/IP address of the (VM) server might therefore be different the next time you work through this book. Doing a quick ipconfig /all to confirm that the TCP/IP address hasn't changed before you restart might save you some nerves.

Did you Know?

Setting this to Bridged was the key final step. The previous setting of NAT (the default) was enough to let the VM connect to the Internet and to be visible from the host system but wasn't enough to enable access from another machine in the same network.

Working with the Administration Site

The installation of SPF 2010 installed two sites:

- Default site called Team Site (accessible with http://SPF1)
- Administration site (accessible with http://SPF1:randomportnumber)

In this book's test installation, the random port number is 41170; in your case it almost certainly won't be. It will however always be a random number (here 41170) unless you specifically change it.

Did you Know?

> Never worry if it takes what seems to be a long time before either the site is opened or the request for authentication comes. This is quite normal.

By the Way

> Sometimes even if all the settings are correct http://192.168.1.2 will still not work. In this case try the address again in the same browser. Experience shows that often the system needs to wake up and only the second attempt will get the necessary authorization pop-up. I also found it useful to use both IE8 and Safari for Windows. IE8 often wouldn't ask for credentials and wouldn't access the site, but Safari did ask for credentials and did then access the site.

Did you Know?

> Amending the networking settings of the VM system also amends the TCP/IP address. Now an ipconfig /all gives a different value. In this case http://192.168.1.2 works from the Mac, from the host system, and from the server.

To see how to work with the Central Administration site, follow these steps:

1. Open the Administration Site with http://SPF1:yourrandomportnumber. Alternatively, on the server, you can also open it with Start > SharePoint 2010 Central Administration.

2. Complete the usual login. Figure 4.6 shows the standard Central Administration page.

By the Way

> Although it is possible to change the port number to something you easily remember, I don't recommend doing so. The procedures that change this port number are supposed to amend everything that needs to be amended because of the change, but I always think that the programmers might have missed something, so I just leave the value as the value that was generated.

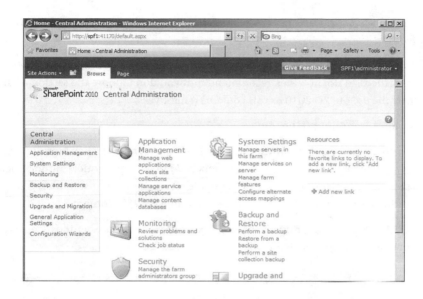

FIGURE 4.6
SharePoint 2010
Central Adminis-
tration

Figure 4.6 is a bit reminiscent of a modern operating system Control Panel as compared to the Classic View of the Control Panel that the MOSS 2007 Central Administration looked like.

So far, apart from the (to old hands) somewhat confusing look, there seems at first
glance to be nothing particularly new there.

As you see in this brief look at some of the Administration options, Microsoft has done
a good job of including the 2010 Central Administration functions that required manual activity (in some cases a lot of nonobvious manual activity) in the 2007 version.

Looking at Some Improvements Compared to Earlier Products

Specifying Where the Search Routine Should Search

The book I wrote on WSS 3.0 (*Sams Teach Yourself SharePoint 2007: Using Windows Share-
Point Services 3.0*) included two actions that need to be done before going further: Alternate Access Mapping (AAM), which is discussed later in this hour, and specifying
which server is running the SPF 2010 search routine, which no longer needs to be done.

Here we look at why we no longer need to specify a server for search. Then we look at
where to restrict the use of SharePoint Designer 2010 (SPD 2010) and when to specify

email parameters. And finally, we look in depth at how Alternate Access Mapping now looks.

If you want to get on with it, you can skip to the section "Configuring Alternate Access Methods." I do, however, recommend that you don't ignore the section on how to restrict the use of SPD 2010 as this could be a lifesaver.

At first sight, everything is the same:

1. From the Central Administration page (refer to Figure 4.6), click Manage Content Databases (2007 = "Content Databases") in the Application Management section. This gives in the case of the single server SPF 2010 installation a screen listing a single database with the default name of WSS_Content.

2. Click that name to bring up the Manage Content Database Settings screen, part of which is visible in Figure 4.7.

FIGURE 4.7
A section of the Manage Content Database Settings page

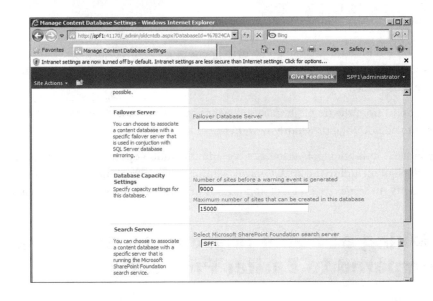

As you can see in the Search Server part of Figure 4.7, the server name SPF1 is already entered in the entry box. In other words, the system—without any manual action— already knows where the content database is located that the search routine will search. In the 2007 version of SharePoint, this value (even though the content database could only be in the only server that we had) needed to be entered before any search results could be obtained (which was the source of many newsgroup questions).

Did you Know?

The database for Search is only specified when a single-server (basic) installation has been done (as we did here). If any other kind of installation is made, there will be no entry here (and a server will need to be selected, because typically in those kinds of installations, the database system is not installed on the same server as SPF 2010 but on a server running SQL Server 2008).

Having the server name specified automatically is a typical example of how the 2010 version concentrates on tidying up the failings of the previous version.

Restricting the Use of SPD 2010 with the SPF 2010 Site

SharePoint Designer 2007 (SPD 2007) was a powerful tool for site customization, but in the wrong hands, it could lead to disastrous results. So it was often necessary to make manual adjustments to the SharePoint system so users could not use SPD 2007 with SharePoint 2007 sites.

In the 2010 products, there's a single page accessed via Central Administration where you can specify exactly what can and cannot be done with SPD 2010. You can access this page by going to the General Application Settings page (see Figure 4.8) and clicking Configure SharePoint Designer Settings.

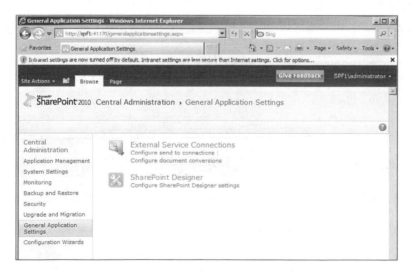

FIGURE 4.8
General Application Settings

As shown in Figure 4.9, not only can you now block users from doing anything with SPD 2010, you also have various options that restrict the rights of site administrators.

There are many more examples of how the Microsoft team has noted problems with the earlier versions of SharePoint and have tried to ensure that they do not occur with SPF 2010 by improving the way Central Administration works. The final example discusses how Microsoft improved incoming email.

FIGURE 4.9
Options for the
use of SPD
2010 with SPF
2010 sites

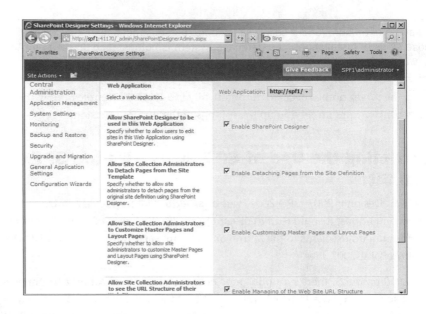

A Useful Small Improvement in Email Specification

Specifying incoming email is simpler if an SMTP server is available, so rather than just assume that everyone knows this, the Microsoft team has added a simple pop-up screen when "incoming email" is selected that warns that Advanced settings need to be selected (which means manual work) if an SMTP server is not available (see Figure 4.10).

FIGURE 4.10
The SMTP serv-
ice warning in the
Incoming Email
Settings page

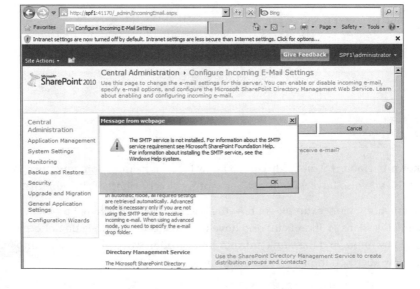

You as Administrator for the entire SPF 2010 system can still use SPD 2010. In many companies the role of site administrator is allocated to a key person in a part of a company whose role is perhaps to control which users can access the sites of that part of the company. Often such users don't have much SharePoint knowledge, yet might be tempted by the seeming ease of use of SPD 2010 to make "a quick change." The settings on the web page shown in Figure 4.9 stop that.

Configuring Alternate Access Methods (AAM)

Most administrators need to configure the alternate access methlods (AAM) at an early stage.

Alternate Access Methods are ways to access a site that are different from the standard way of accessing a site which is to use http://<sitename> (here http://SPF1). It's not always convenient (or possible) to access a site in that way and so there needs to be a way to tell the system which other URLs could also be used.

How, where, and when to specify these alternatives is covered in the main text.

The problem occurs when you access a SharePoint site using a different name than http://<servername> (in our case **http://SPF1**).

At first everything works fine, provided the name you give (perhaps http://sharepoint.mycompany.com) can be converted (using the company's Dynamic Name Server [DNS] perhaps) to the TCP/IP address of the site; then the default page of the site will be accessed as if you were using http://SPF1. After all, that TCP/IP address is the address of http://SPF1, too.

But at some point, you need to access a page internal to the system only known by the address http://SPF1/PathWithinThe Server/default.aspx (for instance) and that page won't be found by a browser looks for http://sharepoint.mycompany.com/PathWithinTheServer/default.aspx or even by a browser that looks for http://<TCP/IP address>/PathWithinThe Server/default.aspx.

To solve this problem, SPF 2010 includes AAM. To use this function, follow these steps:

1. In the Central Administration main page (refer to Figure 4.6), click the Configure Alternate Access Mappings in the System Settings section of the main part of the page (see Figure 4.11).

Oddly, there is an alternative way to get to the same page. Click Application Management (either the heading or the listing in the left column) and you see that Configure Alternate Access Mappings is an option there, too. Equally odd is that

when you click System Settings, you won't see Configure Alternate Access Mappings listed.

As you can see, two sites (the default site and the Central Administration site)
are listed. The following steps amend the default site. The procedure is the same
for the Central Administration site if you want people to access it from outside
the server.

2. Click Edit Public URLs.

Figure 4.12 shows the page you see after the Intranet and the Internet fields have
been completed.

The Central Administration site can be amended by selecting that site in the drop-down at the top right corner of the screen that now shows SharePoint – 80. After Change Alternate Access Mapping Selection, click on Central Administration; write in the same names as in Figure 4.12, but don't forget to include **:41170** at the end of each address.

http://sharepoint.mycompany.com is listed only as an example. It is not necessary to follow this book. What might be useful are additional TCP/IP addresses in different fields. For instance if I connect this PC to my work network, the server will be given a completely different TCP/IP address from the one given to the server in my home network. So it's useful to have specified both these TCP/IP in two different fields.

Here, you can mix addresses such as http://sharepoint.mycompany.com with TCP/IP addresses such as http://192.168.1.2.

What you can't see is that there is no particular reason—beyond good documentation—why the intranet address http://sharepoint.mycompany.com should be entered into the Intranet row.

If you have a single address to enter (apart from default) it can be entered into any of the four rows: Intranet, Internet, Custom, or Extranet. Default however *is* important because that is the address to which the other addresses will be converted.

Summary

This hour looked at the Central Administration site. It showed a few improvements made for this version of SharePoint and how and why to amend the Alternate Access Methods settings so that (in our case) full access to the site can also be available remotely using the address http://192.168.1.2. (Replace this with the TCP/IP address you have for your site.)

Q&A

Q. Are there any other functions of Central Administration that you particularly like?

A. Much of the Central Administration is a tribute to the desire of the Microsoft team to make actions that needed to be done in the earlier versions of Share-Point easier.

One simple thing that I like is the ability with one-click (provided you are on the right page!) to see exactly what SharePoint products have been installed and what their exact version numbers are.

You do this by selecting (again from the basic Central Administration page or Figure 4.6) Upgrade and Migration and then Check Product and Patch Installation Status. That gives a list that at this early stage looks like what is shown in Figure 4.13.

FIGURE 4.13
Patch status

Having this so easily available is useful when providing exact product information to people in forums (or from Microsoft Customer Support Services) trying to help with a problem.

Workshop

Quiz

1. Do you need to be on the server to access Central Administration?

2. Which alternate access box do you need to fill in if users will be accessing your site from an extranet?

Answers

1. No, you can access Central Administration remotely via the browser provided this possibility has not been shut down for security reasons. If it hasn't you should specify suitable AAM settings for the Central Administration site and for the default site.

2. This trick question expects the "obvious" answer that you will need to write the address in the Extranet field, but any of the four fields can be used. Using the Extranet field, however, would be good practice (and would provide good built-in documentation).

We'll come to Language Packs later in the book. Here, note that we thought we had installed one application, and we did (it's the bold Microsoft SharePoint Foundation 2010), but it consists of three separate parts: the core (last line), the main part (first line), and the Language (1033 is U.S. English).

Did you Know?

Planning a Site's Structure

What You'll Learn in This Hour

▶ What sites are
▶ Creating a site
▶ Templates used to create a site
▶ Which site to use for which situation

The site is the basis of all SharePoint installations. You can have one or more sites, and they can be of different types and provide different looks and functions. This hour concentrates entirely on what they are and how to create them, as well as when to use the different kinds of sites.

Basic Information About Sites

Before we can start thinking about a site's structure and contents, we first need to know more about sites in general. Our standard installation of SPF 2010 created two sites: a "normal" one (http://spf1) and a "special" one (http://spf1:41170).

> The words "normal" and "special" are by no means official.

By the Way

The normal site isn't used for any particular purpose and can have subsites. The special site administrates the entire SPF 2010 system using routines provided by Microsoft as part of the software package. This site doesn't include a function for creating a subsite.

> The Central Administration site is the only special site that comes with SPF 2010.

By the Way

SPS 2010, on the other hand, has a few special sites. The one you are most likely to come across in books and the Internet is MySite.

MySite is a site that all users can define for themselves (if not blocked by the administrator). Its dual role is to be a personal page containing information that the user wants to make available to others and a more personal page that the user uses as his usual entry to the system and that contains the information that the user wants to see personally.

Here are a few, often confusing, terms that you will come across:

▶ **Web application**—Any Windows Internet Information Services (IIS) website in the SharePoint system (here, for instance, the default site).

▶ **Top-level site**—A site that is at the top of a site plus subsite structure (even if there are no subsites).

▶ **Site collection**—A set of sites and subsites. There are exceptions to this definition. For example, the Central Administration site is regarded as a site collection even though it has no subsites.

Creating a Site

In this section, you create a subsite to our default site to see what different kinds of sites can be created. The following steps show you how to create a Meeting Workspace site:

1. Start with the default page. (Refer to Figure 2.10 if you can't remember the original look of this). Select Site Actions and then New Site from the drop-down list (see Figure 5.1).

2. After clicking New Site there's a page where information about the name, URL, and what kind of site is to be created needs to be completed. Figure 5.2 shows part of that page. Fill in the three sections that I have added text to but *do not* press Create after doing so.

   The reason you shouldn't yet click Create is that if you do the type of site that will be created will be a Team Site, which is the default type of site (and the most widely used). Here we want to create a Meeting Workspace site.

   Figure 5.3 shows what options are available if the Meetings column head is clicked.

The difference between *sites* and *workspaces* is explained in the section "Q&A."

FIGURE 5.1
The default site showing the Site Actions dropdown

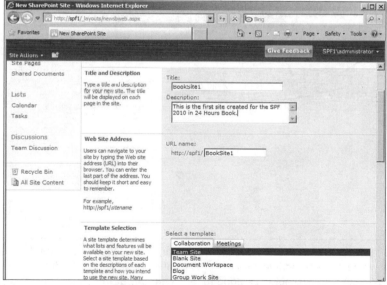

FIGURE 5.2
First steps in creating a site

It is pure chance that there are five different options here and five different options in the Collaboration column, so don't attempt to compare like with like in any way based on position in the respective columns.

Behind each entry in a column is something called a *site template*. A template will be defined later in the hour; for now, just note this as a term that is used. The ones listed at the moment have been created in advance by Microsoft and

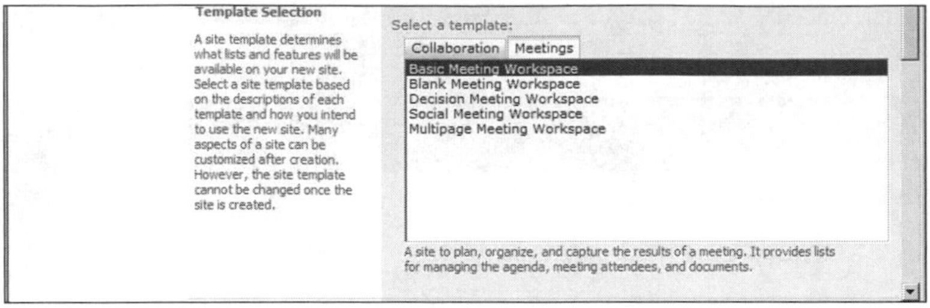

FIGURE 5.3
Meeting sites

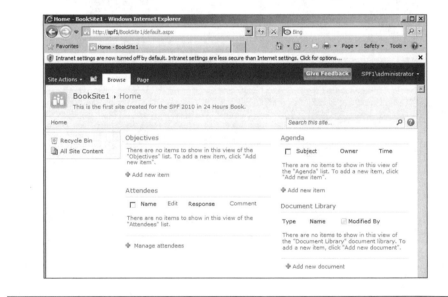

were installed as part of the SPF 2010 installation routine. Each site template
has its own (different) set of functions.

3. Select the standard Basic Meeting Workspace and click Create. Figure 5.4 shows
the newly created Meeting Workspace subsite called "BookSite1."

FIGURE 5.4
Meeting Work-
space–BookSite1

By the Way

> The SharePoint Server 2010 product offers a larger selection of standard sites.
> As shown here, these additional sites are grouped in columns with different ver-
> sions of each type available. It's good to look carefully at the description of a site
> because some have different functionalities than others (and when one function-
> ality is added, another functionality is removed).

By the Way

> This means accepting all the default values that follow the site template section
> on the page. This subsite will inherit the permissions of its parent site. So all the
> users who have access to the default site will also be able to access this Meet-
> ing Workspace with the same access rights.

What you can see in this site's page is covered in the next hour. In this hour, we concentrate on sites and workspaces.

We've already had an example of using a template that wasn't the default "Team Site" template. The next section looks more closely at templates.

Using Templates

A template is a ready-made set of code that is used to create a site. The code contains both a look (site design, colors, fonts) and a feel (what functions are available to use in connection with the site).

In addition to Microsoft providing templates, it's possible to create new templates and have them appear either under the existing Collaboration and Meetings group names or under a group name that we specify.

Typically, templates aren't created from scratch. Instead, they are generally created by amending a site that was created with a standard template and then using the Save As Template function to create a new template with a different name.

> Your browser should be pointing at BookSite1 (see Figure 5.4). If it isn't, type in (if on the server) **http://spf1/BookSite1/default.aspx** or (if in the host system) use your version of my http://192.168.1.2.

By the Way

Let's walk through an example of creating a new template from a site that uses a standard template. Here, we change the color of a site. In this case we use the Meeting Workspace called BookSite1.

1. Select Site Actions (see Figure 5.4) and then (at the bottom of the drop-down list) Site Settings (see Figure 5.5).

2. Select Site Theme in the Look and Feel section (as shown in Figure 5.5).

3. Select Berry from the list of options (as shown in Figure 5.6).

4. Click Apply.

Now you have a page that looks like Figure 5.5 but is horribly garish with a purple top horizontal section and a large, bright yellow section below (and links are in a different color). I chose this Theme because it is so terrible looking that we won't have any difficulty in recognizing it. I don't recommend it for real-life sites.

Let's make another change to the site before we save it as a template.

FIGURE 5.5
Site Settings

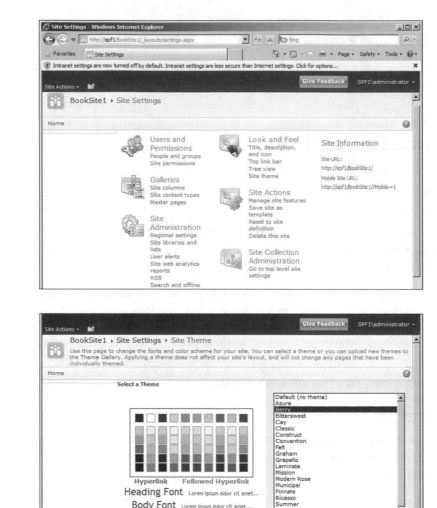

FIGURE 5.6
Selecting the
Berry Theme

In Figure 5.5 (or rather the garish purple/yellow version you have in front of you), perform the following steps:

1. Click Regional Settings under Site Administration.

By the Way

Even though our BookSite1 enables the same people to access it who could access the default site, access, it is still possible to make entries in it look completely different by amending regional settings. Even the simplest thing such as saying that the site is for Finnish and uses a 24-hour clock will make entries in a document library look completely different. (Document libraries will be covered further in Hour 7, "Creating and Using Libraries.")

2. Fill in something different then the original English (U.S.) here (see Figure 5.7). I selected Finnish, which automatically gave a 24-hour clock.

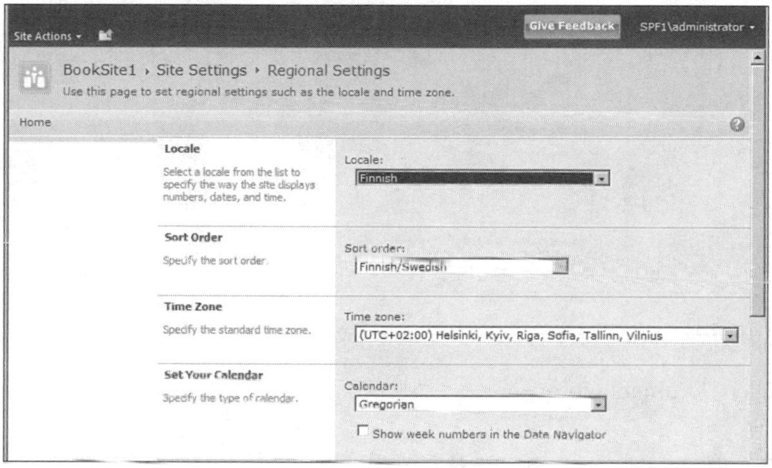

FIGURE 5.7
Specifying different regional settings

3. Click OK.

4. Click BookSite1 (in the large "breadcrumb" at the top of the page) and then on Add New Document, which is under the Document Library section at the right of the site's main page (see Figure 5.8).

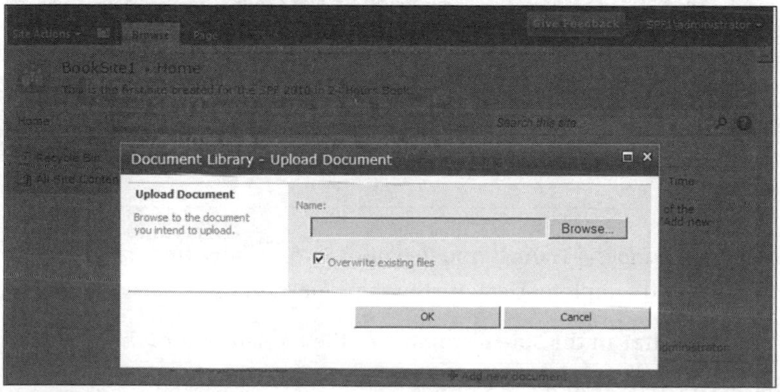

FIGURE 5.8
Adding a file to a Document Library

5. Browse for a .txt file (and text file, we're interested in the date) and add it with OK.

Figure 5.9 shows the revised default page for the BookSite1. (There are no dates here so we can't yet see that this site is using a 24-hour clock and non-U.S. date format).

6. Click Document Library.

If you don't have one in your virtual machine (VM), copy a file from the host system to the desktop of the VM.

Now in Figure 5.10, we can see a Finnish date format (2.12.2009) and a 24-hour clock (18:13) rather than the 12-hour clock of the U.S. settings that we would have seen if we had uploaded the same file to the default site.

With these two changes—Themes and Regional Settings—it's time to save a copy of the revised site as a template. Here are the steps for that:

1. Click BookSite1 in the "breadcrumbs" at the top-left part of the screen.

2. Select Site Actions and Site Settings.

3. This time (you are again at Figure 5.5), click Save Site as Template in the center of the screen; save the template and call it GarishYellow (see Figure 5.11).

4. Click OK (see Figure 5.12).

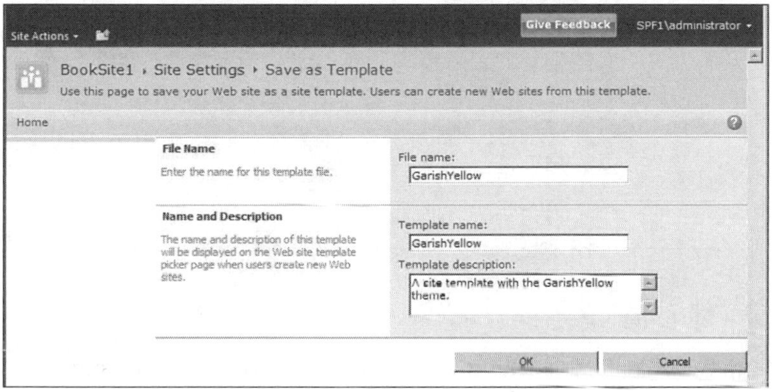

FIGURE 5.11
Saving a GarishYellow template

FIGURE 5.12
The site template has been stored in the User Solution Gallery.

Now that we have saved a site template that includes our two changes (Theme and Regional Settings), we can create a second site called BookSite2 that includes those changes with no additional actions needed on our part. To do this, repeat the steps from earlier in this hour, which were as follows:

1. Go to the default site (Team Site). (There are several ways to do this, one being the Navigate Up button to the left of the Browse tab. Note that the Edit tab is between them if you are logged in as Administrator.)

2. Click Site Actions and then New Site in the drop-down list.

3. Everything is entered as before (replacing BookSite1 with BookSite2 of course), but at the bottom of the screen, you see an additional column called Custom (see Figure 5.13).

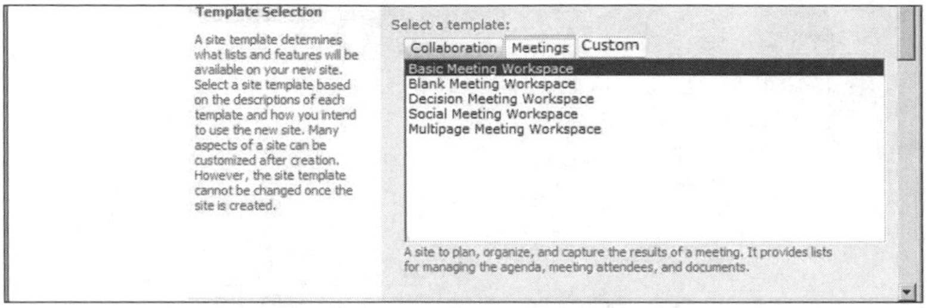

FIGURE 5.13
An additional
Custom column

4. Click Custom.

5. Click GarishYellow, which should be the only entry in that column.

6. Click Create (at the bottom of the page).

Now that you have created a new site, you can check if it has those purple and bright yellow bands, and if you want you can upload a document to the document library as before to check the date and time format.

So now we know that if we want to have a standard look for sites that is different from the look provided by Microsoft, we can do it. Later in the book, we make more comprehensive changes to the look of a site.

Designing Your Site

When creating a site, you have choices. You can choose where to put the site and what kind of site it is.

Creating a Blog or Meeting Site

There are standard templates for blogs, or meetings, so if you want to create one of these types of sites you normally use the standard template provided for them. In each case we have the choice between creating our new site as a subsite to the default site or creating a new top-level site.

For blogs (see Hour 12, "Using Wikis and Blogs"), there's normally no point in having them under the default site in the site structure, so just create a new site. For a meeting site, that could be part of the site structure. If you think it is, create it under the default site.

Always think about why you're creating the site and make it a new site or a site within the existing site structure accordingly. Don't delete the default site. People who do tend to get problems later. Just ignore it if you aren't using it.

Creating a Site for Your Sports Club

Generally, this is going to be an information site. Therefore, you need to choose the Team Site template. In this case, however, because the default site is already a team site, there's no need to create any new sites. Instead, you can just use the default site.

Note the warning about the cost of connecting to the Internet in the "Q&A" section at the end!

Let's close this section on private sites with a couple of thoughts about access rights. When you create a top-level site, you can decide whether anyone can access it (anonymous), or whether you will restrict it to particular users (and which rights they will have). You'll remember that we already created a cross-section of users with different access rights and added them to the site.

When you create a subsite, the default choice is that whoever can access the top-level site (or because subsites aren't necessarily only at level two in a structure, the site above the subsite) can also access the subsite with the same rights. This is known as *inheriting permissions*. The other choice is to not inherit permissions, meaning that no one can access the site until you specifically grant that person access rights on that site.

Now suppose we have our Sport's site and we let everyone access that, but we also want to keep some things private, such as finances. One way is to create a subsite that doesn't inherit permissions and then specify individually those few people who can access and amend that information.

Another way is to create a SharePoint group with standard Contribute rights and then make the finance committee members of that SharePoint group. Then give the group access rights to the subsite. Then when the committee changes, just replace some of the members of that SharePoint group.

Creating a Site for Your Company

With company sites, the main choice is likely to be between a single site (no doubt the default site) with a subsite structure and several different top-level sites (probably also with a subsite structure). The main considerations here are administration needs, the size of those sites, and perhaps even the number of top-level sites the design requires.

You potentially have increased administration needs because the various settings are specified for an entire site collection. If you don't want to have the same settings for all your sites, you must have different site collections (that is, different top-level sites).

The size of those sites is important for backups and restores (for which the size of the content database is important). Each site collection must be contained in a single content database. Therefore, if you have a lot of sites with a lot of data, you might need to use different site collections (which can have their own content databases) to keep the sizes reasonable.

What is *reasonable*? It's difficult to say, but today more than 200GB is considered unreasonable (a couple of years ago, that figure was 50GB).

Finally, it's not advisable to have more than roughly 50 site collections. So, if you are thinking about using a site collection for each subsidiary and you have more than 40 subsidiary companies today, think again. Instead group your subsidiaries together with one group of companies per site collection.

Summary

This hour covered different sites. It showed how to create sites and amend their look. From this new-look site, a template was created from which new sites could be generated.

The hour concluded with a brief look at which kinds of sites are suitable for common private and work areas.

Q&A

Q. *What is the difference between sites and workspaces?*

A. There isn't one. Workspaces are sites, too. The difference is probably historical.

Originally, there were only sites. Then, in SharePoint version 2 products, it became possible to create sites from Office 2003 products (and not just in the browser). Such sites were called document workspaces (connected to Excel, PowerPoint, Word) and meeting workplaces (connected to Outlook).

In present versions of SharePoint, both kinds are called workspaces, even though the meeting workspaces are sufficiently different to justify their own type button.

Q. *I want to connect my private website using SPF 2010 to the Internet. Can I just do it?*

A. No. Connecting to the Internet involves licensing costs. These costs could drive you to using a commercial web host for your site. If you run SPF 2010, an Internet connection license for the server costs a few thousand dollars. This is on top of the normal licensing requirement for the operating system used on the server (and database licensing costs if a full SQL Server product is used).

Workshop

Quiz

1. What are the two main groupings of site templates?

2. How does the Site Settings page change after a subsite has been created?

3. Can we create our own company look and duplicate it?

Answers

1. Collaboration and Meetings.

2. There are more options in the Site Collection Administration Column after subsites have been created.

3. Yes. One way is to make changes to an existing site, save the result as a template, and then use that newly created template when creating all future sites.

HOUR 6

Using Libraries and Lists

What You'll Learn in This Hour

- ▶ Main areas of the default site page
- ▶ Differentiating among a List Type, a List, and a List View Web Part

There is often great confusion even among people who have been using SharePoint sites for a long time as to what the difference is among a List Type, a List, and a List View Web Part. Because of the confusion, this hour, in addition to looking at the basic elements of a site, spends a lot of time looking at the differences among these three kinds of List-related elements of an SPF 2010 site.

Understanding the Basic Site Elements

To understand the concept of lists and libraries, the first section of this hour focuses on the links to list and libraries in the standard website.

The version of the default site you can see now (Figure 6.1) includes the two subsites that you created. These are neatly placed horizontally next to the original Home. If you click BookSite1, this section of the page vanishes, and you need (as you have previously seen) to click the Navigate Up icon to go back to Team Site.

The section vertically below the word Home is the Quick Launch section.

The Quick Launch section created for the default site consists of three main sections (Documents, List, and Discussions) and within them links to one or more other features. These other features with the exception of the first (Site Pages) are all different kinds of Lists.

If you now go to Site Actions > More Options, you see a list of things that can be created, as shown in Figure 6.2. Most of these (apart from the Pages and Sites) are Lists, too.

FIGURE 6.1 Looking more closely at the default page

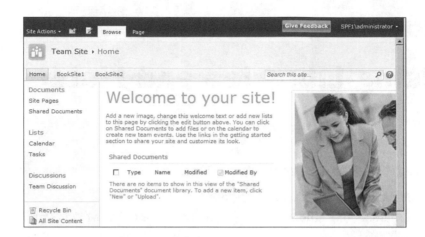

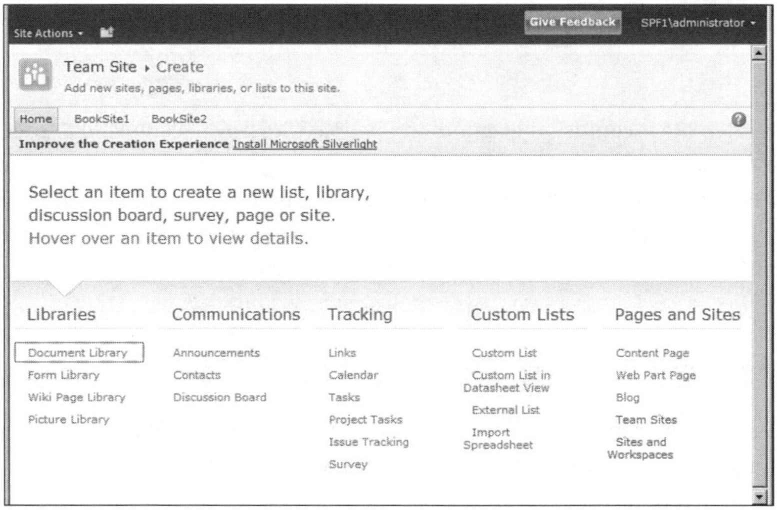

FIGURE 6.2 List types that you can create

This, as stated in the figure caption, is a listing of List Types that can be created.

You should especially note here the following: Document Library, Calendar, Tasks, and Discussion Board, because we'll come back to them after first learning the difference between a List and a Library.

Did you Know?

This is the look you get if you haven't installed Silverlight. It's a clean, practical look (if nonsexy) that is suitable for work done by an Administrator on a server. I therefore don't recommend that you follow the "Improve the Creation Experience" suggestion and install Silverlight (on your server).

Differentiating Between a List and a Library

A List is the basic way in which information is stored in a SPF 2010 site.

All the items in Figure 6.2 when accessed generate a List. Columns 2 through 4 are only there to split up the kinds of Lists that are created into logical groups.

But Column 1 is a separate column because all the items listed are for a special kind of List known as a Library.

The main difference between a Library and a List is that an item in a Library must contain a file.

▶ The main function of a Library is to store files and the accompanying metadata to those files.

▶ The main function of a List is to store data.

The other main difference is that because document libraries always contain a file, it's possible to have versioning of files.

Differentiating Among a List Type, List, and List View Web Part

1. Look again at Figure 6.1 and click Calendar (see Figure 6.3).

2. Now make an entry in the Calendar—say for about 2 weeks from now.

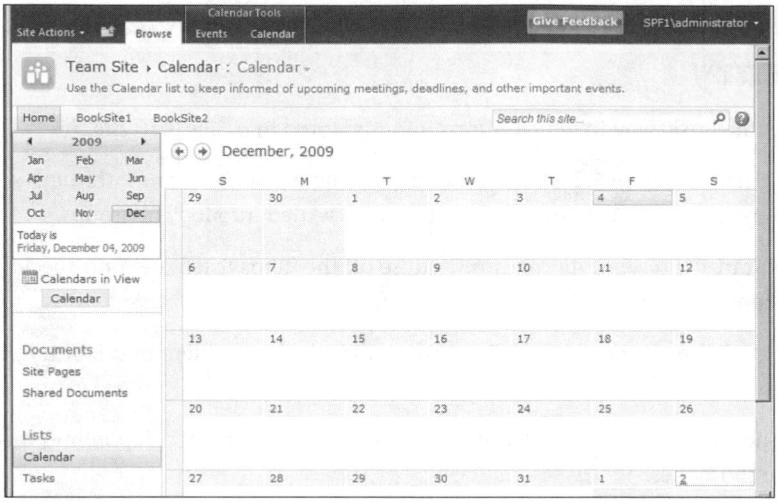

FIGURE 6.3
The Calendar
is included in
the basic
installation.

By the Way

You can add links to one or more files as part of the metadata of Lists. This, while possible, is rare, and the links to the files typically are much less important that the data in the List.

Did you Know?

Don't get too enthused by the idea of using SPF 2010 as a Version Control system. That's not what Versioning is for. Versioning (of major and minor versions) is fine for working on a company document and keeping track of amendments to it, but it is not suited for source code.

3. Double-click a specific day (see Figure 6.4).

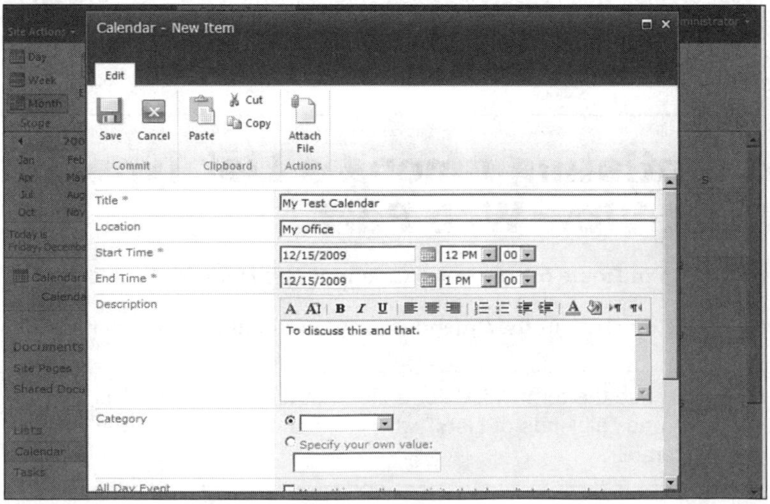

FIGURE 6.4
My Test Calendar

4. Fill in the New Item form, as shown in Figure 6.4.

5. Click Save. The screen now shows a new version of Figure 6.3; this time there is an entry on the 15th of December, 2009 (in my case).

6. Go Back to the default page via the Navigation Up icon and Team Site. No change to that page is visible.

We've done this before in Hour 5, "Planning a Site's Structure," so I won't repeat the screenshots. Look at Figure 5.8, which matches step 3.

By the Way

Next we'll do a similar action with the entry for Shared Documents. Because this is a Library, we'll add a file to Shared Documents. The following steps are the way to do that:

1. Click Shared Documents.

2. Click Add a Document.

3. Browse for a .txt file and upload it to the site.

We now have a library called Shared Documents that includes a single Text file called weeklyblog.txt (see Figure 6.5).

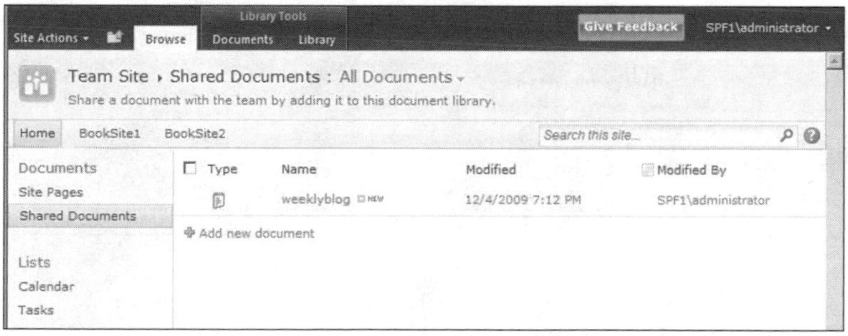

FIGURE 6.5
A list of the files in Shared Documents

Now return to the Team Site page. Figure 6.6 shows that the section of the main part of the page (the heading "Shared Documents") now includes a file called weeklyblog.

So far we have used a Library called "Shared Documents" and a Calendar called "Calendar," both of which were created for us by the installation routine.

We can also create our own. Let's create our own Library called "OurDocumentLibrary." We can do this using Site Settings > More Options (see Figure 6.2).

1. (At Team Site) Click Site Actions > More Options.

FIGURE 6.6
A home page

2. Click Document Library, as shown in Figure 6.7.

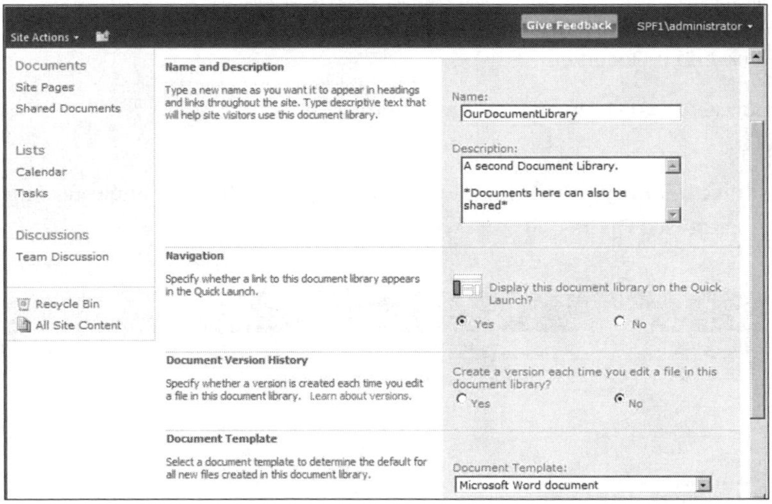

FIGURE 6.7
Creating a new
Document
Library

3. Click Create.

4. Go back to the Team Site (Navigate Up icon again).

The default page now has an additional entry in the Quick Launch section—at the end despite the name.

By the Way

Did you notice the text in the description? Despite its name, the already existing document library called "Shared Documents" is not the only document library where documents can be shared. That name has confused users from earlier versions of SharePoint, but it remains.

Now we have enough material to enable us to give an understandable explanation of the differences between a List Type and a List. (The List View Web Part follows.)

▶ **List Types** are what you saw in Figure 6.2. A List Type is a definition of a kind of List. Earlier in the book, we used the List Type "Document Library" to create a Library called "OurDocumentLibrary." Microsoft, as part of the installation routine, used the List Type "Document Library" to create a Library called "Shared Documents." Microsoft also in the installation routine used the List Type "Calendar" to create a List called "Calendar."

▶ **A List** is created using a List Type. Several Lists with different names can be created from the same List Type. Content is added to a List. Each List is a separate entity. If content is added to a List, that content is only in that one List and not in any other List created from the same List Type (unless also added specifically there).

> If you dislike the order of Items in Quick Launch, you can change it by selecting Search Actions > Site Settings > Quick Launch.
>
> *Site*

I hope that clears up the difference between a List Type and a List. Microsoft did us no favors by sometimes (Calendar, Tasks) creating as part of the installation Lists with the same names as the List Types they were built from and sometimes (Shared Documents, Team Discussion) creating Libraries/Lists with different names to the List Types they were built on.

The Difference Between a List and a List View Web Part

If you were watching carefully earlier, you might have spotted one example of a List View Web Part.

A List View Web Part is a representation in web part form of a List or Library.

When we added a file to the Shared Documents Library, we first saw the List containing the file (see Figure 6.5). We then went back to the default site page (see Figure 6.6) and saw that the Shared Document (main) section of the default site page also showed the same file. This is because what is visible in the main section of the default site page is the same list in a different form. It is officially called a List View Web Part.

> For now, let's just say that a web part is a function that can be added to a page like the default site page.

Now that we've got that straight, let's create our own simple List View Web Part.

We already added an entry to the List called "Calendar" (see Figure 6.4), so let's create a List View Web Part from that List using the following steps:

1. (At Team Site) Click the Edit icon (to the right of the Navigate Up icon), as shown in Figure 6.8.

FIGURE 6.8
Editing the default page text

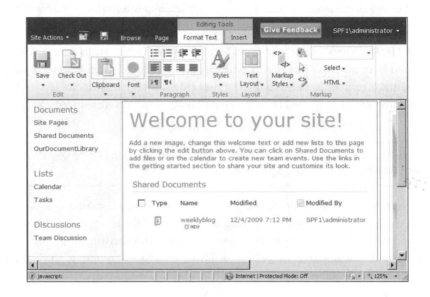

Here for the first time you can see that the 2010 SharePoint products have acquired the same look as Office 2007. (It was there in some other screenshots but hardly noticeable).

This particular set of editing tools that focuses on texts and fonts isn't what we need this time.

2. Click Insert in the top menu line under the Editing Tools heading (see Figure 6.9).

3. Click Web Part (see Figure 6.10).

4. Click Calendar and OK (see Figure 6.11 in a couple of pages).

As you can see, if you scroll down the page, the Calendar has been added to the main section of the default page just above the "Welcome to the Site" section. We won't

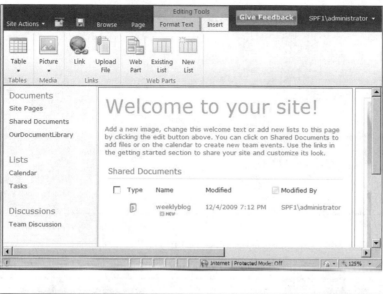

FIGURE 6.9
Editing the
default page
insert

FIGURE 6.10
Editing the
default page—
Web Parts

change that location but note that having the whole calendar there takes up a great deal of space.

The following steps show what to do to convert this into a Summary View that will only show appointments (in this case, one):

1. Click the downward-facing arrow at the end of the line containing the Calendar heading. This arrow is visible if the mouse is hovering above the line following the calendar text.

2. Select Edit Web Part.

FIGURE 6.11
The Calendar
has been added
to the central
section.

3. Move to the right of the screen (see Figure 6.12).

FIGURE 6.12
Modify the Cal-
endar Web Part

4. Change the Current View to Summary View.

5. Change Toolbar Type to No Toolbar.

6. Click OK (see Figure 6.13).

As you can see in Figure 6.13, the entry we made in the Calendar List is visible in this Calendar List View Web Part (LVWP). That's because this Calendar LVWP was based on the Calendar List, and the View of the List we chose to display did not exclude this particular calendar item. (Views are discussed further later in this hour.)

Finally, we need to save the changes we've made under Edit. There are two alternatives (see steps 7 and 8).

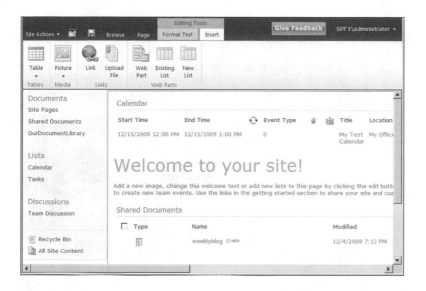

FIGURE 6.13
The Calendar
Summary View

7. Save using the diskette icon, which is in the location where the Edit icon previously was.

   OR

8. Leave Editing (such as via clicking All Site Content in the left-hand-column). Then you will be asked if you want to save your changes.

When you have a screen that looks like Figure 6.13, try clicking some of its sections (Calendar, Shared Documents, and the Image) You can see the menu bar options change accordingly. Figure 6.14, for instance, is part of the menu bar when the image is clicked.

By the Way

If for some reason you decide you don't want to make changes, following step 8, you can choose No to take you back to the state before the Edit.

Did you Know?

FIGURE 6.14
An extended
Menu Bar after a
single click on
the image

Summary

The main part of this hour has been learning about the differences among a List Type, a List, and a List View Web Part. These differences are summarized in the following bullets:

▶ A **List Type** is ready-made code supplied with the product that contains certain functions. When you (or the installation routine) create a List, you decide which List Type you are going to use to provide the functionality of that List.

▶ The **List** is the sole one of List Type, List, and List View Web Part that contains data.

▶ A **List View Web Part** is only a representation of a List. Depending on the View chosen for it, it contains all the data from the list or only some of the data of the List.

Views will be covered properly in Hour 8, "Creating and Using Views and Folders." Here we have just glanced at them.

Did you
Know?

There are two different kinds of List View Web Parts in SPF 2010. The second kind called "XSLT List View Web Parts" or "XLV" will be discussed later. The preceding description (no own content) applies to both kinds of LVWP.

Q&A

Q. *I lost count of the number of times we did things with Calendars. Why were there so many different things that were Calendars, or were they all the same thing?*

A. In the present site, there are four things called Calendar:.

1. There's a Calendar List Type *(code that provides Calendar functionality)*.

2. There's a Link in the Quick Launch section *(a Link that goes to a List called Calendar that the installation routine created using the Calendar List Type)*.

3. There's a List called Calendar *(created by the installation routine using the Calendar List Type)*.

4. There's a List View Web Part called Calendar *(created using the List called Calendar to provide its content)*.

Q. *Are there any differences between the default page of the main site and the default pages of the subsites we created using the default Meeting Workspace template?*

A. Yes, the default site created by the installation package uses the Team Site template. This—in the 2010 products—creates a default page that uses the Wiki page type. The default page created by the Meeting Workspace uses the Web Part page type.

The Wiki page type is more powerful but more difficult to use. In this hour, the Summary View of the calendar would have been better located below the Welcome text, but explaining how to do this is beyond the scope of this hour. As we see later, adding and positioning a calendar to a page of the Web Part type is much more straight-forward.

Workshop

Quiz

1. What is the main difference between a Library and any other kind of List?

2. Is Shared Documents the only Document Library that is shareable?

Answers

1. The main difference is that a Library item must include a file.

   Document Libraries and other kinds of Libraries are thus storage locations for files and the metadata about those files. Other kinds of Lists contain data and cannot contain files. (They can however contain links to files if a file is required to add value to the data in the List.)

2. No. All Document Libraries are as shareable as the Document Library that Microsoft created in the Installation of SPF 2010 by using the Document Library List Type and choosing to call Shared Documents. It is just a name—they could have picked a better name in my opinion as this particular name has confused people in earlier versions too not just in SPF 2010.

HOUR 7

Creating and Using Libraries

What You'll Learn in This Hour

▶ Understanding the different libraries

▶ Creating a picture library and a document library

▶ Different ways to add images and files

There are several different kinds of Libraries. This hour describes the differences between them and shows how to create a library and how to use it.

Different Types of Libraries

The list of libraries shown in Figure 6.2 (in Hour 6, "Using Libraries and Lists") contains the following four library types:

▶ **Document library**. Standard library type used for the majority of file types. This is the most commonly used library type.

▶ **Form library**. Designed to be a storage location for forms created in InfoPath 2010. When you create a form in InfoPath 2010 and "publish" it, it publishes to a form library.

▶ **Wiki page library**. Stores wiki pages.

▶ **Picture library**. Stores images (previously this was called an image library).

InfoPath 2010 is beyond this book's scope, so Form Library is not discussed in this hour.

By the Way

All these library types store files. Each type enables versioning to be specified, but they differ in the kinds of files that they are designed to store.

A picture library differs from a standard document library mainly in the way the files are presented. For example, a thumbnail view and a slide view are available in picture libraries. Neither would make sense in a document library.

By the Way

> Hour 12, "Using Wikis and Blogs," covers wiki pages.

Creating and Using a Picture Library

In this section, we create a simple picture library and add images to it.

Creating the Picture Library

To create the picture library, go to the default site and select Site Actions > More Options; then scroll down to see the image for Picture Library. Click the icon to select Picture Library, add the name **My Own Photos** (see Figure 7.1), and click Create. You now have an empty picture library (see Figure 7.2).

FIGURE 7.1
Creating a picture library

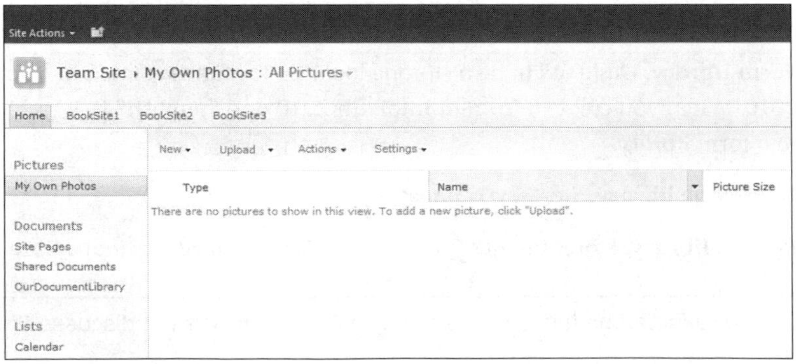

FIGURE 7.2
An empty picture library

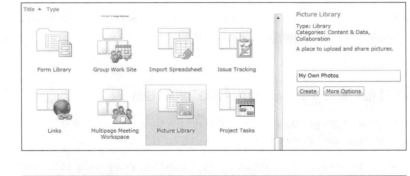

You need to add some files to the picture library. The most common way to add files (and this goes for a document library) is to use the browser.

Using the Single-Upload Method

To add files to your picture library using the single-upload method, you must first select the Upload option.

Although here we use Upload to upload an image to a picture library, the technique is identical for uploading a single file to a document library; thus, these steps are not repeated when we discuss the document library. So even if you don't think you'll use a picture library, read through the instructions in this hour.

Here's how you can upload one document at a time:

1. Select Browse.

2. Find a suitable image file. (A suitable image file can be any image file you have available—for instance a .jpg file).

3. Select the image file.

4. Upload the image file.

Add some more images by repeating the preceding steps. At this point—in TV cook style—I've uploaded three images. Now I'll upload a fourth, still using the single-upload method (see Figure 7.3).

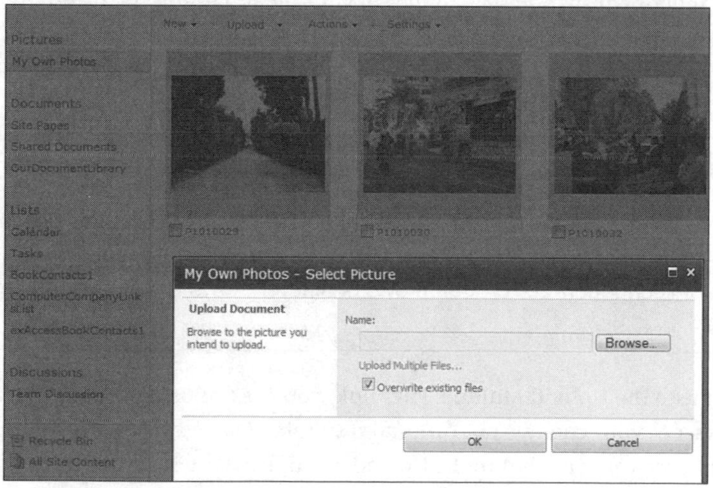

FIGURE 7.3
Adding a picture

When you add a single picture, you get the chance to add metadata. In this case, the fields that can be completed are those included in the picture library as it is delivered. As you add another picture, fill in some of the fields as in Figure 7.4 and press Save to complete the action.

FIGURE 7.4
A single picture
with fields to fill
in

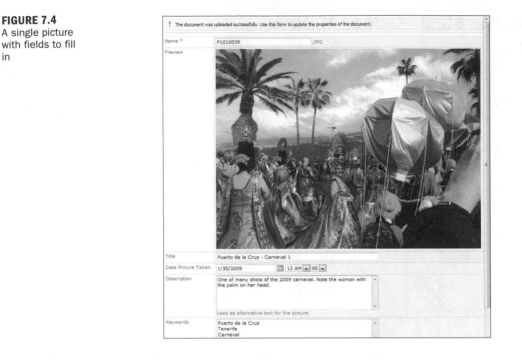

Using the Multiple-Upload Method

You can simultaneously add several files to your picture library by using the Upload Multiple Files link that was an option in Figure 7.3.

For an alternative way to achieve the same result of uploading multiple files (instead of clicking the word Upload in Figure 7.2), select the small arrow to the right of the word Upload. A drop-down list displays with the options to Upload Picture or Upload Multiple Pictures.

SharePoint Foundation 2010 often provides different ways to achieve the same result.

If you can't see the Upload Multiple Files link, you are not using Internet Explorer as your browser or your client is not running a suitable Office version on your client system. (The Office versions that make Upload Multiple Files visible are Office 2003 Pro, Office 2007, and Office 2010.)

Follow these steps to upload multiple files using the Upload Multiple Files link:

1. Choose Upload Multiple Files, as was shown in Figure 7.3.

Figure 7.5 is included so that you are not worried if you see it. (You might not see it. Don't worry about that, either!) If you don't see Figure 7.5, you instead loaded Microsoft Office Picture Manager directly (see Figure 7.6).

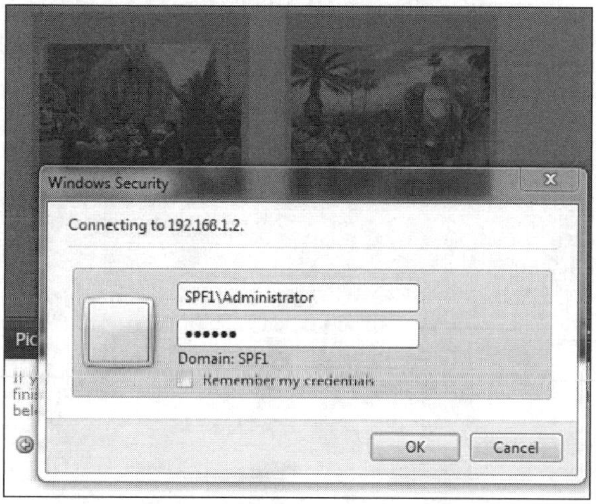

FIGURE 7.5
A request for authentication when starting Office Picture Manager

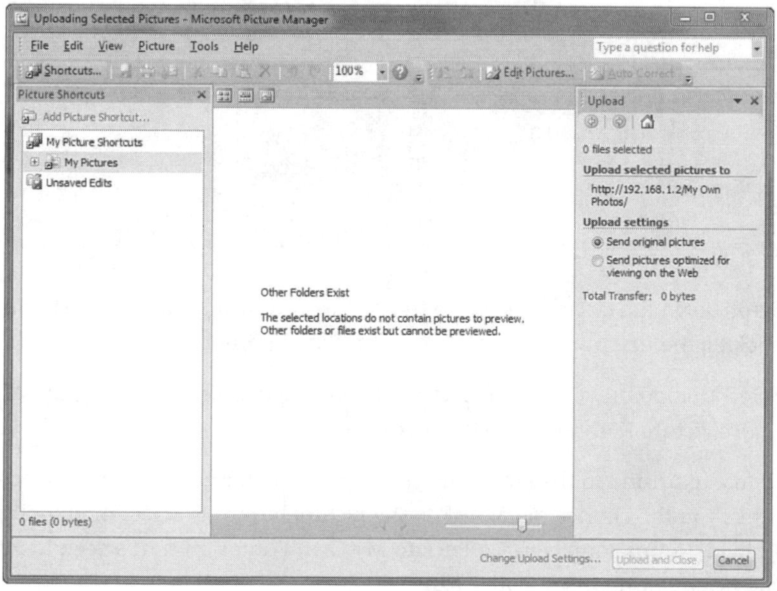

FIGURE 7.6
Choosing a directory in Office Picture Manager

You need certain Office versions on your client PC to use Multiple Upload, which has previously been mentioned; however, the fact that a multiple upload will load the Microsoft Office Picture Manager is yet another reason for that requirement.

The Office Picture Manager screen is likely to show you images from a directory that you don't want to select your photos/images from.

2. If the wrong directory displays, select Add Picture Shortcut (see Figure 7.6) to add to the My Picture Shortcuts list the directory containing the images you want.

In Figure 7.7, I've added (and selected) the MikePics2009 directory (see the left-most column).

FIGURE 7.7
Selecting pictures in Office Picture Manager

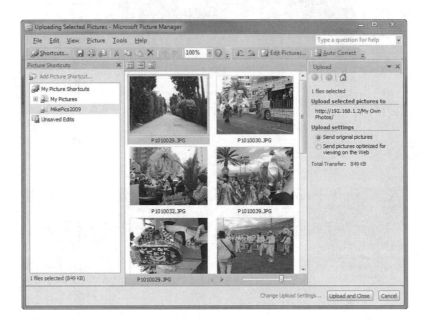

3. Scroll down the central section to the photos you want to use. Select them by clicking the first one and Ctrl-clicking subsequent images.

4. Select Upload and Close. The pictures upload to the picture library, and the Office Picture Manager application closes.

5. Before returning to the picture library, the Picture Library Information screen offers you the chance to go back to the picture library to select more images to upload. In this case, click Go Back to My Own Photos on that screen to return to the picture library (see Figure 7.8).

Although we added metadata to one of those pictures, all the pictures look the same. Nothing indicates that one picture has metadata associated with it.

FIGURE 7.8
The picture library with content

As previously mentioned, if you select Upload Multiple Pictures, the pictures upload to the picture library with empty metadata fields. This is logical. Otherwise, uploading a number of pictures would mean "Stop! Give me metadata for picture 1; Stop! Give me metadata for picture 2;" and so on. The upload would take forever.

By the Way

To see whether you have metadata, double-click a picture. If you want to amend or add metadata, select Edit Item in the menu line (see Figure 7.9).

FIGURE 7.9
Checking and adding metadata for a picture

> The Upload Multiple Pictures option offers a quick way to upload numerous images from a single directory. If you require the images to be itemized, however, the total time needed might be more than that required for single uploads.

You can upload documents to a library in other ways (as discussed in the document library coverage). Even so, only the browser-based, single-upload method means that metadata entry is possible as you upload to the library.

Creating a Document Library

A document library stores documents in the same way as a picture library stores images. Document libraries are more widely used than picture libraries, so throughout the rest of this book we concentrate almost entirely on them.

So that we have something to work with in our document library, I created several files (most with little content) in Acrobat, Excel, PowerPoint, Notepad (so, normal text files), and Word. (I did this on a PC running Office 2010 but saved the Office files in 2003–2007 format.) These files should give enough initial data to see how document libraries are used. If you don't want to create files yourself (or can't), you can find files in different formats on the Internet and use them.

Following are the files, the number of files, and the file types. The filenames indicate which company is associated with them:

▶ Excel (7) 2 HP, 3 IBM, 1 MS, 1 Oracle

▶ PDF (4) 2 IBM, 2 MS

▶ PowerPoint (1) MS

▶ Text (3) 2 HP, 1 MS

▶ Word (5) 2 HP, 3 MS

> **By the Way**
>
> Be patient. It won't be long and you'll see why I created files that are supposed to be from different companies.

We start by creating a new document library (instead of using the existing one, Shared Documents):

1. If you aren't at the default page, click Home and select Site Actions > New Document Library.

2. Add a Name and Description.

3. Leave the default as Display on the Quick Launch but amend the second radio button pair so that we have versions allowed.

(If you forget to do this—or want to fine-tune the Version settings—go to (Library) > Library Settings > Versioning Settings.

4. Leave the final drop-down at its default value. Notice that this specifies the type of document that will be created for this document library if you click New Document when opening the document library.

There is actually one good reason for having a special template here: if you are an administrator and want your users to use a different template when writing documents for a particular document library than they normally use.

One good reason for that is if you want them to always fill in some additional properties whenever they create a new Word document.

In that case, you create a Word document, add properties, and then give all those properties dummy values. You then save the Word document as a template (Our-CompanyTemplate perhaps) and make sure that template is available in the drop-down that appears in Figure 7.10.

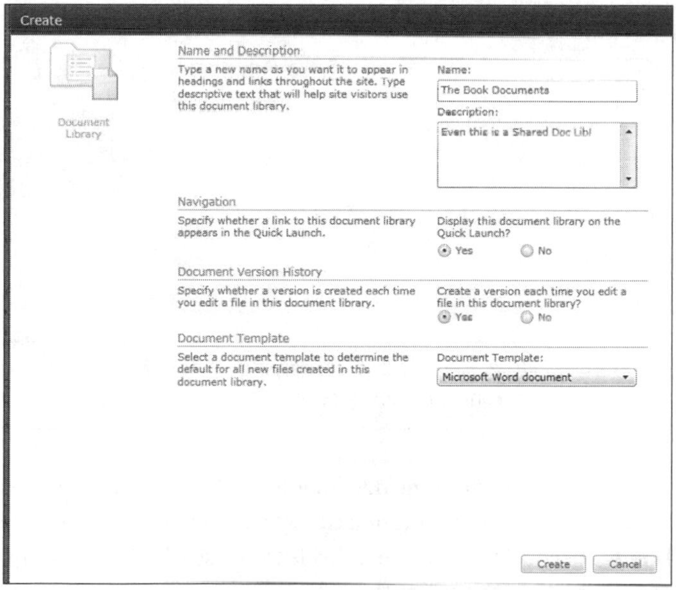

By the Way

FIGURE 7.10
Creating a document library

In this case, I left this at the default value of a Word document (see Figure 7.10).

By the Way

5. Click Create.

Alternative Methods for Uploading Files to a Document Library

You just learned two ways to upload items to a library. In this section, those methods apply to files being uploaded to a document library.

Because the methods are the same, there's no point in repeating them here. Instead, let's look at a couple of alternative methods.

One method involves opening the document library in one window and going to Library > Open with Explorer (what used to be known as the Explorer view). (See the left-most and upper-right part of Figure 7.11.) Then open Windows Explorer in another window and select the files you want to upload (lower-right part of Figure 7.11).

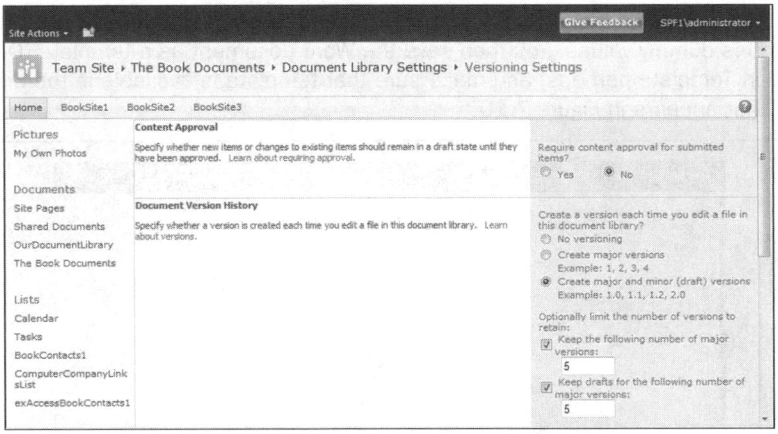

FIGURE 7.11
Copying files to a document library using Explorer View

By the Way

> Don't be confused by Figure 7.11. It is a screenshot that combines in one image the web pages of two different browser copies.

Often, you can just drag and drop the documents (in Figure 7.11). On a few client systems, however, this doesn't work. In that case, select the files and then press Ctrl-C on the right side and Ctrl-V on the left (here, this is top) side (that is, copy and paste)—this alternative method always seems to work.

By the Way

> Don't worry if you see an error message after clicking Open with Explorer that says your client system isn't suitable. Just try again. In almost all cases in which the client system isn't suitable (such as if you use Safari for Windows), Open with

Explorer isn't listed and can't be selected. So if it can be selected, it should work. If you keep getting this message, turn the IE Browser Protected Mode to Off.

Just as with the multiple-upload option in the user interface, you won't have yet had an option to fill in any fields with additional information about the documents being uploaded. All the system knows is that you uploaded the document, when, what the filename is (what kind of document it is), the file size, and a few more things we can't see in Figure 7.12.

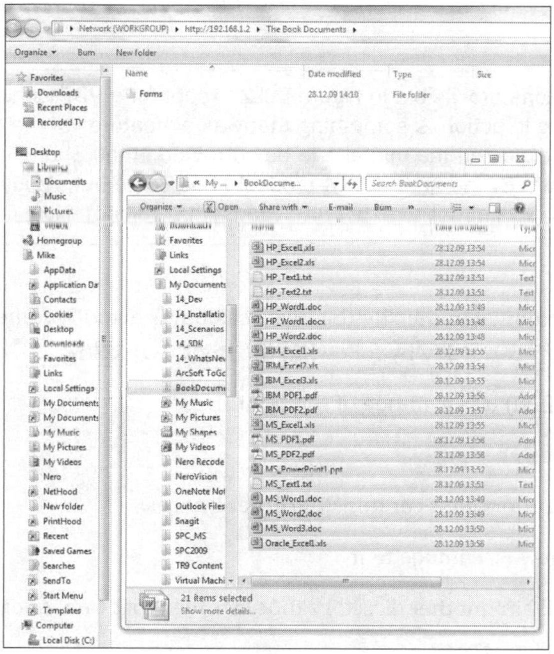

FIGURE 7.12
The refreshed All Documents view

After you copy the files, close the window created by Open in Explorer and go back to the Book Document page. To see the files you have just uploaded to this page, refresh the page and you get the list of files you see in Figure 7.12.

The second main way to perform multiple uploads (there are some less-usual methods that I don't discuss) involves using local drives.

Here is an outline of how to use that second method:

1. Assign a document library to a local drive via a statement in the command line like this (where the URL of the document library is http://servername/xxx/doclib1):

   Net use X: \\servername\xxx\doclib1

(If this isn't enough explanation for you, ignore this method.)

2. Copy your files from (for instance) your PC My Documents folder to X: or use the following method using My Network Places:

▶ Define the document library in My Network Places.

▶ Open the My Network Places entry.

▶ Copy and paste (or drag and drop if it works) the files from Windows Explorer to it.

All the correct icons are visible in Figure 7.12 except for a PDF icon. Having the PDF icon missing in action is something that was a "feature" of the SharePoint v2 products, too. I expected the mistake to be corrected in the SharePoint v3 products, but it wasn't. By the time the v4 products had come out, I'd given up expecting anything. I was right not to expect it because it's still not there.

The problem mentioned in the "By the Way" sidebar is actually something the administrator can fix quickly by following the steps that follow:

1. Create (or find) a PDF image of the right size.

2. Go to the server.

3. Find the directory that contains the other images.

4. Copy the new PDF image to it.

5. Amend a file in another directory that lists file types (and adding a line for PDF files).

If you want more detailed instructions, track down a Microsoft article with more details: Go to www.microsoft.com and use the search term **pdf icon sharepoint**, which should give you KB article 837849.

Summary

Here we looked at a picture library and a document library. It showed how files are uploaded to them, which data is available on those files, and how the files are displayed on the default page for the library.

Q&A

Q. *What is the point of adding metadata? I just want to quickly add content, so surely uploading a lot of files simultaneously is the best method even if I can't in the same process add metadata.*

A. Adding metadata both enables you to set up meaningful views (see Hour 8, "Creating and Using Views and Folders") and to improve the quality of your searches (Hour 14, "Improving Searches").

There's a discussion later (in the section about folders in Hour 8) about why it's not a good idea to attempt to replace the file system by uploading large quantities of files in bulk.

Q. *You talked about creating a template for use in a document library. What are the steps for doing this?*

A. Here is what you do:

1. Open the document library.

2. Choose Library.

3. Choose Library Settings.

4. Choose Advanced Settings (leftmost column).

5. Select Edit Template (second section down on the far-right of the screen).

    This opens the default template in Word, and you can amend it. (It's probably an empty page; see what happens if you write a text into it like My New Template).

6. Save as the template with a new name (MyTemplate.dotx).

This saves the template in Forms alongside default.dot. (That is, both templates are stored in Forms, so default.doc is still available if you want to change back to it.) In this case the new template is a Word 2010 format template. To avoid this, follow the warning on saving the template to specify a template that is compatible with older versions.

You are then taken back to the Advanced Settings page, where you see the effect of the change. You need to change the name of the default template to MyTemplate.docx. Click OK.

Now when you click New in the document library, you see your new template (perhaps with your company logo) rather than the old standard one.

Workshop

Quiz

1. What are two main ways to upload files to a library when using the user interface?

2. When is the Multiple-Upload option not available?

3. What is the major problem with using the Multiple-Upload option?

Answers

1. The single-upload method and the multiple-upload method.

2. If the client system is not running Internet Explorer (5.x and later) or is running Internet Explorer but isn't running Office 2003 Pro, Office 2007, or Office 2010.

3. Metadata cannot be added during the upgrade process when using the Upload Multiple Files option.

HOUR 8

Creating and Using Views and Folders

What You'll Learn in This Hour

▶ Creating and naming a new field

▶ Creating views using the new field's different values

▶ Creating folders even though you should not use them

To present the contents of a list or library to a user, you can use a view. Views are typically used for document libraries to divide the presentation of the library's contents into subsections or to list them in a particular order.

A folder is the equivalent of a directory in the file system. You can add documents to a folder contained within a document library rather than to the document library's main storage level.

Creating a Suitable Column for a View

Later in this hour, we create views. To do that, we need to have a column/field in the document library that we can use when creating those views. So in this section, we create a column called Company and populate it with the name of computer companies. This enables us to later create, for instance, a view where only IBM documents are listed for the user.

Follow these steps to create a column for a view:

1. Go to http://spf1 (or the TCP-IP address you are using) and select The Book Documents.

2. Select Library > List Settings. In the Column section of the page, select Create Column. Figure 8.1 appears.

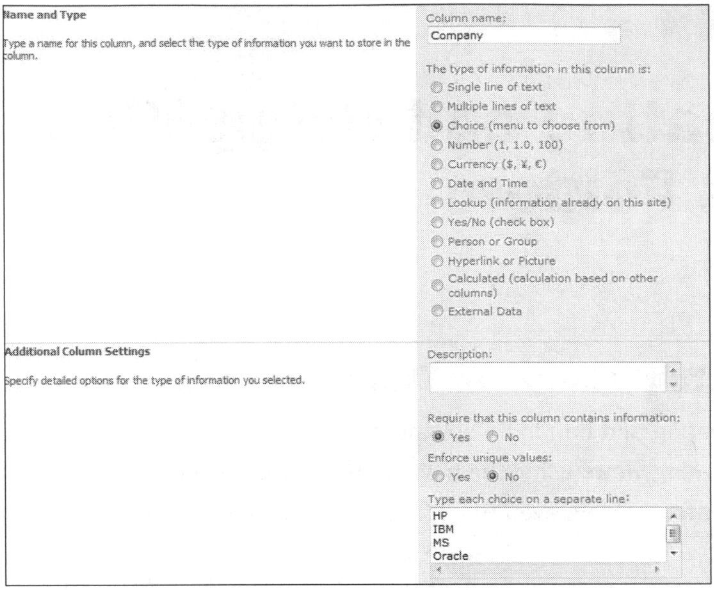

FIGURE 8.1
Creating the Column page

Both words—field and column—are used in documentation. Column is used because when you open a document library, the new field Company appears in the list as a column (if it is selected to be listed, that is).

In the database table where all these things are stored, it's a field, of course. Confusing, isn't it? (I have already added some information to this figure.)

Below the area of the screen shown in Figure 8.1, there is a tricky option: Allow Fill-In Options. If this isn't selected the user is restricted to using one of the values that the administrator has previously defined for this column/field.

If you don't (as an administrator) allow additional values, you open the door to a stream of phone calls or emails asking you to add something.

If you do allow this option, you will be bound to get alternative spellings of the same thing (which, naturally, the system will not regard as being the same thing), and you will have to occasionally tidy the mess.

3. You have many different options for The Type of Information in This Column Is section.

    It would be swamping you with too much information to go through all the options, so here are the ones I use most often on my sites:

    ▶ Single Line of Text

    ▶ Choice (which enables you to specify the possible contents of this field/column)

▶ Date and Time (using the Date Only option for that column)

▶ Yes/No

4. We have the option to Add to Default View. Here, we leave it in.

5. Click OK. That takes us back to the Library Settings page, which is often useful because typically you add several columns before moving on to doing something else. Here, as we are only adding a single column, going back to this page is a minor nuisance.

6. Click The Book Documents at the top of the page (above the section of the page shown in Figure 8.1) in the breadcrumbs. Figure 8.2 displays.

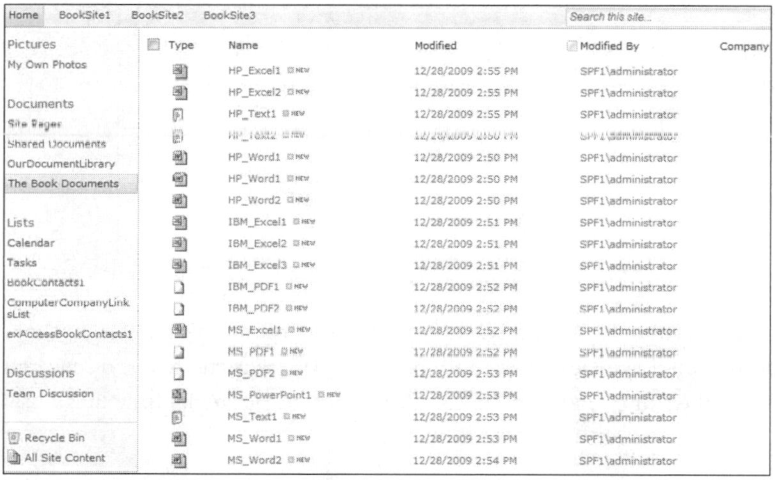

FIGURE 8.2
No values in the column we just added

Can you spot the issue in Figure 8.2? We want to add a value in the Company column for each row in the list, and we don't seem to be able to.

Here's what seems to be a list of our present options:

▶ We can click the icon in the Type column to open the document.

▶ We can click the field name (which is in the Title column) to open the document.

Neither the icon nor the field name enables us to add a value to the Company column. However, as the next section shows, there are actually other less apparent options on that page.

Three Editing Solutions for a View

You have three ways of creating such a view. All three are detailed next.

Editing a View with a Drop-Down

One solution, which is editing a view with a drop-down, requires no changes to the list shown in Figure 8.2. To use this solution, follow these steps:

1. If you move your cursor to the first row under the Name column and then carefully move the cursor beyond the text, you see a box with an arrow at the end of it (see Figure 8.3). (In earlier versions of SharePoint, this worked only if your browser was Internet Explorer 5.5 and upward but now also works in browsers such as Safari for Windows and Firefox.)

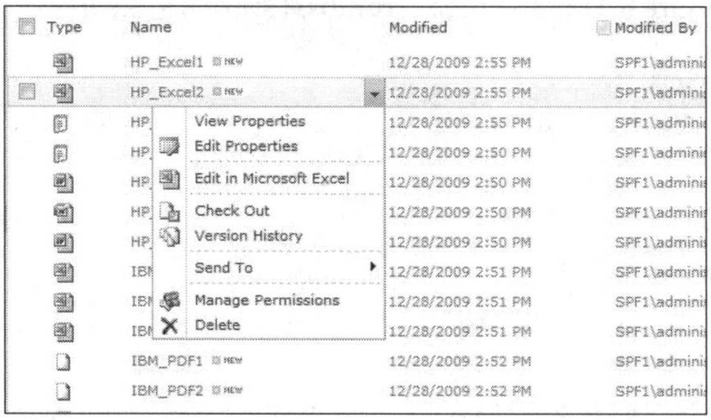

FIGURE 8.3
One way of editing the contents of a row

2. To add a value to Company, choose Edit Properties. I select HP from the Company drop-down (see Figure 8.4). Note that this was created as a required field—the star (*) next to the word Company in Figure 8.4 indicates this.

3. Then click Save.

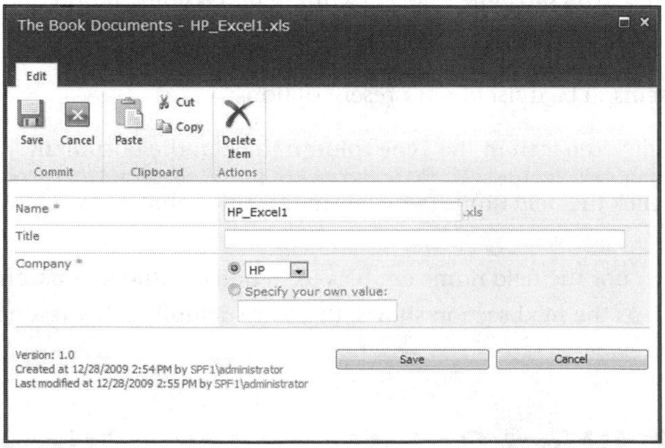

FIGURE 8.4
Changing the contents of a row

Editing a View Using the Existing Edit Column

By the Way

The Name field is the place where the filename is stored; the Title field is where you give a file a meaningful name that can be used in a list.

Do not use Title in a view of a list rather than Name. There is no possibility of right-clicking a Title field in the way we clicked the Name field.

Another solution—editing a view by using the existing Edit column—works even if we have the Title field listed and not the Name field. This solution uses a view of the Document Library that includes an Edit field.

Despite the look of Figure 8.2. there actually is an Edit box. It's just not visible. To make it appear, run your cursor over any of the lines in the main (right) section of Figure 8.2.

Figure 8.5 is a small section of the screen shown in Figure 8.2 including the edit box that appears on the left when the cursor is moved over the line containing the HP_Word1 file.

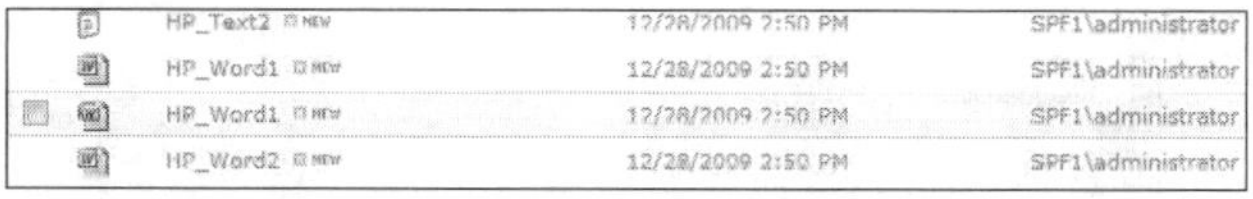

FIGURE 8.5
Seeing the existing Edit icon.

Select the box, and then all the options that were available via the drop-down in the earlier section are now available in the ribbon, as shown in Figure 8.6. (The drop-down is faster to use, which is why I showed it first).

Click Edit Properties to get the same screen you saw earlier (Figure 8.4).

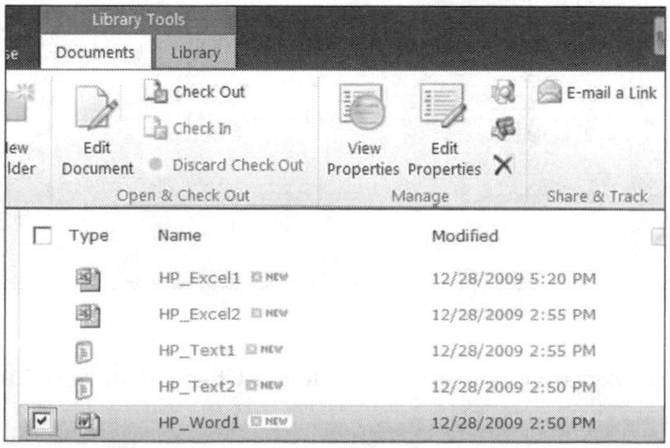

FIGURE 8.6
Seeing the Edit options in the ribbon

Editing a View by Using Datasheet View

Both of these two options enable the addition of HP (or IBM, MS, or Oracle) text to the Company column for a single row at a time. The third option, to use Datasheet View, enables a quicker approach when an identical value needs to be added to several rows.

To do this we need to first create a Datasheet view: Go to Library > Library Settings > Create View > Datasheet View. I named this Datasheet view (Maintenance). The parentheses indicate that it's not actually a view that users are expected to use in normal circumstances.

The key thing with a maintenance view is that it should contain all the columns you want to change the value of and sort on. In this case that means the Name field (for sorting and also for knowing which row this is); the Company field; and the Title field (it has no value yet, but we might later want to add one, so there's no point in not including it). Make sure those views are selected. Do remove the x from the Modified and Modified By fields to deselect them because they are system fields that cannot be amended.

This time, as shown in Figure 8.7, I left the x next to the icon so that column is still listed. I've said that the view should be sorted by name (and that it will not be the

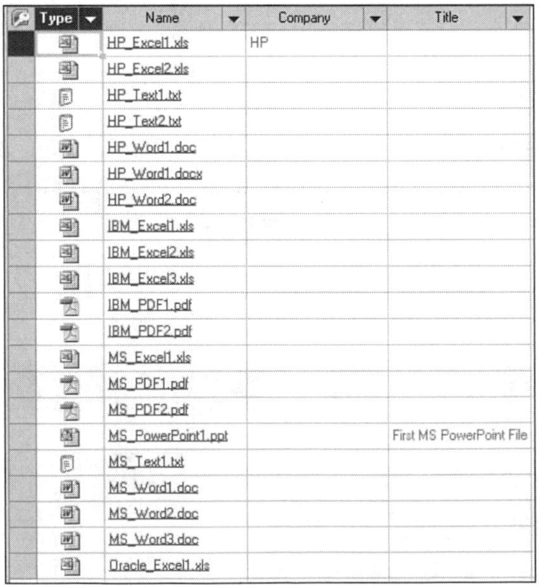

FIGURE 8.7
Using a Datasheet View to add a value to the Company column

Type ▼	Name ▼	Company ▼	Title ▼
	HP_Excel1.xls	HP	
	HP_Excel2.xls		
	HP_Text1.txt		
	HP_Text2.txt		
	HP_Word1.doc		
	HP_Word1.docx		
	HP_Word2.doc		
	IBM_Excel1.xls		
	IBM_Excel2.xls		
	IBM_Excel3.xls		
	IBM_PDF1.pdf		
	IBM_PDF2.pdf		
	MS_Excel1.xls		
	MS_PDF1.pdf		
	MS_PDF2.pdf		
	MS_PowerPoint1.ppt		First MS PowerPoint File
	MS_Text1.txt		
	MS_Word1.doc		
	MS_Word2.doc		
	MS_Word3.doc		
	Oracle_Excel1.xls		

default view). Not being the default view is default here. After clicking OK, you will usually see the screen shown in Figure 8.7.

What you might instead see is a page with the columns you selected in Standard View, that is, the kind of view that we have seen before. At the bottom of that page in Standard View, there would then be the following text indicating the reasons why Datasheet View wasn't possible.

Watch Out!

> Take the following paragraph as a warning not to make Datasheet View a key part of your user experience. An Administrator can afford to spend time getting one of his PCs to work with Datasheet View; he can't afford the time to get all those different user PC configurations working.

The list is displayed in Standard view. It cannot be displayed in Datasheet view for one or more of the following reasons: A datasheet component compatible with Microsoft SharePoint Foundation is not installed, your browser does not support ActiveX controls, a component is not properly configured for 32-bit or 64-bit support, or support for ActiveX controls is disabled.

This message indicates the main possible problems, which are listed in the following bullet points.

- Your browser does not support ActiveX controls; it is not Internet Explorer.

- A component is not correctly configured; Microsoft doesn't know why it's not working.

- Support for ActiveX controls is disabled; it is possible that your ActiveX settings aren't quite what the application expects them to be.

The first couple of these you can't do much about. The first is a certain "No." If you don't have Internet Explorer you can't fix it. The second is so unclear that it is impossible to trace.

That leaves the third one. You can try amending your ActiveX settings in IE for the security zone in which the SPF1 site is located. (Again, if you don't have IE you don't have ActiveX settings you can amend.)

If that doesn't work you may have been hit by the mixed Office versions problem. Datasheet View requires a particular Office application to be installed in the client. If the client is running only one 2007 or 2003 Office application in addition to a full suite of Office 2010 applications, this may have confused Datasheet View into looking for the wrong application (version) and not finding it. If it can't find it, Datasheet View won't work.

By the Way

> Figure 8.7 is taken from a client system running Office 2007 on XPPro where the browser is IE8. When preparing this hour, I couldn't get Datasheet View to run on a client running Office 2010 on Windows 7 despite the browser there also being

IE8. This was a neat confirmation of the suggestion earlier that you should not rely on Datasheet View working for all your users.

The following bullet points give several reasons why using Datasheet view instead of Standard view can be advantageous:

▶ You can change several or all rows and then leave the page.

▶ You can use the drop-down in the column (row) to choose the value.

▶ You can copy the values in cells just like you can in Excel (but only like to like).

Doing a combination of these, we can complete the Company column with the appropriate values in all rows:

▶ There is no OK button, so you must ensure that the changes go through. To do this, select a different view after you fill in the values on the page. At this stage you may get a pop-up saying, "You Have Pending Changes." If so, just click OK and wait until the pending changes are made. Figure 8.8. is the final result.

FIGURE 8.8
The result of using Datasheet View to add a value to the Company column

☐ Type	Name	Modified	☐ Modified By	Company
	HP_Excel1 ☑ NEW	12/28/2009 5:20 PM	SPF1\administrator	HP
	HP_Excel2 ☑ NEW	12/28/2009 6:25 PM	SPF1\administrator	HP
	HP_Text1 ☑ NEW	12/28/2009 6:25 PM	SPF1\administrator	HP
	HP_Text2 ☑ NEW	12/28/2009 6:25 PM	SPF1\administrator	HP
	HP_Word1 ☑ NEW	12/28/2009 6:25 PM	SPF1\administrator	HP
☐	HP_Word1 ☑ NEW	12/28/2009 6:25 PM	SPF1\administrator	HP
	HP_Word2 ☑ NEW	12/28/2009 6:25 PM	SPF1\administrator	HP
	IBM_Excel1 ☑ NEW	12/28/2009 6:25 PM	SPF1\administrator	IBM
	IBM_Excel2 ☑ NEW	12/28/2009 6:25 PM	SPF1\administrator	IBM
	IBM_Excel3 ☑ NEW	12/28/2009 6:25 PM	SPF1\administrator	IBM
	IBM_PDF1 ☑ NEW	12/28/2009 6:25 PM	SPF1\administrator	IBM
	IBM_PDF2 ☑ NEW	12/28/2009 6:25 PM	SPF1\administrator	IBM
	MS_Excel1 ☑ NEW	12/28/2009 6:25 PM	SPF1\administrator	MS
	MS_PDF1 ☑ NEW	12/28/2009 6:25 PM	SPF1\administrator	MS
	MS_PDF2 ☑ NEW	12/28/2009 6:25 PM	SPF1\administrator	MS
	MS_PowerPoint1 ☑ NEW	12/28/2009 6:25 PM	SPF1\administrator	MS

Creating a View That Includes All Documents

Now that we have a Company value for each document, we can (finally) create a view that uses those values. To do this, follow these steps:

1. Choose Library > Library Settings > Create View > Standard View. This time, we focus on the second half of the screen.

Before you scroll down, remove the tick for Company. If we leave it there, we'll have a view called HP in which only items where Company=HP are listed, and we'll have a column called Company, which for all rows will contain HP. That's pointless!

Did you Know?

2. Name this view **HP**. Then scroll down and complete the Sort and Filter fields (see Figure 8.9).

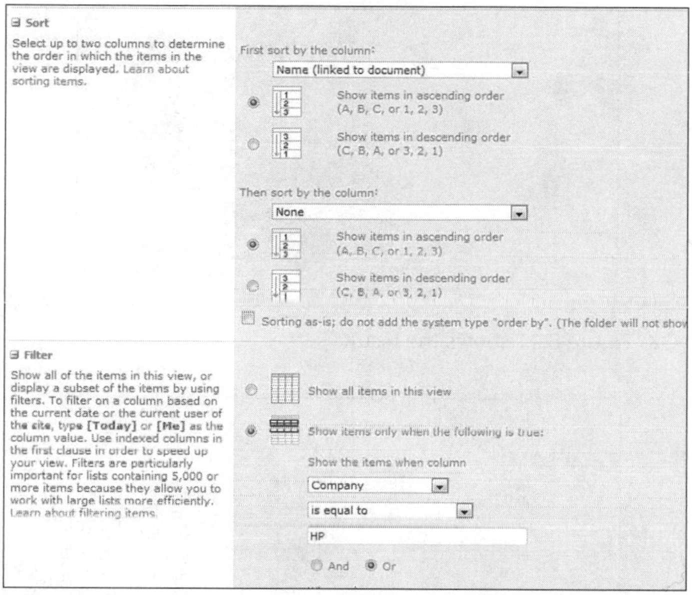

FIGURE 8.9
Setting sorting and filtering for a view

3. Click OK and repeat the whole thing for IBM, MS, and Oracle. You can speed things up by selecting the option to Start From an Existing View and always use the HP view as a model for your other views.

Did you Know?

If you do this for fields/columns where the names are long, enter the name in the View Name field (make sure it is exactly the same name you had in the Choice field) and copy (Ctrl-C) this name and paste it (Ctrl-V) in the Filter field.

I often play it even safer by opening the list in a second browser and then going to Document Settings and the Choice field. That way, I can copy the exact value and then paste this value into first the Name row and then into the Filter row.

Creating a Grouped View

Next, let's create a view that could be used if you want to split a single report into HP, IBM, MS, and Oracle sections:

1. Choose Library > Library Settings > Create View > Standard View. This time call it **Grouped By Company**. Remove the tick for Company and sort the view by name.

2. Do not enter a filter. Complete the rest of the page, as shown in Figure 8.10. (Note that I chose Grouping to be Expanded.)

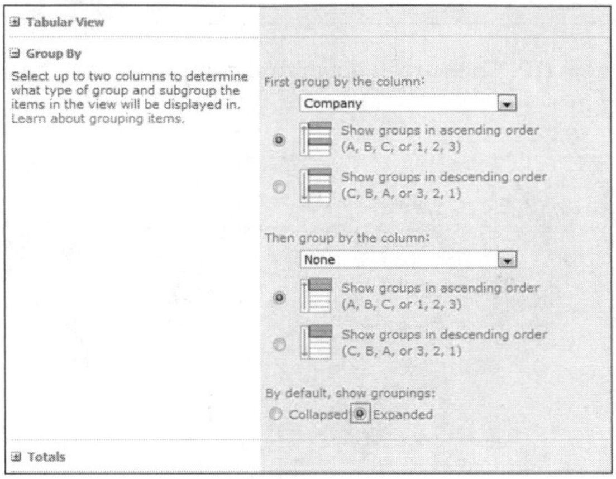

FIGURE 8.10
Looking at the Group By element when specifying a view

3. Click OK. Figure 8.11 shows the result.

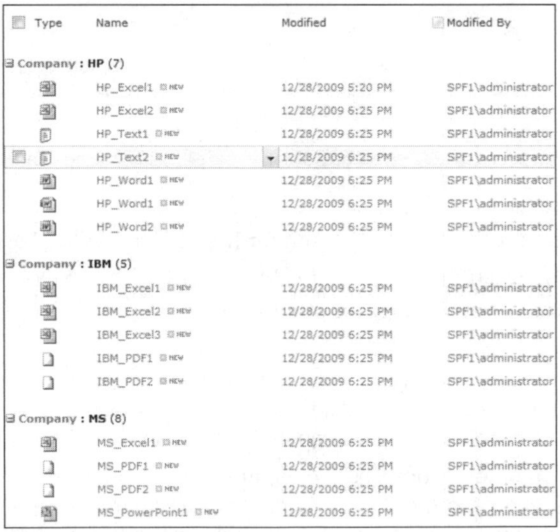

FIGURE 8.11
A completed Grouped By view

Type	Name	Modified	Modified By
Company : HP (7)			
	HP_Excel1 🆕	12/28/2009 5:20 PM	SPF1\administrator
	HP_Excel2 🆕	12/28/2009 6:25 PM	SPF1\administrator
	HP_Text1 🆕	12/28/2009 6:25 PM	SPF1\administrator
	HP_Text2 🆕	12/28/2009 6:25 PM	SPF1\administrator
	HP_Word1 🆕	12/28/2009 6:25 PM	SPF1\administrator
	HP_Word1 🆕	12/28/2009 6:25 PM	SPF1\administrator
	HP_Word2 🆕	12/28/2009 6:25 PM	SPF1\administrator
Company : IBM (5)			
	IBM_Excel1 🆕	12/28/2009 6:25 PM	SPF1\administrator
	IBM_Excel2 🆕	12/28/2009 6:25 PM	SPF1\administrator
	IBM_Excel3 🆕	12/28/2009 6:25 PM	SPF1\administrator
	IBM_PDF1 🆕	12/28/2009 6:25 PM	SPF1\administrator
	IBM_PDF2 🆕	12/28/2009 6:25 PM	SPF1\administrator
Company : MS (8)			
	MS_Excel1 🆕	12/28/2009 6:25 PM	SPF1\administrator
	MS_PDF1 🆕	12/28/2009 6:25 PM	SPF1\administrator
	MS_PDF2 🆕	12/28/2009 6:25 PM	SPF1\administrator
	MS_PowerPoint1 🆕	12/28/2009 6:25 PM	SPF1\administrator

This is a useful overview of the contents of that document library.

Let's say, however, for the purposes of our training here that we don't need to see the date a document was modified and remove it from the view.

By the Way

Views contain the columns you want them to contain. When you initially create a view, you naturally specify those columns in the view that you think your users will want to see. Real-world requirements might turn out to be different from those you envisaged, however, so you need to know how to amend views by adding or deleting columns.

Deleting a Column from a View

To delete the Modified column, follow these steps:

1. Select Library > Library Settings in the menu line. Then scroll the screen to see a list of the views (see Figure 8.12).

Views

A view of a document library allows you to see a particular selection of items or to see the items sorted in a particular order. Views currently configured for this document library:

View (click to edit)	Default View	Mobile View	Default Mobile View
All Documents	✔	✔	✔
DataSheet View (Maintenance)			
HP		✔	
IBM		✔	
MS		✔	
Oracle		✔	
Grouped By Company		✔	
Create view			

FIGURE 8.12
Amending a view

2. Select Grouped By Company, and you can remove the tick for Modified. Click OK to open the Book Documents page without the Modified column (see Figure 8.13).

Type	Name	Modified By
Company : HP (7)		
	HP_Excel1 NEW	SPF1\administrator
	HP_Excel2 NEW	SPF1\administrator
	HP_Text1 NEW	SPF1\administrator
	HP_Text2 NEW	SPF1\administrator
	HP_Word1 NEW	SPF1\administrator
	HP_Word1 NEW	SPF1\administrator
	HP_Word2 NEW	SPF1\administrator
Company : IBM (5)		
	IBM_Excel1 NEW	SPF1\administrator

FIGURE 8.13
A revised view

Using Folders

Now that you've seen how views can be used to separate the documents stored in a single document library into subdivisions, let's look at folders, which are an alternative method of doing this.

Most people with several years of experience with SharePoint do not recommend using folders. Instead, they prefer having several document libraries or using views. (They usually prefer to use both combined.)

However, we have two problems with folders:

- Implementation isn't particularly good.
- Folders encourage bad habits—specified in more detail later in this hour—when transferring data from "normal" systems (that is, from the file system).

A quick demonstration can show you a few problems with folder implementation:

1. Go to BookSite1 and open the document library.

By the Way

It's called Document Library in this site template (not Shared Documents). The Microsoft people obviously ran out of inspiration.

2. Select Documents in the menu line and then New Folder from the ribbon (see Figure 8.14). Name this folder **HP**.

Library Tools
Site Actions
Browse
Documents
Library
New Document
Upload Document
New Folder
New
Edit Document
Open & Check Out
View Properties
Edit Properties
Manage
E-mail a Link
Share & Track
Type
Name
Modified
weeklyblog
2.12.2009 18:13
Add new document

FIGURE 8.14
Creating a folder

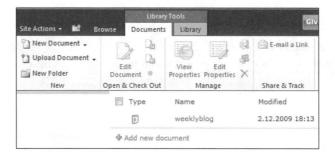

3. Repeat this process to create folders for **IBM**, **MS**, and **Oracle**. Figure 8.15 shows the result.

Type
Name
Modified
Modified By
HP
29.12.2009 10:25
SPF1\administrator
IBM
29.12.2009 10:25
SPF1\administrator
MS
29.12.2009 10:25
SPF1\administrator
Oracle
29.12.2009 10:25
SPF1\administrator
weeklyblog
2.12.2009 18:13
SPF1\administrator
Add new document

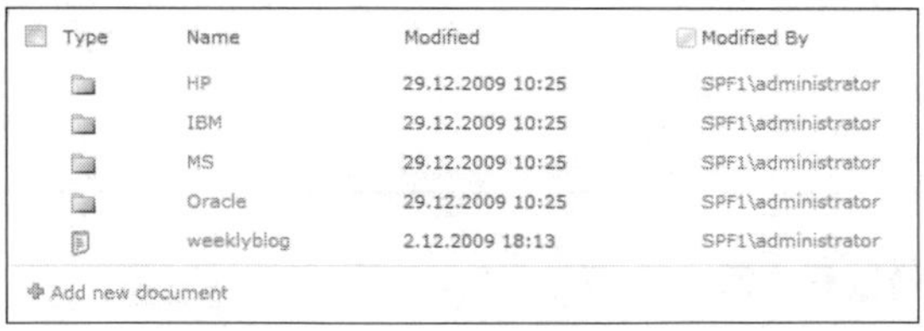

FIGURE 8.15
Folders are now available for use.

4. Populate the folders with the same test files we used earlier in this hour. To do so, click the folder icon before the word HP or on the word HP itself to open the folder. Then use the upload actions we've used before. Repeat this process for the IBM, MS, and Oracle files.

Use the Navigate Up section next to Site Actions. Click Document Library to go back to a screen where you can open the next folder.

5. Now go back to the Document Library level and upload some other files (preferably with more appropriate names for your business than those shown in Figure 8.16).

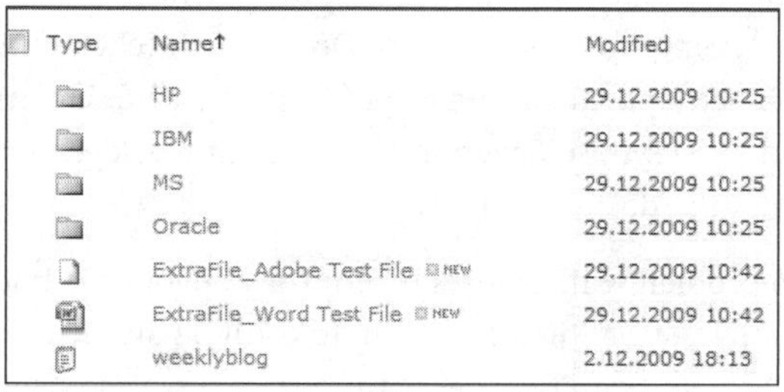

Type	Name↑	Modified
📁	HP	29.12.2009 10:25
📁	IBM	29.12.2009 10:25
📁	MS	29.12.2009 10:25
📁	Oracle	29.12.2009 10:25
🗋	ExtraFile_Adobe Test File ⊠ NEW	29.12.2009 10:42
📄	ExtraFile_Word Test File ⊠ NEW	29.12.2009 10:42
📄	weeklyblog	2.12.2009 18:13

FIGURE 8.16
A document library with both views and folders

6. Click Name at the top of the column. This sorts the contents of the document library in name order (first ascending and after a second click on Name, descending).

7. The folders all come first, followed by all the files (see Figure 8.16). Click Name again, and all the files come first and then all the folders. That's perhaps acceptable.

8. Now open the IBM Folder and create a file in Notepad and add it to the IBM folder.

9. Go back to the Document Library level and click Modified (twice).

After we click Modified, which sorts the date and time at which something in Share-Point was added or amended, we expect to first see the folder IBM, the contents of which have been modified last, followed by the individual files we uploaded, followed by the other folders. In fact, we see the screen shown in Figure 8.17.

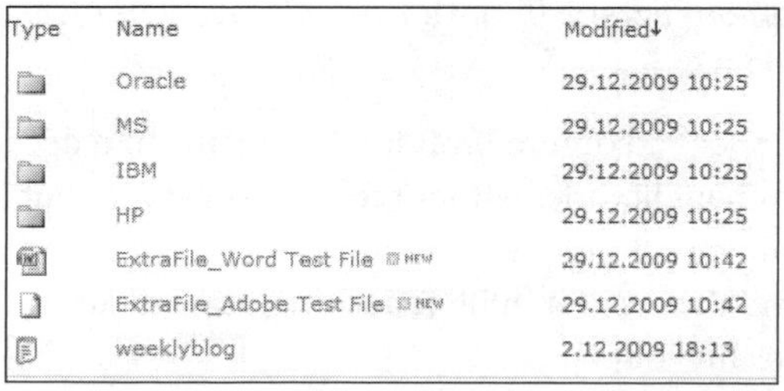

Type	Name	Modified↓
📁	Oracle	29.12.2009 10:25
📁	MS	29.12.2009 10:25
📁	IBM	29.12.2009 10:25
📁	HP	29.12.2009 10:25
📄	ExtraFile_Word Test File ⊠ NEW	29.12.2009 10:42
🗋	ExtraFile_Adobe Test File ⊠ NEW	29.12.2009 10:42
📄	weeklyblog	2.12.2009 18:13

FIGURE 8.17
Problems with sorting when folders are involved

From Figure 8.17, you also have no way of seeing that new content has been added to the IBM folder.

The software sorts only according to when the folder was created; when the contents of the folder were amended is completely ignored. In addition no matter when the folders or the files were created, the folders are always listed first.

That's one of the functionality problems with folders. Another one, that was in earlier versions of SharePoint, no longer occurs. Do a search (click Browse in the menu line, and the search box appears at the top-right part of the screen), and the search now identifies the document itself even if it is stored in a folder. Earlier only the folder was specified and not the document itself.

However, the main problem with folders is that they encourage bad habits. They encourage you to copy your entire file system to a single SPF 2010 document library, which also means that you don't bother getting rid of documents that no longer are relevant.

The process of creating a view, on the other hand, means that you need to analyze the files in the file system first (to create suitable views). This means that during the analysis process, you become aware of irrelevant files and sets of files and do not upload them to the SPF 2010 document library. You also divide your relevant files into different document libraries.

Summary

This hour showed you how to create views and folders. It showed you the benefits of using views to subcategorize the documents in a document library, and you learned some of the disadvantages of using folders.

Q&A

Q. *I've heard that if I use folders I can have up to 4 million documents stored in a single document library. If that's true, why are you recommending that I don't use folders?*

A. The recommended maximum limit for documents in a document library is 2,000 for document libraries without folders. However, that limit is 2,000 x 2,000 for document libraries with folders (2,000 folders and 2,000 documents per folder), and thus your 4 million documents when using folders. So that statement is technically correct.

Some papers say this limit is 5 million. This is a hard number, whereas the 2,000 number that leads to the 4 million total is a "recommended maximum" only. You can have 2,001 or 2,002 and so on.

There are many reasons why this wholesale transfer of files from the file system is not desirable, including the following:

- Ease of use when accessing the files

- The results of searches

- The storage space required (up to 80 percent more space can be needed for storage in the SharePoint databases than is require for the same files in the file system)

- Backup requirements

Q. *Are there, in your opinion, any good uses for folders?*

A. In my opinion, just one.

You might want to consider folders if you have a copy of a website that was created by a fairly old tool, such as Site Sweeper. These old tools typically created a single index.htm file with links to files that were placed in folders one level below the index.htm file.

The index.htm file can be uploaded to the document library, and the files it references can be uploaded to a folder in the document library.

The reason this is a good use of folders is because it can't be done any other way, given the way these Site Sweeper-type applications work.

Workshop

Quiz

1. When creating a view, which type of column do I use when I want to ensure that it always contains specific text strings?

2. With folders, what main functionality problem area is still there?

3. Why is it a bad idea to copy the file system to a SPF 2010 document library that uses folders?

Answers

1. I use the Choice type of field because in this field type I can specify a list of possible values (and, incidentally, a default value).

2. Sort.

3. It's a bad idea to copy the file system because this encourages the mass copying of files, which means that no effort is made to weed out documents that are no longer relevant or active (or duplicates).

HOUR 9

Looking at List Types and the Included Web Parts

What You'll Learn in This Hour

▶ Purpose of list types

▶ Which web parts are delivered with SPF 2010 that are not just representations of lists and libraries

▶ Purposes of standard and nonlist web parts

A lot of different ready-made types of lists come out-of-the-box when you install SPF 2010. Surprisingly, often people aren't aware of the less commonly used of these built-in list types and spend time working out solutions to problems that could easily be solved just by using a built-in list type. This hour saves you that time in the future by giving you an overview of those less common list types and briefly working through where you can use them.

Understanding List Types

The SPF 2010 product includes several list types. This section discusses some of these list types.

Refer to Figure 6.2 in Hour 6, "Using Libraries and Lists," for a complete list of the possible list types. They're shown in columns called Communications, Tracking, and Custom Lists.

By the Way

The Announcements List

The Announcements list is intended for use as a web part on a website's default page to present readers of the site with up-to-the-minute and important information. The

Announcements list is almost always on the default page so that as many people as possible see this information. Be wary of changing the default view. The standard default view is designed especially for use on the site's default page. Amending it might mess up the look, and it's impossible to create a new view with the same look.

The Contacts List

The Contacts list contains useful contacts for readers of the website. So, for instance, if a computer services company uses the site for one of its customers, the Contacts list would consist of contact information for people in that customer company (and also probably for people from the computer services company who work with that particular customer).

Watch Out!

You cannot combine the contacts information in the site's Contacts list with your Outlook contacts. Even if it is possible, there will be two separate Contacts items in Outlook, not just one that combines both sources. (For more information, see Hour 16, "Using Outlook 2010 with SPF 2010.")

The Discussion Board

Naturally, the Discussion Board is used for discussions. There are both threaded and nonthreaded options for the look of this list.

The Discussion Board hasn't improved much since SharePoint Team Services (2001), so don't expect much functionality beyond the simple write-a-message, get-a-reply level of functionality.

The Links List

The Links list's main function is to list useful web addresses with accompanying descriptions. I use it in my websites to list and link to both useful SharePoint articles and Knowledge Base articles.

The problem with the Links list is that the URL field consists of two parts: the URL and the description. So, for instance, when you open a Links list, you see a description listed in the URL field. When you click the description, the system actually uses the URL to go to the web page.

This isn't a problem for users who tend to be happy to see something meaningful rather than an obscure website address; however, it can be a problem for administrators because Datasheet view (which normally enables bulk changes) does not list a

Description field. It's impossible to populate the Links list in bulk from, say, an Excel spreadsheet containing a URL column and a Description column.

The way around this is to add an additional column, perhaps called Site Description, and use this in the Datasheet view along with the URL column. In this way, you can bulk populate a Links list.

If you do this, all you will have is a URL field containing a URL (unless you copy the cells from a Datasheet View of another SharePoint Links list, in which case the URL columns you copy transfer both the URL and the Description). In other words, there's no corresponding description. In such cases, Figure 9.1 displays where only the URL field has a value; the description field is empty.

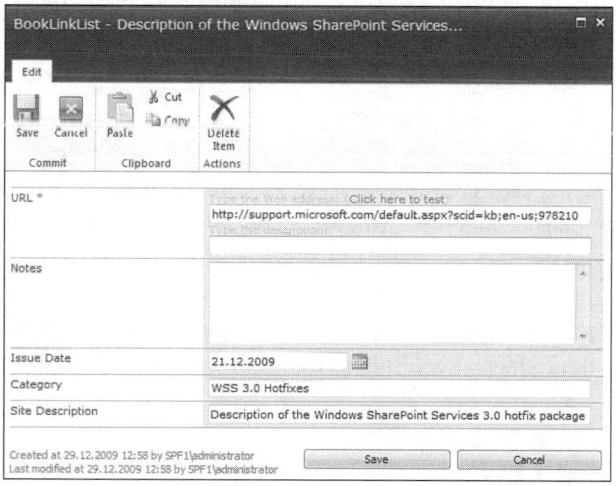

FIGURE 9.1
Editing a single
Links list item

Figure 9.1 is what you see when adding an item to a links list of the type previously described with three additional columns/fields. When adding an item to a standard links list, the three rows in Figure 9.1 starting with "Issue Date" would not be visible.

By the Way

After a bulk populate, it's usually necessary to edit each item individually because then the Description field is available. In such a situation, it would be possible to copy the contents of the Site Description field into the second box in the URL section. It might not be the fastest process overall, but it's not that demanding. If you don't do this, the description will be assumed to be the same as the contents of the URL field, and that URL will be what you see in views of the list. So this tidying up process is important because most users want to see the description (in this case of a Knowledge Base article) and not a less meaningful URL.

The Calendar List

Typically, the Calendar list is used as a calendar only for the area covered by the website (for instance, for the customer company in the preceding example).

Like the Contacts list, the Calendar list is not merged with any Outlook calendar. If the Outlook version allows it (see Hour 16, "Using Outlook 2010 with SPF 2010"), however, this calendar can appear in Outlook alongside the Outlook user's own calendar.

The Tasks List

The Tasks list relates to workflow. Workflows are covered in Hour 21, "Creating Workflows in SPF 2010," and Hour 22, "Using SharePoint Designer 2010 to Create Workflows," and are not mentioned further here.

Survey

A Survey consists of a series of manually created questions, each of which typically has multichoice, prespecified responses (with free text an alternative) the creator of the Survey can specify. New in SPF 2010 is the ability to branch to a later question than the next one in the normal order depending on the response to a question. The built-in surveys are even so rather simple, and it's wise to look for more powerful third-party add-in products if you intend to use surveys in your SharePoint sites often.

The Custom List

A Custom list isn't as custom as you might think. It's just a list that doesn't already (in contrast to the others) have a predefined role.

Typically, it stores simple data. I use it to store FAQs, where I have a Single-Line Text field for a question and a Multi-Line Text field for an answer.

Import Spreadsheet

In SPF 2010, the Import Spreadsheet option provides a way for you to move an existing Excel spreadsheet to an SPF 2010 site. If you use this option, a list is created from a set of cells contained in a spreadsheet. The result is a list in which each field/column name matches its respective column in Excel.

The list created using the Import Spreadsheet option and the Excel spreadsheet from which it's derived are not connected. Changes made later to the spreadsheet are not reflected in the list. When the list is compiled, the spreadsheet and the list are two completely independent entities.

Always delete the spreadsheet after you create the list from it. This forces your users to update only the SPF 2010 list.

Using Standard Web Parts with the Team Site

Now that you understand the various list types, let's look at the standard web parts listed when you add a web part (see Figure 9.4 later in this section). To study these standard web parts, we set up a separate site for testing them.

Creating a Site to Test Web Parts

If you want a site where you can test web parts, you must first create one. Let's start at the default page by following these steps:

1. To create the site, select Site Actions > New Site.

2. Name the (Blank) site **Web Parts Test** and specify the URL as **http://spf1/ WebPartsTest** (see Figure 9.2).

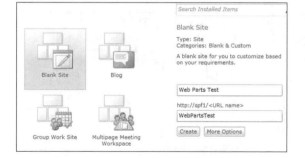

FIGURE 9.2
Creating the Web Parts Test site

I chose the Blank Site type for two reasons:

▶ It is a web part page, and web parts can be added easily to it.

▶ It is empty (unlike say a Meeting Workspace), so we can concentrate on the (test) web parts we add to it.

3. Click Create.

Adding Web Parts to the Test Site

To add a web part to your test site, follow these steps:

1. After the previous Create, you see an almost empty Web Parts Test site. Select Page in the menu bar (Tab).

2. Select Edit Page from the ribbon (on the far left). The screen shown in Figure 9.3 displays.

3. Click Add a Web Part in the left column. There's a selection of four groups of web parts available at the moment for this site. (If we used one of the existing sites based on the Meeting Workspace, there would be more options in particular web part versions of the Lists in those sites.) Figure 9.4 displays.

To the right of Figure 9.4, you can see on your screen an Add Web Part To section with a drop-down showing Left. Even though we clicked the Add a Web Part over the left column, we can still change our minds and have the web part added to the right column. In the next section, we actually add the web part.

Understanding Different (Nonlist) Standard Web Parts

This section introduces some of the web parts included in the Blank Site template that are not just representations of lists or libraries.

The Content Editor Web Part

The Content Editor web part is a way to include data in a section of a SharePoint web page that differs in look and feel from the rest of the SharePoint web page. The following steps will make what I mean by that clearer:

1. At Figure 9.4, click Content Editor to select it.

2. Click Add. What you now see is a Content Editor web part listed below the Add a Web Part section of Figure 9.2.

3. Click the downward arrow to the end of the line that starts with Content Editor.

4. Select Edit Web Part. Figure 9.5 displays where I expanded the Appearance section.

FIGURE 9.5
Defining a Content Editor Web Part

5. Change the name of the Title to **Test Content Editor Web Part**. An area on the screen displays named Test Content Editor Web Part.

6. Save the changes made by clicking OK.

The following steps are one way to create a suitable URL to put in the Content Link box, as shown in Figure 9.5:

1. Open Notepad while in the server.

2. Enter this HTML code into Notepad.

```
<H3><center><color="#FF0000">Key Personnel</color></center></H3>
<center><table border=2 cellspacing=2 cellpadding=5>
<tr><bold>
<td>Finance</td><td>IT</td>
<td>Manufacturing</td><td>Personnel</td>
</bold></tr><tr>
<td>Jim McPherson</td><td>Woody Winchester</td>
<td>Robin Goodfellow</td><td>Lucius Cassio</td>
</tr>
</table></center>
```

3. Save the file in C:\ as TextContentEditor.txt.

4. Create in the WebPartsTest site a document library called WPT Doc Lib by click-ing the Documents link; then click Create and specify Document Library.

5. Upload the C:\TextContentEditor.txt file to the WPT Doc Lib document library, as shown in Figure 9.6.

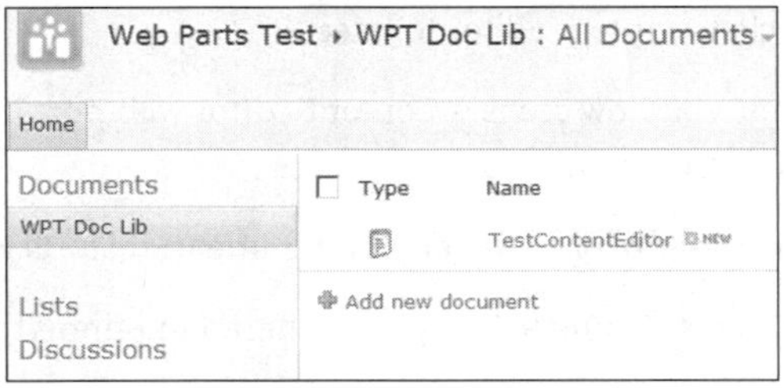

FIGURE 9.6
Putting the Con-
tent Editor file in
a Doc Lib to
give a URL

6. Right-click the name TestContentEditor and select properties. Copy (Ctrl-c) the URL that is listed there.

7. Go back to the home page of the WebPartsTest site, and again modify the web part (steps 3 and 4 before Figure 9.5).

8. This time paste (Ctrl-v) the URL of TestContentEditor into the Content Link sec-tion and test the Link.

   Links of type file:/// are not accepted in the Content Link field, so we couldn't directly refer to the TestContentEditor.txt file in its original location. By putting the file in a document library in the same site, we ensure that people with rights to access the site can access the file and that the web part would function as we intended.

9. Click OK, and Figure 9.7 displays.

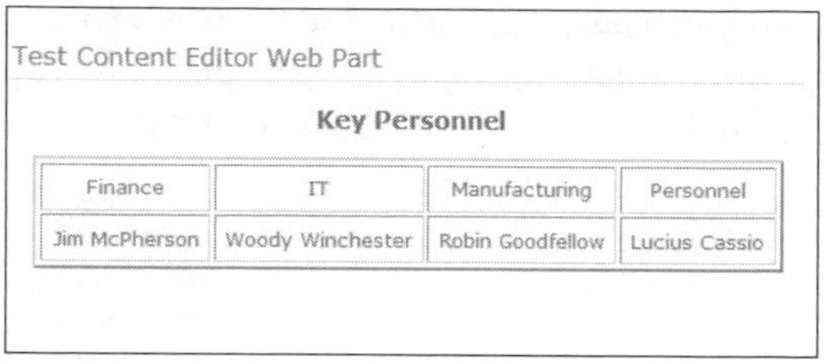

FIGURE 9.7
An example of using the Content Editor web part

10. The final step could be to remove the name and leave just the Key Personnel diagram. Check out the options in the right-hand section of Figure 9.5 to see how to do that if you want to experiment with this; otherwise, just move on.

The HTML Form Web Part

The HTML Form web part is a single entry box with a Go button (refer to the left half of Figure 9.8). It doesn't look like much, but as you'll see, even the simplest version of this web part type (which is all we look at here) is useful.

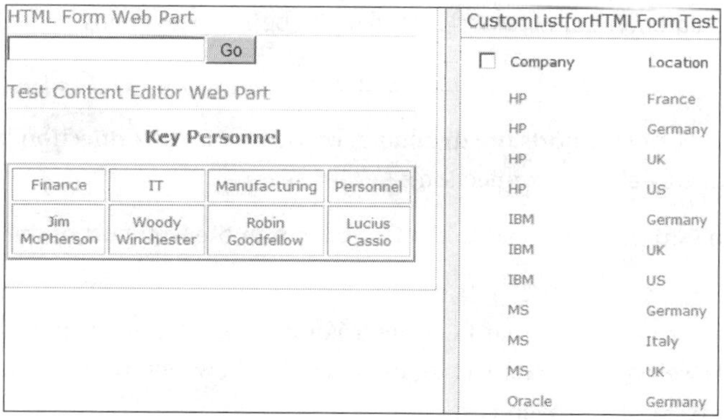

FIGURE 9.8
Stage one of showing how to use the Form web part

To use the Form web part, we first need some data, and then we run through how web part connections work (something else that is simple but useful).

To show how this works, I created a custom list, added two columns to it (Company and Location), and populated the columns with some data. (If you want to do this, look at the right half of Figure 9.8 to see which columns and values were added.) When that was done, a web part of that new list was available.

In the same page used for earlier exercises, I did the following:

1. I selected Add a Web Part in the rightmost column.

The list of possible web parts appeared, and the new web part was now listed. (A new section was available in Figure 9.4 [in Categories] called List and Libraries that included both the newly created WPT Doc Lib and the Custom List I called CustomListforHTMLFormTest.)

2. I selected it.

3. I clicked OK.

The rightmost column of Figure 9.8 contains the web part version of that new List; that is, I created a new view called WebPartView where I had removed both the Title column and the attachments column from the View when I created the Custom List.

Now add an HTML Form Web Part with a similar technique. (Don't bother changing the name of it.)

1. Add a web part in the left column.

2. Select the HTML List Web Part for the web part types listed.

3. Click OK.

Now that that both web parts are available, we can set up a connection between them (a so-called web part connection):

1. Click the small arrow next to the Edit button in the web part of the list we just created.

2. Then on Connections, select Get Filter Values From. Often we have a number of possible web parts to connect to. In Figure 9.9, however, we have just one choice: HTML Form Web Part.

FIGURE 9.9
Starting web part connections

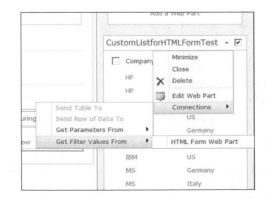

> When adding content to the list, the Title field is compulsory. So I used dummy values of 1 to 12. The key data in this list for this HTML Form Web Part test is the repeated company names and the non-repeated (for each company) locations.

By the Way

3. Select HTML Form Web Part. A pop-up appears (see Figure 9.10).

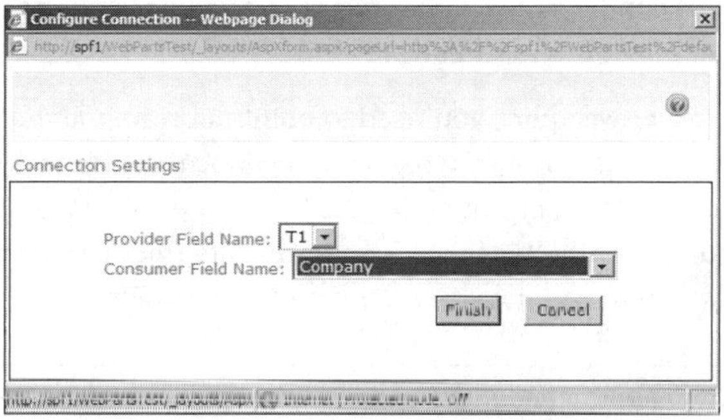

FIGURE 9.10
Configuring the web part connection

4. There is only one column in our standard HTML Form web part, so that drop-down has a single entry (T1). We then need to decide if we want to link the HTML Form Web Part to Company or Location (the drop-down lists all fields in the list, not just those). We decide on Company.

5. Click Finish.

6. Click Stop Editing.

Now we see Figure 9.8 again. The CustomListforHTMLFormTest web part (in the text that follows I use CL1 for this list) still shows all possible Items.

7. Write IBM into the HTML Form Web Part field and click Go. You now see Figure 9.11 (compare this with Figure 9.8).

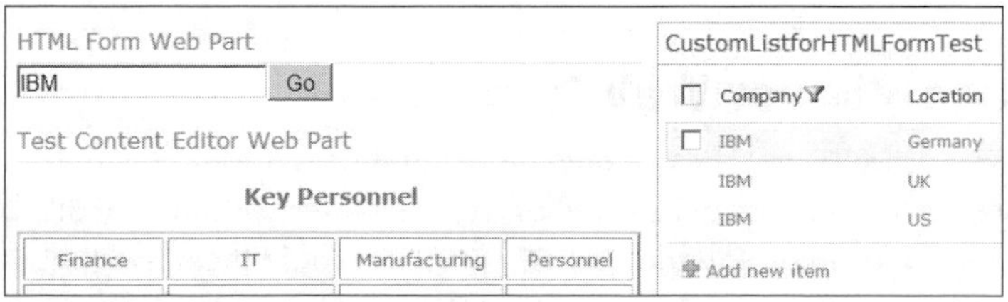

FIGURE 9.11
The result of entering IBM into the Form web part

Entering IBM in the HTML Form web part connected to CL1 has filtered the information that CL1 shows us. CL1 the list still contains rows for HP, IBM MS, and Oracle, as does CL1 the web part of that list (because we are using a nonfiltered view for it).

However, CL1 the connected web part displays only the information about the company the user of this page chose to specify in the HTML Form web part.

The Image Viewer Web Part

The Image Viewer web part enables you to position an image on any part of a page to which a web part can be added. Other methods of adding images to a page require coding changes, so they are less straightforward.

With the Image Viewer web part, you need to point at an image that all the people accessing the page have the rights to see. One such location is the /_layouts/images/ directory, which is the storage location for the homepage.gif image (the photo of some people). You can verify this by looking at the Site Image web part (which is a standard Image web part that has been renamed) via Modify Shared Web Part.

> One way to get an "appropriate" version is to open the image library and right-click one of the images that, at this point, appears in a reduced-size form. Select Copy Link Location. Enter this link into the URL field of the Image web part (Ctrl-v) and click Test Link.
>
> You'll probably see more than you want to (not just the image, but the image's metadata). So on this test image, again right-click. Select Copy Location and enter this new value into the URL field of the Image web part. Now at least you'll just have an image being displayed.

Another way to guarantee that everyone can access the image is to create a site (or subsite) that everyone has access rights to (safest way is to allow anonymous access; see Hour 10, "Learning About Authentication and Access Rights") and within that site create an image library. Upload your images to this newly created image library. Then use an appropriate version of the image from the image library in the URL field of the Image web part.

The Page Viewer Web Part

The Page Viewer web part does just one thing, but it does it well. It enables you to incorporate any page that can be accessed from the Internet into your SPF 2010 site. For instance, a page in an Internal Dell SPF 2010 site could include a (public) HP Hardware Announcements web page so that Dell people can quickly see new HP announcements.

To see the example shown in Figure 9.12, follow these steps:

1. Add a Page Viewer web part to the page.

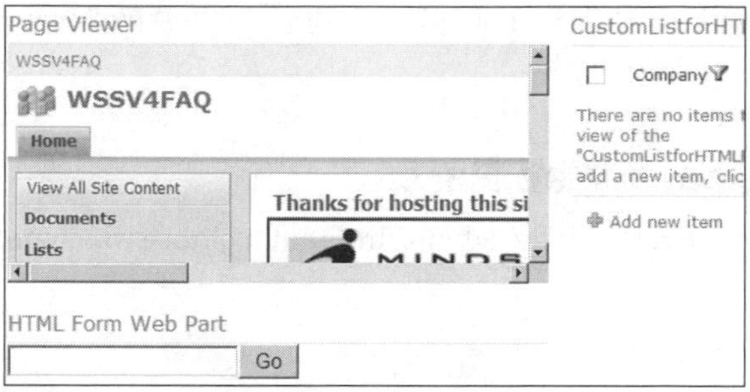

FIGURE 9.12
An example of using the Page Viewer web part

2. Select Edit Web Part.

3. Enter **http://wssv4faq.mindsharp.com** into the URL field.

4. Click OK.

5. Click Stop Editing.

The Picture Library Slideshow Web Part

The Picture Library Slideshow web part shows a slide show of images and photos from a picture library. (You'd never have guessed!)

The Relevant Documents Web Part

A relevant document is a document that the user who is accessing the page ("me") has done something with. The choices are Has Created, Has Checked Out, and Has Last Modified (see Figure 9.13).

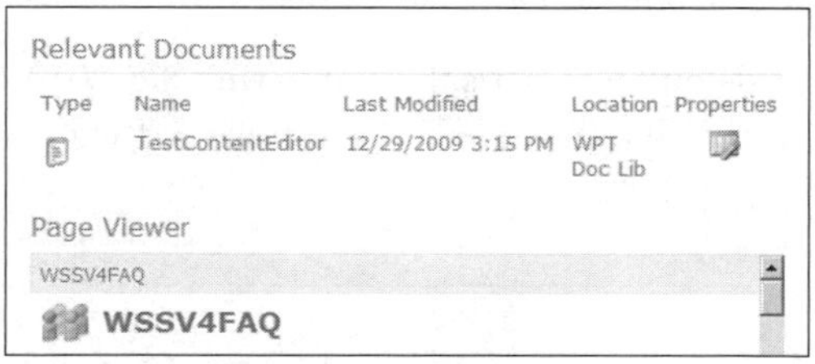

FIGURE 9.13
An example of using the User Tasks web part (in the right column)

The Silverlight Web Part

The Silverlight web part is beyond the scope of this book because using it requires programming knowledge. The sole parameter for it is a URL that contains the address of a Silverlight Application Package (.xap file).

I suspect that over time we'll see a lot of user-supplied .xap packages both useful and not (and free and not).

The Site Users Web Part

The Site Users web part shows the administrator at a glance which groups of users can access the site.

Some possible options are

▶ Show People in This Site's Member Group

▶ Show People in the Group: (Where You Specify the Group)

The User Tasks Web Part

The User Tasks web part is similar to the Relevant Documents web part (see Figure 9.13) in that it shows only items that have been entered elsewhere (in this case, naturally, in a Tasks list rather than in a Documents list).

The XML Viewer Web Part

The XML Viewer web part is similar in operation to the Content Editor web part.

Because writing XML code is beyond the scope of this book, I'll leave it to the XML experts among you to wonder about how you could use XML code in a web part.

Summary

We looked at the list types that haven't been mentioned earlier and examined what they are good for and potential problems associated with their use.

We then looked at the default web parts that come with SPF 2010. We saw when each of them is used (when appropriate) in actual examples of their use.

Q&A

Q. *I can't find the /_layouts/images/ directory. Where is it in the file system?*

A. Find this directory: C:\Program Files\Common Files\Microsoft Shared\web server extensions\14\TEMPLATE\LAYOUTS.

Q. *How do I transfer web parts from one column to another?*

A. Use the following steps to move a web part from the left column to the end of the right column:

1. Click the arrow on the top right of the web part you want to move and select Edit Web Part.

2. In the new box on the right of the screen, expand the Layout section.

3. Change the Zone to Right and the Zone Index to 10.

It's helpful to use increments greater than 1 when specifying the position of a web part in the zone. Using 10 is perhaps overkill, but it ensures that the web part is at the bottom of the list, even when other web parts are added to the zone.

By the Way

Workshop

Quiz

1. What do the Contacts list and the Calendar list have in common?

2. I want to add a web part to my page. When I choose Site Actions > Other, however, I don't see any web parts that were discussed in this hour.

Answers

1. Both lists can be synchronized with some versions of Outlook, and yet the copy of both lists in Outlook is separate from your Outlook Contacts and your Outlook calendar.

2. You don't see any web parts because what you do see when you select Create are lists and library types (and sites!) from which you can create a new list or library or site. To add a web part to a page, start by going to Site Actions > Edit Page.

Learning About Authentication and Access Rights

What You'll Learn in This Hour

▶ How anonymous users and authenticated users can be allowed access to our sites

▶ Getting familiar with the built-in authorization levels (SharePoint groups)

▶ User levels and the rights associated with them

This hour expands on Hour 3, "Adding Users and Giving Them Rights," by looking at how you can give anonymous users or all authenticated users access to a site. It also looks at how to change the logged on user when accessing the site and the differences logging in with a different level of user makes to what can be seen and what can be done.

> We created new users and assigned them to SharePoint groups in Hour 3. Refer to that hour if you need to refresh your memory about SharePoint groups and their privileges.

By the Way

Learning About Anonymous Access and All Authenticated Users

This section looks at a few special cases of groups of users: anonymous users and all authenticated users.

Anonymous Access

It is possible to have anonymous access to a site. As installed, SPF 2010 does not enable anonymous access, so the ability to access anonymously needs first to be specified, and then it is possible to say what anonymous-access users are enabled to do.

Anonymous access is a two-step process set at the Web Application level:

1. Specify that anonymous access is possible by selecting the web application in Central Administration and then choosing Authentication Providers in the ribbon. Then select an Authentication provider (typically Default is the only one) and for that provider specify that Anonymous Access is enabled.

2. You need to specify what anonymous users are allowed to do.

When anonymous access is possible, select Anonymous Policy in the same (Web Application) ribbon; then specify what anonymous users can access from a choice of Entire Web site, Lists and Libraries, and Nothing.

As this is set at the web application level, it applies for all site collections (and all sites in them) in the web application, something that might be forgotten later when creating a site. So be careful.

Allowing anonymous access isn't a sensible choice for many sites. You may decide that you don't want anonymous users to access even a restricted amount of your site's information. If that's the case, you can restrict access to the site to only users who have specifically been given rights to the site, or you can consider giving all the users who are logged in to your domain such rights. In the latter case, you should, instead of specifying anonymous access, give authenticated users access rights to your site.

By the Way

> The "Q&A" section gives information on creating a web application and site collection for you to test anonymous access in a completely separate site of sites.

Authenticated Users

The Authenticated Users group is a special set of users available when an SPF 2010 server is in a domain. In WSS 3.0 and MOSS 2007 there was a simple link on the left side of the screen, "Add All Authenticated Users," which gave this group access to a site quickly and easily. In SPF 2010 this link has been removed (pity, because I thought it was useful), and now you have to give a user access rights in the normal way and then specify that you want to add this group (write **Authenticated Users** and then Ctrl-K to get the name checked).

The good thing about adding this group is that it includes everyone who is logged in to the domain rather than anyone who can access the site, so it's an easy way to restrict access to company insiders.

Understanding the Rights of Different Kinds of Users

So far, even though we've created different users and assigned them to one of the existing SharePoint groups or to a new specially created SharePoint group, we've always been logged in as administrator. I use this access right throughout this book unless otherwise stated.

The rest of this hour describes how we can log in as someone else and the effect of doing so on what we can do in the site and what we can see of the site.

Logging In to a Site as Someone Else

In SPF 2010, logging in as someone else is simple. Just as with Windows 7 (or Vista), you can use the authority of a normal user most of the day and "run as an administrator" when you do something "special."

When accessing SPF 2010, you can switch users as follows:

1. Go to the Home page. Look at the upper-right corner of the screen. You see text similar to SPF1\administrator, with a small arrow to the right of the text. Click the arrow (see Figure 10.1).

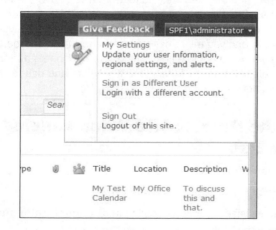

FIGURE 10.1
Signing in as a different user

2. Click Sign in as Different User. The standard login box displays, as shown in Figure 10.2.

FIGURE 10.2
Starting to log in
as MyReader

3. Click Use Another Account. The standard login box displays, as shown in Figure 10.3.

FIGURE 10.3
Logging in as
MyReader

Notice that SPF1\administrator is replaced by SPF1\myreader at the top-right part of the screen. Otherwise, everything seems to be the same. Or is it?

By the Way

If this doesn't work, don't immediately suspect that you have the wrong password. First make sure you have specified the preceding SPF1\; second, make sure you have given the user access rights to the site (in Hour 3, you gave several users access rights, and you might have missed one); third, maybe the password you remember is wrong, and if you can't guess the right one, go in the server to Administrative Tools > Computer Management > Users and right-click the User Name to specify a new password.

Effect on the Default Site When Logging in as Somebody Else

The screen shows little difference compared to before, and you have to look closely to see what is now missing:

► Near the upper-left corner when logged in as administrator, there was an Edit button (before the Link to Browse). Now there isn't.

▶ Before, there was a Recycle Bin at the bottom of the left column just above All Site Content. Now there isn't.

It's clear why these two items have gone:

▶ The user MyReader has Read rights, and a reader can't edit pages.

▶ The user MyReader has Read rights, and readers can't delete anything or add anything, so there is no need for a Recycle Bin for them.

The main difference, however, is behind the scenes. If you now (as MyReader) click Site Actions you see two options only (Figure 10.4). If you remember, Site Actions for the administrator had approximately ten options.

FIGURE 10.4
The reduced Site Actions list when logged in as MyReader

Here, too, the reason there is a difference is clear. All the other functions are not valid for a person with only Read rights.

Now log in as MyContrib. Before you do and before you look at Figure 10.5, however, think about whether any of the two previously mentioned items will then be present

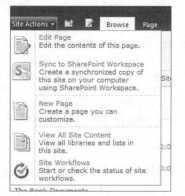

FIGURE 10.5
The Site Actions list when logged in as MyContrib

or whether they will both still be missing—and whether Site Actions will offer any more alternatives and if so, what.

The Recycle Bin is back (in its usual place) because a contributor does have Delete and Add rights. The Edit button is back, as shown in Figure 10.5, and Site Actions now has three extra functions, one of which (Edit Page) is just a repeat of the Edit icon just above it; the second is Adding a Page that is also clear; and the third is about workflows, discussed in Hour 21, "Creating Workflows in SPF 2010," and Hour 22, "Using SharePoint Designer 2010 to Create Workflows."

What is the situation if you give someone Design rights? We look at this next.

By the Way

> Microsoft failed to include a group called Team Site Designers, so first create this group and give that group Design rights. When you've done this, you can add it and they get Design rights. If you want to try this out, use the techniques that were specified in Hour 3 to create the user, MyDesign. Then, in this site (logged in as an administrator), use People and Groups to add MyDesign to the new Team Site Designers group. Assign this group Design rights with Site Actions > Site Permissions > Grant Permissions (see Figure 10.6).

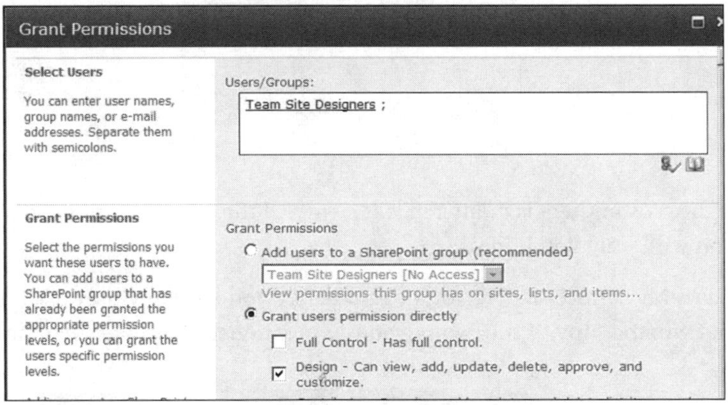

FIGURE 10.6
Granting permission to Team Site Designers

Did you Know?

> When you are investigating someone else's site, it is worth spending the time to look at exactly which permissions have been granted to each group that is listed. Even though some groups are included when the product has been installed, even they could have had their access rights amended by an earlier Administrator, and of course any new groups they added (such as the ReadPlus group you added in Hour 3) could have any set of access rights (and the name of the group could be misleading!).

Effect on Site Settings When Logging In as Somebody Else

Let's closely look at what happens to the Site Settings screen and compare the situation when logged in as administrator or when logged in as designer. Select the same menu item (Site Actions) and select the same item from the drop-down list (Site Settings):

▶ Logging in as the administrator displays the screen shown in Figure 10.7. It's a long list.

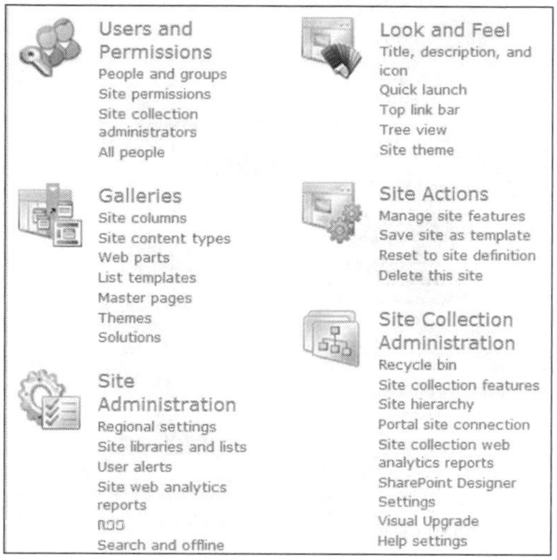

FIGURE 10.7
Site Settings
when logged in
as administrator

▶ Logging in as a person with Design rights displays Figure 10.8. It's a short list.

FIGURE 10.8
Site Settings
when logged in
as MyDesign

Not much left of all those options in Figure 10.8, is there? Again, the screen is changed to reflect just what that particular user (within or not within a SharePoint group) has rights to do.

If the user doesn't have rights to do something, then (almost without exception) the user will not see it.

Remember that Administrator was the name of the administrator of the server (or VM) on which we installed SPF 2010. Also recall that SPF1\Administrator is also the site collection administrator for the main site. So what happens if we have someone with Administration rights who isn't a site collection administrator, for instance, if we are signed in as MyAdmin?

Sign in as MyAdmin and have another look at Site Settings.

Figure 10.9 shows more possibilities than Figure 10.8 (Site Administration has been cut off at the same point as Figure 10.7 when creating the image), but the entire Site Collection Administration section is missing compared to Figure 10.7, as is the Site Collection Administrators link in the User and Permissions section.

FIGURE 10.9
Site Settings
when logged in
as a mere site
admin

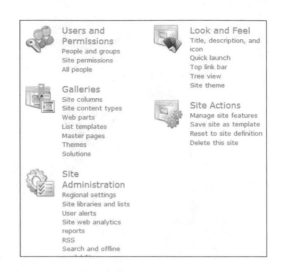

Both of these omissions are fairly obvious, but it's interesting that a site administrator isn't even allowed to see who the site collection administrators are.

Many readers probably have just one name and password combination to access Share-Point sites. For those readers, were the preceding sections a complete waste of time?

Not necessarily. You might be wondering why your friend Joe, who works just down the corridor, can see more on his screen than you can. You might also be trying to follow another SharePoint book and are wondering why you don't see the options it describes. This is actually a tricky one. One of the usual reasons for this is that the book you are reading is describing something in SPS 2010 that doesn't even exist in SPF 2010. In that case, even Joe (if he is using SPF 2010) won't see it.

I believe it's better to be open about these things rather than to hide them. So, no, you didn't waste your time reading the preceding sections. Now if you discover that you are missing access to something you need in your work, you know (if Joe has that access) that you just need to be moved to a different SharePoint group, which has the same rights that Joe already has (or which Joe is a member of). I'm not saying that will happen if you ask, but if you don't ask, you certainly won't be moved.

General Security Principles Apply

Of all the users we created together in Hour 3, one has so far not been used: MyDocLib. We haven't used it because I want to use MyDocLib as an example when showing you how to restrict access to a list within a site to a particular group.

First, however, there's one thing about SharePoint security that you need to know: SharePoint security does not break any standard security rules. Therefore, when restricting access to a document library, you can allow someone to access only the document library in question who also has the rights to access the site (or subsite) in which the document library is located. If you want someone to be allowed to access a document library but not be allowed to access the site containing it, the only solution is to create a special site that the person can access and put the document library there.

Treat "access" here as an example. You can't give them Contribute rights to the document library if they have only Read rights to the site. Again, doing so would break standard security rules.

By the Way

Specifying Special Access Rights for a Document Library

Now that you know the general principles, check again that MyDocLib has been given rights to the main site. Go back to being the administrator and access People and Groups / Team Site Members. You should see mydoclib listed along with mycontrib. If mydoclib is not listed there, add it (as MyDocLib).

Now that we know that MyDocLib has access rights to the main site, there is nothing stopping us from giving MyDocLib access rights to a document library in the site. To do this, follow these steps:

1. We have two libraries, so let's open Shared Documents from the link in Quick Launch. It already has one document in it, so using this Document Library is a reasonable test.

2. Access Library Tools > Library (tab) and Library Settings (ribbon). Figure 10.10 displays the top part of what you'll see.

List Information

Name:	Shared Documents
Web Address:	http://spf1/Shared Documents/Forms/AllItems.aspx
Description:	Share a document with the team by adding it to this document library.

General Settings	Permissions and Management	Communic
Title, description and navigation	Delete this document library	RSS settings
Versioning settings	Save document library as template	
Advanced settings	Permissions for this document library	
Validation settings	Manage files which have no checked in version	
	Workflow Settings	

FIGURE 10.10
Customizing a document library

3. In the center column (Permissions and Management), select Permissions for This Document Library item. You see Figure 10.11, which is warning you that

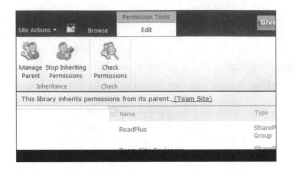

at the moment the Document Library is inheriting its permissions from the site
it is in.

Clearly the first step needed is for this document library to stop inheriting
permissions.

4. Click Stop Inheriting Permissions. You receive a warning that you are going to
   specify permissions for this document library. Click OK.

   As Figure 10.12 shows, this is the same list of SharePoint groups and users
   shown in Figure 10.11. Now, however, there are several different ribbon items
   and a clearly visible check box next to each SharePoint Group.

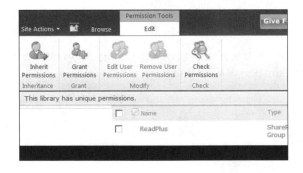

In this case, we intend to end up with a document library that can be accessed
by all the administrators (members of the Team Site Owners SharePoint group)
and MyDocLib.

5. Select all the rows except Team Site Owners and select Remove User Permissions
   (see Figure 10.13).

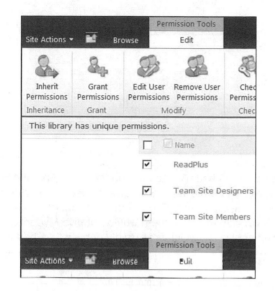

FIGURE 10.13
Removing some
user permissions

6. Click OK when the warning message appears.

7. The list now shows only Team Site Owners. The final step is to add MyDocLib, so select Grant Permissions.

Figure 10.14 shows the situation before checking the username you've typed in (always a good idea). Figure 10.15 shows an extract of the same screen after the username has been checked.

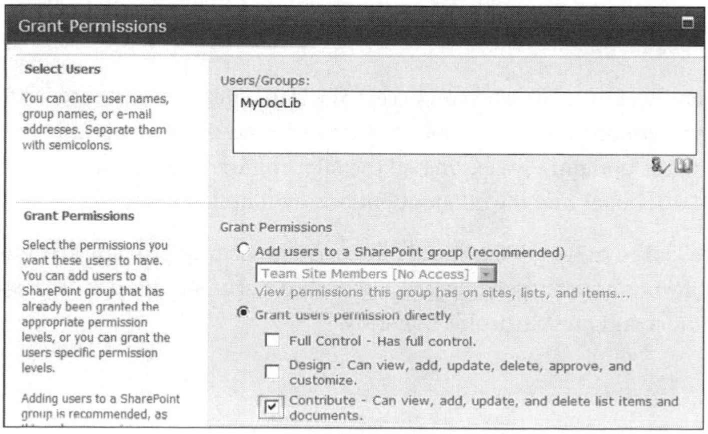

FIGURE 10.14
Adding a user to
Shared Docu-
ments

FIGURE 10.15
Adding a user after having checked the username

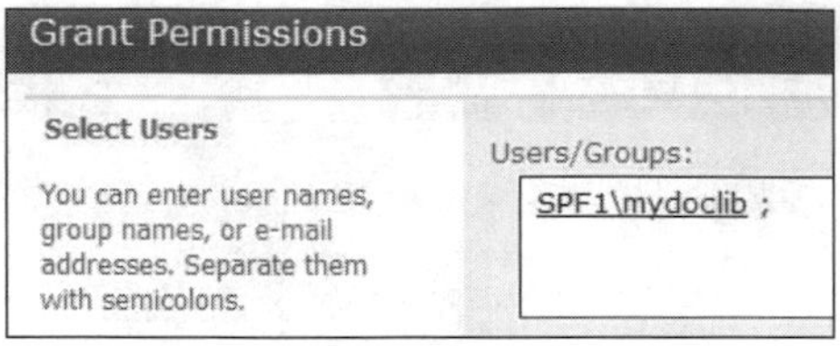

Grant Permissions

Select Users

You can enter user names, group names, or e-mail addresses. Separate them with semicolons.

Users/Groups:

SPF1\mydoclib ;

Look at your options if you had tried to add the user to a SharePoint group. You could do this, but except for the Team Site Owners newsgroup that has access rights to the site, all the other SharePoint groups are listed as <Name> (No Access). Adding MyDocLib to any of them would not give MyDocLib any access rights to the document library, which is certainly not what we had in mind.

Note that I have given this user direct permissions.

We have achieved our goal, and both the administrators and this single user can access the content in this document library (see Figure 10.16). No one else apart from Site Owners can, though!

FIGURE 10.16
Only the administrators and one user have access rights

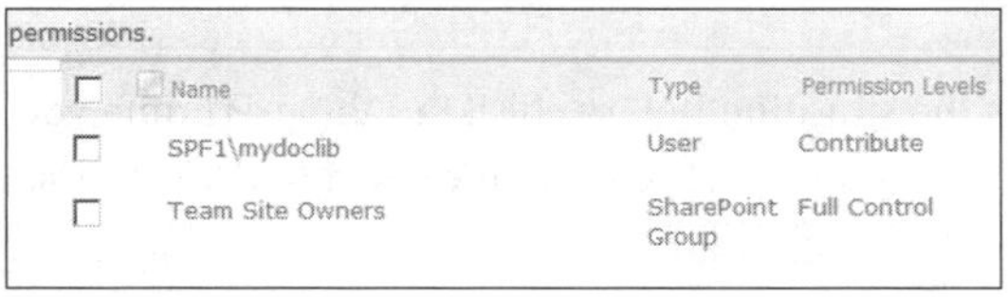

permissions.

	Name	Type	Permission Levels
	SPF1\mydoclib	User	Contribute
	Team Site Owners	SharePoint Group	Full Control

Summary

The different types of users who can access SPF 2010 sites were discussed. After briefly covering anonymous access and the All Authenticated Users group (all the users logged in to the domain), we examined the effect different permissions have on the look of SPF 2010 sites and the different options available.

Finally, we looked at how SPF 2010 applies general security principles, using an example of what happens when access rights to a document library are restricted to administrators and one particular user only.

Q&A

Q. *Anonymous access is specified at the web application level. What is a web application, and how do I create one?*

A. A web application is a bunch of sites accessible via the same port.

The basic installation created one web application (http://spf1) at port 80 (that is, the default site). All the sites we have added so far have been subsites to that site and are thus included in that same web application.

Even if we were to add a new "top-level" site to start off a new site collection (which, remember was a top-level site with its subsites and sub-subsites), that top-level site would still be in the same spf1 web application.

Here we look at creating a web application because it is good practice to separate anonymous access content from the normal content. As anonymous access is set at the web application level (see previous text), you can either allow anonymous access for all the sites below the default site (probably not a good idea) or create a new set of sites containing data that is suitable for anonymous access. This "new site of sites" must be contained in a site application.

Here are the basic instructions for creating a new web application where you specify that anonymous access is allowed, followed by the instructions for creating a new top-level site (site collection):

1. Open Central Administration > Manage web applications (in the Application Management section).

2. New (In the ribbon, upper left).

3. A long way down the page you need to Register New Managed Account. Do this (using SPF1\Administrator) and return to the Create New Web Application screen.

4. Note the port number and accept the defaults until halfway down the page.

5. Change Allow Anonymous (in the Security Configuration section) to Yes.

6. Near the bottom of the page, specify SPF1 (the only selection in the drop-down) as the location of the Search server.

7. Turn the Customer Experience Improvement Program off. (Check back to see that Require Use Remote Interfaces Permission is turned off).

8. Click OK.

After a long wait, sometimes so long on a slow machine that it times-out, in which case just redo the creation, we now have a web application and anonymous access has been specified for it. The next steps create a top-level site:

1. From the Central Administration main page (or the Applications Management page), in the center of it, is a Create Site Collections link. Click it.

2. Make sure the web application listed at the top of the page is the one you want to use; otherwise change it. Give the top-level site a name (I used Anonymous Website and specified AnonWebSite for the URL).

3. Select Team Site.

4. Specify Administrator as the Primary Site Collection administrator. (Note that the site collection administrator could be anyone. For a site created for the Personnel department, it would be useful if it were someone within the department and not you. In this case of a site for anonymous access, however, the administrator of the server is fine.)

5. Note in passing that each site collection has its own set of (different) quotas but only if you have already created a separate quota template. Here we have only one listed.

6. Click OK.

7. The site is created and can be accessed via http://spf1:<portnumber>. (Mine is 42641, so http://spf1:42641 is what I can see.)

Q. *I already have a web application, and I didn't specify anonymous access when I created it. How can I do so now?*

A. Complete the following steps:

1. Go to Central Administration > Manage web applications (in the Application Management section).

2. Select the web application that you want anonymous access to be allowed for.

3. Select Authentication Providers in the ribbon.

4. Select (usually) Default, and the Anonymous Access section should be visible on the page. (Then refer to the beginning of this hour for how to say what anonymous users an do).

Workshop

Quiz

1. Name the couple of "special" sets of users discussed in this hour.

2. Do all users always see the same things when they access the same page?

3. Why when we grant a specific user rights to a document library (or list) should we specify the user permissions directly rather than assign the user to a Share-Point group?

Answers

1. Anonymous access and the Authenticated Users group.

2. No, what they see depends on which rights they have.

3. Yes, you should specify user permissions directly. If the user is assigned to a group, that group will have access rights to the document library (or list). That is not what we want in this case.

HOUR 11

Using What We've Learned So Far in a Site

What You'll Learn in This Hour

- ▶ Collecting data to create a site
- ▶ Assigning data to appropriate SharePoint lists and libraries, and accepting when data isn't suitable
- ▶ Deciding what to place on the default site page
- ▶ How a user accesses information

This hour works through the actions needed when creating a website for a particular work scenario.

Brainstorming What Information a Site Could Contain

Now that we learned the concepts of building a website using SPF 2010, let's put them into practice by setting up a site for a particular purpose.

Let's build a site that can be used as a model for large teams investigating a serious crime. The first thing is to brainstorm what kinds of information the team is likely to have and need. So, just at random, a few things come to mind:

- ▶ Eyewitness reports
- ▶ Interviews with suspects
- ▶ Interviews with relatives
- ▶ Photographs of suspects

- ▶ Photographs of witnesses
- ▶ Soundtracks of interviews
- ▶ Videos of interviews
- ▶ Videos of the crime scene
- ▶ Photographs of the crime scene
- ▶ Fingerprints
- ▶ DNA samples
- ▶ Links to other computer systems
- ▶ General information to the team members
- ▶ Restaurant and hotel information for out-of-area members of the team
- ▶ Images of menus
- ▶ Recommendations from local members of the team
- ▶ Dates of press briefings
- ▶ Dates of internal meetings
- ▶ Method for the boss of the team to report to his superiors

This gives you the general idea. Include anything and everything connected with issues related to the site, even if it later ends up being rejected.

Making Sense of the Mass of Data

Brainstorming should lead to a mass of hodge-podge ideas. The next step to starting a website is to collate this date and assign it to SharePoint "things." We start with the documents previously listed (but we could start anywhere).

Thinking About Documents

Here's our first attempt at a list of the documents:

- ▶ Eyewitness reports
- ▶ Interviews with suspects
- ▶ Interviews with relatives

At this point (and this is normal), we discover that we forgot that the team will produce various reports, so we add them to the list:

▶ Weekly summaries

▶ Progress reports

▶ Text of press releases

▶ Transcript of press briefing

▶ Reports from the team boss to higher management

It's fairly clear that all these documents will go into SharePoint document libraries. What is not clear is how many document libraries, because we might think of some more documents later in the process.

We need to think about whether we need a document library that includes all these documents, some (fewer than eight) document libraries to contain them, or eight different document libraries (one document library listed item).

In other words, think about consolidation. To do that, consider the names of the previously listed categories. Interviews with eyewitnesses, interviews with suspects, and interviews with relatives should go in the same document library because

▶ They are all interviews.

▶ There is a floating line between a suspect and an eyewitness (or relative): Being one doesn't exclude being the other.

We can put all three categories in an Interviews document library. Then we need something that makes it possible for us to mark someone as both an eyewitness and a suspect, for example.

I often do this by having three Yes/No fields:

▶ Suspect: Yes/No

▶ Eyewitness: Yes/No

▶ Relative: Yes/No

Perhaps you think there will be a demand for the latest three weekly summaries and the latest three progress reports to be visible on the same page. In this case, you need two document libraries.

By the Way

Go back to Hour 6, "Using Libraries and Lists," and you see that you can have two web parts on the same page that show content from the same document library and yet show different content.

In other words, these two setups solve the demand for the latest three summaries and the latest three progress reports: two document libraries and a single document library with two non-overlapping views.

By the
Way

As well as using premade views, you can also use (in real time) filters on one or more fields to get the same effect. The problem is that before moving on you have to spend time resetting the filters back to the All settings.

This makes it possible to easily create views, such as Suspect (condition is Suspect = Yes) or even a combined view, such as Suspect and Eyewitness (first condition is Suspect = Yes; second condition is Eyewitness = Yes).

Another option is to have a Choice type field with three choices (Suspect, Eyewitness, and Relative) and make this Choice type field (unlike the one we used in Hour 8, "Creating and Using Views and Folders") have multiple choices.

The Interviews document library reduces the list by three items. Five items are left! We can immediately cross another one off: reports from the team boss to higher management. This won't be available to team members other than the boss, so it can't be located in the same document library as anything else. So we create a document library called Reports to Senior Management. We can decide later what to do to keep it secure. Four items left.

Because two of the four items relate to the press, both of them can be in a document library called Press Documents. To keep the two kinds of documents apart but still within the same document library, we can use the same technique as in Hour 8 and use a Choice field called, perhaps, Type of Document. In this, we have two alternatives: Press Releases and Press Briefing Transcripts. Of course, we'll pre-prepare views for each of those two values (just as we did in Hour 8 for HP, IBM, and so on). Two left.

Both the two left, despite the completely different names in the list, are reports made on a regular basis. We can put them in the same document library using a Choice field (and views) to keep them apart.

Finally, we discover that we completely missed one set of documents. Regular team meetings will no doubt be written up. Because of the size of the team, there will probably be team meetings of subteams and team meetings of the entire squad. So we need one document library for team meetings with an extra field, Team Name, to categorize them and ease the use of views.

The end result (at least for now) are the following document libraries:

- Interviews
- Press Documents
- Summaries and Progress Reports
- Team Meetings
- Reports to Senior Management

The Reports to Senior Management document library needs to be separate.

Pictures

In the original list, we have four sets of pictures:

- Photographs of suspects
- Photographs of witnesses
- Photographs of the crime scene
- Images of menus

The first three involve solving the crime; the fourth does not.

The first two—following the ideas previously stated—can go into a single picture library. In this picture library, there must be a way (as previously, with the Yes/No fields) to decide whether someone is a witness or a suspect or both.

In fact, we now realize that we will have photographs of relatives, too, so this picture library will include them and be the equivalent of a document library.

> You'll often find, when trying to making sense of your collection of things and deciding what to include in a site, that you want other things to appear in a site, too.

By the Way

The images of menus need their own picture library. For the moment, we can't think of any other social usage for a picture library. Also it might prove useful if the out-of-town members of the squad (that is, those for whom the images of menus were conceived) can recognize the other members of the squad. In other words, we need a third picture library (with photographs of squad members). Let's also add descriptions to the photographs in the picture library.

The end result is that we have four picture libraries:

- Suspects, Eyewitnesses, and Relatives

▶ Crime Scene

▶ Menu Images (and other social bric-a-brac)

▶ Squad Member Pictures (with brief descriptions)

> My preference is to keep the crime scene pictures in their own picture library. It's only a preference, but it seems logical because they are a completely different set of pictures (from those of people).

Now let's look at some of the easier items to categorize.

Announcements

One item obviously goes in an Announcements list: general information to the team members. This can be used both for general information about how the investigation is proceeding and for information for out-of-town squad members about interesting things about to happen in the town. Given the seriousness of the investigation, it's best to keep them apart.

We'll have two Announcements lists:

▶ General investigation information announcements

▶ Announcements about interesting local events

Dates

Two date items were previously listed: dates of press briefings and dates of internal meetings. These are obvious candidates for different Calendar lists.

Did you Know?

> Make the date items different because they are of different priority to different people.

At this point, there could be a third calendar—one giving the local events for the out-of-towners' free time.

Now, we have three different Calendar lists:

▶ Press Briefings

▶ Internal Meetings

▶ Local Events

Unformatted Information

A few items listed in our original list are both in the social category and haven't been covered:

▶ Restaurant and hotel information for out-of-area members of the team

▶ Recommendations from local members of the team

Both items are likely to be free format, with a title and a brief description from the local squad member, so they are suitable for the Custom list format with a title such as Bob's Café and a description.

I see no reason why we can't combine these items if they are strictly free-formatted information. If the restaurant/hotel information is official (and so probably laid out within a certain number of set fields) and the recommendations are strictly off-the-cuff ones, however, there should be two Custom lists (with different fields). Again, it's a decision for the site designer based on the designer's sense of how this information is going to be provided.

So we have two different Custom lists:

▶ Local Hotel and Restaurant Details

▶ Local Tips

Other Information

Here's what's left from the original list:

▶ Soundtracks of interviews

▶ Videos of interviews

▶ Videos of the crime scene

▶ Fingerprints

▶ DNA samples

▶ Links to other computer systems

Links

Links to other computer systems may seem to be the only obvious Links library required; however, fingerprints might be stored in a national (perhaps) fingerprint system rather than in our SharePoint site. Therefore, there ought to be a link to the fingerprint system.

I obviously don't watch television enough, because I have no idea where DNA information is stored and accessed. Let's assume that the information is similar to fingerprints and thus requires us to access another system.

From this, we can calculate that we will have one Links library, which contains several entries, such as the following:

▶ Links to Various Police-Related Organizations

▶ Link to the Fingerprint System

▶ Link to the DNA System

Just because we have listed something (about what the site should provide) in our brainstorming, we need to remain flexible and remind ourselves constantly that not everything needs to be stored in our own system. What is important is that our team can access the information, not that it is stored in our system. Links lists are often the solution to this "problem."

Audio and Video

We're left with audio and video. There is no list or library specifically for audio and video as there was for pictures. So the logical place to put these files is in a document library (or libraries)—that is, if we put them in a library at all. Whereas MP3 audio files are small and are not going to be a problem for a document library, video files are large and are a potential problem for (for instance) backups. One option, therefore, is to keep video files in the file system.

The other thing is that the SharePoint v4 systems do not as delivered provide any functionality for playing back video files in a window within the browser. Typically, either software additions are required (if third-party additions to the basic SharePoint software are available), or a video file will open a completely separate copy of software capable of playing back the video format we use.

In addition, it might first be necessary to check which file formats can be uploaded to a document library. The first question in the "Q&A" section shows how to check the file formats enabled in document libraries and how to amend that list.

Otherwise, if MP3 (for instance) is on the list of file types that are "banned," any attempt to upload a single MP3 file (or a batch of files containing at least one MP3 file) will fail.

For the purpose of this site-creation exercise, let's just assume that we've covered all the bases and that both audio and video files will be added to document libraries.

To be as logical as possible, let's have three separate document libraries:

- Soundtracks of Interviews
- Videos of Interviews
- Videos of the Scene of the Crime

Summary of Lists/Libraries

So far, our final tally of lists and libraries is as follows:

- Document libraries (8)
- Picture libraries (4)
- Announcements lists (2)
- Calendar lists (3)
- Custom lists (2)
- Links lists (1)

Placing the Lists/Libraries into the Web Pages

We've brainstormed our lists and libraries, so now we must create them and add fields (as appropriate) for each list. Then we must decide which lists/libraries should appear in the Quick Launch section and which lists/libraries need to appear in web part form in the main section of the page.

Deciding on One Site or Several Sites

First, consider whether one site is enough for your needs. If you look at our list, it is because the only thing we have that is of restricted access is one single document library; we can assume that there is nothing to stop the top management having rights to access the rest of the site. Therefore, we can also give them rights to that one Reports to Senior Management document library (following the rules outlined in Hour 10, "Learning About Authentication and Access Rights").

However, although that approach is possible, we can always expect to have missed something when doing the brainstorming and follow-up design sessions. This means that we could have missed some other piece of information needed for contact between the senior management and the squad leader.

By the
Way

I thought about a Discussions list for the squad team. In the end, however, I decided that they'll be in a big room and will hold their discussions in person.

In fact, we probably missed that they need to communicate. These days, many senior managers communicate via a computer. Therefore, a Discussions list open only to senior management and the squad leader is certainly a possibility we should add to our design.

So now we have both a Discussions list and a document library that have restricted access. The obvious solution is to put them in a subsite that does not inherit permissions.

By the
Way

When an item is created (or in this case a document is added to a document library), both the Created and the Modified fields contain the time and time it was created. When an item is changed, the Modified field is amended, but the Created field stays the same.

Usually, you want to know both about the latest new and the latest amended articles. Therefore, you use the Modified field.

If you want to see in one part of the screen the latest New documents and in another part of the screen the latest Modified (but not New) documents, however, you need to use two web parts from the same document library with two different views.

You want one view just sorted on Created; that gives the latest New documents. You want a second view that is sorted on Modified to give all documents that have been modified but which includes a filter that keeps out newly added documents. (To do this you create a calculated field called NotMod whose value is "=Created-Modified" and then have a filter that is defined as NotMod not equal 0).

In that subsite, we have so few lists/libraries that we might as well put both web parts in the main section of the screen. We can place the Discussions list on the left, and on the right the document library, the web part for which should, perhaps, use a view that specifies something between 10 and 20 items.

Did you
Know?

Typically, the best sort order for the main page of a site is by the Modified field in descending order. (So specifying an item limit of 5 in a view will show the latest 5 items.)

I find 5 to be a useful limit if the page is crowded and 10 to be more suitable if it isn't.

Allocating Lists/Web Parts to the Default Page

What about the main site? It's obvious that we have so many lists and libraries that we are not going to fit the web parts for all of them in the center section. So what we look for there are the lists/libraries that need to be "in your face."

This knocks out most of the document libraries because we expect people to regularly look through them without prompting. For instance, the meeting reports and so on will automatically be read by people who were away at the time (or missed most of the meeting because they were daydreaming). Therefore, they don't need to be in the main section. And, in any case, there's a technique called alerts (discussed a bit later in this hour). With alerts, you can tell people when something has been changed in a document library (or list).

For both these reasons, we'll use what little space we have in the main section of the screen for some other lists. The first obvious candidates are one of the two Announcements lists and two of the three Calendar lists.

Why not both the Announcement lists and all three Calendar lists? The reason is that the ones I don't plan to include on the standard page are the ones intended only for out-of-towners because those lists are almost entirely uninteresting for local squad members.

By the Way

You can tweak the calendars to make sure they don't take up too much space.

Did you Know?

Of the rest, only one list/library should be included in the main section of the page: the Links list. That is there because people will be using it often as a way to go directly to other systems, and they won't want to first open it from Quick Launch.

Specifying What Will Be Listed in the Quick Launch Section

As for the question of which items to list in Quick Launch, it depends on how many lists/libraries you have. At a minimum, you should have a link there for every list/library that you have not included as a web part in the main section of the screen. If you have the space, however, there's nothing wrong with having even the list/libraries behind those web parts present in the main section of the page (or some of them) listed in the Quick Launch section.

To some extent, in a company environment this can be decided by the size of the monitors in use and the standard screen resolution. Just as an overfull screen looks a mess, so does a nearly empty one.

Positioning the Web Parts in the Web Page

So far, there's been no discussion about how to position those web parts that we selected for the main section of the page. A good start is to get rid of the standard picture (if you are using a site template that includes it)! It does nothing useful and just fills up otherwise useful space. Follow that, if you have two Announcements lists, by placing (one each!) at the top of the two columns.

For some reason, it's a good standard to have the Links list on the rightmost side of the screen. (Because we want all the links in the list to be visible here, that should be the rightmost section completed.)

That leaves the two calendars, which can then be placed only in the leftmost screen section (with the more important one first).

Here the view called Calendar does look nice, I agree, but it takes up a lot of space. So you should at least consider making one or both of your web parts use another more boring view. Figures 11.1 and 11.2 illustrate this point.

FIGURE 11.1
Using small-size calendars

FIGURE 11.2
Using at least one "real" calendar

In Figure 11.2 (and only a small part of the second calendar is actually on screen), the second calendar dominates the entire screen (even though it contains no more information than the first calendar). So use full calendars with care. If you want them to dominate, fine. But if you don't, use more minimal versions.

That's enough for setting up the site. Now let's look at the needs of the people who require access to a site's information.

Additional Functions for the Users of the Site

People tend to use a site in three different ways:

- ▶ They access the site regularly and check what's new there.

- ▶ They want to be told when things are new.

- ▶ They want to search for things from the site.

Of course, people might also want to do a combination of any of the things previously listed. Let's look at these briefly.

People Who Access the Site Regularly

People who access the site regularly want to see at-a-glance information. The information they see directly is what the site designer decides they are likely to be most interested in.

People Who Want to Be Prompted for Updates

In the earlier releases users could specify alerts at List or Library level, and they would then receive email whenever anything happened in the List or Library. This restriction (which is still valid, although alerts are now possible on Views) on having Alerts only at List or Library level was something that caused a lot of queries to SharePoint administrators.

Often, therefore, site administrators didn't tell their users that alerts were possible because, from the point-of-view of the administrator, alerts did nothing but cause him work. Another reason was that the administration of alerts was a mess because the only person who could create an alert was the user and the administrator had no picture of how many alerts were in place and for what. That has now been improved but users complaining about getting too many alerts (or not getting any) remains.

For alerts to function, the SharePoint system needs to send emails. This is something that our system hasn't been set to do, so instead of going through how to create an alert, we go through how to create an RSS feed because this doesn't require the administrator to do anything. (Sneaky perhaps, but these days I tend to rely more on RSS feeds than on emails, so I'm helping you to do what I do.)

(Very brief information on how an administrator can specify outgoing email, which is what is required for alerts to work, is in the "Q&A" section.)

Here are the steps for creating an RSS feed for The Books Documents document library:

1. Open The Book Documents library.

2. Select Library (menu line).

   As you can see in Figure 11.3, the RSS feed is in the Share & Track section. (If your administrator has already specified support for outgoing email, this section would be the place where an icon for Alert creation would appear.) It doesn't appear in Figure 11.3 because outgoing email hasn't been specified; it wouldn't be possible to use even if it were there, so SharePoint, as usual, doesn't show it.

FIGURE 11.3
Choosing
RSS feed

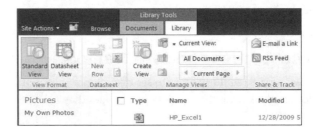

3. Click RSS Feed. Figure 11.4 shows the top section of the page.

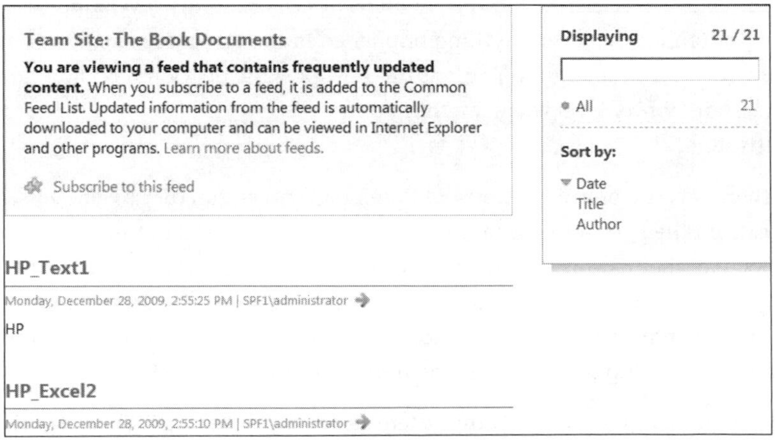

FIGURE 11.4
The RSS feed

4. There are now two alternatives:

   ▶ You can copy the URL and then go to your RSS Reader; create a new feed; and specify the URL you just copied. (This is what I do.)

   ▶ You can click Subscribe to This Feed.

This option is a big disappointment. What you expect, based on your experience of creating RSS feeds from many non-SharePoint sites, is a selection of different RSS readers so that you can directly add this feed to your RSS Reader. Instead all this function does is add the feed to a folder in the copy of IE on the PC you are using at the time. So you need to add it to your own RSS Reader by hand anyway.

People Who Want to Search the Site

The final category of typical users consists of those who neither want to visit a site regularly nor want to receive email about changes to it. These people typically access a site only when they want something specific; therefore, they tend to use the Search function.

Searching a SPF 2010 site is covered in both in Hour 13, "Using SF 2010 Search and Installing Search Server 2010 Express," (for simple out-of-the-box searches) and Hour 14, "Improving Searches," (for more complicated searches after Search Server 2010 Express has been added).

Summary

This hour covered basic site design. It started with brainstorming data and then assigned this data to suitable kinds of SharePoint lists and libraries. The hour then examined where to place the data in the site and how typical users might access the data.

Q&A

Q. *How do I find out which file formats are on the banned list (and how do I add new formats)?*

A. Go to Central Administration > Security > Define Blocked File Types. You see a screen similar to Figure 11.5.

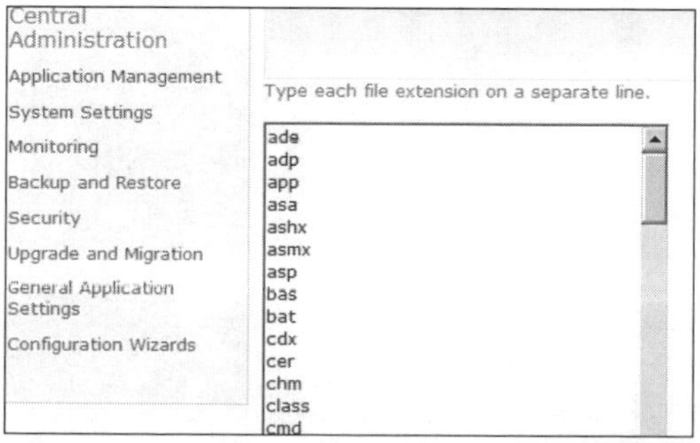

FIGURE 11.5
List of Blocked File Types

Scroll down the list to see whether MP3 files are blocked. They are not, and neither are such files such as AVI, MP4, and WMV file types that many administrators of business sites might well want to ban. However (and to my mind, oddly), Microsoft help files (.chm) are banned.

(Before you do anything else, check that you can't upload .chm files.) So delete CHM from the list of file types in Figure 11.5 and click OK. Now you can upload Microsoft help files.

By the Way

Readers of my earlier book on WSS 3.0 will notice that in SPF 2010 when CHM is removed from the list, there is no longer a warning. As I pointed out in the equivalent hour of that book, the warning was about something that wasn't true. Did they spot this for themselves, or did someone in the Microsoft development team read my book?

Adding file types such as MP4 to the list of file types is equally trivial. Just insert a line feed at the correct alphabetical location (for ease of use); add MP4 and click OK.

Q. *How can administrators make alerts possible?*

A. To create alerts, the administrator needs to allow the SharePoint system to send email; otherwise, there is no link available in the Share and Track group in the ribbon. This is done in Central Administration > System Settings > Configure Outgoing e-Mail Settings.

The main requirement is the need to have an SMTP server available. Typically, this is Exchange Server, but it could be any SMTP server (even a small, free one installed on the same server as your SPF 2010).

Getting the name of that SMTP server correct is the usual stumbling block in what otherwise is a relatively simple process (unlike setting incoming email settings).

Workshop

Quiz

1. Is the data we have gathered in the brainstorming phase the totality of data for the site?

2. If I have only a single document library that is of restricted access, should I locate it in the standard site and specify special access rights for it?

3. Can I specify that I get an email alert when a single item in a list or document in a document library changes?

Answers

1. It's not likely to be. The subsequent processes (of assigning the data to lists and libraries and of then deciding what to include on the default page) all tends to throw up new data that was previously overlooked.

2. It is one option you have. Unless you are 100 percent sure that you will not have any more lists or libraries with restricted access, however, it might be a better option to create a special site (with restricted access) for it.

3. Not as such. If the item in question is the only one in a view and you have specified alerts for a particular view, then yes, you can. But typically, the standard options, views, lists, and such mean that an alert can act on several items or documents, not just on one.

Using Wikis and Blogs

What You'll Learn in This Hour

- ▶ Definition of wikis and blogs
- ▶ Which site types are based on the wiki page type
- ▶ How best to create and use wiki functionality
- ▶ How to create a simple blog site

Wikis and blogs were introduced to the SharePoint range in 2007. Whereas blog functionality hasn't changed much for SPF 2010, wiki functionality has improved a lot, so the emphasis in this hour is on wiki functionality. Basic blog functionality is still covered, but look out (in Codeplex) for an "Extended Blog Edition" for SPF 2010 and SPS 2010 (at the time of writing only available in a 2007 version) as a way of improving on the basic blog functionality.

Wikis and Blogs in SPF 2010

To most of you, the terms blogs and wikis are already familiar. Blogs are a way for people to write an open letter to (potentially) the world. Wikis don't get as much attention as blogs, so we discuss them first.

An example of a wiki is Wikipedia, which is an online encyclopedia that depends on the contributions of the masses to produce quality entries. For example, someone describes a pop artist's background and posts it. This description can then be amended and expanded on by anyone who knows more about the subject. Wikipedia defines a wiki as follows (http://en.wikipedia.org/wiki/Wiki):

> "A wiki is software that allows users to collaboratively create, edit, link, and organize the content of a website, usually for reference material. Wikis are often used to create collaborative websites and to power community websites."

In the v3 products, both wikis and blogs had only basic functionality built-in, and quickly two CodePlex projects arose to try to improve on that functionality. The wiki project never made it past the beta stage, but the blog project quickly provided useful and stable additional functionality to blog functionality.

Despite the basic functionality available, people still used the wiki functionality unless they required much more, in which case they went to third-party products. However, here we look at wiki functionality in the SPF 2010 product, and it—to say the least—is confusing. So how it was before is briefly described and then we go on from that (clear) starting point to describe how it is in SPF 2010.

In the v3 SharePoint products there was the choice of selecting a Wiki Site Template when creating a site or of creating any kind of site and then in that site specifying a Wiki Library. When you created a Wiki Site, your first page was "Welcome to Your Wiki Site," and you could click How to Use This Wiki Site to see some explanatory text on how to add (wiki) content. That How to Use page was stored in a Wiki Library!

In other words, the only main difference between creating a Wiki Site and creating a Wiki Library was that if you created a Wiki Site, it already contained a Wiki Library (in fact it contained *only* a Wiki Library), and by going the Wiki Site route you in effect "forced" yourself to have a separate site that contained all your wiki information. If you created a Wiki Library you could have (it was your choice) included that in another kind of site that contained other things beside wiki pages.

This, to my mind, wasn't as good an administration solution, so I therefore recommended in my earlier book that a wiki site should be created so that all the wiki information was stored in the same site.

In the v4 products (SPF 2010 and SPS 2010), there no longer is a Wiki Site Template in the list of Site Templates you can choose from. There is still a Wiki Library (now called a Wiki Page Library) List/Library type you can choose. So you can still decide whether to create a site just for wikis or to add a Wiki (Page) Library to an existing site.

Later in this hour, we learn how to do that. We add a Wiki Page Library to a site we previously created for convenience, but it's best in production to create a new site just for wikis.

The pages of a Wiki Page Library look just like the pages of a Wiki Library in the v3 product. So at first glance there is little difference between wiki pages in SPF 2010 and those in WSS 3.0—basic wiki functionality, looking very much like a Wikipedia page with mainly text and links.

Let's start this hour by creating a Wiki Page Library and using it to create a simple Wikipedia type set of pages. When that is done we look at what Microsoft in this version of SharePoint has added to that basic concept.

Creating a Basic Wiki in SPF 2010

Start creating a basic wiki by going to the WebPartsTest site:

1. Go to Site Actions > More Options.

2. Click Wiki Page Library.

3. Name the library **Wiki Library Test**. Figure 12.1 is standard for the creation of any type of Library.

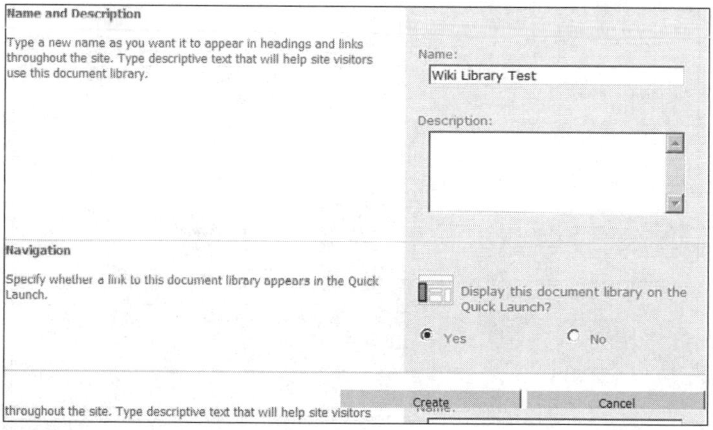

FIGURE 12.1
Creating a Wiki Library

4. Click Create.

The Home web page of a Wiki Page Library contains a brief description of what a wiki is (see Figure 12.2).

At this point, you can click How to Use This Wiki Library to see a page with all the things you can do with your wiki (see Figure 12.3). (We concentrate on a few basic things in this hour.)

To add information to a wiki, follow these steps:

1. Go back in the browser or just click one of the two Home options you see.

2. Click the Edit icon in the ribbon.

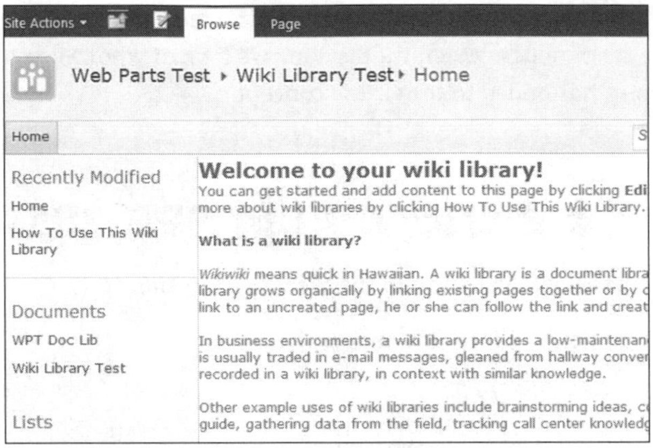

FIGURE 12.2
The Starter Page of a wiki library

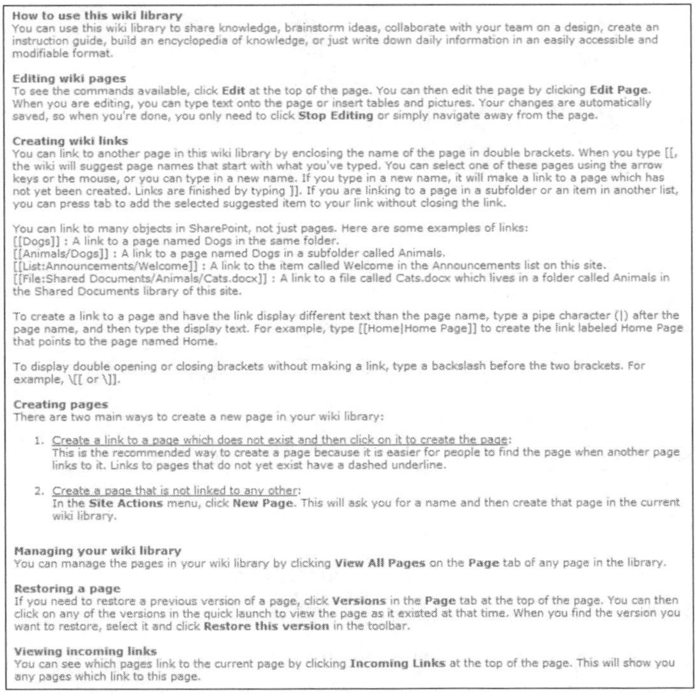

How to use this wiki library
You can use this wiki library to share knowledge, brainstorm ideas, collaborate with your team on a design, create an instruction guide, build an encyclopedia of knowledge, or just write down daily information in an easily accessible and modifiable format.

Editing wiki pages
To see the commands available, click **Edit** at the top of the page. You can then edit the page by clicking **Edit Page**. When you are editing, you can type text onto the page or insert tables and pictures. Your changes are automatically saved, so when you're done, you only need to click **Stop Editing** or simply navigate away from the page.

Creating wiki links
You can link to another page in this wiki library by enclosing the name of the page in double brackets. When you type [[, the wiki will suggest page names that start with what you've typed. You can select one of these pages using the arrow keys or the mouse, or you can type in a new name. If you type in a new name, it will make a link to a page which has not yet been created. Links are finished by typing]]. If you are linking to a page in a subfolder or an item in another list, you can press tab to add the selected suggested item to your link without closing the link.

You can link to many objects in SharePoint, not just pages. Here are some examples of links:
[[Dogs]] : A link to a page named Dogs in the same folder.
[[Animals/Dogs]] : A link to a page named Dogs in a subfolder called Animals.
[[List:Announcements/Welcome]] : A link to the item called Welcome in the Announcements list on this site.
[[File:Shared Documents/Animals/Cats.docx]] : A link to a file called Cats.docx which lives in a folder called Animals in the Shared Documents library of this site.

To create a link to a page and have the link display different text than the page name, type a pipe character (|) after the page name, and then type the display text. For example, type [[Home|Home Page]] to create the link labeled Home Page that points to the page named Home.

To display double opening or closing brackets without making a link, type a backslash before the two brackets. For example, \[[or \]].

Creating pages
There are two main ways to create a new page in your wiki library:

1. Create a link to a page which does not exist and then click on it to create the page:
   This is the recommended way to create a page because it is easier for people to find the page when another page links to it. Links to pages that do not yet exist have a dashed underline.

2. Create a page that is not linked to any other:
   In the **Site Actions** menu, click **New Page**. This will ask you for a name and then create that page in the current wiki library.

Managing your wiki library
You can manage the pages in your wiki library by clicking **View All Pages** on the **Page** tab of any page in the library.

Restoring a page
If you need to restore a previous version of a page, click **Versions** in the **Page** tab at the top of the page. You can then click on any of the versions in the quick launch to view the page as it existed at that time. When you find the version you want to restore, select it and click **Restore this version** in the toolbar.

Viewing incoming links
You can see which pages link to the current page by clicking **Incoming Links** at the top of the page. This will show you any pages which link to this page.

FIGURE 12.3
How to use a Wiki Library

Nothing seems to change in the text section, but the ribbon is replaced by one suitable for editing, and you can now delete the existing text (which you couldn't before).

3. Select the existing text and delete it. Now we have a clean sheet to work with. We start with the Title.

This is the Wiki Page Library's top page, so you might want to write some information to your users describing how your company (or whatever) will use the wiki functionality.

If you use an English language version of SPF 2010, but your users don't have English as their mother tongue, this is a good place to explain the wiki concept in their language (perhaps by writing a translation of the "How to Use a Wiki Library").

4. Add some text. (As you can see, it's similar to working in Word.)

   ▶ Write the heading text.

   ▶ Select the text.

   ▶ Center it.

   ▶ Make the font larger.

   ▶ Add an underline.

Let's assume that the wiki site will be used to share (internally) information about customer staff who work with us and the products installed at the customer company.

Figure 12.4 is a page in which that has been done and where you can also see what the drop-down at the top right of the ribbon is for.

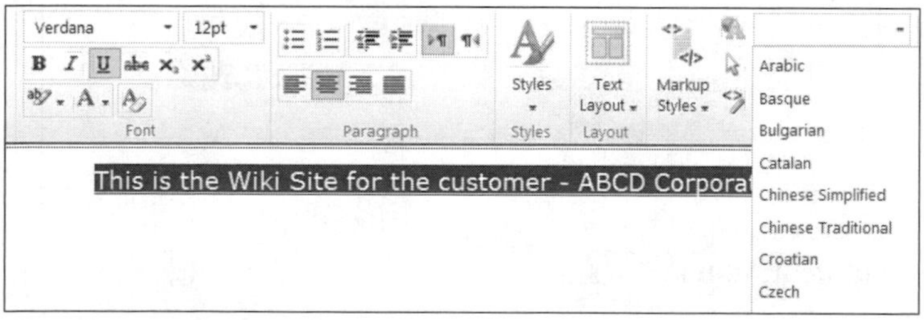

FIGURE 12.4
Starting to create a wiki home page

Or can you see what it is for? It's certainly for selecting a language, but what can you do with this drop-down that you couldn't do before? Nothing much actually. It adds a piece of code to the page (not visible) that advises programs that evaluate the page's contents which language all (or some selected part) of the text is in.

There's another possibly key function in the ribbon that is not directly obvious. There are two A icons in the Font section on the left of Figure 12.4. The left of the two actually leads to a choice of colors.

(The reason I find this difficult to see is that when installed the color of that A is the same as that of the other A. If it were, for instance, bright red, it would be obvious that this icon means change color.)

5. Add more text to the page following the guidelines from Figure 12.3. (See Figure 12.5 for the result of that.) While you are doing this, a few "helpful" pop-ups appear that you can ignore.

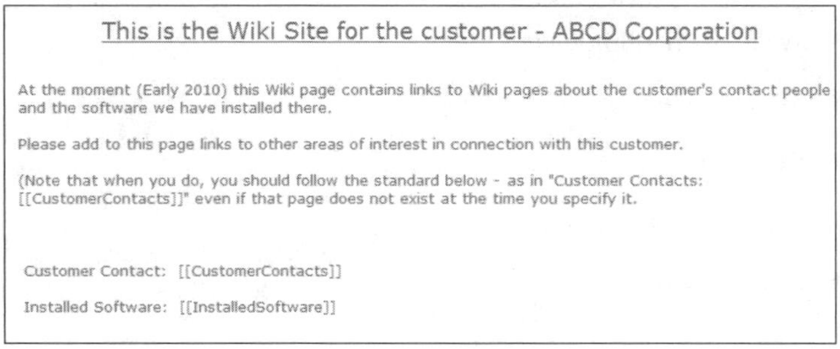

FIGURE 12.5
The full text of the page

This is the Wiki Site for the customer - ABCD Corporation

At the moment (Early 2010) this Wiki page contains links to Wiki pages about the customer's contact people and the software we have installed there.

Please add to this page links to other areas of interest in connection with this customer.

(Note that when you do, you should follow the standard below - as in "Customer Contacts: [[CustomerContacts]]" even if that page does not exist at the time you specify it.

Customer Contact: [[CustomerContacts]]

Installed Software: [[InstalledSoftware]]

6. Click Save at the left of the Ribbon.

See Figure 12.6. It's a mess, isn't it?

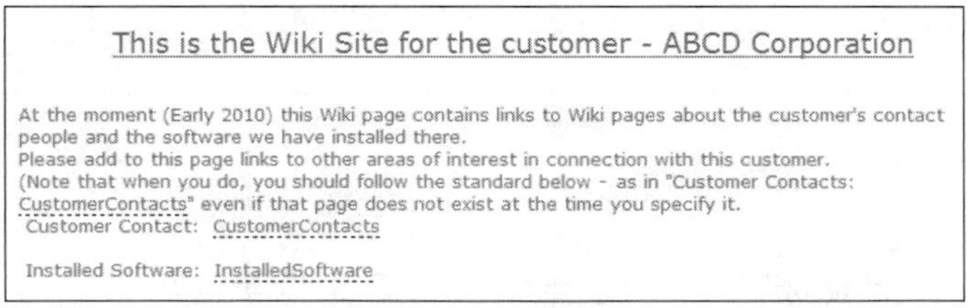

FIGURE 12.6
Not very pretty

This is the Wiki Site for the customer - ABCD Corporation

At the moment (Early 2010) this Wiki page contains links to Wiki pages about the customer's contact people and the software we have installed there.
Please add to this page links to other areas of interest in connection with this customer.
(Note that when you do, you should follow the standard below - as in "Customer Contacts: CustomerContacts" even if that page does not exist at the time you specify it.
  Customer Contact: CustomerContacts

Installed Software: InstalledSoftware

So what went wrong?

▶ The first thing is that only the formatting is wrong. We lost all the line feeds that made Figure 12.5 look reasonable.

▶ The other thing that appears wrong is that we have three things that are underlined with a dotted line (and in a color book would also appear in blue). The dotted underlining means that these are links to pages that don't exist. When we create those pages, the dotted underlining disappears.

▶ Two of the underlined links should go to other pages. The first though should indicate to readers that to create a link to another page, you need to write two open square brackets, then the Title of the page you link to, and then two close square brackets. We can remove that problem by spelling it out rather than using the symbols.

7. Click Edit again.

The problem is that the function ignores line feeds; you need to move the cursor to the correct line and then write the text in. (The opposite of what you'd expect, isn't it?)

There are two main solutions.

If you are happy using HTML, you can use the HTML button and amend the code by adding in <p></p> wherever you want an empty line. The HTML window is however extremely messy, so this would be the alternative to choose if trying to adjust the page by (a loop of) changing something followed by saving (and finding something still wrong) was driving you mad.

Remember the old (SharePoint v2 editor!) favorite of needing to have two empty lines in your edit form when you actually only need one?

(After rewriting the text and including two empty lines when I wanted one—and removing an extra line when I suddenly had two empty lines—I did the final step 6.)

8. Click Save.

Now you should see Figure 12.7.

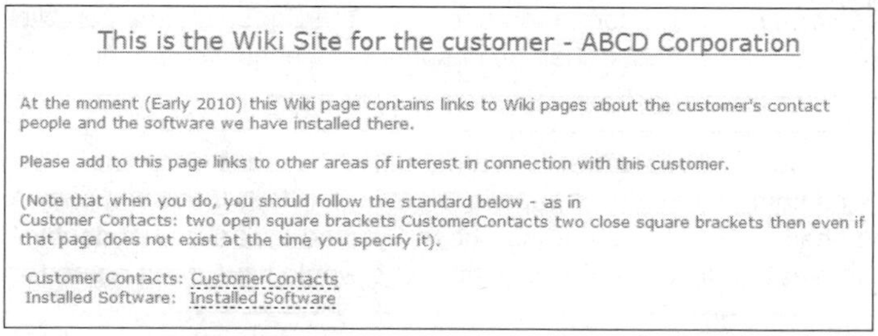

This is the Wiki Site for the customer - ABCD Corporation

At the moment (Early 2010) this Wiki page contains links to Wiki pages about the customer's contact people and the software we have installed there.

Please add to this page links to other areas of interest in connection with this customer.

(Note that when you do, you should follow the standard below - as in Customer Contacts: two open square brackets CustomerContacts two close square brackets then even if that page does not exist at the time you specify it).

Customer Contacts: CustomerContacts
Installed Software: Installed Software

FIGURE 12.7
The first page correctly spaced

9. Click the CustomerContacts link.

Even though the link to CustomerContacts is underlined because there is no CustomerContacts page, you can still click the link. Figure 12.8 displays that you want to create a Customer Contacts page, after which you can add some data to it (see Figure 12.9).

FIGURE 12.8
Creating a new
Customer-
Contacts page

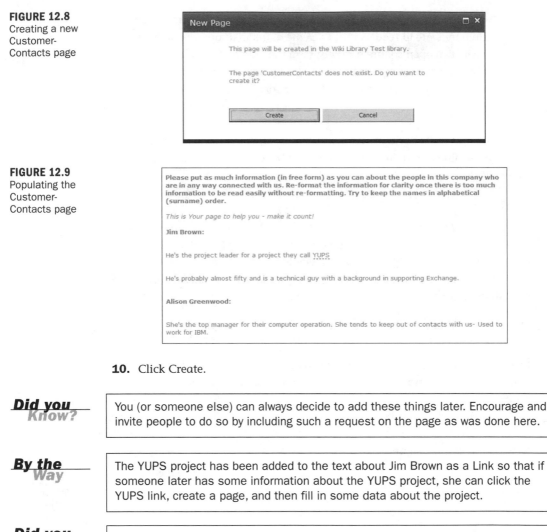

FIGURE 12.9
Populating the
Customer-
Contacts page

> Please put as much information (in free form) as you can about the people in this company who are in any way connected with us. Re-format the information for clarity once there is too much information to be read easily without re-formatting. Try to keep the names in alphabetical (surname) order.
>
> *This is Your page to help you - make it count!*
>
> **Jim Brown:**
>
> He's the project leader for a project they call YUPS
>
> He's probably almost fifty and is a technical guy with a background in supporting Exchange.
>
> **Alison Greenwood:**
>
> She's the top manager for their computer operation. She tends to keep out of contacts with us- Used to work for IBM.

10. Click Create.

Did you Know?

> You (or someone else) can always decide to add these things later. Encourage and invite people to do so by including such a request on the page as was done here.

By the Way

> The YUPS project has been added to the text about Jim Brown as a Link so that if someone later has some information about the YUPS project, she can click the YUPS link, create a page, and then fill in some data about the project.

Did you Know?

> We didn't put double square brackets around IBM because everyone knows IBM, so there's no point in creating a page in the Wiki for IBM. If the company Alison Greenwood had worked for earlier had been SysFred Inc., a use of double-brackets to create a link to a SysFred Inc. page would have been a good idea.

Wiki Pages (and Sites) in SPF 2010

When you install SPF 2010, the system creates a default site, and when it creates that default site, it uses the Team Site site template. When creating additional sites later, you decide which site template to use, so although you could create a site using the default Team Site template, you also have the choice of another nine other site templates.

The relevance to wikis is that the Team Site site template creates a site where the default page is a wiki page. The default pages for all the other site templates are not wiki pages but "web part pages" or pages where the main concentration is on adding web parts in zones on the page. You might also see the term Zone Pages used for them.

Those are the page types we've mostly used so far in the book because they are the easiest to use when adding web parts to a page in a controlled fashion. As we saw when we amended the default page of the Home (Team Site-based) site, we could add web parts, but it wasn't so controlled. That, too, wouldn't be too complicated if that were as far as it went because it would mean that if you wanted to have your default page be a wiki page, you would use the Team Site site template, and if you didn't, you would use any other site template. However, there is an added complication.

In each kind of site, there is the possibility of adding a page (Site Actions > New Page), and no matter whether you have a site where the default page is a Wiki Page or is a Web Part Page > Zone Page, that new page will always be a Wiki Page.

Just for completeness note that this applies only to creating a new page. If you, for instance, create a document library—even in a site based on the Team Site template—and then Edit a page of the document library (for instance, the default View), the page you see is a page of the Web Part Page type.

In the next section, we create a wiki Page in a site that isn't of type Team Site.

Creating a More Advanced Wiki in SPF 2010

Here we create a more advanced wiki. To do that we use the WebPartsTest site again for adding a page. You may remember from Hour 9, "Looking at List Types and the Included Web Parts," that this site was created using the Blank Site template.

1. Go to the Home page of the WebPartsTest site.

2. Click Site Actions > New Page. Figure 12.10 is one reason why I decided to use the WebPartsTest site.

Create V4 Pages Library

In order to create wiki pages on this site, there must be a default wiki page library and a site assets library. Would you like to create those document libraries now?

Create   Cancel

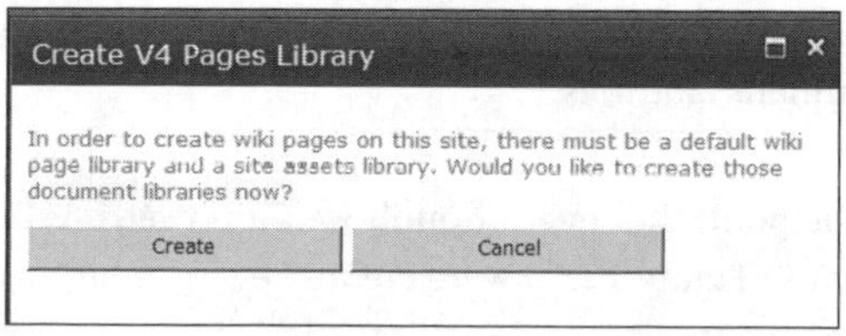

FIGURE 12.10
Needing a default wiki library

We already created a Wiki Page Library in the WebPartsTest site, but that isn't good enough for this function. It has spotted that the website was not created on the basis of the Team Site template and therefore didn't have a default Wiki Page Library (and a site assets library) installed from the start.

3. Click Create. Figure 12.11 that follows is worth showing because there is no further action required from you in creating the Wiki Page Library and the Site Assets Library.

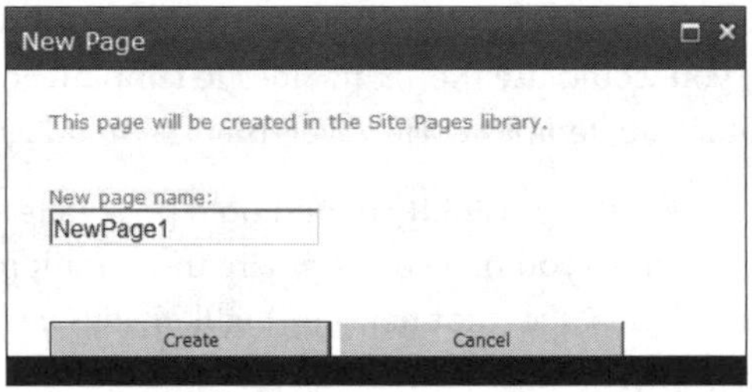

FIGURE 12.11
Creating the first
(wiki) page

New Page

This page will be created in the Site Pages library.

New page name:
NewPage1

Create   Cancel

4. Click Create. What you see is the same kind of wiki page we previously had (refer back to Figure 12.4) when we created a Wiki Page Library.

Now let's do a few checks:

Check 1: Look at the URL.

The URL is http://spf1/WebPartsTest/SitePages/NewPage1.aspx.

The URL of the Customer Contacts page we had earlier was http://spf1/WebPartsTest/Wiki%20Library%20Test/CustomerContacts.aspx.

In other words, this page isn't stored in the Wiki Page Library we previously created (Wiki Library Test); it is stored in a new library called Site Pages.

Check 2: Click the link to Site Pages.

It shows the standard (for a Wiki Page Library) starter page of Welcome to Your Wiki Library (refer back to Figure 12.2).

Check 3: Click Site Actions > View All Site Content.

Figure 12.12 shows that both Site Pages and Site Assets were created behind the scenes as Document Libraries.

The checks proved the point that even though we didn't see anything, the two additional libraries shown in Figure 12.10 were created even though we already had a Wiki Page Library in this site.

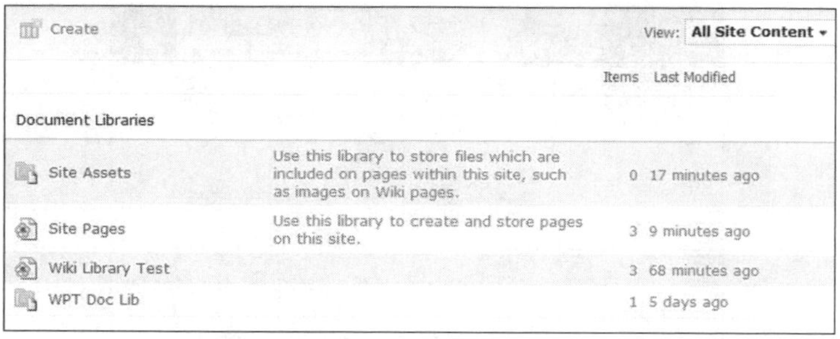

Create		View: **All Site Content** ▾
		Items Last Modified
Document Libraries		
Site Assets	Use this library to store files which are included on pages within this site, such as images on Wiki pages.	0 17 minutes ago
Site Pages	Use this library to create and store pages on this site.	3 9 minutes ago
Wiki Library Test		3 68 minutes ago
WPT Doc Lib		1 5 days ago

FIGURE 12.12
All Site Content after New Page

Also notice that Site Assets is there as a location for "files which are included on pages within this site, such as images on wiki pages." This solves the old problem of where to put images so that everyone who should see them can.

To use an image in a wiki page, you first upload that image to the Site Assets Library. For completeness, let's do that, and as a test we can then use that image in the Wiki Page Library page that we previously earlier (Wiki Library Test), not the one created by the system (in Site Pages).

How to Add an Image to Site Assets and Use That in a Wiki Page

The following steps show how to add an image to Site Assets and then use that image in a wiki page:

1. Click Site Assets. (You should be at Figure 12.12.)

2. Click Add New Document.

3. Select a file via Browse.

4. Click OK. The file is now in Site Assets; now let's add it to a wiki page in Wiki Library Test.

5. Click Wiki Library Test in Quick Launch.

6. Select (Tab) Editing Tools > Insert (see Figure 12.13).

7. Put the cursor a couple of lines below the Installed Software row.

8. Click Picture.

9. Select From Address. Now you need to find the address of the .jpg file in Site Assets.

10. In another browser copy, open Site Assets.

FIGURE 12.13
Adding a picture
to a wiki page

11. Find the image you want and right-click at the end of the line.

12. Select View Properties (which displays as in Figure 12.14).

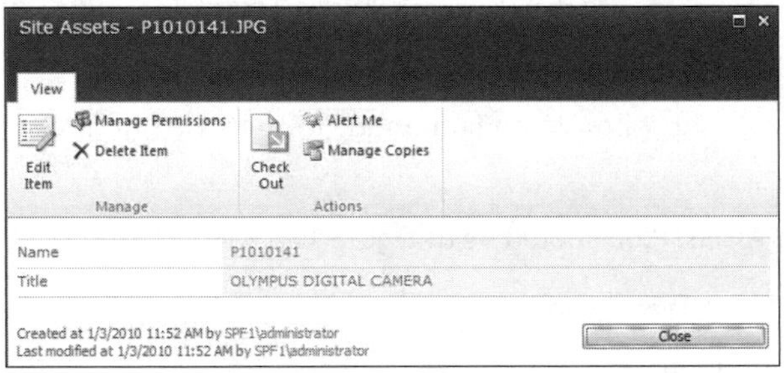

FIGURE 12.14
Zooming in on
the picture to get
its URL

13. Right-click P101041 and select Copy Shortcut.

This displays http://192.168.1.2/WebPartsTest/SiteAssets/P1010141.JPG, which you can enter into the box you had at step 9. The final result, after adjusting the size of the image by manipulating the Horizontal Size, looks like what is shown in Figure 12.15.

14. Change the Tab to Editing Tools > Format Text to see the Ribbon icon Save.

15. Use Save from the drop-down or use Save and Keep Editing if you have more changes you want to make to the page.

The process of capturing the correct web address was a bit messy, so is there another way?

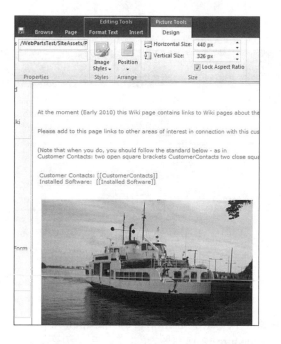

FIGURE 12.15
The wiki page
including image

How to Add an Image Directly to a Wiki Page

The following steps are alternative steps to the preceding 15 steps. This time we don't start by going to Site Assets to add the image.

1. Click Wiki Library Test in Quick Launch.

2. Select (Tab) Editing Tools > Insert (see Figure 12.13).

3. Put the cursor a couple of lines below the Installed Software row.

4. Click Picture.

5. Select From Computer.

6. Fill in the location of the image file. (Site Assets is the default value, as shown in Figure 12.16.)

FIGURE 12.16
Selecting a picture from your computer

7. Click OK. Then you see Figure 12.17.

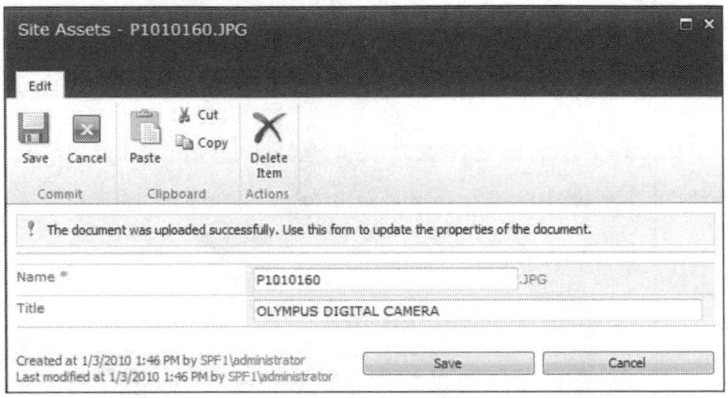

FIGURE 12.17
Giving the image
a Title before
adding to the
Library

8. Click Save (perhaps after amending the Title).

Now you are taken immediately to the wiki page where the Image has already been added. (There is no fussing about trying to obtain a web address for it).

Again (after adjusting the size of the image by manipulating the Horizontal Size), the final result looks like Figure 12.15.

Watch Out!

Don't forget that because this is a Wiki Page you need to save the change! (See steps 14 and 15 regarding Figure 12.15.)

As with many alternative methods in SharePoint, the end result of both methods is exactly the same.

Making a Wiki Not Look Like a Wiki

What we have so far is a normal-looking, text-based basic wiki with an image added to it. However, if you take another look at Figure 12.13, you can see that in addition to adding an image, you can also add Tables, Links, External Files, Web Parts, and existing Lists. You can even create a New List (which is similar to the way we added an image directly to the wiki page).

Rather than go through all these options, Figure 12.18 shows part of a wiki page that uses some of them that you might recognize.

Yes, even though it looks nothing like a wiki page, the default page of the SharePoint installation was a wiki page that now includes both a Text (Welcome); three Lists (Calendar, Shared Documents, and even though it doesn't look it, a Links

There are currently no upcoming events. To add a new event, click "Add new event".

FIGURE 12.18
A Wiki page—
or is it?

List—Getting Started); and an Image, most of which are on the page you see immediately after installing SPF 2010.

So wikis aren't quite what they were in WSS 3.0 after all.

Differences in the Tabs and Ribbons of the Wiki Page Type Compared to "Normal" Pages

At this point, I'd like to thank Todd Bleeker of Mindsharp for encouraging me to look deeper into wikis than I had planned.

The conversation with him started with some early comparisons he had made between the two different sets of menu lines and ribbons used by (1) wiki pages and (2) web part pages. He came up with several oddities of which he mentioned three main groups of differences in connection with Editing a Page.

The following are some of those differences put in my own words. (Earlier in this book, I have used the words "menu line" for what is officially a Tab; here I'll use "Tab" because it is shorter.)

▶ When you want to edit a Page, in (1), you use (Tab) Page and (Ribbon) Edit. In (2), this is (Tab) Page and (Ribbon) Edit Page.

▶ When (after you have specified Edit) you want to insert a web part using the Tab, in (1) you use a Tab Item Editing Tools (with two sections, Format Text and Insert), but in (2) the equivalent Tab is Page Tools (with only one section, Insert).

▶ After finishing editing your page, you find in both (1) and (2) a Stop Editing button. In (1) this means abandon your changes, but in (2) it means nothing more than stop editing, and the changes you have made are safe.

When you add something to a page of the Web Part Page type, changes to pages are saved automatically—all changes are done immediately—but if you add something in a page of the Wiki type, the drop-down (from the Save ribbon item that the Wiki page type has, but the Web Part page doesn't have) that includes the Stop Editing option also includes a Save option and even a Save and Keep Editing option. Press the wrong option, and you lose (all) your changes since you last saved.

Creating Blog Support in Standard SPF 2010

In this section, we work through the standard functionality for blogs provided by SPF 2010 out-of-the-box.

> About a month after WSS 3.0 was released, there was an Extended Blog Edition provided in codeplex (so free) that added useful additional functionality to blogs and that was stable. At the time of writing this book, this wasn't available for the SPF 2010 blog function, but look for it if you are reading this book from the end of 2010 onward.

Here are the steps to create a Blogs Site. To keep things simple we're going to add it as a subsite to the WebPartsTest site. Just as with wikis, in real life, you would probably create the Blogs Site as a completely new top-level site, possibly even in a new web application. (See also Hour 10's "Q&A" section.)

1. Go to Home > Site Actions > New Site.

2. Name the site **Blog Test Site** and specify its URL, **http://spf1/BlogTest**.

3. Specify a template of type Blog (in the Collaboration column).

4. Accept all the defaults for the remaining fields except Display This Site in Quick Launch of the Parent Site, which I always specify for test sites because it makes getting to them quicker.

5. Click Create. (Figure 12.19 gave a brief description about what a blog is. By now, this shouldn't be particularly useful information for most of the people who see it.)

6. Click Create a post. Avoid the pitfalls new bloggers can fall into. (See the text in italics in Figure 12.20.)

7. You can either Save as Draft, in which case you can't see it and need to go to Manage Posts, as shown earlier in Figure 12.8, to see what it looks like.

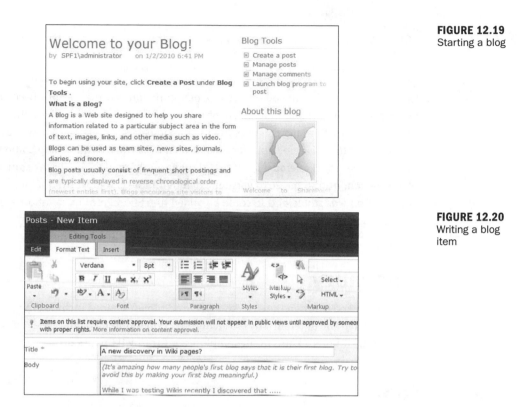

FIGURE 12.19
Starting a blog

FIGURE 12.20
Writing a blog
item

Alternatively, which I recommend, you can go straight to Publish. You can, after all, correct it immediately if it looks terrible. It's a good idea to do something about the Category Names in use. See Figure 12.21 for one good reason.

FIGURE 12.21
Your first blog
post appears in
the site.

8. Click Home to see your blog site as other people will see it. At this point, you'll notice how pointless the standard "Welcome to Your Blog!" post now looks, and you'll rush to delete it (use Manage Posts).

> Only when logged in as Moderator will you see the right column. Your users won't see it.

Compared with wikis, the out-of-the-box blog function is rather simple. Because it doesn't need much explanation, I spent most of this hour on wikis where there is a lot of added functionality compared to the previous (2007) version. As I wrote at the beginning of this hour, look out for a 2010 version of the Extended Blog Edition. That (in its 2007 version) offered a lot of useful additional functionality to the standard blog function, and so the 2010 version when available is well worth adding. The 2007 version was stable and so could be added to a SharePoint installation even by people who usually would avoid free tools.

Summary

Here we worked through the standard wiki and blog functions included in SPF 2010. We considered the different ways to create wiki pages and also noted the differences between the different kinds of site templates as far as wiki pages are concerned.

Q&A

Q. *I have Word 2010 on the client machine. How can I use that to create blogs offline?*

A. Here are the steps:

1. Click (on the Blog page) Launch Blog Program to Post.

2. The first time you do this, Word 2010 opens at an empty document, and you see a series of pop-ups starting with Figure 12.22 to register your copy of Word 2010 with that particular blog.

3. The options you select in the screens that follow are what you would expect; because this is a Q&A I won't include them here. At the end of the process that probably includes you signing in to the SharePoint site, your Word 2010 copy is registered as being connected to this particular blog site.

4. Figure 12.23 is a basic example of a new blog item showing that you can use Word 2010 functionality to add an Image. (The image which no doubt confuses some of you is of a log-in screen!)

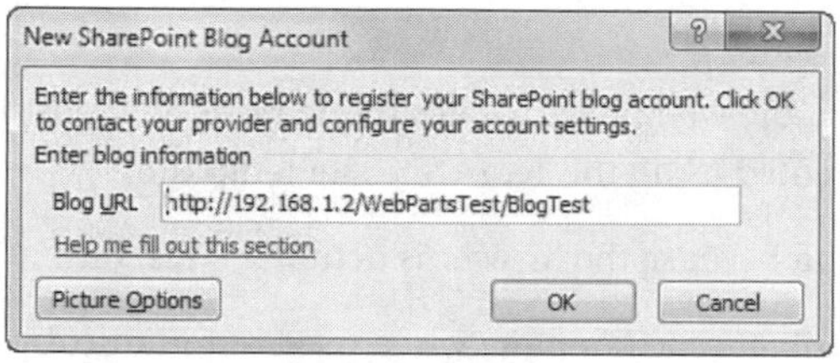

FIGURE 12.22
Starting the registration process

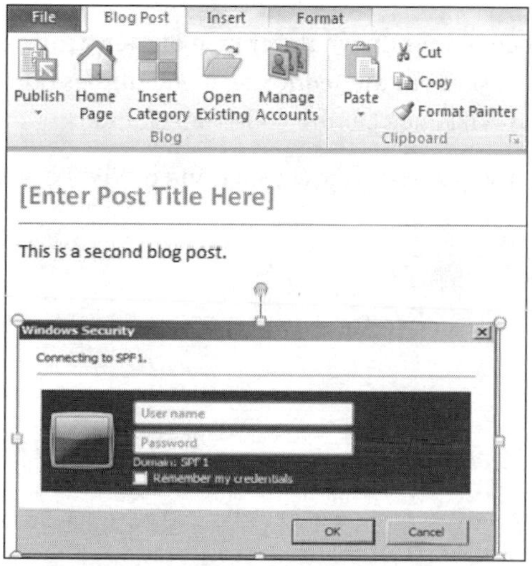

FIGURE 12.23
A sample blog created in Word 2010

5. Click Publish, as shown in Figure 12.23, and Word connects to the blog site and posts the blog.

6. Check that this has happened by going to the blog site.

Workshop

Quiz

1. Is it necessary to create a Team Site to get wiki pages?

2. Do I need to create a Wiki Page Library to get wiki pages?

Answers

1. No. You can create wiki pages in sites made from different site templates, not just in sites created using the Team Site site template.

2. A trick question because the answer is actually, "Yes, but..."

   ▶ The Team Site site template when used automatically creates a Wiki Page Library and a wiki page.

   ▶ Add a Page always (in whatever type of site) creates a wiki page, but in all types of sites but the Team Site, it will also as part of the process create a new Wiki Page Library called Site Pages.

   ▶ You can also get wiki pages by creating a Wiki Page Library.

PART II

Search

HOUR 13

Using SPF 2010 Search and Installing Search Server 2010 Express

---

What You'll Learn in This Hour

▶ How SPF 2010 Search works and how it compares to Search in SPS 2010
▶ Adding Search Server 2010 Express to the SPF 2010 server

Here we look first at how the search that is built in to SPF 2010 works. Then, as preparation for Hour 14 ("Improving Searches"), we work through the installation of Search Server 2010 Express on top of SPF 2010. Hour 14 then uses that installation to show the additional search options that the combination of the two products make available.

SPF 2010 Includes a Basic Search Function

One of the main differences between the free versions of SharePoint and the expensive ones (previously mentioned in the book as the Services line and the Server line) has been in Search.

Just as in all the previous products in the Services line, SharePoint Foundation 2010 can search only data stored in its own databases. That is, it can search only data that has been added to the SharePoint sites created after SPF 2010 has been installed.

This means that when you are positioned in your browser at a site—perhaps, at the default page of a site—you can search only the site. This means that the search results will be matching items that come from all the Lists and Libraries that are part of the site. However you are positioned in your browser at a List or Library—perhaps you have just opened a Custom List in your browser—you can either decide to search just that List/Library, or you can decide to search the site that List/Library is a part of.

In addition to being restricted to searching only the content of its own sites, the search routine is also simple. You enter a value in the Search box and get a set of results. You cannot, for instance, use filters in any way to restrict what is searched and where you search. You also cannot search for people (users of the sites).

The "expensive" product SharePoint Server 2010, like its predecessors in the server line, also offers the possibility of, in addition to searching its own content, searching many other locations such as websites, file system, Exchange databases, etc., and People Search.

This hour discusses the basics of using the built-in SPF 2010 search function. You then learn how to install the Search Server 2010 Express function on top of SPF 2010. This is a necessary first step before reading Hour 14, about searching when Search Server 2010 Express has been added to SPF 2010. As we you see in that hour, the combination of two free products offers almost as much search functionality as the expensive SharePoint Server 2010 and yet with none of the CALs requirements that product has.

Using the Standard Search Function

We already have some documents stored in The Book Documents document library in the default site, so let's start by going to the default site (http://spf1) and then going to the Search box at the top-right corner of the page.

As you can see in Figure 13.1, it's not quite the top-right corner of the screen, but it's actually the top-right corner of the menu section of the screen.

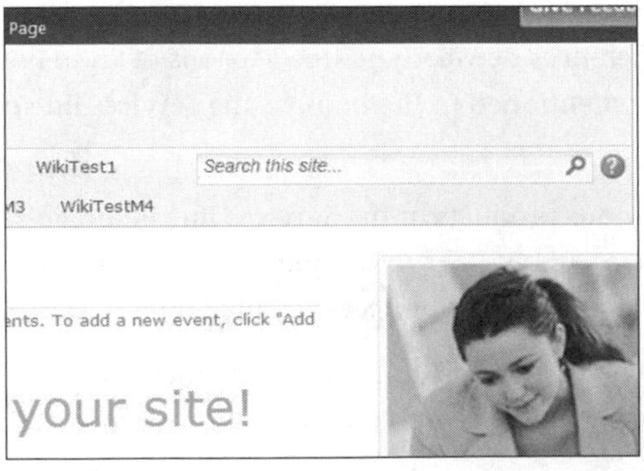

FIGURE 13.1
The Search this site box

You can no doubt recognize the image as being the top-left corner of the standard image, so if reading this offline you should have a good idea of where you'll find the Search this Site box. It's a Search this Site box because we are located at site level and therefore have the option of only searching the site.

Now enter **MS** in that box and click the magnifying glass. You can see in Figure 13.2 the first section of the search results.

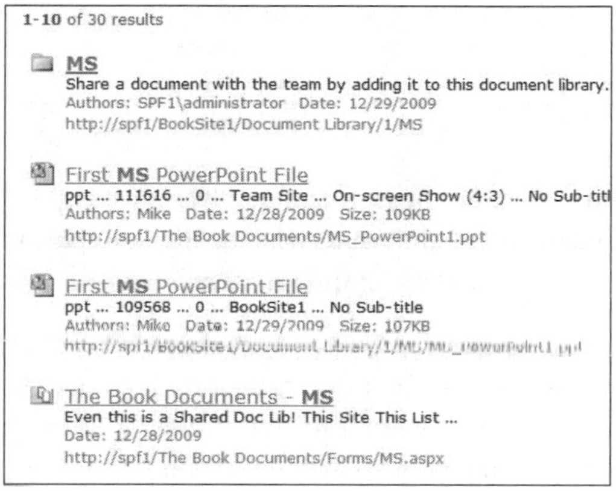

FIGURE 13.2
The results of searching the site

Here are some of the things to particularly notice in that list:

▶ A search of a site also searches all the subsites of that site. (There are hits from http://spf1 and from http://spf1/BookSite1.)

▶ A search of a site will not only search the contents of lists and files, but it will also search folder names and View names:

  ▶ Contents: First MS PowerPoint File (2,3)

  ▶ Folder: MS (1)

  ▶ View name: The Book Documents: MS (4)

Next we look at what happens when we move down to a document library in the default site. This time the process is a bit longer, so I use numbered steps to make it clearer:

1. Click Team Site to go back to the default page.

2. Click The Book Documents in the Quick Launch section.

   As you can see in Figure 13.3, now the Search box really is at the top-right of the screen (or near enough). The reason is that this is a page of the Web Part

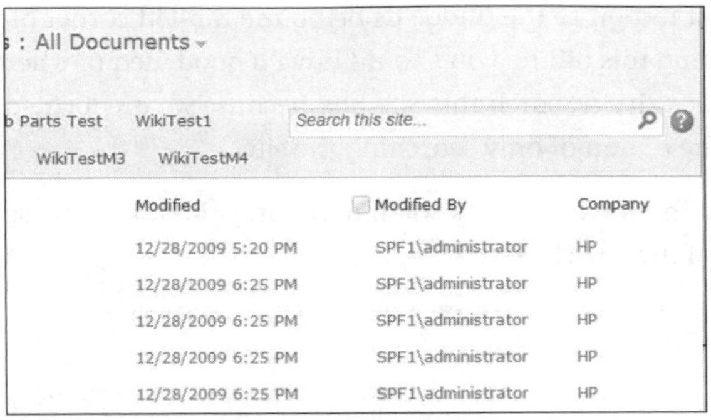

FIGURE 13.3
Searching a doc-
ument library

Page type, and all sections of such a page always add up to 100% width, which makes the menu section here just as wide as the data part (unlike the page in Figure 13.1, which was a page of the Wiki Page type).

At this point, if you've just read my introduction, you ought to be confused. You'll be wondering why—when we are now at document library level—the Search box is still saying "Search this site...". Well, this might be different in the version of SPF 2010 you have in front of you, but for now let's assume that because we are located where we are (in a document library in http://spf1), we will not get the same results as we did when we were at the top of http://spf1.

3. Enter **MS** in the Search Box.

Do we see (in Figure 13.4) the same results that we saw in Figure 13.2?

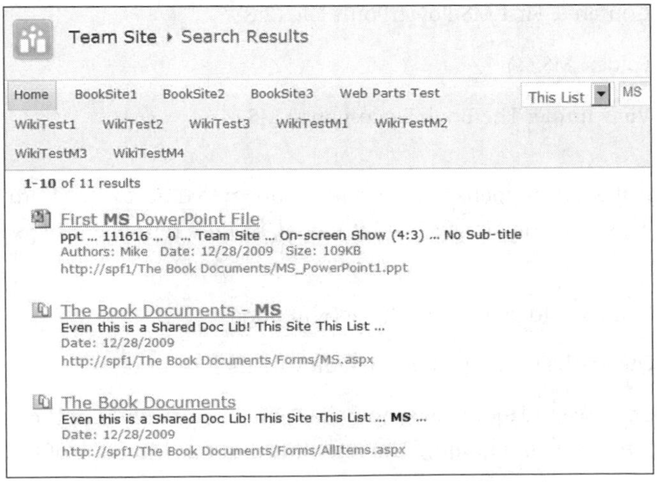

FIGURE 13.4
Results of
Searching a doc-
ument library

Instead of the 30 results we had in Figure 13.2, we now have only 11, and (if you scroll down the page, you can check this) all of them are from The Book Documents.

Now look at the top-right part of Figure 13.4, and you'll see the reason. When we searched this site in Figure 13.3, we were actually searching This List, as shown in Figure 13.4.

There remains only one further test. What happens if we change that drop-down that is now showing This List?

4. Go to the drop-down and change it to (the only other option) This Site.

5. Click the magnifying glass again.

What you see, as shown in Figure 13.5, are the same first four hits that we had in Figure 13.2, so even though we are now located within a site, we are still getting hits from subsites to that site. It looks as if a search on a site is the same whether it's down from the site (default page) or from within a List or Library. Well, it would except for one oddity. Figure 13.2 shows there were "about 30 results," and Figure 13.5 shows there are "about 390 results." What's going on?

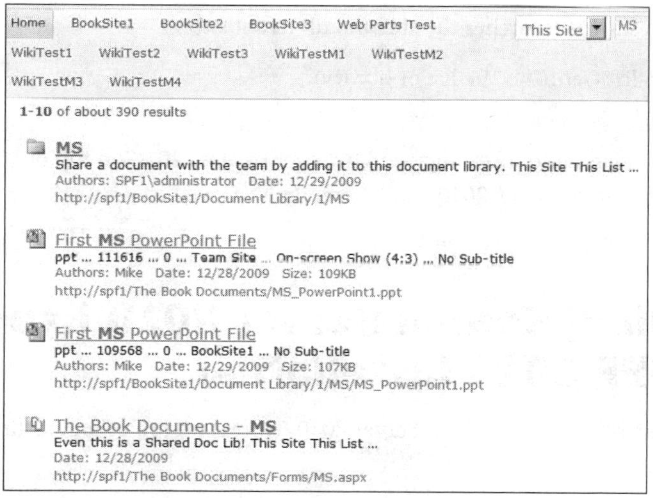

FIGURE 13.5
Results of searching the site from a document library (1)

6. Click 2 (at the bottom of the page) to go to the second page of hits. Figure 13.6 then indicates what the difference is.

Both these hits are from a different web application. They are from Central Administration that was created by the installation routine as a new web application (using

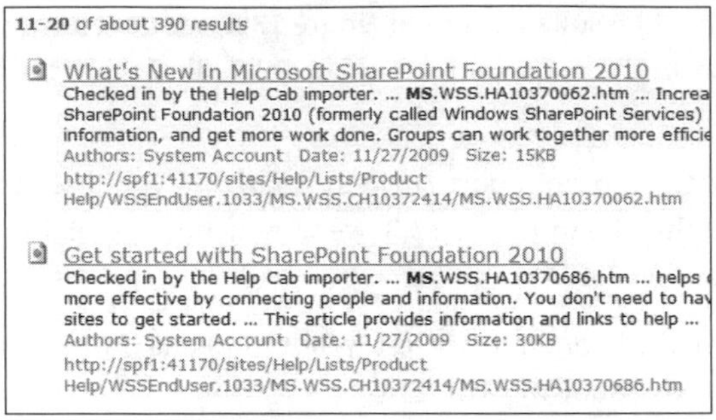

FIGURE 13.6
Results of
searching the
site from a docu-
ment library (2)

```
11-20 of about 390 results

 What's New in Microsoft SharePoint Foundation 2010
    Checked in by the Help Cab importer. ... MS.WSS.HA10370062.htm ... Increa
    SharePoint Foundation 2010 (formerly called Windows SharePoint Services)
    information, and get more work done. Groups can work together more efficie
    Authors: System Account  Date: 11/27/2009  Size: 15KB
    http://spf1:41170/sites/Help/Lists/Product
    Help/WSSEndUser.1033/MS.WSS.CH10372414/MS.WSS.HA10370062.htm

 Get started with SharePoint Foundation 2010
    Checked in by the Help Cab importer. ... MS.WSS.HA10370686.htm ... helps
    more effective by connecting people and information. You don't need to hav
    sites to get started. ... This article provides information and links to help ...
    Authors: System Account  Date: 11/27/2009  Size: 30KB
    http://spf1:41170/sites/Help/Lists/Product
    Help/WSSEndUser.1033/MS.WSS.CH10372414/MS.WSS.HA10370686.htm
```

the random port number 41170 here) and with its own (site collection) set of sites and
subsites. That explains the difference in the number of hits. If you go back and redo
the search when located in the default site, you can see that all 30 results are from
that site and from its subsites; none of the hits are from any other web application.

Another thing to notice in Figure 13.6 is that the two hits shown are both Help files.
You might not want Help files to show up in your results, but when using SPF 2010
you can't restrict the search apart from restricting it to site or list.

▶ Search site (1) (searches all web applications' site collections)

▶ Search site (2) (searches the site and all its subsites)

▶ Search list (searches the list or library)

But now we move on to installing Search Server Express 2010 on top of SPF 2010, so
our searches even with SPF 2010 can be greatly improved.

Installing Search Server 2010 Express in a SPF 2010 Installation

The following steps install Search Server 2010 Express on top of an existing SPF 2010
installation:

1. Go to the server.

2. When there, search for the free download for Search Server 2010 Express at
either http://www.microsoft.com/downloads or at my own site, http://wssv4faq.
mindsharp.com, where it will be in the V4Articles section. Figure 13.7 shows
the equivalent page for the public Beta version of the application, which is
what I used when testing and writing the installation instructions.

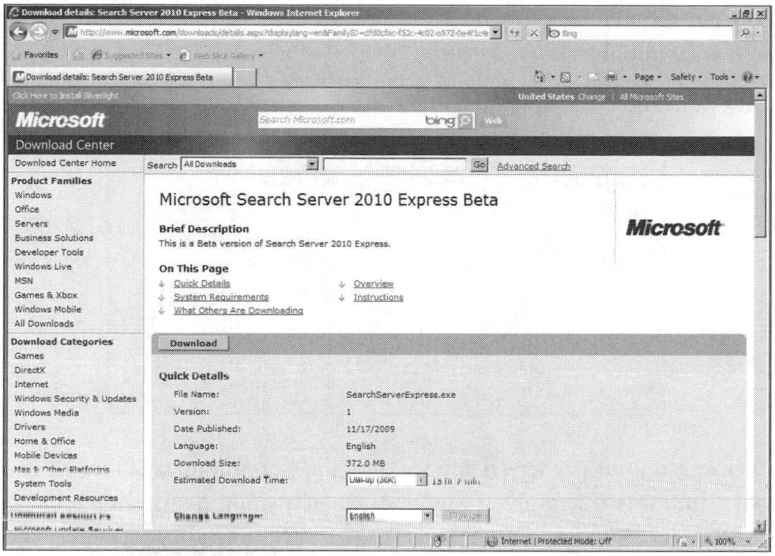

FIGURE 13.7
The download page for Search Server Express 2010

3. Click Download (making sure that English is selected in the Language section at the bottom of Figure 13.7). There is only a single (x64) version of Search Server 2010 Express available, so there is no decision to be made about whether to use a 32-bit or a 64-bit version.

You next see Figure 13.8. Here there is a decision to be made. If you think that you might want to repeat the Search Server 2010 Express installation (perhaps

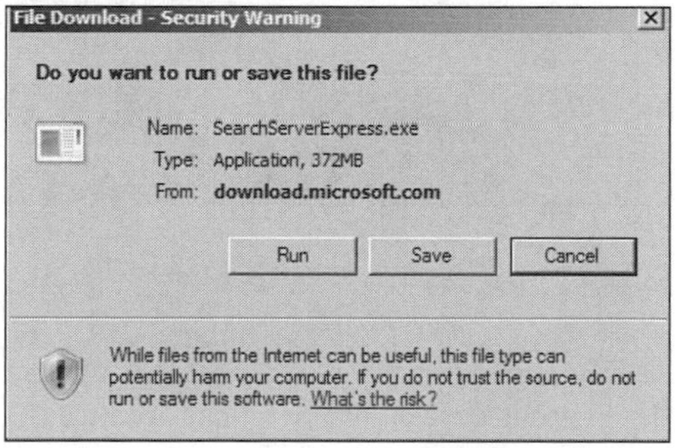

FIGURE 13.8
Run directly or Save first?

you've just made a snapshot of your VM, so you can go back to the situation before you started downloading Search Server 2010 Express), use Save and then run the downloaded file later from your hard disk. If you are optimistic that everything will go smoothly, just do step 4.

(The download takes quite a while, more than ten minutes, so only having to do it once might be a good idea.)

4. Click Run. After a long wait, you see another small screen (Figure 13.9).

FIGURE 13.9
A second Run

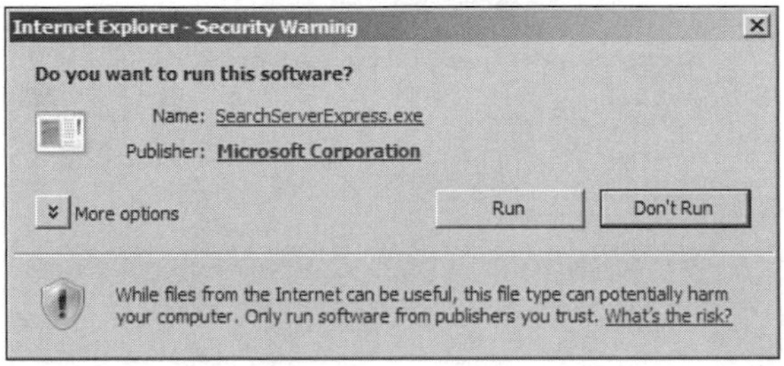

5. Click Run again. The screen you see after the second Run is Figure 13.10. It looks similar to a screen you would see when installing any SharePoint product.

FIGURE 13.10
The installation page for Search Server Express 2010

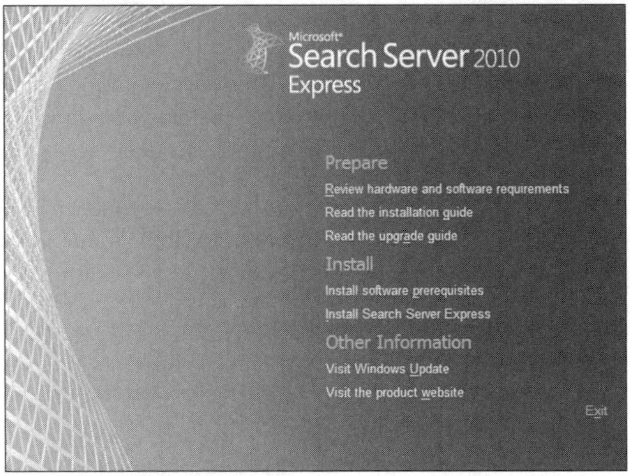

It all goes back to the previous version of SharePoint (WSS 3.0 and MOSS 2007) where Microsoft created a version called MOSS 2007 for Search (naturally—this was Microsoft after all—with a Standard version and an Enterprise version). I presume that under those names they didn't sell too well, so they were revamped with better search routines as Search Server 2008 (Standard and Enterprise), and in order to introduce people to these "new" products, the free Search Server 2008 Express was invented. It was in effect WSS 3.0 with most of the search functions from MOSS added. It had however a 4GB database size limit, which

WSS 3.0 didn't have so wasn't a full replacement for that product. However it could be added to it.

The reason that Figure 13.9 looks like a SharePoint screen is that Search Server Express 2010 is a SharePoint product. (So, yes, you can just install it and you have installed SharePoint).

Let's now go back to our installation. Because Search Server 2010 Express is a SharePoint product, the hardware and software requirements and the software prerequisites are the same as they were for SPF 2010.

When installing always play it safe and never assume anything. In this case my tests showed that installations done without doing Install Software prerequisites looked fine, until I had created a new Search site and tried to search. Then it didn't work. Don't do as I did (once!)—don't skip the install software prerequisites step.

6. Click Install Software Prerequisites. Accept all the screens that follow until the process is complete and you are back at Figure 13.10.

7. Click Install Search Server Express.

8. Click Continue after accepting the typical licensing requirement that follows.

   The File Location page follows (see Figure 13.11).

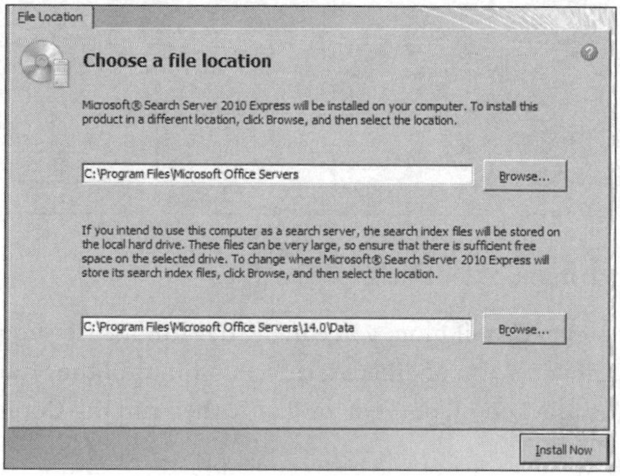

FIGURE 13.11
The File Location page

9. Click Install Now to accept the standard locations.

The next part of the installation takes quite a while, and you see Figure 13.12 before any progress is shown (in Figure 13.12 a small amount of progress is shown) for long enough to think something is wrong.

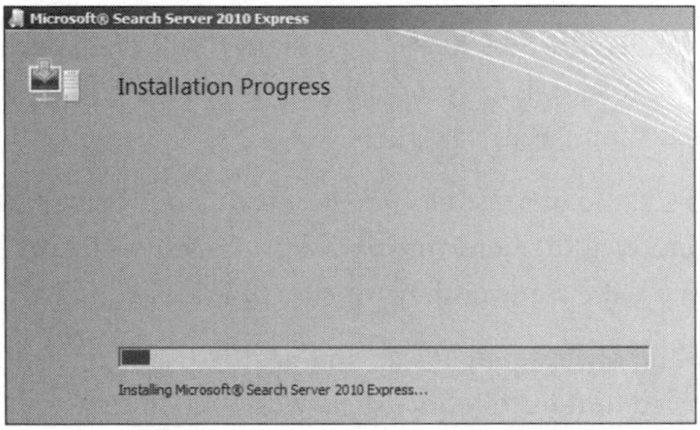

FIGURE 13.12
Waiting for the installation to progress

Finally, Figure 13.13 displays.

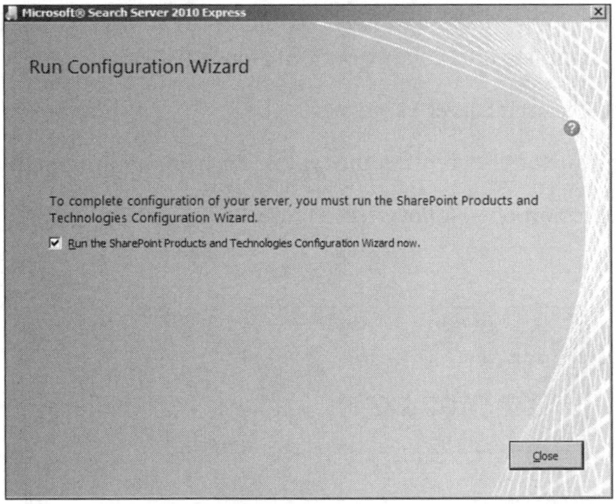

FIGURE 13.13
Run the Configuration Wizard

10. Leave the tick in place and click Close.

(In a single server installation, you can always run the Configuration Wizard at once. If you have a farm of different servers, wait until the SharePoint 2010 product is installed on all of them, and only then run the Configuration Wizard.

There will here be a brief pause between Figure 13.13 disappearing and Figure 13.14 appearing. Most likely you will then see Figure 13.10 again and think, "Oh, that was a quick installation," and move to click Exit. Don't! Just wait another few seconds.

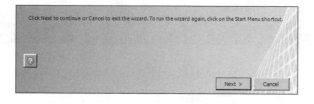

FIGURE 13.14
The lower part of
the Welcome to
SharePoint prod-
ucts screen

11. Click Next.

12. Approve the need to stop and start three services (screen not shown here) by clicking Yes. (Make 100% sure you only click once.)

Now with the next screen we are at a crucial stage of the installation. So be careful not to automatically click Next in Figure 13.15. (Figure 13.5 shows only the top half of the screen; Next is at the bottom of the screen).

FIGURE 13.15
Do *not* overwrite
the existing site.

We already have data at http://spf1, so we definitely don't want to use that default choice for Search Server 2010 Express. But do we need a new site for Search Server (the second choice) or no site (the third choice)? My preference is to keep things simple and to create a new site.

13. Be very careful! Select the section option No, do not overwrite the existing site.

14. Note the port number.

15. Now (and only now) click Next. But recheck first that you have selected the second option.

16. After the wizard has gone through its 11 steps, click Finish on the Configuration Successful screen (not shown here).

If at this stage (after Finish) you get a screen about communication problems, just click the URL (http://spf1:27951 in my case) again in the browser. This time you should get a login screen. Login in as SPF1\Administrator, and you will then see Figure 13.16, which is the search page of Search Server 2010 Express (and which is what you will see immediately if you didn't have communication problems).

Did you
Know?

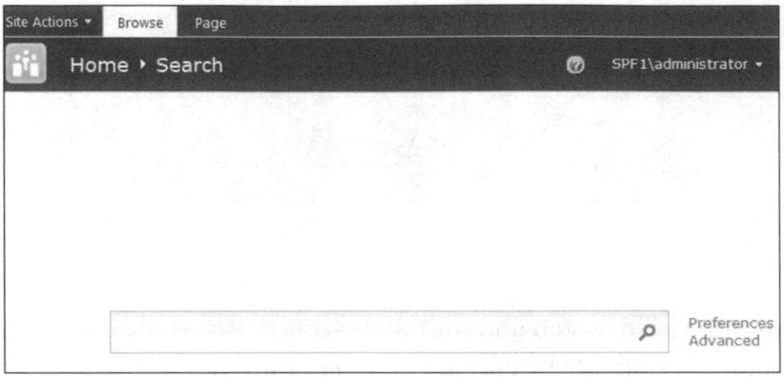

FIGURE 13.16
The Search
Server search
page

We'll leave it there for this hour. The next hour looks at what new search possibilities are available and how to use them.

Summary

In this hour, we went through how the search function provided with SPF 2010 worked. We also installed Search Server 2010 Express on the same server as SPF 2010. The additional search functionality available in this free product (and the few restrictions associated with it) are covered in the next hour.

Q&A

Q. *I heard that the SPF 2010 Search routine is powerful, yet you don't indicate this. What's the real story?*

A. It depends what you are comparing. If you used the basic installation (free database system) of Windows SharePoint Services 2.0, Search didn't work . To get Search, you had to either use SQL Server 2K (or later SQL Server 2005) and get only a simple full-text search or pay for a third-party search tool.

Since WSS 3.0, the search function provided with the free SharePoint product has been essentially the same as the search routine provided with the more expensive SharePoint products of the same version level. Only the ability to search outside the SharePoint sites was removed.

Search in the v4 products is even more powerful. Whereas search in WSS 3.0 was based on the rather under-performing Live.com search, SPF 2010 is based on Bing. You can see this improvement in the information provided in the page containing the hits.

Workshop

Quiz

1. What's the usual recommendation about how long to wait after adding content to a site and doing a search, and is this wait really necessary?

2. If you are located in your browser at a list, which two search scope options do you have?

Answers

1. About 24 hours. In most cases, it isn't necessary to wait that long.

2. This List and This Site (but only after you have done a search—your first search box says Search the Site but actually searches the list).

HOUR 14

Improving Searches

What You'll Learn in This Hour

▶ Three main aspects of searching
▶ Adding IFilters
▶ Customizing Search Server 2010 Express
▶ Improving all your searches

This hour delves deeper into SharePoint searching with the emphasis on the additional functionality that Search Server 2010 Express provides.

Searching Aspects

Following are three main aspects to searching:

▶ **Crawling**—Looking for documents, files, and data. A site—such as Google, which lives by providing information from everywhere—wants to crawl as many locations as possible. If you have a site on the Internet that you don't want crawled, specify that in some way.

In the case of a crawl of a company site, the intention is usually to crawl only meaningful locations for data. In that case, restrict what is crawled. As discussed in this hour, you want to define what you want to be crawled and what shouldn't be crawled.

▶ **Indexing**—Before you can index all the files that the crawl process finds, you need to "translate" the contents of file formats into words that the indexer can understand.

▶ **Searching**—Making sense of what you have indexed so that you have quality links high on the results listing.

Using IFilters to Translate the Contents of Files

This section looks at IFilters—how they are used and how new IFilters can be added.

What Are IFilters?

Microsoft uses pieces of code, called IFilters, to make sense of the contents of files that its search routines find. Some IFilters are built in to Microsoft's search products. For instance, SPF 2010 and Search Server 2010 Express both include IFilters for many common file formats out-of-the-box.

The situation with WSS 3.0 and Search Server 2008 Express was that Search Server 2008 Express contained several more IFilters than WSS 3.0 out-of-the-box (because it came out more than a year later), but you could add all those missing IFilters (and more) by installing a free Filter Pack from Microsoft.

SPF 2010 and Search Server 2010 Express, as they were released the same time, contain the same basic set of IFilters. In addition you may have noticed (Hour 2, "Installing SharePoint Foundation 2010," Figure 2.6) that one of the things that the Prerequisites function installs is Filter Pack 2.0, which is the latest version of the Filter Pack that could be added to WSS 3.0. Even so there will be some cases where you have files of file types for which you don't have an IFilter installed. In that case although the files will be found by the crawl process, their contents will not be indexed by the index process.

Files created by most main Microsoft products already have IFilters included either in the product or in the Filter Pack, but there are some that are not covered (such as Office template files). Similarly although standard file types such as .zip and .txt also have IFilters included, the file types of most non-Microsoft products are not supported by built-in (or Filter Pack) IFilters; so if you have files of such types, you need to find IFilters for them if you want to search the contents of those files.

The usual place to go is the manufacturer of the product that you use because it has an incentive to provide such a filter, but sometimes it either can't be bothered or provides a poorly working IFilter; then you need to look for third-party companies specializing in creating IFilters. By far the most common file format for which an IFilter needs to be found is the .pdf format used by what used to be called Adobe Acrobat.

Microsoft seem to delight in making working with Adobe products difficult; you may remember that they do not provide icons in the SharePoint products for the .pdf file type even though you can create documents from Word 2007 and 2010 saved in the

.pdf format. That situation is true for IFilters, too. Microsoft has never provided IFilters for the .pdf file type and instead suggest you go to Adobe or to a third party for them. Until recently (in 2009) Adobe repaid the compliment by making it impossible to have an IFilter in a SharePoint system without you needing to install the entire Adobe Reader product on the server. Luckily this has now changed.

The following section gives some information about Adobe's own 64-bit IFilter support for its pdf format, before mentioning where a third-party IFilter for pdf support is available. Test both if you have the time. If you don't and you can afford the small cost of it, use the third-party product. It is generally considered to be faster and more accurate than the free version from Adobe, and likely if it hadn't existed Adobe would never have bothered making its own (separate product) version available.

Even if you intend to use the chargeable product, read the following section because it gives details of how in an installation of SPF 2010 + Search Server 2010 Express you get to the Administration Pages for Search. It's by no means as simple as it was in the previous version (WSS 3.0 + Search Server 2008 Express).

Adding an IFilter for the Adobe Acrobat (PDF) File Type

Thanks to customer pressure over many years, Adobe finally in 2009 made available a separate 64-bit IFilter for .pdf files. Earlier there had been a 32-bit IFilter for versions of .pdf up to and including version 6.0 of Adobe Acrobat that could also be used for 64-bit systems, but for files of version 7, 8, and 9 to be indexed, you needed to install the Adobe Reader product. You still need to do this for older versions of SharePoint running on 32-bit systems if you don't want to use the chargeable product.

This new (and separate) Adobe IFilter for file types up to version 9 is here: http://www.adobe.com/support/downloads/detail.jsp?ftpID=4025. Because the instructions on that page were written in 2009, they do not say that it is for SPF 2010 or SPS 2010. It is!

The installation procedure is straightforward. (Just click the file and let it go.) Following the installation of the IFilter, PDF needs to be added to SPF 2010 as a file type that will be included when files are crawled. (Without doing this, you have the ability to index a file type that isn't included in the set of files you are indexing!)

To find where file types are listed, we first need to find the main page for Search Administration. Following are the steps you need to take:

1. Open Central Administration (see Figure 14.1). (If in the server, click the menu item; if on a client, specify http://spf1:portnumber in your browser.)

The reason that I have bothered with a screen here is that what you will
quickly become aware of when you use Central Administration is that the
options listed in the main section of the page under each heading are *not* all
the options available. To see all the options, you need to first select the item in
the left column.

Here we will be using a function of General Application Settings that is not the
single item listed under the General Application Settings header in the main
section of the page.

2. Click General Application Settings in the left column (see Figure 14.2).

The screen in the previous version only listed Configure Send to Connections. (It's a confusing page design, in my opinion.)

3. Click Farm-Wide Search Administration. (Ignore that our "farm" is a single server; it's still a farm.) There's not much here yet (see Figure 14.3), but the next screen will satisfy all our search configuration demands.

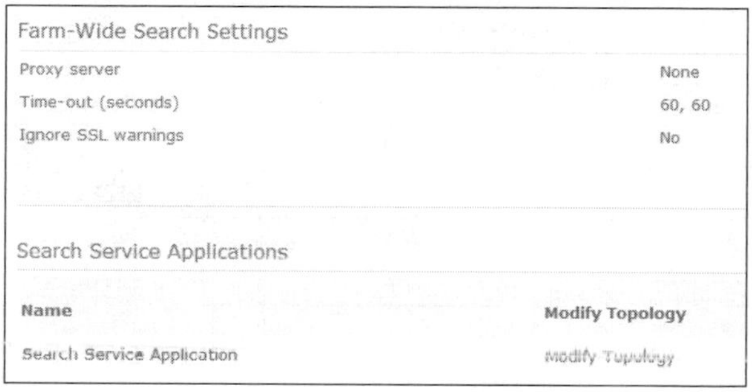

FIGURE 14.3
The Farm-Wide page

4. Click Search Service Application. (What you then see is shown in Figures 14.4, 14.5, and 14.6.)

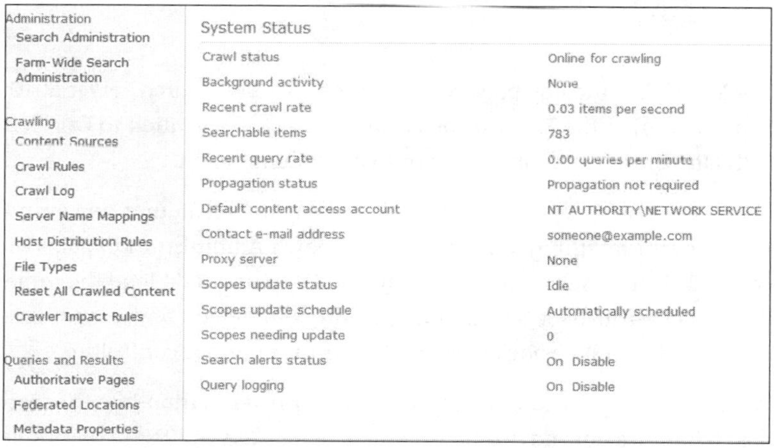

FIGURE 14.4
The top half of the Search Administration page

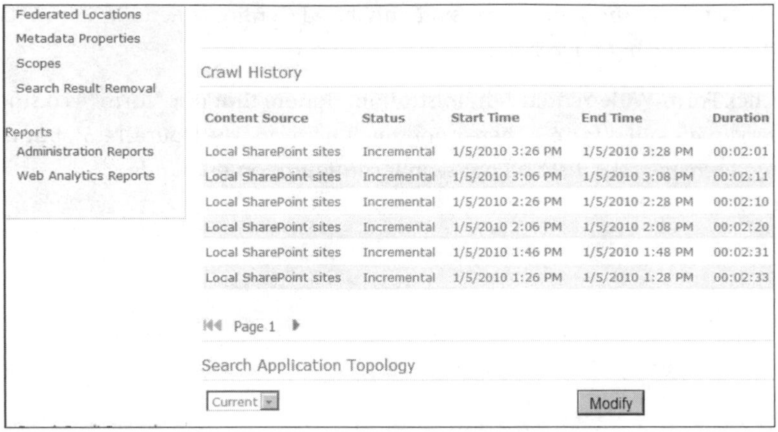

FIGURE 14.5
Most of the
lower half of the
Search Adminis-
tration page

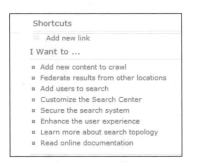

FIGURE 14.6
The I Want To
section of the
Search Adminis-
tration page

The Modify Technology page confirms that Microsoft Search Server 2010 Express Restricts the Topology of a Search Service Application to One Server with One Crawl Component and one Query Component.

There's a lot on this page, which is why I created three figures and even then didn't cover everything. It is actually the Search Administration page, and if you click Search Administration at the top-left part, you'll load the same page. If you click Farm-Wide Search Administration at the top of the left column in Figure 14.4, you'll be back at Figure 14.3. How's that for confusing?

We look at this page later when we do further investigation into the search possibilities we now have after installing Search Server 2010 Express, but here we want the list of file types. That is listed in Figure 14.4 under the Crawling section of the left column.

5. Click File Types (see Figure 14.7).

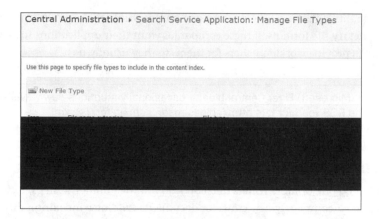

FIGURE 14.7
The top of the
File Types page

To avoid needing to have a large image so that you can see all the file types mentioned here—and remember these are only the file types that will be crawled; it is not necessarily a list of the file types that will be indexed—I'll list them:

ascx, asp, aspx, csv, doc, docm, docx, dot, eml, exch, htm, html, jhtml, jsp, mht, mhtml, msg, mspx, nsf, nws, odc, odp, ods, odt, one, php, ppt, pptm, pptx, pub, tif, tiff, txt, url, vdw, vdx, vsd, vss, vst, vsx, vtx, xls, xlsb, xlsm, xlsx, xml, zip

Now we just need to add pdf to the list here, and we're almost finished.

6. As shown in Figure 14.7, click New File Type.

7. Click OK on the Add File Type screen, which is not shown here.

8. Check the list in Figure 14.7 to see that pdf is now listed (without an icon).

Another alternative is to use the commercial 64-bit (pdf) IFilter from Foxit Software. You can get this at http://www.foxitsoftware.com/pdf/ifilter/. These Foxit IFilters cost (early 2010) $330 per server. As noted they are reputed to be considerably faster (and better) than the Adobe ones so are well worth considering. There is a download link for the Foxit Software 64-bit IFilter here: http://mirrors. foxitsoftware.com/pub/foxit/ifilter/desktop/win/1.x/1.0/enu/ FoxitPDFIFilter10_X64_enu.msi.

Adding an IFilter for Other File Types

IFilters of varying quality for other file types are available from various commercial and noncommercial companies. Just search for them.

The best-quality ones tend to come from companies whose main product uses their own proprietary file formats. If these companies want their applications to be used, they need to provide working IFilters for them, so they usually do.

Follow the (Microsoft) Filter Central blog; it occasionally mentions newly available IFilters. The RSS feed for it is http://blogs.msdn.com/ifilter/rss.xml.

Actions Needed After Installing IFilters

After installing one or more IFilters and carrying out the additional steps, restart the server and do a completely new crawl for documents (and new indexing); this ensures that these document types are included in the indexes.

An alternative approach is to do the following:

1. Net stop osearch

2. Net start osearch

3. Iisreset

I prefer doing completely new crawls in such situations.

Crawling and Indexing in SPF 2010 and Search Server 2010 Express

This section compares the methods used to crawl when using SPF 2010 and when using Search Server 2010 Express.

Crawling SPF 2010

Crawling in SPF 2010 can be done at the command line. Open a command prompt and go to C:\Program Files\Common Files\Microsoft Shared\web server extensions\14\BIN. Run the following command:

```
stsadm -o spsearch -action fullcrawlstart
```

Crawling Search Server 2010 Express

To crawl in Search Server 2010 Express, do the following:

Work your way down from Central Administration (via Figures 14.1, 14.2, and 14.3) until you reach Figure 14.4.

1. As also shown in Figure 14.4, click Content Sources (see Figure 14.8).

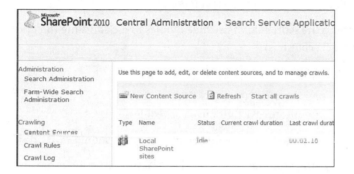

FIGURE 14.8
Starting a new crawl after adding an IFilter

2. Click Start All Crawls.

Using Other Search Server 2010 Express Options

Search Server 2010 Express provides more flexibility than SPF 2010 in determining what exactly we want to search. Let's look at some of those additional functions.

For both SPF 2010 and SPS 2010, these (manual) crawls are typically done only after installing a new IFilter to create a completely new index. The first crawls are done automatically when the Search function starts.

Things are sometimes not what they seem to be. The Search Administration page has a Crawl History section (see Figure 14.5), which shows the latest six crawl results. There are also other pages you can go to so that you can see progressive older crawl results. At least that is what it looks like. In fact you can only use the right-arrow on that screen section to go to a single extra page (i.e., the second page, which also shows six crawl results). If you want to see all the crawl results you need to select the Crawl Log in the Search Administration page's Quick Launch section (see Figure 14.4) and then select Crawl History there.

After those two important notes, another thing to watch out for is how to do a new Full Crawl. It looks as if this ought to be done using the Reset All Crawled Content link (again in the Quick Launch section of the Search Administration , Figure 14.4). In fact that, in the (slightly revised) words of Woody Windischman who kindly answered a question I had on this:

Essentially, it will return the Search indexes to a "known clean" state by

1. Deleting the existing file-system indexes

2. Resetting the search database index tables to a clean state (including resetting unique ID counters)

It does not:

1. Delete content source definitions or schedules

2. Start new crawls (though defined crawls from #1 should start on schedule)

3. Stop any crawl that might already be underway (though it may wait until it is done before it actually does anything)

The way to start a Full Crawl is to select Content Sources; click the single Content Source ("Local SharePoint sites"), which is provided as part of the installation, and then go to the bottom of the page where there is a Start Full Crawl section. Select the check box and click OK.

The Reset All Crawled Content option should be used only when the search indexes are in a mess and search is clearly not working properly.

Let's now look at how to define which locations we can search using Search Server 2010 Express. Here are the steps required:

1. As shown in Figure 14.9, select Content Sources. This time, look at what we can add as locations to be searched.

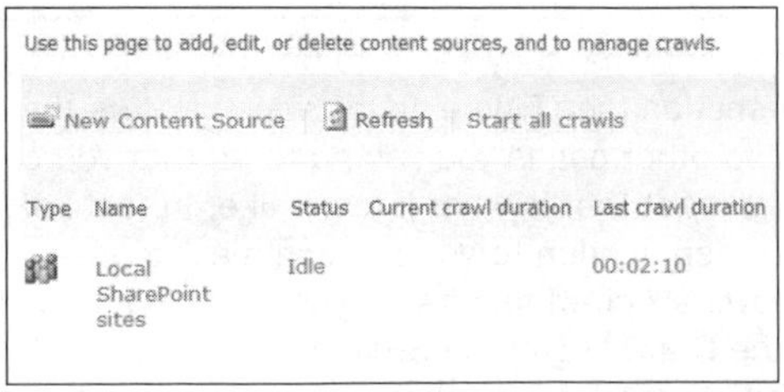

FIGURE 14.9
The Content
Source page

Use this page to add, edit, or delete content sources, and to manage crawls.

New Content Source   Refresh   Start all crawls

Type	Name	Status	Current crawl duration	Last crawl duration
	Local SharePoint sites	Idle		00:02:10

2. Click Local SharePoint sites, which is the only content source that has been installed by the Search Server 2010 Express installation routine. You can either amend the existing content source or create new ones using New Content Source, or do both. Here we look at the existing source to see what has been specified for it.

Figure 14.10 shows two key sections that are needed when saying what is to be crawled.

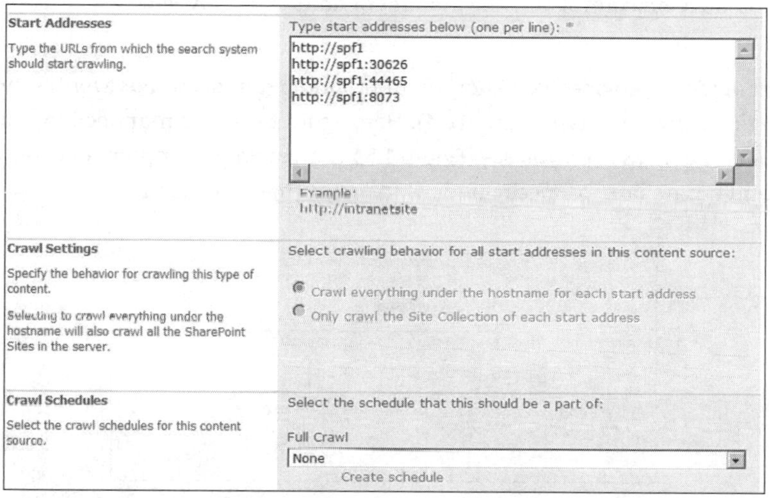

FIGURE 14.10
Where to search

The Start Address section includes all the top-level sites that were in existence when Search Server 2010 Express was installed with the exception of the Central Administration site. Addresses are not removed from this box if one of those top-level sites is later deleted (as was the case here with http://spf1:44465). In such cases, you can avoid unnecessary error messages by removing the addresses of deleted top-level sites from the table in Figure 14.10. You need to do this manually. The system will not do this for you when you delete a top-level site.

The Crawl Settings section enables you to decide if you want to crawl all sites (that is, subsites) below the top-level site (site collection) or whether you want to just crawl the top-level site.

Finally, Crawl Schedules does not by default set a schedule for when Full Crawls are to take place. When Search Server 2010 Express was installed, a single Full Crawl was automatically done using the above Start Addresses. Since then only Incremental Crawls have been done according to the default schedule that can also be changed in the same screen that Figure 14.10 shows a section of.

It is wise in production situations to Create a new schedule for Full Crawl so that it occurs at a suitable time, during the weekend for instance. The default value (when a schedule is specified) of every 20 minutes is suitable only for Incremental Crawls, where it is also the default and should not be selected for Full Crawls.

Normally, three main problems exist when you crawl "foreign" websites:

▶ You might need rights to access them.

▶ The sites' administrators might have blocked crawling.

▶ You have no control over the amount of data to be crawled.

The first of these (provided you know an appropriate name and password) is handled by selecting crawl rules (see Figure 14.4). Here again Microsoft managed to confuse us because the first screen you see (Figure 14.11) gives only the option of choosing paths and has no box for specifying how to access these locations.

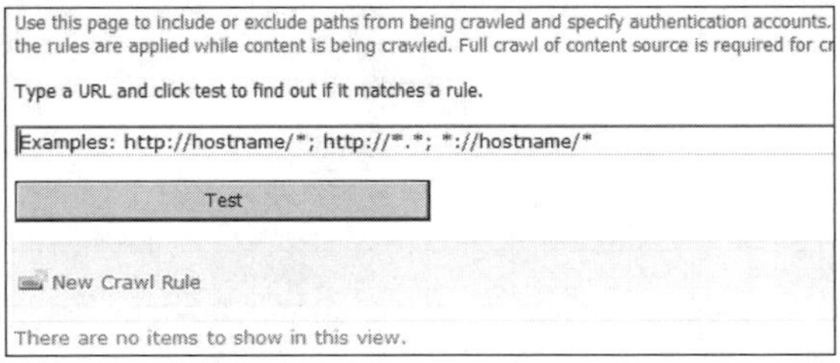

FIGURE 14.11
A misleading
Crawl Rules page

At first glance, this screen seems to indicate that the only Crawl Rule you can set is which locations should be crawled. This is just an intermediate page that enables you to test various URLs. To actually specify, for example, the Administrator account and password for crawls, we need to create a New Crawl Rule using the link in Figure 14.11. (This leads to Figure 14.12.)

In addition to selecting paths that are not to be crawled, there is now also the possibility of giving name and password access information (or alternative access information) for paths you want to be crawled. The items in the Specify Authentication section are grayed out (and thus inaccessible) until the radio button in the Crawl Configuration section is changed to Include All Items in the Path.

I won't go into the other options here. If you are serious about search, there are specialist books available only on Search. Here the intention is to introduce you to the options available rather than go through each option in detail.

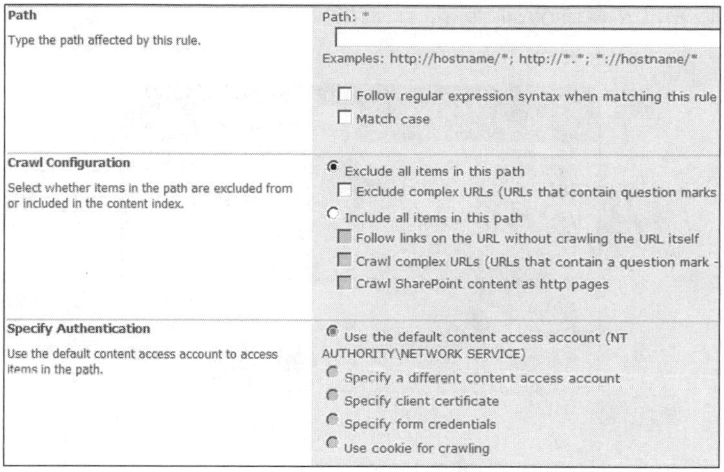

FIGURE 14.12
Full Crawl Rules

Next, we look at how to do searches using the data we will have indexed in the crawling/indexing phases.

Using the Search Server 2010 Search Function in the SPF 2010 Site

Here it seems logical to do our search from the newly created Search page—which is the default page of the new site we created in Hour 13, "Using SPF 2010 Search and Installing Search Server 2010 Express," (see Figure 13.16). When we go to that page, we see a simple entry form for searches.

Entering a search term there gives us a different (and probably slightly better) search than we would get from the standard SPF 2010 search. However, it's messy to always need to go to this page when we already have search boxes in our existing sites, so let's consider what happens if we search in the default site that SPF 2010 created.

What actually happens is that, unlike the situation with the v3 products where you had to fiddle with the system to get this to work, the Search in the default SPF 2010 site by default will use the Search Server 2010 search function.

You can check this (or turn it off if you want to keep the two kinds of searches strictly separated) with the following steps:

1. Go to Central Administration.

2. Select Manage Web Applications.

3. Select http://spf1:80 (see Figure 14.13).

4. Click Manage Features (Figure 14.14).

As can be seen (lower option), using the Search Server Service is now (by default after installing Search Server 2010 Express) the active option for searching the sites we created in SPF 2010. Because Search Server 2010 Express has been installed, we also have the possibility to search many other sources of enterprise data even from within the SPF 2010 sites. Now that we've checked that, here's a quick look at the key additional search functions available to us in our searches.

The Queries and Results section enables us to improve the quality of our searches. Apart from again restricting searches and also specifying on which page the search results appear (using Scopes), there are a couple of useful new functions:

▶ **Authoritative Pages** enable you to specify which parts of the areas being searched contain the best quality information.

▶ **Federated Search** is a useful function that enables you to use ready-made search functions (available on the Internet; search for them in Bing or Google using Federated Search Locations or Federated Search Connectors) for searching particular locations. These ready-made search functions are fully configurable so that, for instance, you can have a web part on a page that uses a Federated Search Connector for Bing. You can then make a couple of special versions of this web part that are further restricted; perhaps the first could search only http://social.technet.microsoft.com (TechNet Forums) and the second could only search www.microsoft.com.

Summary

In this hour, you learned that searching actually means deciding where to look for data; grabbing, interpreting, and indexing all the files within the scope we set; and finally having a search function to find suitable data for our needs from the mass of base data provided by the indexing stage.

You also learned both how to restrict your search by specifying only particular places to look for information and how to extend your search by adding IFilters to enable your indexing software to extract sensible data from more file formats.

Finally, you learned how adding Search Server 2010 means that its extended search functions are also available for your searches in the SPF 2010 sites.

Q&A

Q. *Is SPF 2010 plus Search Server 2010 Express better than the search provided by the much more expensive SPS 2010?*

A. No. But the functionality provided is virtually the same.

Q. *Search Server 2010 Express is free and seems to be powerful. Why should I bother paying for Search Server 2010?*

A. Search Server 2010 and Search Server 2010 Express are identical in functionality, but Express is limited to running on a single machine.

Workshop

Quiz

1. What are the three main aspects of searching?

2. What is the purpose of an IFilter?

Answers

1. Crawling, indexing, and searching.

2. An IFilter is needed so that contents of a file in a particular file format can be understood by the indexing program. Without it, the indexing program usually can't extract meaningful data from a file.

PART III

Working with Office Products

HOUR 15

Using Different Versions of the Main Office Products with SPF 2010

What You'll Learn in This Hour

▶ Stating the rules for the interaction of Office products with SharePoint products

▶ Storing documents in document libraries

▶ Creating document workspaces in Office 2003 and Office 2007

▶ Differentiating between the workspaces in Office 2003 and Office 2007

▶ How files attached to Outlook 2003 and Outlook 2007 email messages can be stored in a SPF 2010 site

This is the first of a number of hours about the inter-relationship between SPF 2010 and Office products. At first glance, the bullet points at the start of this hour look out of place in a book written about a SharePoint 2010 product, which mostly considers the interaction between various Office 2010 products and SPF 2010. The explanation is a simple one—what is covered in those is functionality that has been removed from Office 2010. It is thus available only for users of previous Office products.

This book, unlike some others, does not start with the assumption that all the users accessing SPF 2010 systems are also using Office 2010 on their PCs; therefore, there is coverage in the book of both Office 2003 and Office 2007 where it is warranted. The now missing functionality was both important and useful, so I spend time in this hour covering it in depth.

Office Products and SPF 2010: The Rules

The interaction between an Office product and a SharePoint site varies depending on which version of Office and SharePoint you use. In this section, I define the "rules."

The standard rule is that the full functionality available in each Office version works only with the equivalent SharePoint version:

▶ To get the most out of SharePoint Team Services (STS) 2001, you need to run Office XP on your client.

▶ To get the most out of WSS 2.0, you need to run Office 2003.

▶ To get the most out of WSS 3.0, you need to run Office 2007.

▶ To get the most out of SPF 2010, you need to run Office 2010.

The second rule is that all the Office versions are backward-compatible. If you use STS and Office 2010, Office 2007, or Office 2003, you have the same functionality you had with Office XP but no more. Whereas if you use WSS 2.0 and Office 2010 or Office 2007, you have the same functionality you had with Office 2003, but no more; naturally if you use WSS 3.0 with Office 2010, you get the same functionality you had with Office 2007 but no more.

There are also a couple of exceptions to the preceding rules: The first exception is that any Office application might offer no more functionality when used with Share-Point than an earlier version of that particular Office application. The second—and perhaps less-expected—exception is that a later Office application might offer less functionality with SharePoint than an earlier version. This is rare; although worry-ingly at the time of writing several Office 2010 applications have lost functionality when working with SharePoint sites compared to the equivalent Office 2007 product. (See the "Creation of Document Workspaces" and "Files Attached to Outlook" sec-tions at the end of this hour for two examples of this).

This hour starts by looking at Word, Excel, and PowerPoint. Despite being principal Office applications, their functionality, when used with SPF 2010, has hardly changed since Office 2003 (or Office 2007).

Let's investigate three main interaction areas of these Office products with SPF 2010:

▶ Storing documents in document libraries

▶ Creating document workspaces

▶ Adding attachments to Outlook messages

Storing Documents in Document Libraries

You might ask, "It's obvious that you can store Word (and so on) documents in a document library, so why discuss that?" The answer is that when these documents are stored in a document library, some differences exist as compared to the way other document types are stored in document libraries.

These differences are

▶ Edit available in Microsoft Word/Excel/PowerPoint but not in Acrobat

▶ Standard Word/Excel/PowerPoint templates available for use (and more, see the "Available Templates" section)

▶ SPF 2010 column information included with the Word/Excel/PowerPoint file

Different Editing Options

The most obvious difference is that there is an "Edit in Microsoft XXX" (where XXX is Word, Excel, or PowerPoint depending on what kind of file it is) entry in the drop-down when you click the area to the right of a Word, Excel, or PowerPoint document's name in a view (see Figure 15.1).

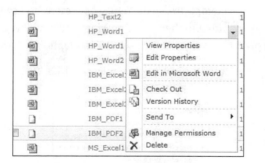

FIGURE 15.1
Edit in Microsoft Word

When selecting an Acrobat file in the same library, there is no equivalent Edit in Acrobat option (see Figure 15.2). This is true even if you have the commercial version of Acrobat that enables changes and saving.

There is no PDF icon in Figure 15.2. To add it, get a pdf icon from the document at http://www.adobe.com/misc/pdfs/TM_GuideforThirdPartiesFinalPrint.pdf. Then scale it to 16 x 16 pixels, and save it as a gif file (icpdf.gif). (The icon is in the "Adobe PDF File Icon" section of that paper that also gives the rules for its

IBM_Excel3
IBM_PDF1
IBM_PDF2
MS_Excel1
MS_PDF1
MS_PDF2
MS_PowerP
MS_Text1
MS_Word1
View Properties
Edit Properties
Check Out
Version History
Send To
Manage Permissions
Delete

FIGURE 15.2
No edit capability in Adobe Acrobat

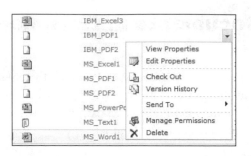

> use on websites.) Then save it to the server at C:\Program Files\Common Files\Microsoft Shared\web server extensions\14\TEMPLATE\IMAGES.
>
> Open C:\Program Files\Common Files\Microsoft Shared\web server extensions\14\TEMPLATE\XML\DOCICON.XML in Notebook; copy the PNG row and change (twice) PNG to PDF. Save. Finally, run iisreset in the command line.

Available Templates

A Document Library has a New Document function. When this is used an empty document is created that uses a template specified when the Document Library was created. The only applications for which templates are included in the SPF 2010 installation are all Office products.

To see the list of available templates, create a new document library by going to Site Actions in the menu line tab and then selecting More Options. If you want to create a document library, give it a name and then select More Options (in that screen this time).

The list of possible templates is displayed as in Figure 15.3.

None
Microsoft Word 97-2003 document
Microsoft Excel 97-2003 spreadsheet
Microsoft PowerPoint 97-2003 presentation
Microsoft Word document
Microsoft® Excel® spreadsheet
Microsoft PowerPoint presentation
Microsoft OneNote 2010 Notebook
Microsoft SharePoint Designer Web page
Basic page
Web Part page

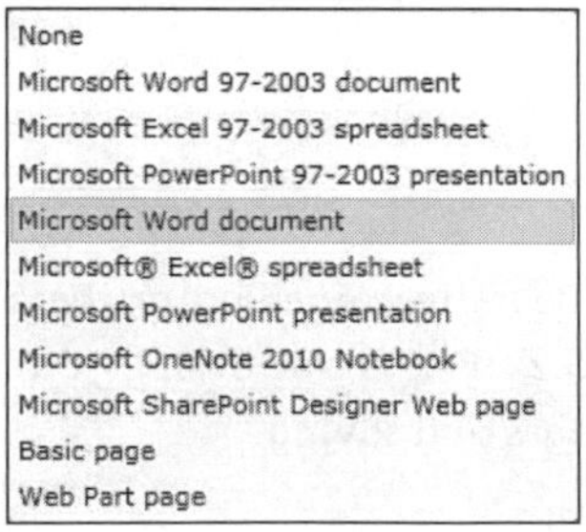

FIGURE 15.3
List of document library templates

The four items at the end of the list were also available (the OneNote template was of course for 2007 and not for 2010) in the previous versions of SharePoint. It's perhaps indicative of the usual use of templates—namely for Office products—that I thought at first were new features of the SPF 2010/SPS 2010 implementation!

Figure 15.4 shows what happens if you use New Document while in a document library that has the web part page template specified.

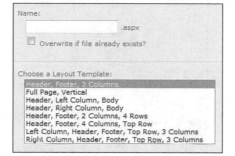

You have the full options that would be available to you if you went through the normal (and longer) process of Creating a web part page and then specifying this document library to contain it.

This is a good use of the document library template function. The best practice when creating web part pages is that they are stored in a single document library that contains only web part pages. To do this you need to create a new document library. Specifying a different template to the default Word template for that document library takes a single click, once. Yet this saves several clicks every time a web part page is later created in that document library.

By the Way

There are different templates in Figure 15.3 for the Excel/PowerPoint/Word file types for the 97–2003 format (.doc) and for the 2007–2010 file format (.docx). That isn't a major problem because the administrator will know which file format he can use in his company. The problem with these templates is that they aren't typically as straightforward as the web part page example was. There are a couple of reasons:

▶ Creating a New document using such a template often requires logging in to the server.

▶ When you say that you are saving to a SharePoint site's document library (see Figure 15.5), it works straightforwardly only if you have already done saves to that document library from the client PC. If the site and document library you want to save to isn't already listed in the Recent Locations section that you see after clicking Save to SharePoint, as shown in Figure 15.5, you need to write in the **http:// address of the server + document library** (plus the filename you want to use) when saving the file. Some users won't be happy having to do this.

To avoid the possible need for manually entering the document library's URL in the Save field following the use of New Document, encourage your users to create their documents in their own copies of Word (or other Office program) and then upload them to a SharePoint document library by accessing the SharePoint document library in their browsers. In most cases (using a noncustomized, blank template) the end result looks exactly the same. Only if you have created a special company template for your users does using the New Document function offer any advantages, and even those advantages can be reduced by making sure all the users can access that (Word and such) template in their own PCs' copies of the Office product.

Missing from the list of templates in Figure 15.3 is a template for earlier versions of OneNote. The OneNote 2007 and 2010 formats are completely different, and OneNote 2007 cannot read OneNote 2010-formatted files. Unless you are sure that all your users have OneNote 2010, this would be a good reason for advising your users not to use the OneNote (2010) template and to create their OneNote files in the product (and specify when saving the OneNote 2007 file format).

SPF 2010 Column Information

A relationship exists between additional fields/columns in a document library and the properties of a Word/Excel/PowerPoint document that doesn't exist with a non-Office document.

Here's the situation in brief: A non-Office document (perhaps a PDF) has its own properties that are part of the document. When you add an Acrobat file to a document library, that document library might have extra columns/fields, and you will give those fields values. So you might have a Company field and give it the value HP.

By the Way

If you move documents from a document library in one site to an (already existing) identical document library in another site, you need—in the case of PDF files—to copy both the files (typically from Explorer view to Explorer view) and the columns and their data (typically from Datasheet view to Datasheet view). Doing so is the only way to get the file, the file's own properties, and the SPF 2010 column information across (at the files level).

Now let's take that document offline so that we can edit it. The file is copied to our hard disk, and that Acrobat file includes both the document and the document's properties. However, the (SPF 2010 document library) Company field no longer exists, so it no longer has a value. The information is lost.

Compare this with an Office document. One difference is that an Office document can be edited and then copied back to the SharePoint site. This naturally means that none of the column data is lost. However it is also possible to save a copy of an Office document to your hard disk, Even then the file you have on the hard disk contains the data from those SPF 2010 columns. They are not lost.

All this becomes clearer if we work through an example:

1. Create a new Document Library by clicking Site Actions > New Document Library.

2. The Document Library is Open. Click Library > Library Settings.

3. Add two new columns: Subject and Formula One Cars. These were carefully chosen. Subject is the name of a standard Property of a Word document. Formula One Cars clearly isn't the name of a standard Property.

If you want to check that Subject is the name of a standard Property, open Word 2010 in your client PC and create a new blank Word document. Then select File > Info. Now look to the right side of the page (also shown in Figure 15.7) and select Properties > Show All Properties, and you see Subject listed.

By the Way

4. Create a simple document in Word 2010 (one line of text is enough), and upload it to the document library you just created. You will be asked to fill in the two new fields (columns), as shown in Figure 15.6.

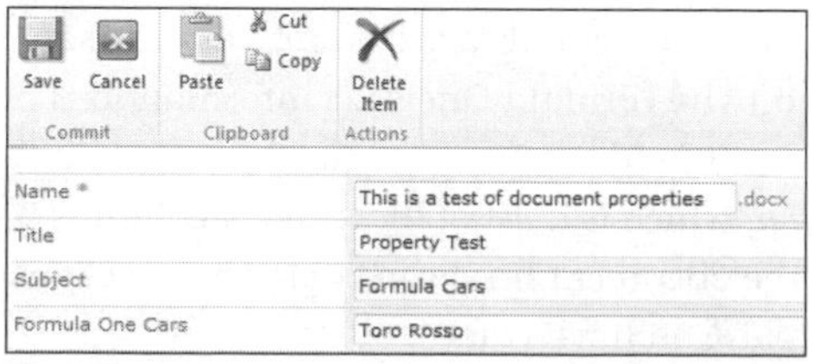

FIGURE 15.6
Adding values to two document library columns

5. Save the document. This saves it to the document library.

6. Now (using IE) right-click the actual name of the document in the Document Library view and select Save Target As. This copies your amended document to a location in your client PC. The file is now completely separated from the document library.

7. Open the document in your client copy of Word 2010.

8. Select File > Info.

9. Go to the right of the screen and select Properties (Figure 15.7).

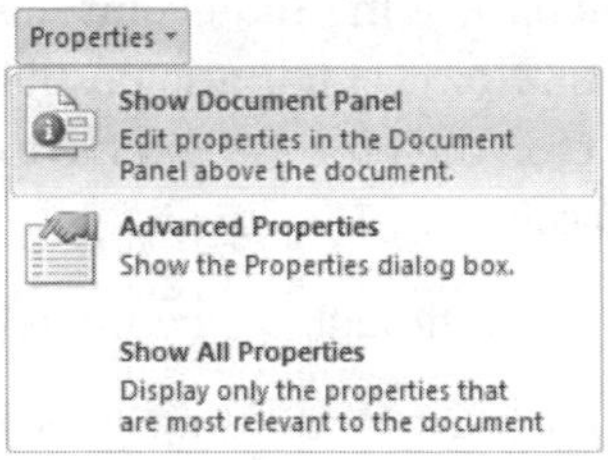

FIGURE 15.7
Where to check the properties of a Document

10. Click Show Document Panel. A document panel, Document Properties - Server, opens at the top of the document (see Figure 15.8).

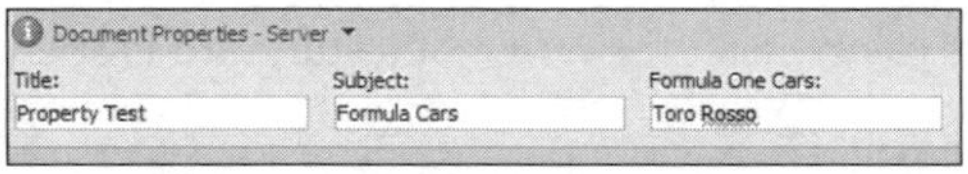

FIGURE 15.8
Document Properties - Server

11. Click the drop-down arrow, as shown in Figure 15.8, and select Document Properties (see Figure 15.9).

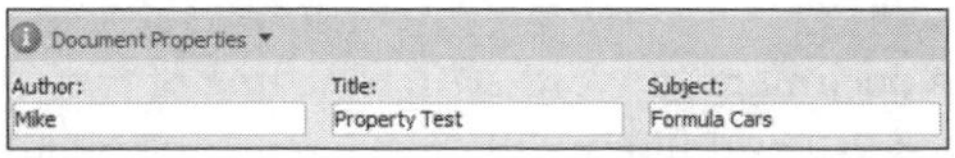

FIGURE 15.9
Document Properties shows only standard properties.

As you can see in Figure 15.9, the standard document property Subject now contains the value we added in a document library column with the same name. (Actually the Title field does, too.) The Formula One Cars information is not listed in Document Properties. Instead it (and the Title and the Subject fields) are listed in Document Properties - Server, which is a list of those fields/columns included in the document library. Even if the document has been copied to the client PC's hard disk and opened there, these fields still have values.

Following is a summary of the way this works between Office 2010/2007 and Office 2003:

▶ **Office 2010 (and Office 2007)**—If the column name is the same as an Office document property, the value entered into the column is transferred to the document property with the same name (accessed via Document Properties).

   If the column name is not the same as an Office property, the value entered is retained as a server property (accessed via Document Properties - Server).

▶ **Office 2003**—If the column name is the same as an Office document property, the value entered into the column is transferred to the document property with the same name. (There are a few standard document properties for which this doesn't apply, but we won't discuss them here.)

   If the column name is not the same as an Office property, a document property is automatically created with that value.

If you move Office documents from a document library in one site to an identical document library in another site, you need to copy only the files (typically from Explorer view to Explorer view). After all, those files contain the file, the file's own properties, and the SPF 2010 column information.

By the Way

The exercise helped you see one advantage that can be gained by combining Office products (rather than non-Office products) with SPF 2010.

Another main function that is restricted to Office products is the capability to create websites to discuss a particular document. This is something that was available in Office 2007 and Office 2003 but has been removed from the Office 2010 products. See the "Q&A" section for brief information on what replaces it. Because it is a useful function, it is discussed next for both Office 2007 and Office 2003, both working with SPF 2010.

Creating SPF 2010 Document Workspaces in Office 2007

As previously mentioned in this hour, some kinds of interaction with SharePoint products that were in earlier Office products are no longer available in Office 2010. Creating Document Workspaces (in effect a site for storing and discussing a single document) were possible in both Office 2003 and Office 2007 when working with the 2007 and 2003 versions of SharePoint.

This section shows how to continue to create them with SPF 2010 if you have Office 2007 on your client systems. The following section gives the equivalent details for when you have Office 2003 on your client systems.

To create a document workspace in Office 2007, follow these steps:

1. Open Word and create a document. I use the text "Test document for a document workspace."

2. When in Word 2007, click the (Office) icon at the top-left corner of the page; select Publish, and then select Create Document Workspace (see Figure 15.7).

    Figure 15.10 appears on the rightmost side of the screen. As you can see, you have two choices:

    ▶ Specify a name for the document workspace. (Call it **BookDocWS1**.) Currently, it has the name of the document (which hadn't been saved and was thus Document5).

    ▶ Say where the document workspace should be created.

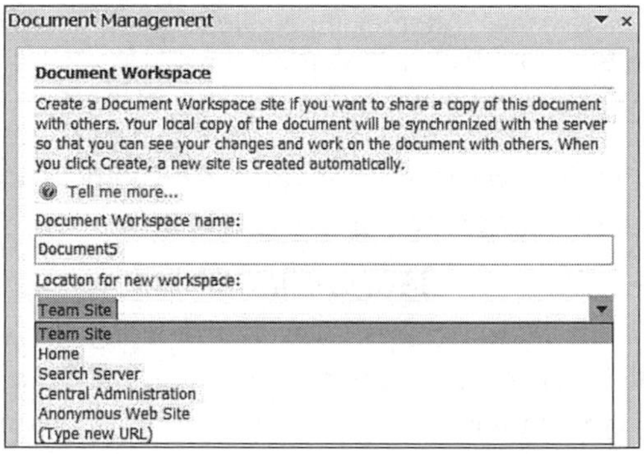

FIGURE 15.10
Selecting a location and name for the document workspace

This example shows that it is good to call websites something recognizable. The only one in this list that is recognizable is our Anonymous Web Site; the others are too general. (All the sites listed are top-level sites, the default site of a site collection.)

By the Way

3. Accept the offered Team Site with Create.

    If you aren't offered a SharePoint site here, you'll see only Type New URL. Type **http:/SPF1** (or the TCP-IP equivalent). If you are told the site needs to be a trusted site, go to your browser's Internet settings and add the address you just typed to the list of trusted sites in the security section. Then return here and click Create again.

4. If you haven't saved the document, you'll be asked to. Then, you'll be asked for authorization with the typical Name/Password box.

5. The document workspace is created. You see Figure 15.11 in the rightmost panel.

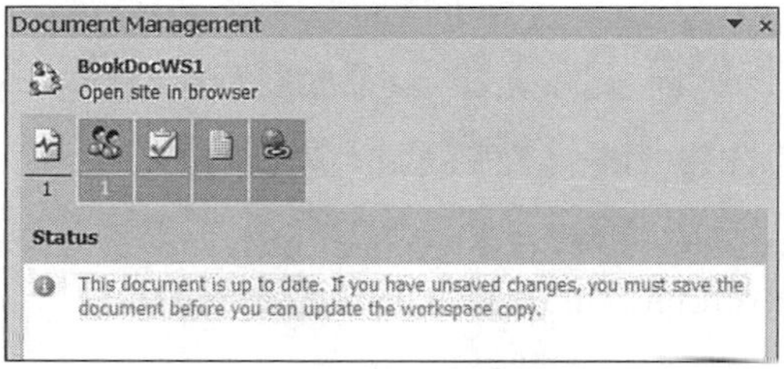

FIGURE 15.11
The Document Management panel

Don't be worried if the authorization process happens twice.

By the Way

6. Select Open Site in Browser to see what we have.

Figure 15.12 shows the site that has been created. The Navigate Up list shows that it is located under the default Team Site.

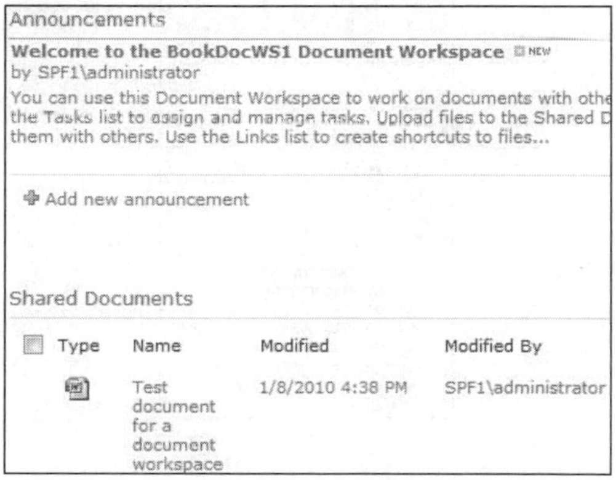

FIGURE 15.12
The default page of a document workspace

Unlike the subsites previously created, this site did not inherit by default permissions from the Team Site, and instead the only user at the moment is the administrator who created the document and decided to store it in a document workspace. (Figure 15.13 is obtained by clicking Site Actions > Site permissions.)

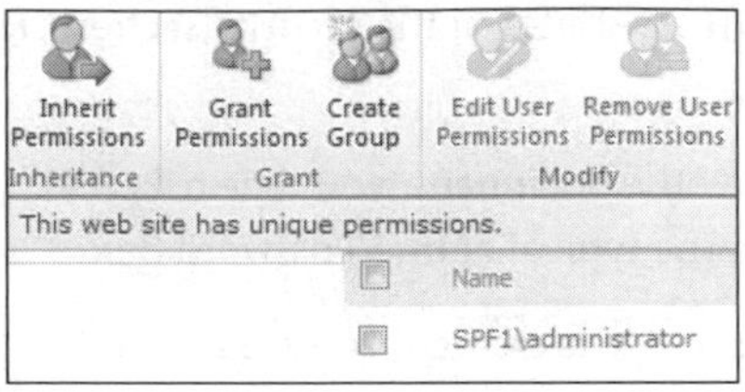

FIGURE 15.13
The only person
with access
rights is the
administrator

Creating SPF 2010 Document Workspaces in Office 2003

Here are the details that were promised earlier for creating a document workspace when your users are running Office 2003 on their clients:

1. Create and save a document. Access Tools on the menu line and select Shared Workspace.

2. Team Site is selected (see Figure 15.14). The drop-down shows various Share-Point servers that this workstation running Office 2003 has been connected to in the past.

FIGURE 15.14
Selecting the
site and docu-
ment name in
Office 2003

3. The default name of the document workspace comes from the document name, but it can be changed. We'll change it to **BookDoc2003WS1**.

4. Accept the default value TeamSite by clicking Create. The result (shown in Figure 15.15) is similar to the Word 2007 equivalent. If you click Open Site in Browser, the website looks similar to that in Figure 15.12.

FIGURE 15.15
The Shared
Workspace panel
in Word 2003

Never mix Office 2007 and Office 2003 applications on the same client system!

Watch Out!

Differentiating Between Office 2007 and Office 2003 Document Workspaces

Although creating a document workspace is a similar process in both 2003 and 2007, there are several differences. The main difference is that, in the Word 2003 version of the Shared Workspace panel, there is an extra icon.

If you click any icon and look at the bottom of the Shared Workspace panel, you see that it's possible to do administration tasks directly from Word with this new (document workspace) site.

That missing icon on the right for Word 2007 means that these options are no longer available in Word 2007. The unavailable options are

▶ Restrict Permissions

▶ Alert Me About This Document

▶ Version History

All are however—like all the other options here—available when accessing the document workspace in a browser (as administrator).

To summarize, there is little difference between Office 2003 and 2007 when creating document workspaces. The main differences are

▶ The creation of a document workspace fails often from Office 2003; it works better from Office 2007.

▶ In Office 2007, you don't have to rely entirely on the list of sites available in the drop-down of where the document workspace is to be created; you can also specify a URL of a site or subsite.

Otherwise, the end result is the same. A site is especially created for a document, and it is possible to administer it with the Office product or by using a browser and accessing the site.

By the Way

> Several users could have the document open at the same time, and some of them could have it open for editing. (Only one person at a time can have it open for editing if the file is accessed from the SPF 2010 document library. However, several people using Word could have the linked Word copy open for editing.)
>
> To avoid possible conflicts among competing edits, use the checking-out option for the document so that only one person can have it open for editing at a time; the others can still read it.

The default settings (when using both Word 2003 and Word 2007) are to be asked before changes made to a document (in either the website version of the document or in the Word version of it), which produces an updated document in the site. Automatic updates are possible but may lead to a better version being overwritten.

Although these new document workspaces are not listed in our default site (in the Sites section of the Quick Launch), you can select Site Actions > View All Site Content when at the Team Site. You then see a Sites and Workspaces section where they are listed (see Figure 15.16).

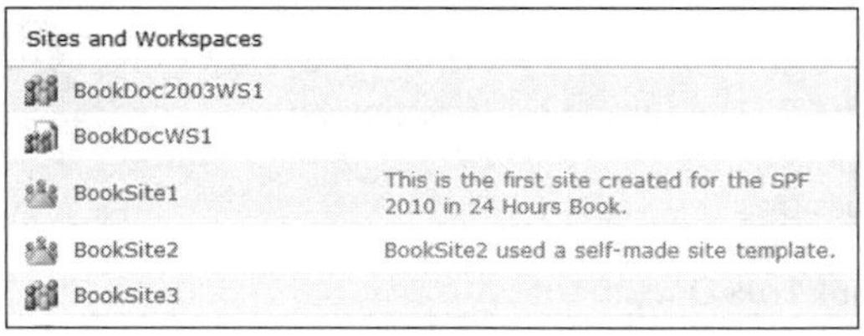

FIGURE 15.16
Sites and Work-spaces

Sites and Workspaces	
BookDoc2003WS1	
BookDocWS1	
BookSite1	This is the first site created for the SPF 2010 in 24 Hours Book.
BookSite2	BookSite2 used a self-made site template.
BookSite3	

By the Way

> There's a second way to display these two workspaces listed on the default page. Go to the "Q&A" section if you want to know how to do this.

Storing Email Attachments in a SharePoint Site

Another function removed from Office 2010 that was available in Outlook 2007 is the capability to store email attachments in a SharePoint site rather than only as part of the email. In Outlook 2007, when you add an attachment, if you just select Attach File, the attachment is sent with the email. If the recipient opens the email, say, a few weeks later, the recipient may see an old version of the document because in the meantime you've updated it. There are, however, alternative ways to attach.

Click that strange icon to the right of Include. You get a new pane on the rightmost side of the screen (see Figure 15.17).

FIGURE 15.17
Attachment Options pane in Outlook 2010

This Attachment Options pane looks familiar. It's exactly the same list of sites as in Figure 15.10. However, Central Administration has moved two places up the list.

The point is that it's the same technique. The attachment will now be stored in its own subsite of the Team Site, so the issue with the recipient opening the message two weeks after you sent is resolved. The recipient always sees the latest version upon opening the message.

At the same time, anyone who receives the email including the message can see the info panel, as shown in Figure 15.18.

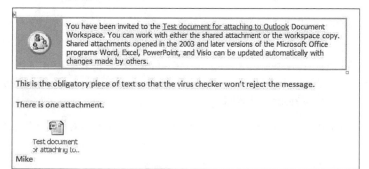

FIGURE 15.18
An email invitation to the document workspace

All the email recipients that can be added (see the following "By the Way") are added to the list of users for the workspace that contains the document.

This list usually contains domain users. In this case, my Hotmail address couldn't be recognized by the SharePoint site, and the sender got a message to that effect.

> The workspace has already been created, as you can see by again clicking Site Actions > View All Site Content from the Team Site.

Summary

In this hour, we looked at some of the ways in which Office 2003, Office 2007, and Office 2010 documents combine with SPF 2010 systems and especially at the differences when non-Office document formats are used.

We concentrated on three main areas: storing and editing documents stored in document libraries; creating document workspaces, which are sites created for discussing a document; and adding attachments to Outlook emails so that the attachment is not just the version available at the time the message was sent but is (through being stored on a server) the latest version.

We discovered that unless Microsoft has reconsidered by the time you read this book and added functionality back, some functions for cooperation with SharePoint systems are missing from some Office 2010 products compared with the equivalent Office 2007 (and Office 2003 to a more limited extent) products.

Q&A

Q. *How can I have both sites and workspaces listed on the default page?*

A. To do this, all you have to do is add a tree view to the leftmost column (or perhaps better still, replace Quick Launch with it) with the following steps:

1. Go to the default site. Select Site Actions > Site Settings.

2. The fourth option in the second column is Tree View. Select it (see Figure 15.19).

In Figure 15.19, notice that I have selected the existing selection of Quick Launch and Enable Tree View. They are check boxes, so you can of course have both or one (or none) selected.

Now the leftmost side includes all the subsites of Team Site, including the two document workspaces (see Figure 15.20). I don't know about you, but I think it's much messier than Quick Launch.

By the
Way

Did you notice the option for Quick Launch in the Site Settings? A common question in the newsgroups has been how to remove the Quick Launch section from the page.

People saw the Quick Launch option (which enables you to change the order of items in Quick Launch) and expected a Remove Quick Launch option. It's not obvious that to get to that option you need to select Tree View.

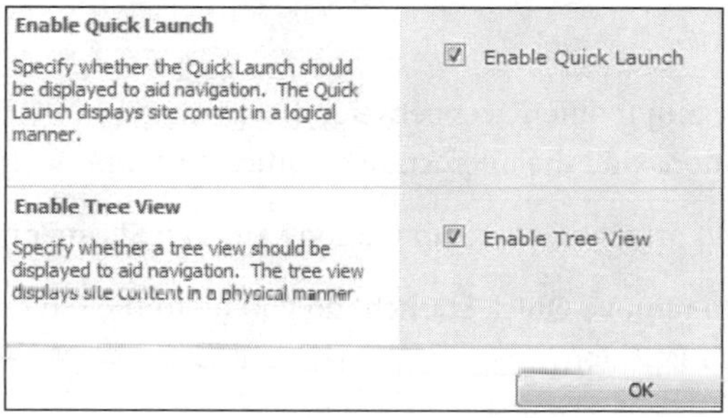

Enable Quick Launch

Specify whether the Quick Launch should be displayed to aid navigation. The Quick Launch displays site content in a logical manner.

☑ Enable Quick Launch

Enable Tree View

Specify whether a tree view should be displayed to aid navigation. The tree view displays site content in a physical manner

☑ Enable Tree View

OK

FIGURE 15.19
Specifying Tree View

Site Hierarchy

▷ BookDoc2003WS
▷ BookDocWS1
▷ BookSite1
▲ BookSite2
  ▷ Document Libra
    Agenda
    Attendees
    Objectives

FIGURE 15.20
The look of Tree View

Tree View, which lists the entire structure of the site, is however more powerful. (You can go directly from this page to a library/list that's in a subsite or workspace). It's up to the site designer or the customer requirements to decide what is chosen.

Q. *Earlier, we learned that Office 2010 applications no longer can create document workspaces. What has replaced this?*

A. It wasn't in the beta version of the Office 2010 products, but Microsoft expects to have something called Co-Authoring available by the time the applications go into production. It is only available for the users of Office 2010 products, however. That is fine if all your users run Office 2010, but if you have mixed

Office 2007 and Office 2010 users, you have major problems because there are certain requirements (that is, compulsory checkout is not possible if you use Co-Authoring) to suit Co-Authoring that don't suit Office 2007 users.

Workshop

Quiz

1. Are there any major differences between the interaction of Office 2003 or Office 2007 applications and the interaction of Office 2010 applications with SPF 2010?

2. Why is adding attachments to an Outlook email a SharePoint issue?

3. If you want to remove Quick Launch, do you go to the Quick Launch item in Central Administration?

Answers

1. There are major improvements when using Outlook 2010 (or Outlook 2007) and Access 2010 (or Access 2007) with SPF 2010 compared to using the 2003 versions. There are also (at the time of writing) several useful functions in some Office 2007 products that are not in the equivalent Office 2010 products.

2. Because one option using Outlook 2007 is to store the attachment in its own document workspace.

3. No, go to Tree View.

Using Outlook 2010 with SPF 2010

What You'll Learn in This Hour

▶ Linking SPF 2010 document libraries to Outlook 2010

▶ Linking SPF 2010 Calendars to Outlook 2010

▶ Linking SPF 2010 Contacts to Outlook 2010

▶ Using Outlook 2007 instead of Outlook 2010

▶ Using Outlook 2003 instead of Outlook 2010

Having in the previous hour, looked at something (attachment storage) that is no longer possible when the user is running Outlook 2010, this hour looks at what is possible when using Outlook 2010 with SPF 2010.

The hour focuses on how document libraries, calendar lists, and contact lists from SPF 2010 sites appear and function in Outlook 2010. It concludes (in the "Q&A" section) by briefly looking at a situation when the user is using Outlook 2007 or 2003 rather than 2010.

Linking Document Libraries to Outlook 2010

With Outlook 2010, you can link a SPF 2010 document library to Outlook. There are a couple of reasons for doing this:

▶ It enables you to take the files offline to work with them (using standard Outlook 2010 functionality).

▶ It enables you to use Outlook 2010's built-in Viewer to see inside your documents (only for formats supported by the Outlook 2010 Viewer).

> Both these functions are also possible with Outlook 2007. They are not, however, possible with Outlook 2003.

To have some documents in a document library that we can use to demonstrate this, I'll copy some files into the document library of BookSite2 using the techniques used earlier in Hour 7, "Creating and Using Libraries."

Following that, Figure 16.1 shows what we have on the default page of that site.

FIGURE 16.1
The document library in Book-Site2 after uploads

	Give Feedback	SPF1\administrator ▾

Browse Page

There are no items to show in this view of the "Objectives" list. To add a new item, click "Add new item".

⊕ Add new item

Attendees

☐ Name   Edit   Response   Comment

There are no items to show in this view of the "Attendees" list.

⊕ Manage attendees

☐ Subject   Owner   Time

There are no items to show in this view of the "A[...] list. To add a new item, click "Add new item".

⊕ Add new item

Document Library

Type Name ☐ Modified By

Windows 7 Application Compatibility List for IT Pros ☒ NEW   SPF1\adm

weeklyblog ☒ NEW   SPF1\adm

solo_mini_manual ☒ NEW   SPF1\adm

Paul Galvin Wild West ☒ NEW   SPF1\adm

MyBookCover ☒ NEW   SPF1\adm

CompleteRealWorld ☒ NEW   SPF1\adm

> The following steps must be taken in a client system that is running Outlook 2010; otherwise, Connect to Outlook, although listed, is not available for use.

Follow these steps to link that document library to Outlook 2010:

1. Open the document library by clicking the Document Library heading in Figure 16.1.

2. Change the ribbon to Library (in the Library Tools section).

3. Move across to the right to the Connect and Export section.

   Figure 16.2 shows what you see if you move the cursor over the top icon in this section.

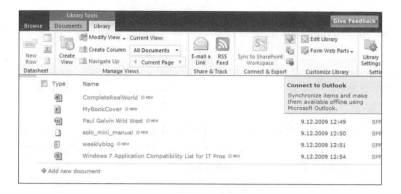

FIGURE 16.2
Finding Connect
to Outlook

It might be that you don't see exactly the same ribbon (as shown in Figure 16.2) on your screen. For instance, in the Connect & Export section in Figure 16.2, there is a column of three icons. On large screens and bigger windows, those icons have labels (Connect to Outlook, Export to Excel, and Open with Explorer). Another less useful change is that the small icon in Figure 16.2 for Edit Library can become a large icon like that used in Figure 16.2 for RSS Feed.

By the Way

The ribbon only works when using a recent browser. If you are still using, for instance, IE6, you get a message warning you of limited functionality, and you cannot follow any of the following steps. (IE6 is not officially supported as a browser for SPF 2010.)

By the Way

4. Click the Connect to Outlook icon.

5. Control is likely to be transferred to a pop-up IE window asking you to confirm that you want the website to open the Outlook program (see Figure 16.3).

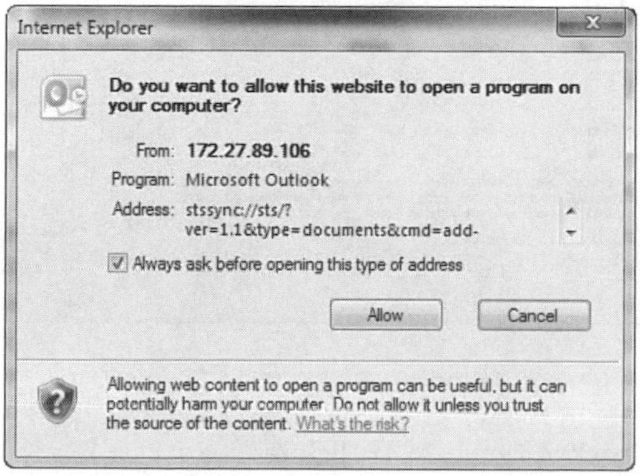

Internet Explorer

Do you want to allow this website to open a program on your computer?

From: 172.27.89.106
Program: Microsoft Outlook
Address: stssync://sts/?
ver=1.1&type=documents&cmd=add-

☑ Always ask before opening this type of address

[Allow]   [Cancel]

Allowing web content to open a program can be useful, but it can potentially harm your computer. Do not allow it unless you trust the source of the content. What's the risk?

FIGURE 16.3
Outlook requires
permission.

6. Click Allow.

7. A similar second pop-up box might appear; click Allow there, too. (This second pop-up is to allow the transfer of content.)

Did you Know?

I logged in using 172.27.89.106, the TCP/IP address of the SPF1 server at the time, rather than SPF1.

After this second Allow with the background of the website, Outlook 2010 opens, and on top of that there is a new pop-up window that again asks if we actually want to do this (see Figure 16.4).

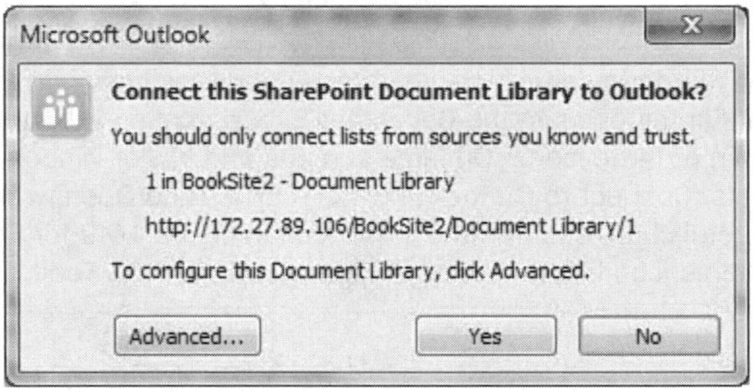

FIGURE 16.4
Approving the connection of the document library to Outlook

Microsoft Outlook

Connect this SharePoint Document Library to Outlook?

You should only connect lists from sources you know and trust.

1 in BookSite2 - Document Library

http://172.27.89.106/BookSite2/Document Library/1

To configure this Document Library, click Advanced.

[Advanced...]   [Yes]   [No]

8. Click Advanced and change the default name to SPF1 Book Documents (see Figure 16.5).

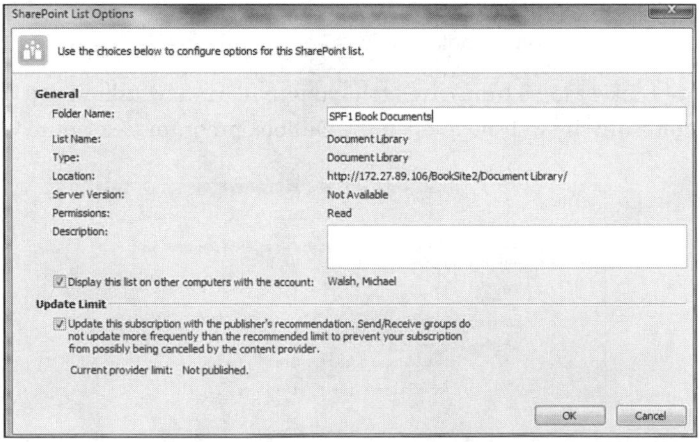

FIGURE 16.5
Specifying the name in Outlook 2010 of the document library

SharePoint List Options

Use the choices below to configure options for this SharePoint list.

General

Folder Name:	SPF1 Book Documents
List Name:	Document Library
Type:	Document Library
Location:	http://172.27.89.106/BookSite2/Document Library/
Server Version:	Not Available
Permissions:	Read
Description:	

☑ Display this list on other computers with the account: Walsh, Michael

Update Limit

☑ Update this subscription with the publisher's recommendation. Send/Receive groups do not update more frequently than the recommended limit to prevent your subscription from possibly being cancelled by the content provider.

Current provider limit: Not published.

[OK]   [Cancel]

9. Click OK.

10. This takes us back to Figure 16.4. Click Yes.

11. Now you need to Log In (again) to the website (see Figure 16.6).

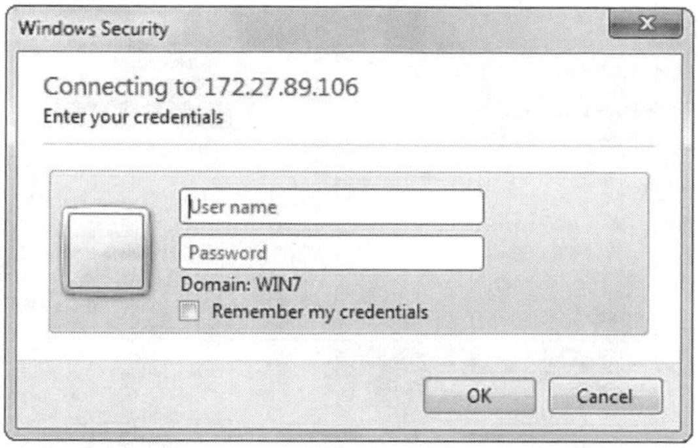

FIGURE 16.6
Authorizing
access to the
website

12. Enter User name in the form **SPF1\Administrator**. (Otherwise WIN7 would be
taken as the "domain.")

Don't worry if you need to enter the proceeding text twice before you move on.

Did you
Know?

What now happens is that the pop-up disappears, and one-by-one the files from the
document library are (slowly) copied across and listed on the page. When all the six
files that were in the BookSite2 document library are copied, you see something like
Figure 16.7 (which is the center section of the page).

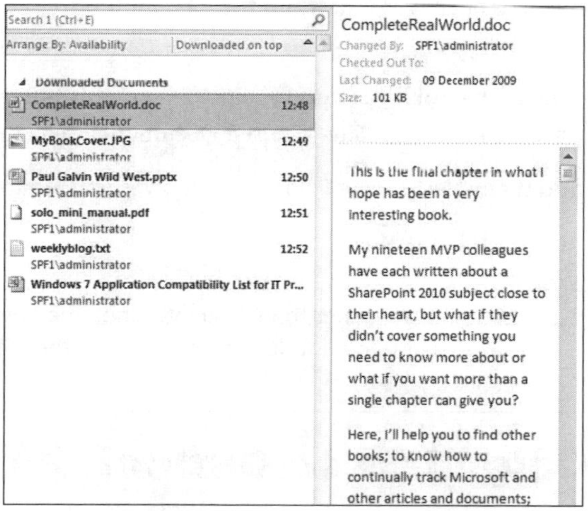

FIGURE 16.7
The document
library as shown
in Outlook 2010

Here, in addition to the list of documents, you can see a new pane containing the
content of the first document in the list. Figure 16.8, for instance, shows what the previewer for Excel files makes of the last item in the Document Library.

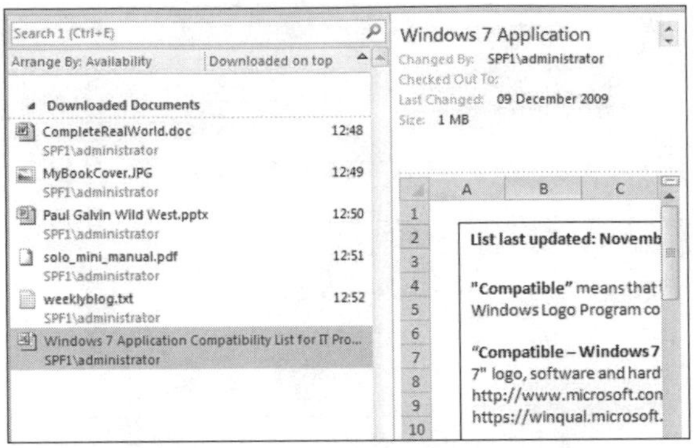

FIGURE 16.8
Another preview
example

FIGURE 16.8
Another preview
example

By the
Way

Previewers are available for most standard basic file formats—here for instance
.txt and .jpg—and for all Microsoft Office products. At the time of this writing,
there was no Previewer available for pdf files; however, this is expected by the
time the product is fully released. (There is a pdf viewer in Outlook 2007.)

Deleting Connections to Old Servers

At some stage, you should remove from Outlook 2010 some of your connections to
old (or test) Lists because they are no longer needed and, by still being there, take up
useful screen space. To do this, follow these steps:

1. With Outlook 2010 open, scroll down in the left column to the SharePoint Lists
   section.

2. Select the name of the link you want to remove; here this link is to an old test
   document library called Team Site—Shared Documents (see Figure 16.9).

3. Right-click and then select Delete Folder, which gives you Figure 16.10.

4. Click OK, and the Link is removed.

Did you
Know?

The text in Figure 16.10 is much scarier than it ought to be. The key paragraph is
the second one—namely that you are not deleting the List on the (SharePoint)
server.

Linking Calendars to Outlook 2010

Another useful way to combine Outlook 2010 with SPF 2010 is to link calendars
between the two. This section goes into the details of how to set that up.

1. Open a Calendar List in SPF 2010 and select Calendar in the Calendar Tools
   section. As shown in Figure 16.11, I have selected the Calendar entry from the
   (default) Team Site because there is already an entry there.

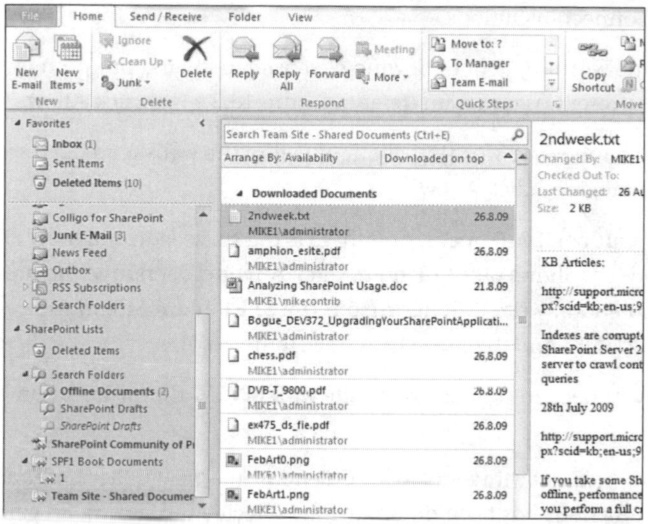

FIGURE 16.9
Selecting a List to be disconnected

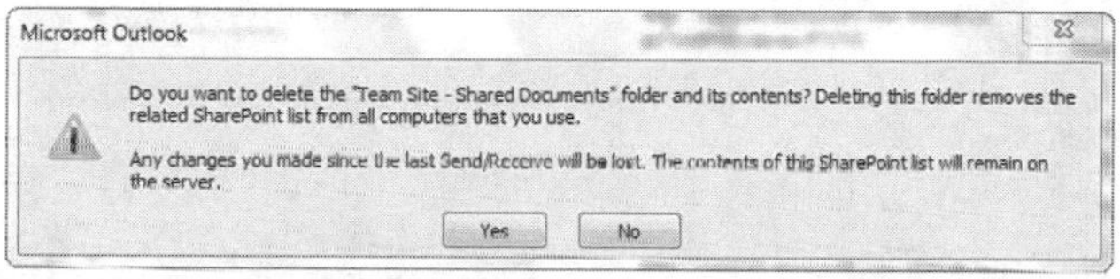

FIGURE 16.10
A scary warning

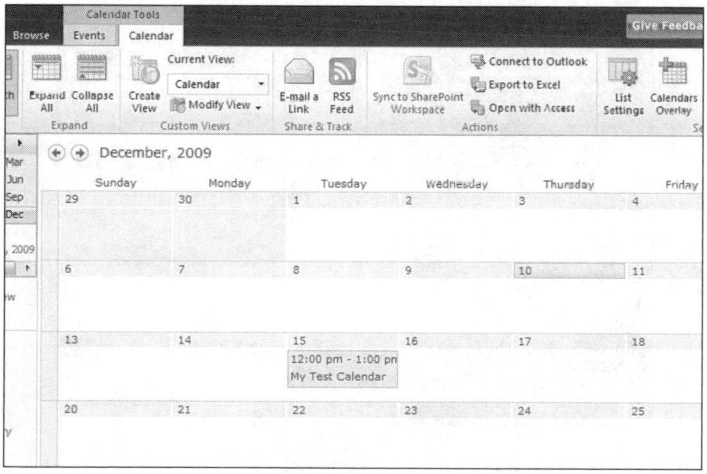

FIGURE 16.11
The Calendar List in SPF 2010

On the far right of this extract (see Figure 16.11) of the ribbon is an item Calendars Overlay. This enables you to overlay SharePoint Calendars within SharePoint. As you see in Outlook 2010, you can overlay SharePoint Calendars with the Outlook Calendar.

By the Way

2. Select Connect to Outlook.

3. The same warning about allowing a website to open a program on your computer is present as a pop-up (refer to Figure 16.3). Just click Allow.

4. The same follow-up warning about allowing the website to open web content comes here, too. Click Allow.

5. Finally Outlook 2010 opens, and there is the same warning as in Figure 16.4, only now for SharePoint Calendar. Click Advanced, change the name to SPF1–Calendar, write **Calendar from the SPF1 Team Site** in the description field, click OK, and then select Yes (see Figure 16.4).

6. Again you need to connect to the site with SPF1\Administrator and password.

7. You now have a Listing for SPF1—Calendar in a new Other Calendars section. SPF1—Calendar has been automatically selected for display, so your Outlook now displays both the Outlook Calendar and the SPF 2010 Calendar (see Figure 16.12).

FIGURE 16.12
Outlook 2010
Calendars

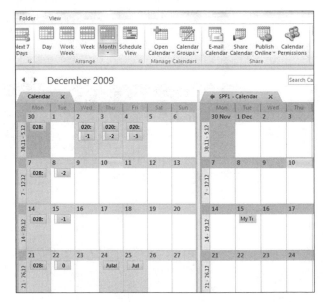

To get an overlay view of the two calendars, click the leftward-facing arrow at the top of the SPF1—Calendar section of Figure 16.12. The Overlay View obtained is shown in Figure 16.13.

FIGURE 16.13
Overlay View of the Outlook 2010 and the SPF 2010 Calendars

By the Way

It's up to you when using Outlook 2010 to decide which of these alternatives (Overlay or Non-Overlay) you choose to see at any time. You can also see only one of the two calendars, or you can include one or more calendars from the My Calendars and Shared Calendars sections.

By the Way

Synchronization occurs at the frequency specified. To see the synchronization in SPF 2010, you need to reaccess or refresh the page containing the Calendar List (or containing a web part list view derived from it).

Did you Know?

Overlapping two or more SharePoint calendars with your own calendar is a perfect way to solve the problem of being a member of several different projects, each of which has its own calendar located in SharePoint sites. Although there are alternatives using only SharePoint, using Outlook 2010 to overlay them is both easier and more powerful.

Synchronization between SPF 2010 and Outlook 2010 for SPF 2010 calendars that are stored in Outlook 2010 is two-way. So it is possible to add a new item to a calendar in the Outlook 2010 copy of a SPF 2010 calendar and then have it synchronized automatically to the SPF 2010 site. (Changes made to the SPF 2010 calendar naturally also synchronize to the Outlook 2010 version of the Calendar.)

To see this in action, we need to take the following steps:

1. Access the Outlook 2010 copy of the SharePoint Calendar (SPF1—Calendar). Do this by removing Calendar from the Overlay View, as shown in Figure 16.13.
2. Add a new entry. Here I'm adding a meeting for the December 30, 2009 (called End of Year Meeting).
3. Now open the calendar in SPF 2010. Here I'm going directly to http://172.27.89.106/Lists/Calendar/calendar.aspx. Your TCP/IP address will be different of course. Figure 16.14 displays a small section of the page.

6
7
8
9
10
13
14
15
16
17
12:00 pm - 1:00 pn
My Test Calendar
20
21
22
23
24
27
28
29
30
31
10:00 am - 1:00 pm
End of Year Meetinç

FIGURE 16.14 A calendar in SPF 2010 that includes an entry made in Outlook 2010

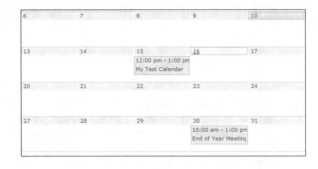

4. Click Team Site in the breadcrumbs near the top left of the Calendar page, a part of which was shown in Figure 16.14. Figure 16.15 shows a revised section of the default page of the (default) Team Site.

Calendar
Start Time
End Time
Event Type
Title
Location
12/15/2009 12:00 PM
12/15/2009 1:00 PM
0
My Test Calendar
My Office
12/30/2009 10:00 AM
12/30/2009 1:00 PM
0
End of Year Meeting
Welcome to your site!
Add a new image, change this welcome text or add new lists to this page by clicking the edit butto
to create new team events. Use the links in the getting started section to share your site and custo
Shared Documents
Type
Name
Modified
weeklyblog
12/4/2009 7:12 PM

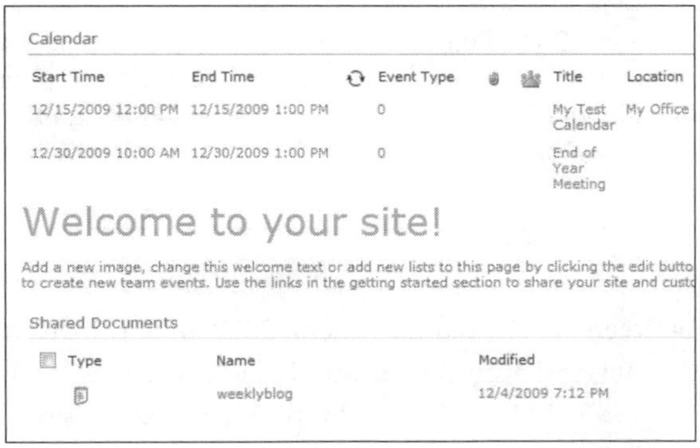

FIGURE 16.15 The List View web part of the SPF 2010 calendar also contains the new entry.

Did you Know?

If the calendar was already open in your browser, you need to refresh the page because you will see only the initial entry.

Linking Contacts to Outlook 2010 (and Learning How to Delete a List)

At the moment, we don't have a Contacts List in our site, but we need one to check functionality with Outlook 2010, so follow these steps to create one. We create one in the (default) Team Site, but it could be created in one of the other sites if preferred; just amend the steps for using it.

1. Go to the Team Site if you aren't already there.

In Hour 6, "Using Libraries and Lists," I recommend that you don't install Silverlight on your server because the "Improve(d) Creation Experience" it offers is in this case not an improvement. On your client system you probably have no choice because other applications or websites may require Silverlight.

Figure 16.16 is what the More Options page looks like when the SPF 2010 site is accessed from a client system where Silverlight has been installed. Figure 6.2 in Hour 6 is what it looks like when accessed from the SPF 2010 server where Silverlight hasn't been installed.

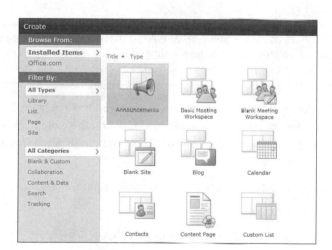

FIGURE 16.16
The More Options page in a system with Silverlight

2. Select Site Actions and then More Options from the drop-down (see Figure 16.16).

3. Going through this All list of things that can be created would take forever, so click List in the left column to make the list of options more manageable (see Figure 16.17).

FIGURE 16.17
All the different
List types

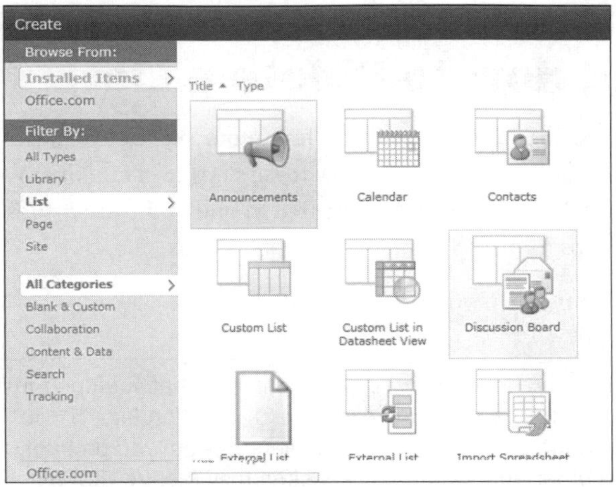

4. This is just a list of all the items from the Communications; Tracking and Custom Lists columns are in the non-Silverlight version in Figure 6.2. (The second copy of External List will probably be gone in your copy of SPF 2010.) Click Calendar.

5. Specify **BookCalendar1** as the name of the Calendar in the right section of the screen. Create now becomes an available option.

6. Click Create.

By the Way

> Around this time if not before, you'll have realized that we wanted to create a Contacts List and we've created by mistake a Calendar List. I've done this to show you how to delete a List you've created by mistake because it's not that obvious.

7. After the BookCalendar1 list has been created, you have only the horizontal menu selection, but nothing has been selected, and therefore there is no thread visible. Select Calendar in the Calendar Tools section. (Refer to Figure 16.11— again, no misprint!)

8. Select List Settings to the right of the screen (see Figure 16.18).

9. Click Delete this List.

10. Click OK to approve that the List is sent to the Recycle Bin.

11. After that small detour, go back to the screenshot shown in Figure 16.16, and this time select Contacts.

12. This time specify **BookContacts1** as the name and again select Create. To use it, add some new names using Add New Item, as shown in Figure 16.19.

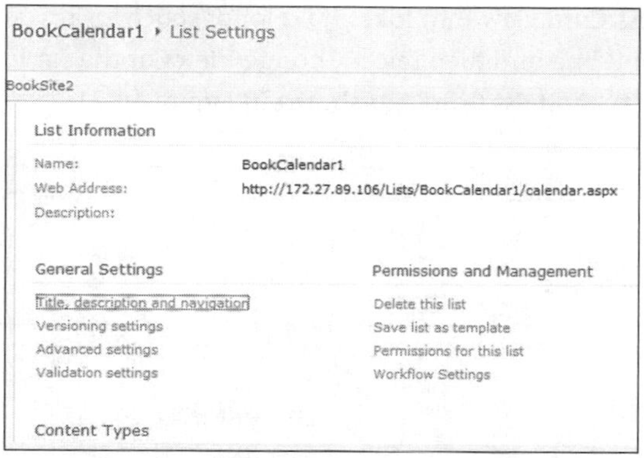

FIGURE 16.18
List Settings

FIGURE 16.19
A new Contacts
List

13. Then in Figure 16.20, select Connect to Outlook.

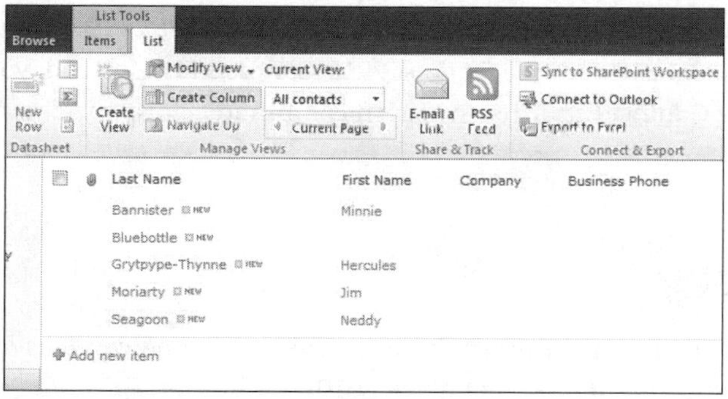

FIGURE 16.20
The populated
Contacts List in
SPF 2010

The same three "do you want to" screens come that we've already seen when connecting a document library and a calendar. Proceed through those screens as before.

14. Again select Advanced in the third screen to change the name to SPF1—BookContacts1 before finally seeing the BookContacts1 List in your copy of Outlook 2010.

You see the Business Card view that takes up a lot of space for no good reason, so go to View on the menu line and then select Change Views at the far left of the ribbon. I've amended this to "Address Card," as shown in Figure 16.21.

FIGURE 16.21
The populated Contacts List in Outlook 2010

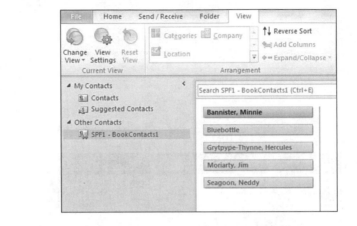

Just as with calendars, the link between the listing in the Other Contacts group in Outlook 2010 and the SharePoint Contacts List is synchronized in both directions.

By the Way

> The choice of which View is to be used for a Contacts set in Outlook 2010 is individual to the particular Contacts set. You could have, for instance, Contacts as a List and SPF1—BooksContents1 as Address Card.

Unlike with calendars, however, you cannot overlay the SPF 2010 Contacts List you copied to Outlook 2010 with the Outlook 2010 Contacts List. Instead, you can select only one of the Contact lists listed in the left column to be displayed in the center of the screen.

Summary

In this hour, we looked at document libraries, calendars, and contacts and how you can use them in connection with Outlook 2010.

Q&A

Q. *I have Outlook 2007—can I still get this functionality?*

A. Connecting these lists to Outlook 2007 is almost identical with copying them to Outlook 2010. Also the options available when the lists have been copied to Outlook 2007 are similar. With Outlook 2007, synchronization is two-way, and with Outlook 2007, too, you have preview software for files in document libraries that can overlay calendars but cannot overlay contacts.

Q. *I have Outlook 2003—can I still get this functionality?*

A. With Outlook 2003 on the client PC, functionality is cut down severely:

▶ There is no longer a Connect to Outlook option for document libraries if Outlook 2003 is used.

▶ You can no longer overlay a SharePoint calendar with an Outlook calendar if Outlook 2003 is used.

There is only one-way synchronization between a SharePoint calendar in Outlook 2003 and the same calendar in the SharePoint site. One-way here means that changes made in the SharePoint site are reflected in the Outlook 2003 copy of the calendar but not vice versa.

▶ There is only one-way synchronization between a SharePoint Contact List in Outlook 2003 and the same contacts list in the SharePoint site. One-way here means that changes made in the SharePoint site are reflected in the Outlook 2003 copy of the contacts list but not vice versa.

Q. *I have some file types in my Document Library that are not shown in the Preview screen in Outlook 2010. Why not?*

A. Microsoft provides in Outlook 2010 preview software for most common file types. If there isn't preview software included for a particular file type, the contents of files of that file type will not be displayed in the Preview pane.

Check the main Office page (http://www.microsoft.com/office) to see if preview software for any new file types is available. This might also come as part of an Outlook 2010 (or Office 2010) Service Pack.

Did you Know?

Workshop

Quiz

1. How can you use Outlook 2007/2010 to view the contents of a document stored in an SPF 2010 document library?

2. What is the main difference between using SPF 2010 calendars and contacts lists with Outlook 2003 and Outlook 2007/2010?

Answers

1. Both these Outlook products have a viewing frame with built-in Viewers for many standard file types. If an SPF 2010 document library is also listed in Outlook 2007/2010, this viewing frame can be used to view the contents of most of the documents in that document library.

2. Outlook 2003 has only one-way synchronization for these lists. Outlook 2007/2010 has two-way synchronization.

Sharing OneNote 2010 or OneNote 2007 Notebooks with SPF 2010

What You'll Learn in This Hour

▶ Using OneNote 2010 with SPF 2010
▶ Using OneNote 2007 with SPF 2010

This hour looks at the various ways of using the OneNote product with SPF 2010. Because there are quite large differences between the usage with OneNote 2010 and with OneNote 2007, I cover each case separately.

Why Combine OneNote 2010 with SPF 2010

I've been a keen user of OneNote since its early days, and I hope by covering its use with SPF 2010 in this book encourages more people to start using it. OneNote 2010 is included in every version of Office 2010 except the Starter Edition, which should help.

OneNote is the modern equivalent of the Borland product Sidekick that was installed in many client systems in the early DOS days. It ran in the background, and you could use it for quickly copying text to and having it saved automatically.

I use OneNote (both OneNote 2007 and OneNote 2010 on different machines) as a structured location for keeping (private) copies of important sections of web pages and articles. Other people use it as a storage location for videos, slide shows, and so on. It's a versatile product with imaginative developers, and its main strength is that you can copy and paste almost anything to it while not needing to explicitly save what you have copied.

For most OneNote users, the information they store in it is important to them, and therefore they want access to it wherever they are. Storing OneNote 2010 notebooks in SPF 2010 allows access to them from any PC running its own copy of OneNote 2010 (or OneNote 2007 if the Notebooks have been stored in that format).

There are three main ways to use OneNote 2010:

> **Option 1.**   Store and use them on a single client PC running OneNote 2010.
>
> **Option 2.**   Store them in a USB stick and use them from any client PC running OneNote 2010.
>
> **Option 3.**   Store them in an SPF 2010 (or SP 2010) server and use them from any client PC running OneNote 2010.

Option 1 is clearly a solution only when you can guarantee that you will have that PC available to you when you want to access your OneNote files. That won't be the situation for most people.

Option 2 works all the time, provided the PCs where you are have USB ports that you have access to (and provided you don't lose the USB stick!). In effect this means everywhere except an Internet café or other location where you can't attach USB sticks.

Option 3 works all the time provided your SPF 2010 server is available to you via the Internet.

By the
Way

> Although this is a SharePoint book and I describe how to set up option 3, what I personally use is option 2. The reason for this is, because I use a lot of different PCs, I do not always have access to a server running my SharePoint storage of OneNote notebooks, and I have found synchronization of those OneNote notebooks between different client systems to be challenging. The "Q&A" section in this hour describes how to setup the USB stick method of using OneNote 2010.

Unlike the situation with OneNote 2007 where it was only possible to share a new notebook, with OneNote 2010 you can also change an existing notebook to shared and thus can also move an existing OneNote notebook to a SharePoint site. So following are two slightly different sets of instructions for each of those two scenarios.

How to Create a OneNote 2010 Notebook and Store It in SPF 2010

Here are the steps for creating a new OneNote 2010 notebook and storing it in an SPF 2010 system:

1. Open OneNote 2010.

2. Select File > New > Network.

3. Fill out the new Notebook page in a similar way to Figure 17.1 (being careful with the Network Connection field).

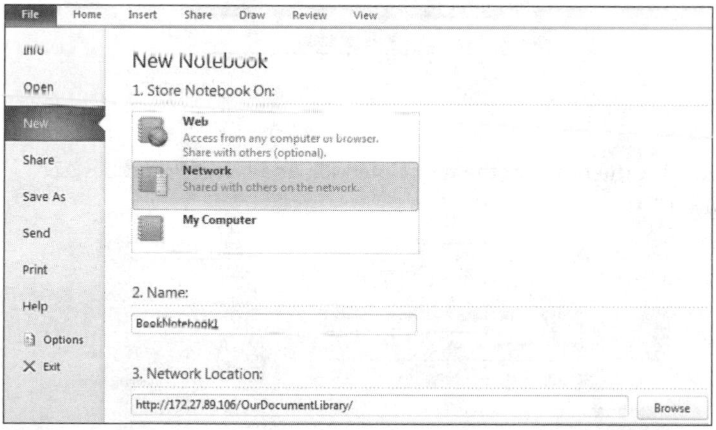

FIGURE 17.1
Specifying the Name and Location of the new Notebook

> If you can only remember the name of the site and still want to use this function, you can specify the site here and then click Browse. This will (after requests for you to give name and password) give you a list of document libraries. Select one and the correct full address (as shown previously) will be visible in the Network Location field and you can proceed with step 3.

By the Way

> It's important here that you choose the address of a Document Library. If you specify only the address of the SharePoint site, this won't work.

Did you Know?

4. Click Create Notebook.

   At this point, you typically see one or more boxes asking you to log in to the SPF 2010 site. Don't forget the need to specify the full SPF1\Administrator as the name.

You will probably see a temporary pop-up informing you that you are connecting to the site, and then you see Figure 17.2, which requires input.

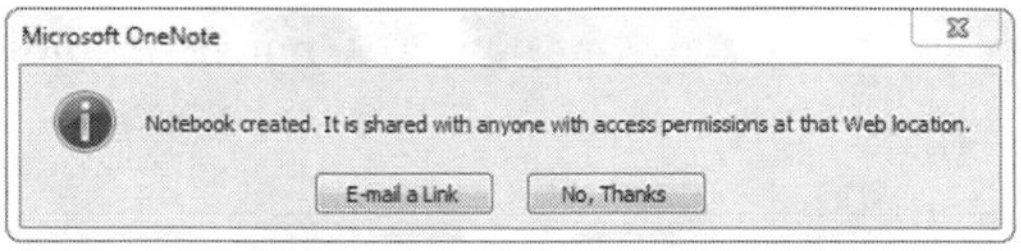

FIGURE 17.2
Asking if an
email is required

5. Select No, Thanks. (There's no need to send an email to yourself as administrator.)

6. Scroll to the bottom of the Notebook column on the left (of OneNote 2010), and you see Figure 17.3. (If necessary, widen the column to see the full name.)

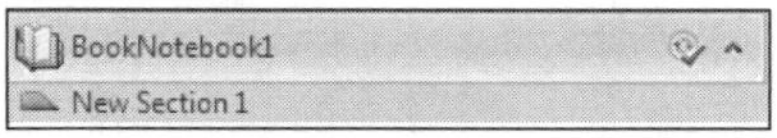

FIGURE 17.3
Checking the list-
ing of the newly
created shared
Notebook

7. Right-click the name of the new Notebook and select Properties (see Figure 17.4).

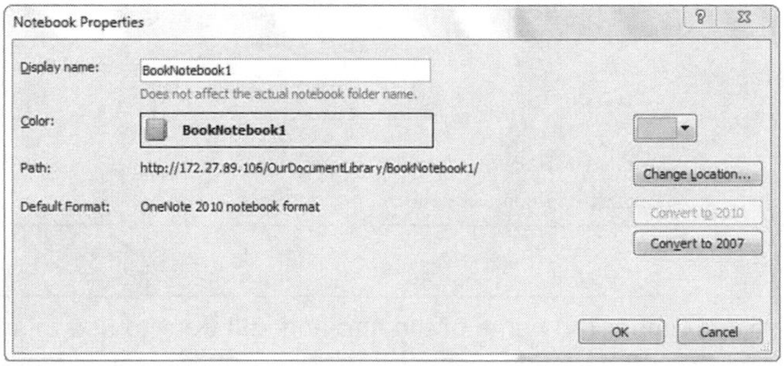

FIGURE 17.4
Properties of the
new shared
Notebook

There is one possible problem. Without asking us the system has created a OneNote notebook that is in Office 2010 format. This is fine if you can be sure that all the people accessing it will be running OneNote 2010 on their client machines but is a disaster if some users are running OneNote 2007 because they can't open the file and see the data.

Did you Know?

Check the OneNote site by going to http://office.microsoft.com/en-us/default. aspx and then accessing Products and finally OneNote for more information about what is new when using the OneNote 2007 format. (Try first the direct link, which at the time of writing was http://office.microsoft.com/en-us/onenote/ FX100487701033.aspx).

8. To make sure that all our users can access this workbook, continue from Figure 17.4 and select Convert to 2007 (see Figure 17.5).

By the Way

It is possible to wait and do this later. There are two good reasons for doing it now:

▶ No user will get a message saying that he/she can't access the data.

▶ A conversion done now before content is added will take less time.

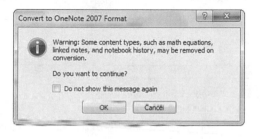

FIGURE 17.5
List of features lost on conversion

By the Way

The OneNote 2010 Guide notebook installed with every OneNote 2010 installation gives lots of useful information about what is in OneNote 2010 but doesn't go into details about what is only available in the 2010 file format.

Figure 17.5 lists some of the features that are only available with the 2010 format and which therefore will be lost with this conversion. Because we have not yet added any data, we won't lose any content, just the ability to uses these features.

9. Click OK.

Did you Know?

This conversion, even of an empty notebook, can take quite a bit of time. Time enough for a short coffee break perhaps. Following the conversion, right-click the name of the Notebook and again select Properties just to make sure that the equivalent of Figure 17.4 displays OneNote 2007 notebook format. It's also useful at this stage to give the New Section 1 section a proper name.

To complete this exercise, open the website in your browser and access the document library where you stored the OneNote notebook (see Figure 17.6).

▼ Name	Modified	☐ Modified By
BookNotebook1	12/15/2009 10:18 AM	SPF1\administrator

FIGURE 17.6
Document Library containing a OneNote 2010 notebook

How to Convert an Existing OneNote Notebook to Shared and Store It in SPF 2010

The following steps show how to share the OneNote 2010 Guide notebook that is installed as part of a standard OneNote 2010 installation. As part of the process of converting the notebook to shared, it will be stored in a SPF 2010 document library.

1. (In OneNote 2010) Select File > Information.

2. Click the Settings drop-down next to OneNote 2010 User Guide (see Figure 17.7).

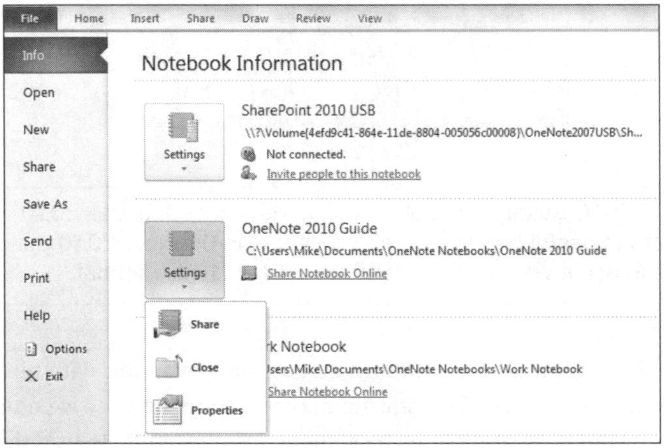

FIGURE 17.7
First step in sharing an existing OneNote 2010 notebook

3. Click Share.

4. The Share Notebook page offers us the choice of Web and Network.

5. Select Network.

   Figure 17.8 offers us the same location that we used last time we stored a notebook to an SPF 2010 document library. Then we were creating a new notebook; this time we are making a nonshared notebook shared *and* moving it to be stored in a location where shared makes sense. (Clearly making something shared and then leaving it in a place where only one person could access it wouldn't make any sense.)

   We want to store this newly shared notebook in the same location.

Did you Know?

It's useful to have a single document library that contains only the OneNote notebooks that you are storing in the SharePoint site.

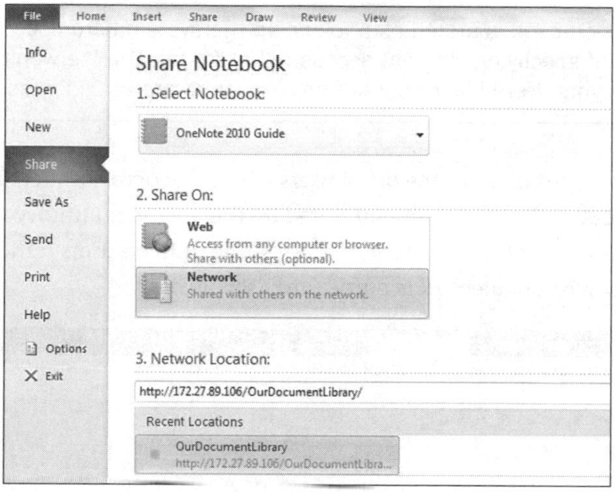

FIGURE 17.8
Prespecified
Document
Library for the
shared notebook

6. Click Share Notebook.

You see Figure 17.9 for a short while followed by Figure 17.2 where again No, Thanks can be clicked.

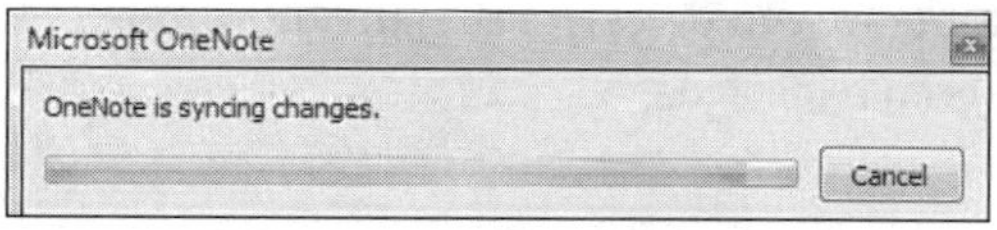

FIGURE 17.9
OneNote is sync-
ing changes.

If you want, you can check in two ways that this change of type and location has succeeded:

1. Check in OneNote 2010 the properties of the notebook after right-clicking the notebook name. The Path will be specified as http://172.27.89.106/ OurDocumentLibrary/OneNote 2010 Guide/.

2. Open the OurDocumentLibrary document library in the browser and right-click OneNote 2010 Guide. Then select Manage Permissions (see Figure 17.10).

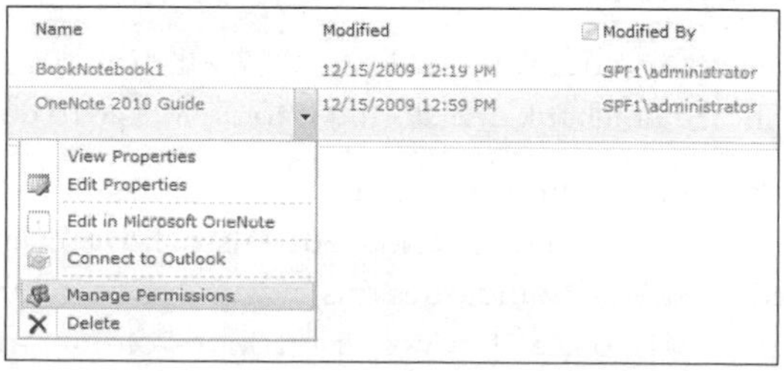

FIGURE 17.10
Checking the
status of the for-
merly nonshared
notebook

The OneNote notebook is stored as a folder, so the system here uses the standard function of specifying different access rights for folders. We won't specify any different rights. Here I just wanted to make you aware of this possibility.

Accessing Permissions gives us the list of users who have access rights to the site and where these access rights have been inherited by the document library (as shown in Figure 17.11). If we want, we can then remove some of these users if the information in our shared OneNote notebook is particularly sensitive.

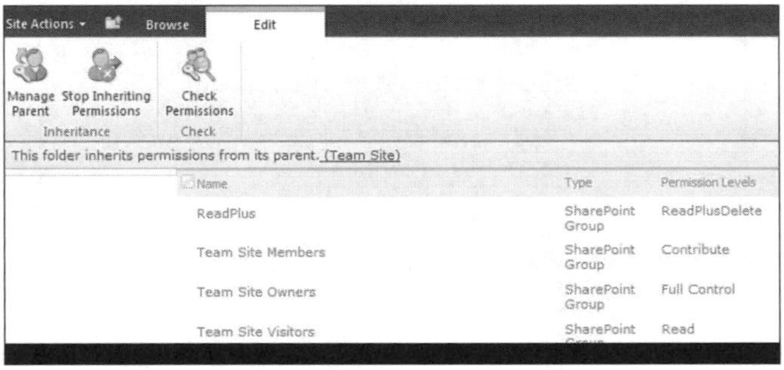

FIGURE 17.11
Possible to amend access permissions for a OneNote notebook

Because we can give this Notebook different access rights confirms that it is now shared, and the fact that we can access it using the browser in a document library confirms that it has been relocated.

Users of OneNote 2007 have access to the same notebooks that an administrator using OneNote 2010 has created provided that the administrator has either specified that she wants to create a notebook in OneNote 2007 format or has converted an existing notebook that was already created in OneNote 2010 format to OneNote 2007 format.

The Basics of Using OneNote 2007 with SPF 2010

In this section, where we look at using OneNote 2007 with SPF 2010, we concentrate on creating a new shared notebook and storing it in an SPF 2010 document library.

Apart from a slightly less appealing user interface, OneNote 2007 users also lose out in one useful OneNote function that OneNote 2010 users have, even if OneNote 2007 format files are used. Figure 17.12 indicates this, using OneNote 2010 and one of the private notebooks that I use to keep track of useful SharePoint information.

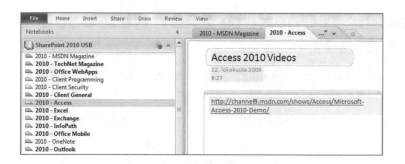

FIGURE 17.12
One benefit of
OneNote 2010
compared to
OneNote 2007

> When using OneNote 2007, to share an existing Notebook, you need to right-click the Notebook > Notebook Properties > Change Location and then specify http://spf1 and select a suitable document library from those listed in a screen similar to Figure 17.16, which you'll see later in this hour.

By the Way

You'll have noticed in Figure 17.12 that some of the sections in my SharePoint 2010 USB notebook (see the "Q&A" section for what this is) are bold and some aren't.

OneNote 2010 indicates with bold a section that contains items that haven't been accessed in this client system. This means that the items have been added in a different client system (that could have been running either OneNote 2010 or OneNote 2007) and then have later been synchronized with this client system. Similarly in the right column (further to the right than what you can see in Figure 17.12), the items in the section that haven't been read are bold until read. This small change is amazingly useful in what might well be a common scenario.

At work you see an interesting web page, and you have time to copy/paste it into the copy of OneNote that you are using on the work machine but no time to read it. Throughout the days of the week, you do the same several times, and at the weekend you take the USB stick home and connect it to your home machine (and it syncs). Now, provided you had already read (or marked as read) everything that was already on that client system, you can see highlighted only those (sections and) items that you haven't yet read, and you can read them at your leisure over the weekend.

Using OneNote 2007, you have to remember them and hunt for them, and you'll probably forget where half of them are. However, the USB stick method is in the "Q&A" section, so the following section is a description of how to create a Shared Notebook when using OneNote 2007 and store that in a SPF 2010 document library. I'm well aware of the difficulties people working in (especially) large companies have in getting permission to upgrade their Office versions. (I can't help OneNote 2003 users though, sorry).

Sharing a OneNote 2007 Notebook with SPF 2010

Here, we go through the process of creating a Shared Notebook in OneNote 2007, adding it to SPF 2010, and using the notebook from SPF 2010:

1. Open OneNote 2007 and select Share > Create Shared Notebook (see Figure 17.13).

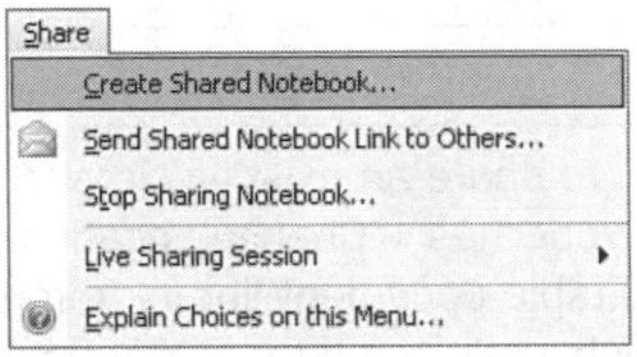

FIGURE 17.13
Creating a
Shared Notebook

2. In Figure 17.14, I chose the Personal Notebook style to give it some built-in properties.

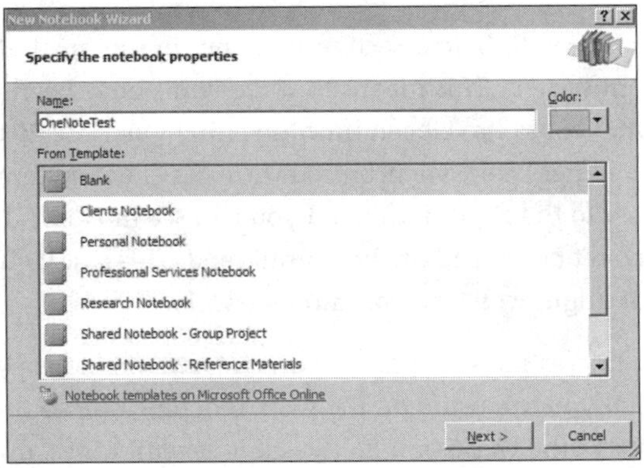

FIGURE 17.14
Specifying the
notebook's
properties

3. Figure 17.15 shows the available options for sharing a notebook. Choose the default options. Click Next.

4. In the Confirm Notebook screen that follows, section http://spf1, click Create to display the screen shown in Figure 17.16.

5. Select Shared Documents.

6. Click Select.

This creates a folder called OneNoteTest in the Shared Documents document library, but first we need to confirm our choice of document library (see Figure 17.17).

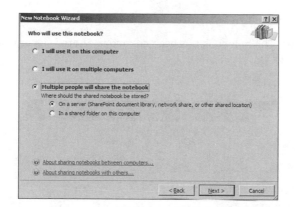

FIGURE 17.15
Sharing a
notebook

FIGURE 17.16
Specifying the
document library
for the notebook

FIGURE 17.17
Sharing a
notebook

7. Deselect Create an e-mail...

8. Click Create. The notebook has been created in Shared Documents as a folder (see Figure 17.18).

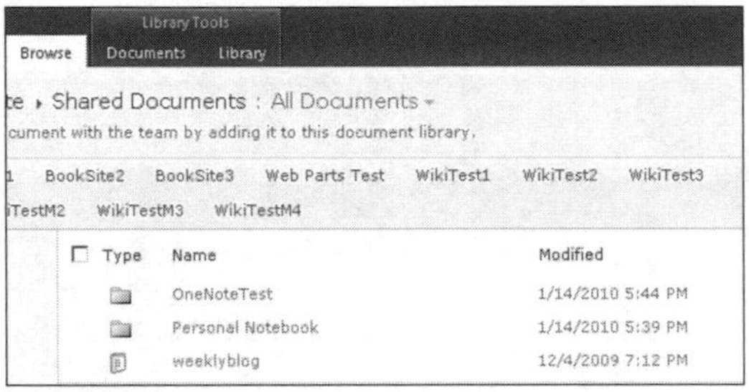

FIGURE 17.18
The Shared
Notebook in the
document library

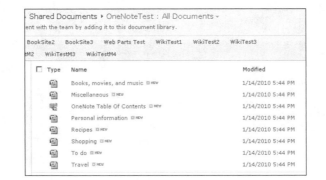

9. Open the folder and you see the sections and items that came standard with the Personal Notebook we selected in Figure 17.14 (see Figure 17.19).

FIGURE 17.19
Inside the
Shared Notebook

10. Finally, click Books, movies, and music, and after a couple of warnings OneNote 2007 opens in your client machine at the first item in that section, as shown in Figure 17.20.

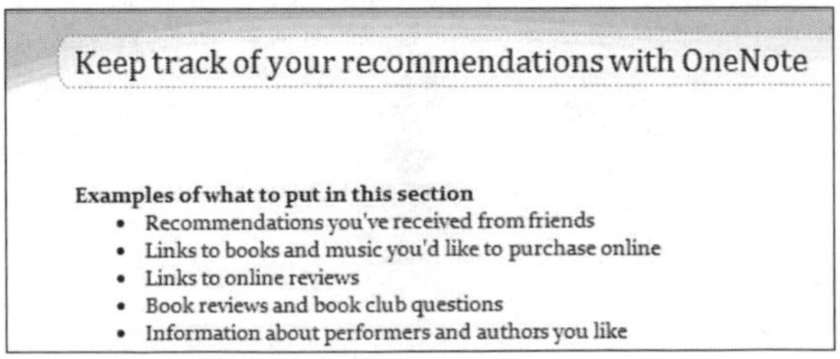

FIGURE 17.20
The first page of
Books, movies,
and music

Keep track of your recommendations with OneNote

Examples of what to put in this section
• Recommendations you've received from friends
• Links to books and music you'd like to purchase online
• Links to online reviews
• Book reviews and book club questions
• Information about performers and authors you like

Summary

In this hour, we've learned why it is useful to use OneNote 2010 and how to store its Notebooks in SharePoint Foundation 2010 document libraries so that they can be shared. We've done this for OneNote 2010 and (more briefly) for OneNote 2007.

Q&A

Q. *What are the details of your preferred method of installing OneNote 2010 on a USB stick?*

1. Make sure that you have an empty reasonably sized USB stick. (I used an 8GB stick, but I don't store videos or PowerPoints in OneNote 2010.) One that is brightly colored and is the only USB stick you possess of that bright color is preferable. (I have mine on a small, black USB stick. I have misplaced it several times.)

2. Create a new Notebook using the following steps:

   ▶ Open OneNote 2010.

   ▶ Select File > New > My Computer and Specify a name (for example, BookNotebook2) but don't click OK yet!

   ▶ Amend the storage location so that it points at your USB stick (in my case the F: drive).

   ▶ Click Create Notebook.

   ▶ BookNotebook2 opens at New Section 1; give it a different name and add some content.

3. Now pull the USB stick from the computer. Do *not* use Safely Remove Hardware and/or Eject.

4. (Later) Close OneNote 2010.

It is important that OneNote 2010 is still open on the computer when the USB stick is pulled from the computer. This means that the computer's cache still contains the OneNote 2010 notebook, so when you next open OneNote 2010 (or if you have left it open), you can still see the contents of the notebook and add new content to it even with the USB stick not available.

Here are the steps for using this USB stick-based notebook on a second (or third...) computer. (Steps 1 and 2 can be done in any order.)

1. Open OneNote 2010 if not open.

2. Attach the USB stick.

3. In OneNote 2010, select File > Open >/ Open Notebook.

4. Select the Notebook folder on the USB stick.

5. Add content if you want.

6. Pull the USB stick.

7. Close OneNote 2010. (Again, this Notebook is available when the USB stick isn't connected.)

Finally, here are the steps for synchronizing the USB-based notebook:

1. Open OneNote 2010 if not open.

2. Attach the USB Stick.

3. Go to the USB-based Notebook (BookNotebook2).

4. Right-click the Notebook itself and not on any item in it.

5. Select Synch This Notebook Now.

Q. *What special precautions do I need to take if some of my computers are running OneNote 2007 and others are running OneNote 2010?*

A. The problem is that OneNote 2010 files have a different format than OneNote 2007 files, and these naturally are not backward-compatible.

Did you Know?

Go to a OneNote site to find a list of the improvements when using the OneNote 2010 format.

If you have both OneNote 2007 and OneNote 2010 installed on different PCs and cannot for various reasons (cost or company regulations, for example) upgrade all these copies to OneNote 2010, you should make sure that your notebooks are all OneNote 2007 format notebooks.

This means two things:

▶ You must either create your Notebook when using OneNote 2007 or convert any Notebook that you have created when using OneNote 2010.

▶ You must not convert an existing 2007 format Notebook to OneNote 2010 format when you access the Notebook for the first time when using that copy of OneNote 2010. (You will be asked, and the default is to convert, so be careful. Note too that you will be asked if you want to convert the notebook for every different computer running OneNote 2010 that opens this Notebook for the first time.)

Provided you follow these rules, you will have no problems accessing and synchronizing (which in OneNote 2007 works as mentioned) your USB stick OneNote notebooks.

Sharing Access 2010 Tables with SPF 2010

What You'll Learn in This Hour

▶ Benefits of having SharePoint Lists stored in Access 2010

▶ Creating a linked Access 2010 Table from a SharePoint List

▶ Importing a SharePoint List to become an Access 2010 Table (one-off)

▶ Exporting an Access 2010 Table to become a SharePoint List (one-off)

▶ Starting with an Access 2010 Table and creating a linked copy as a SharePoint List

▶ Creating a SharePoint List while in Access 2010

▶ The differences between using Access 2010 with SPF 2010 and using Access 2007 or Access 2003

Using Access 2010 with SPF 2010 is made perhaps unnecessarily difficult by there being several ways of doing it (and by unclear names in the ribbon). Each of these methods have their own benefits and restrictions, which is why this hour works through all the options and notes their plusses and minuses.

> As we'll see in Hour 19, "Producing a Report from a Single SPF 2010 List," and (especially) Hour 20, "Creating a Report from Several SPF 2010 Lists," which deal with the creation of reports on SharePoint Lists, it is easier using Access 2010 to create reports from multiple SharePoint Lists than it was when using Access 2007.

By the Way

Benefits of Having SharePoint Lists Stored in Access 2010

The possibility of storing any SharePoint list (except surveys and discussions) as a table in Access is something that first became available in Access 2007. This hour includes a description of how to do this when using SPF 2010 and Access 2010. Differences when doing this using Access 2007 are outlined in the "Q&A" section.

The main reason for storing a SharePoint list in Access 2010 is because Access 2010's reporting facilities can then be used on those tables. This provides a way of creating reports from one or (combining) several SharePoint lists that SharePoint doesn't provide.

A secondary reason for storing a SharePoint list in Access 2010 is because people who want to do all their work in Access 2010 can then edit the SharePoint list in Access instead of needing to go to the SharePoint site.

> These reasons are valid whether a List is transferred to Access permanently or if a synchronizable copy of a List is made available as a table in Access 2010. This works in reverse, too. Most Access 2010 tables can be stored as SharePoint lists.

Prepare for the following section by creating a Links list (ComputerCompanyLinksList) in the default site and populating it with some entries. (I use HP www.hp.com, IBM www.ibm.com, and Microsoft www.microsoft.com for the examples that follow.) You have created Lists several times by now, so I won't give details beyond the start (Site Actions > More Options > Links).

Scenario 1: Creating a Linked Access 2010 Table from a SharePoint List

To store a SPF 2010 list as a linked Access 2010 table, follow these steps:

1. Open Access 2010; use the Blank Database option (see Figure 18.1).

2. On the right of the same screen (and lower), there is an entry box for the database name. Change the name to **BookDatabase1.accdb** and click Create (see Figure 18.2).

3. Select External Data.

4. SharePoint List is no longer (as in Access 2007) visible in the Import section, so you need to first access the drop-down by selecting More in the Import Section (see Figure 18.3).

5. Click SharePoint List (see Figure 18.4).

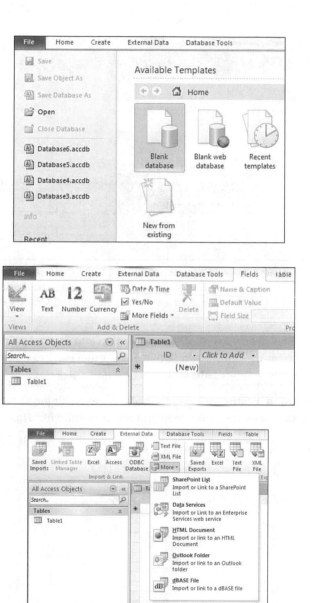

FIGURE 18.1
Using the Blank
Database option

FIGURE 18.2
An empty data-
base

FIGURE 18.3
External
Data–SharePoint
List

6. Change the name of the site address so that it actually is a SharePoint site. Here that means changing the name to http://SPF 1 or, depending on your working environment, to the TCP/IP address.

If it doesn't work (Can't Connect), try again—once. If using the TCP/IP address still doesn't work, but for instance you can access the site in your browser using

Did you Know?

FIGURE 18.4
Source and destination of the data

Get External Data - SharePoint Site

Select the source and destination of the data

Specify a SharePoint site:

Site Address
http://Mike1

http://Mike1

Specify how and where you want to store the data in the current database.

○ **Import the source data into a new table in the current database.**
If the specified object does not exist, Access will create it. If the specified object already exists, Access will append a number to the name of the imported object. Changes made to source objects (including data in tables) will not be reflected in the current database.

◉ **Link to the data source by creating a linked table.**
Access will create a table that will maintain a link to the source data. Changes made to the data in Access will be reflected in the source and vice versa.

> the same TCP/IP address, the probable reason is that TCP/IP address isn't listed in your list of Alternate Access Methods (see Hour 4, "Using the Administration Site"), so add this TCP/IP address to AAM; run iisreset, and then try again.

7. You can leave the default value of Link to the Data Source by Creating a Linked Table. This sets up a two-way link that is the usual way we want to use the SharePoint List / Access 2010 table combination. Click Next.

8. You'll be asked as usual to log in to the SPF1 site (don't forget to make sure the domain is listed as SPF1), and then you see something like Figure 18.5.

FIGURE 18.5
A selection of Lists for import to the database

Get External Data - SharePoint Site

Choose the SharePoint lists you want to link to
http://172.27.89.106

Select the lists you want available in the database:

Link	Type	Name
☐	⊞	Announcements
☐	⊞	BookContacts1
☐	⊞	Calendar
☐	⊞	ComputerCompanyLinksList
☐	⊞	Links
☐	⊞	OurDocumentLibrary
☐	⊞	Shared Documents
☐	⊞	Site Assets
☐	⊞	Site Pages
☐	⊞	Style Library
☐	⊞	Tasks
☐	⊞	UserInfo

By the Way

> Both alternative names have their disadvantages. SPF1 is fine provided your client system can find SPF1. TCP/IP is fine as long as you continue to have the

same TCP/IP address for your SPF 2010 server. Clearly, for synchronization to work, there needs to be contact between the server and your Access 2010 client.

Did you
Know?

If you didn't create a new Links list, you can instead select the default Links list. It's empty, so you'll need to add some entries to it after it has been imported to Access 2010.

9. Here for simplicity we just import one list, although because these are check boxes, it would be possible to import several lists. Select the new Links list I suggested you create at the start of this section. Click in the Link box for Computer-CompanyLinksList and then click OK.

10. Double-click the item ComputerCompanyLinksList listed under Table1. You see Figure 18.6.

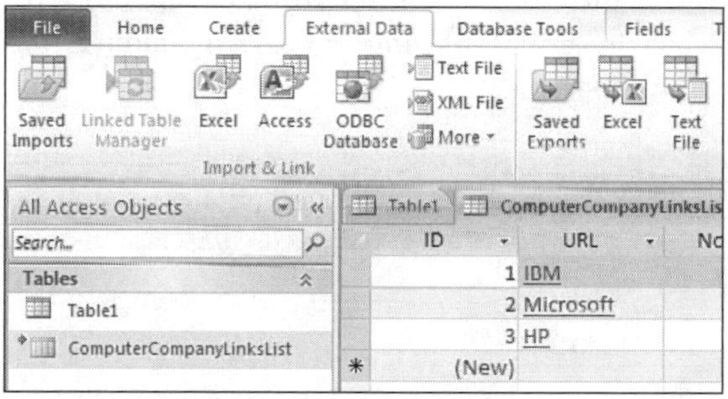

FIGURE 18.6
A new Access 2010 table from SharePoint

By the
Way

This illustrates why the Links list is not a list type that is suitable for maintenance that will only be done in Access 2010. A more normal type of List would have two columns, one for URL and one for the Description, and we would maintain it in Access 2010. Here we have only one URL column with dual functions, so to correctly specify each row, we would need to go to the List in SPF 2010 and amend each added row individually with Edit so both a URL and a description could be specified.

Let's see what happens to it if we add a value to this table. Because the table has now been created in Access 2010, we can start a new set of actions by following these steps:

1. Click the square under HP.

2. Type in Oracle. You notice that Access 2010 automatically thinks the URL is http:/Oracle.

3. Type in **www.sun.com** in the next line. Access thinks this is the description.

In Access 2007, there was a Refresh List option. This is no longer needed because if you now go to your SharePoint site and open this Links list there, you see two additional entries (Figure 18.7).

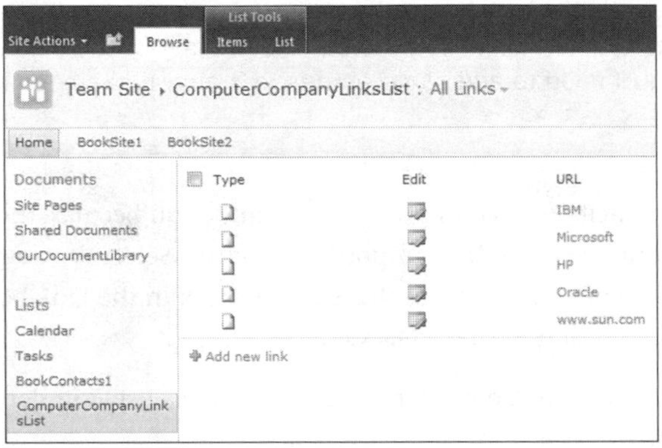

FIGURE 18.7
The revised
SharePoint List
with data from
the Access
2010 table

Clicking the Edit icon in the row that says the URL (description) is www.sun.com displays Figure 18.8 where the error that came because of adding a row in the Access 2010 copy of this list can be corrected.

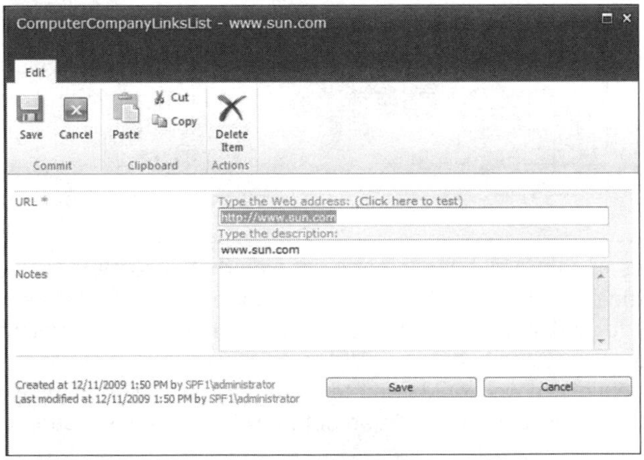

FIGURE 18.8
Correcting a
Links List item
added in Access
2010

By the Way

The snag with the Oracle item is that (as shown in Figure 18.7) it looked completely okay and not in need of any change. So if you add a link to a Links list when in Access 2010, always do that by entering the correct URL rather than the correct description. As we saw in Figure 18.7, it was clear when in SharePoint that the description of www.sun.com needed fixing—with "Oracle" it was not so clear.

Change the description in Figure 18.8 to **Sun**; repeat for the Oracle item (there you change the URL field), and all is well.

Scenario 2: Importing a SharePoint List to Become an Access 2010 Table (One-Off)

To do this, you need to initially follow the steps from the previous section. Here are those same steps in short form referring to the previous diagrams:

1. Open Access 2010; use the Blank Database option (Figure 18.1).

2. Find the entry box for the database name and change the name to **BookDatabase2.accdb**. Click Create. (Figure 18.2, apart from the name of the database, is identical to what you see here.)

3. Select External Data.

4. Access the drop-down by selecting More in the Import Section (Figure 18.3).

5. Click SharePoint List (Figure 18.4).

6. Change the name of the site address so that it actually is a SharePoint site. Here that means changing the name to **http://SPF 1** or, depending on your working environment, to the TCP/IP address. From now on things will be different.

7. This time do not accept the default value but select instead the alternative of Import the Source Data into a New Table in the Current Database.

After a possible interim request to log in to the site (if you work through this entire hour in one session, you might not need to), you again see Figure 18.5. This time select a different list—say BookContacts1—and click OK.

One different thing that happens compared to the first scenario is that this time there is the opportunity to save these steps so that they can be repeated (see Figure 18.9).

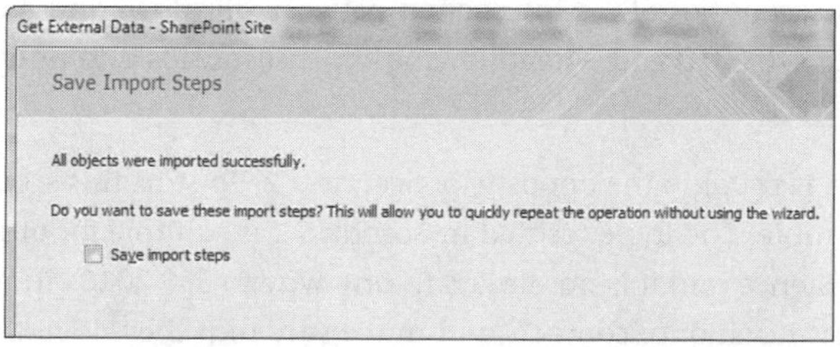

FIGURE 18.9
Save Import Steps

At first, you may wonder why this scenario has this step but the first scenario doesn't. A moment's reflection gives the answer.

The first scenario establishes a permanent link between the SharePoint list and the Access 2010 table. There is thus no need to repeat the action.

This second scenario is a once-only copy of a List from SharePoint to Access 2010.

If we, for instance, want to create a report from a List (see Hour 19), we might want this report irregularly; in such a case there would be no good reason for having a permanent link between the List and an Access 2010 table. So we would copy the list across, use it (in Access 2010) to create the report, and then delete the Access 2010 table. In a few months' time we might want a new report using new data, so we would then copy the list to Access 2010 again. The import steps are not many, but not needing to do them again after saving them with Figure 18.9 can cut down on the time this would take.

By the Way

> This sounds logical, but you still need to create the report in the second scenario. If you have a linked table, you can create the report once, save it, and reuse it again, and it always uses the latest data. My tip therefore is to use this transfer method only for genuine one-off actions.

The database and table combination created as a result of following the preceding instructions differs from Figure 18.6 in two respects:

- ▶ It contains the contents of a different List.

- ▶ Although you can add new items to the table (and edit or delete), these changes will never be visible in the original List.

Scenario 3: Exporting an Access 2010 Table to Become a SharePoint List (One-Off)

The previous two scenarios of the interaction between SPF 2010 and Access 2010 both originated at the SPF 2010 end. The following three scenarios originate at the Access 2010 end.

The first of them is roughly the opposite of Scenario 2. To start this scenario we need an Access 2010 table. The table created in Scenario 2 is suitable for our use because it is already in existence and it is not linked in any way to SPF 2010. To make quite sure of that, add a few additional contacts and make sure that they do not appear in the equivalent List in SPF1. They don't, so we can use this completely separate table (see Figure 18.10).

Do the following steps:

1. Select External Data.

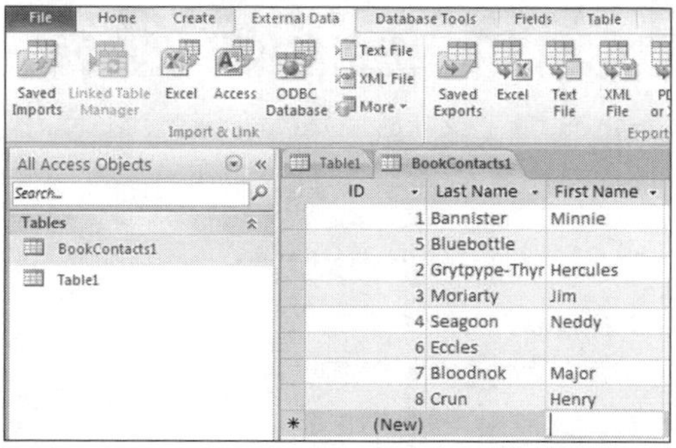

FIGURE 18.10
The new Access 2010 only Book-Contacts1 Table

2. In the Export Section, select More.

3. In the More drop-down, select SharePoint List. This displays the Export screen (see Figure 18.11).

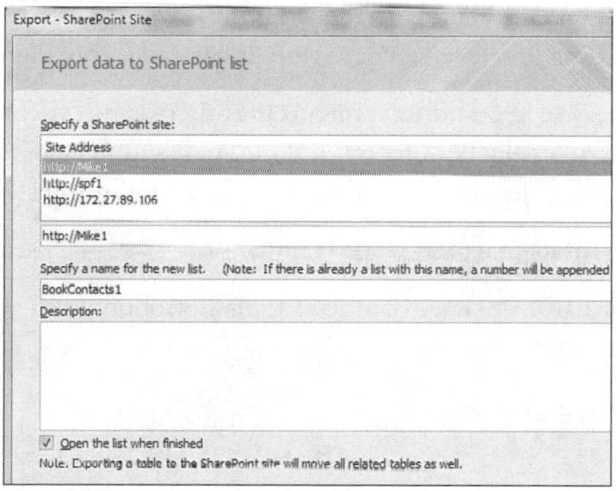

FIGURE 18.11
Export data to SharePoint list

4. Change the Site address if necessary (here to **http://172.27.89.106**).

5. Change the name of the List to **exAccessBookContacts1**.

6. Leave Open the List When Finished selected.

7. Click OK.

The Team Site opens, and there's a new List (see Figure 18.12).

There is no link to this new list in the Lists section. If you want to fix this, click List > List Settings > Title Description and Navigation and select the radio button Yes in the Display This List on the Quick Launch section of the page.

By the Way

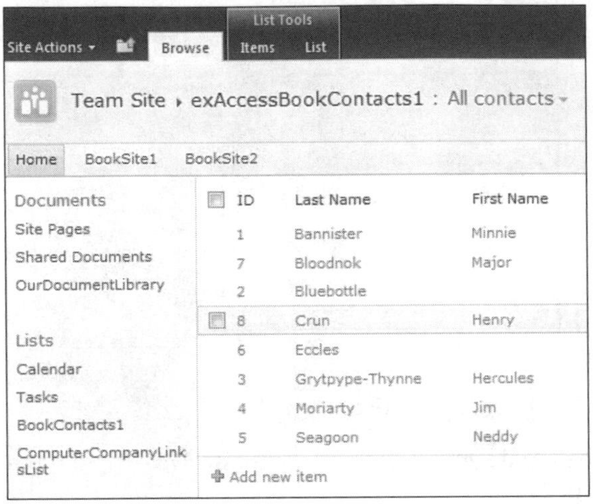

FIGURE 18.12
The newly transferred List

Following the creation of the site, a screen similar to that shown in Figure 18.9 appears; only this time the screen is for saving Export steps (just close it).

Logic says that this, like in Scenario 2, means that there is no synchronization between the List exAccessBookContacts1 and the Access table BookContacts1, but let's do a couple of brief tests just to make sure. Perform the following steps:

1. Add a new contact in exAccessBookContacts1.

2. Go to Access 2010. The BookContacts1 table is probably still open and looks like Figure 18.13.

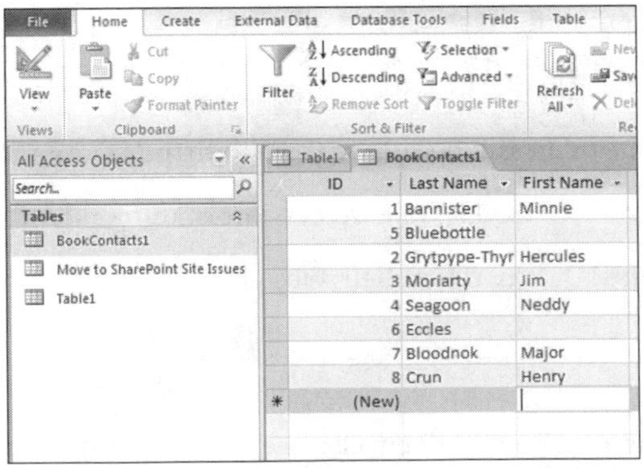

FIGURE 18.13
The revised (in Access 2010) table

3. Try Refresh All (Figure 18.13). Nothing happens.

4. Try closing the database, opening it again, and then selecting BookContacts1. Still no change.

So we have now satisfied ourselves that this third scenario means that there is a once-only SharePoint list copy of an Access 2010 table that is created when using Share-Point List from the More drop-down in the External section of the External Data menu item. We need to look elsewhere for a linked (and synchronized) list.

Scenario 4: Starting with an Access 2010 Table and Creating a Linked Copy as a SharePoint List

This is the second scenario starting at the Access 2010 end. It's roughly the opposite of Scenario 1; that is, after this scenario is complete, there will be synchronization between an Access 2001 table and a SharePoint list.

To start this scenario, we again need an Access 2010 table. The table created in Scenario 2 is still suitable for our use because it is already in existence, and it is still not linked in any way to SPF 2010, despite copying it to become a SharePoint list in the Scenario 3.

In Scenario 3, we added a few additional contacts, so Figure 18.10 (or Figure 18.13) that includes those extra contacts is our starting point here again.

Here are the steps to accomplish this:

1. Open the latest database in Access 2010. (It might still be open if you haven't taken a break.)

2. Click the menu item Database Tools. (Not exactly obvious is it?)

3. There's a SharePoint icon in the move section; look at the following By the Way (and Figure 18.14) and then move on to step 4.

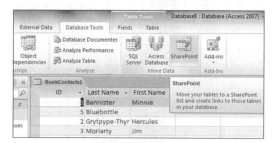

FIGURE 18.14
A clear (?) information box

> If you wonder why this is in the Move section when we want to create a Share-Point list that is also linked to an Access 2010 table that we are expecting to stay

By the Way

in Access, select the SharePoint icon before clicking it. This displays a small information box that will confuse you even more (see Figure 18.14) because it says Move Your Tables but still includes Create Links.

There is no alternative. We'll have to continue the steps and see what the end result is.

4. Click SharePoint.

You now see the usual kind of request to specify the site where the List should be created. Figure 18.15 also gives us some information that to a certain extent clears up the confusion.

FIGURE 18.15
Move your data

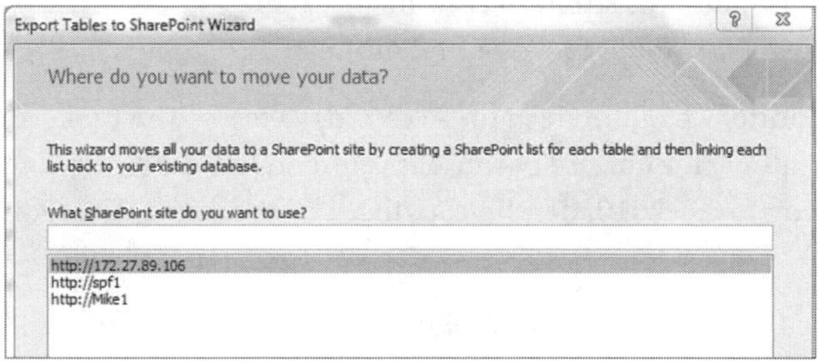

Export Tables to SharePoint Wizard

Where do you want to move your data?

This wizard moves all your data to a SharePoint site by creating a SharePoint list for each table and then linking each list back to your existing database.

What SharePoint site do you want to use?

http://172.27.89.106
http://spf1
http://Mike1

What is moved is only the data not the database table itself. (However, does this mean the database will be empty at the end of the process?)

Did you Know?

Don't be worried if your site can't be found. You might want to go into your browser and access the site using the same TCP/IP address to wake it up. Then try Next again. If you get the box asking for Windows authorization, you will be okay. If not wake up the server a bit more!

5. Enter the site you want to use.

(I'm going to use http://192.168.1.2 here because I've switched networks between Scenarios 3 and 4.)

6. Click Next.

The next screen is just a confirmation screen enabling you to click Finish to, well, finish, but it also contains a check button for Show Details. You might as well select this because all that happens is that a text appears in the same Finish screen (see Figure 18.16).

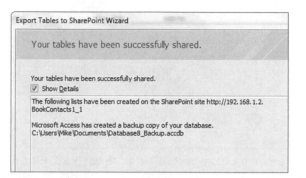

FIGURE 18.16
Export Tables
Details

7. Click Finish.

At the end of this process, you are still in Access 2010, and you can double-click Book-Contacts1 to see that indeed no Data has been lost. It might have been Copied to a SharePoint List, but it hasn't been moved.

The next step is to check the SharePoint site to see if there is a new List that has been created there. One thing that was different in this scenario was that we were not asked for the name of a List. So either data has been added to the List of the same name, or we see two Lists with the same name.

Take a minute away from the computer and try to work out which of the preceding two alternatives apply (and if it's the second one, how to tell the Lists apart).

Did you Know?

There's a new set of steps to follow (now in the browser):

1. Open or refresh the site (at the home page).

What you'll see is a list of Lists in the Quick Launch section that includes only one List called BookContacts1. This doesn't fool us into thinking that this means there is only one list with that name because previously in this hour, we saw that you can have Lists created that are not listed in Quick Launch without some manual action on our part.

2. Click All Site Content (below the Quick Launch area).

Scroll down the page, and you'll see something like Figure 18.17.

There is another way to tell the difference. BookContacts1 is the original list created and updated in Scenario 1. It should therefore contain five names. BookContacts1_1 is a copy of the table revised in Access 2010 by adding two

By the Way

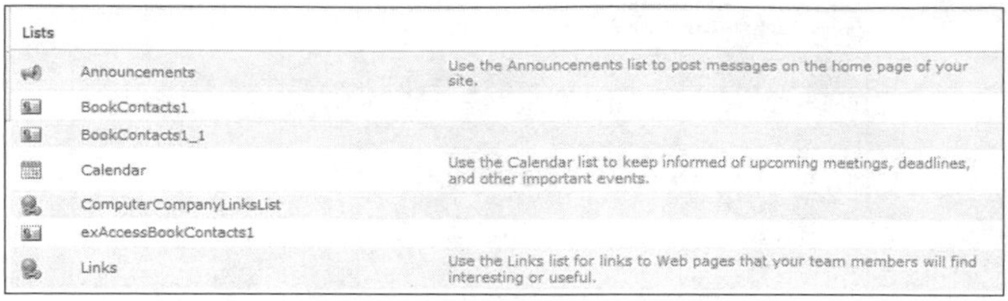

FIGURE 18.17
An extract from
All Site Content

Lists		
🔲 Announcements		Use the Announcements list to post messages on the home page of your site.
🔲 BookContacts1		
🔲 BookContacts1_1		
🔲 Calendar		Use the Calendar list to keep informed of upcoming meetings, deadlines, and other important events.
🔲 ComputerCompanyLinksList		
🔲 exAccessBookContacts1		
🔲 Links		Use the Links list for links to Web pages that your team members will find interesting or useful.

> more names. It should therefore contain eight names (5 + 2 + the one we added in step 1 before Figure 18.13). Check them both by clicking the listing in Lists. (Did I really write that?!)

So that solves both questions. There are two lists, and the way to tell them apart is that the new List created in this scenario has _1 at the end of the name.

Scenario 5: Creating a SharePoint List While in Access 2010

The final thing you can do with SharePoint when in Access 2010 is to create a SharePoint List. For completion, I'll cover this method by giving a brief guideline to it although, in my opinion, people who don't create SharePoint lists in SharePoint are odd.

The steps in brief (and with no images) are the following:

1. (In Access 2010) Click Create in the Menu line.

2. Click the SharePoint List icon; there is a choice of the List types (not all) that can be created.

3. Select Events.

4. On the next screen, specify the address of the SharePoint site and give the list a Name (compulsory—without a name OK is not accessible) such as **EventsfromAccess**.

5. Click OK.

   At this point, we are still in Access 2010 where there is an EventsfromAccess table. So we need to go to the site again.

6. Access the site.

7. Click All Site Content. EventsfromAccess is listed in the Lists section.

8. Click EventsfromAccess. An empty calendar appears.

9. Specify an event over several days.

10. Click OK.

The calendar now shows the new Event.

Now to see if this new List is linked to the Database table we also created with the first few steps:

11. Open Access again.

12. Select the EventsfromAccess table.

13. Right-click.

14. Click More Options (see Figure 18.18).

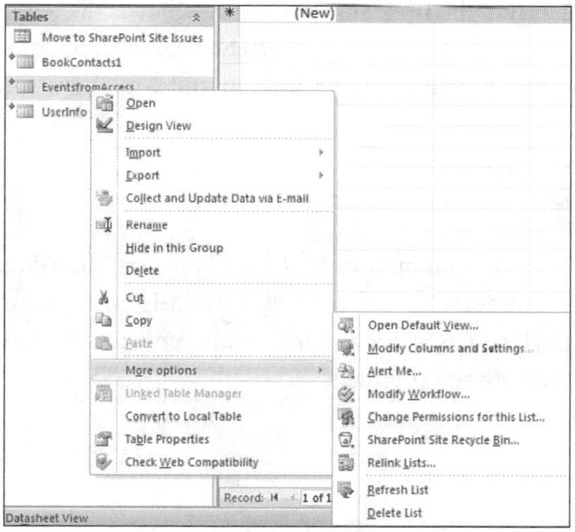

FIGURE 18.18
DB table right-click plus More options

15. Ignore the small pop-up asking for parameter values by pressing OK.

I still don't like the idea of creating a SharePoint list in Access 2010, but there is one advantage to doing so, provided you can accept the restrictive list of List types you can choose. The advantage is that, with one action, you both create an Access 2010 table *and* a SharePoint 2010 List and also link the two.

Finally, what about the final option in the list of List types you can choose? Existing SharePoint List.

This is actually nothing new. All that happens is that you get the same next screen that you also get when following Scenarios 1 and 2 via External Data > More > SharePoint List (refer to Figure 18.4).

The Differences Between Using Access 2010 with SPF 2010 and Using Access 2007 or Access 2003

The options when using Access 2007 are similar to those when using Access 2010. Access 2007 also had the ribbon, and the SharePoint icons were in equally odd locations and had equally confusing "helpful" pop-ups.

The five scenarios that were dealt with in detail in the Access 2010 + SPF 2010 section are also available in Access 2007. The major difference is that Scenario 4 when using Access 2010 includes the synchronization of data, whereas the equivalent scenario in Access 2007 synchronizes only heading name changes but not data changes. Access 2003 does not have any functionality for linking tables to SharePoint.

Summary

In this hour, we looked at both options for creating Access 2010 databases from SPF 2010 and at all three options for creating SPF 2010 Lists from Access 2010. We also looked closely at in which cases the resultant tables or lists were linked and could thus be synchronized between products.

Q&A

Q. *Why did you spend a whole hour on connecting Access 2010 and SPF 2010?*

A. You need to know how to do this to create quality reports from SharePoint Lists (refer to Hours 19 and 20). The creation options in both products are rather confusing and difficult to find, so it is important to know when to use a method that links the two products and when to use a one-off transfer solution.

The names of the icons and screens and even the supposedly helpful explanatory texts provided by both products (use of the word Move, for example, when Copy is all that takes place) means that a detailed guide is necessary.

Q. *If I already have an Access table, why would I want to have a copy of it in SharePoint?*

A. You do it so that your data is stored in a server and accessible from different locations via a browser. The users of the data don't need a copy of Access 2010 installed on their PC, which would otherwise be necessary.

Using a synchronized list would usually make the most sense, but a nonsynchronized SharePoint list would be a better alternative if the intention were to provide, for instance, monthly summary information.

Workshop

Quiz

1. What is the reason (in one word) why it is good to have a synchronized copy of a SharePoint list stored as a table in Access 2010?

2. Why could the creation of a SharePoint List while in Access 2010 not be a good idea?

3. Why could the creation of a SharePoint List while in Access 2010 be a good idea?

Answers

1. Reporting. This is covered in detail in the next hour.

2. Because there is a limited number of List types that can be chosen.

3. Because in one set of actions you create an Access 2010 table and a SharePoint List and also link them.

Producing a Report from a Single SPF 2010 List

There is a clear difference in the techniques that should be used when producing a report using Access 2010 from a single list and producing a report from two or more lists. This hour shows how to best create a report from a single list. The following hour shows how to best create a report from two (or more) lists.

Alternative Approaches to Creating a Report from a SharePoint List

We now discuss the alternative approaches to creating a report from a SharePoint list.

Creating a Report of a View While in SPF 2010

SharePoint Lists are designed to be viewed on a screen. Most views of SharePoint Lists have restrictions in the number of items that you can view on a single (screen) page.

Printing from SharePoint Lists that use standard views is therefore unsatisfactory. It is however possible to create a view that is more suitable for printing.

Here are the main points that need to be considered:

▶ Ensure that the width of the view is not wider than can fit onto a page.

▶ Given that when you create SharePoint Views you aren't allowed to specify the width of fields when they display, the only easy way to control this is to reduce the number of fields to the minimum. (More controlled but more difficult is to use SPD 2010 to edit the source code of the View page.)

▶ Change the default value for the number of lines to be shown on a page.

This is done by amending the value in the Item Limit parameter when specifying the View you want to use for printing.

The paging function in the operating system ensures that there is a page feed when one is needed by using a large number that is more than the number of items in the list; only the printing function controls page breaks.

▶ Make clear in the name of the view that this view is intended for printing only.

This is essential to make sure that users don't select this view by mistake and then wonder why it takes a long time for the page to appear on the screen (and why it is so long and doesn't contain many columns). The simplest methods are the best here. Just call the view something like **Only for Printing**.

By the Way

> The lists produced by this quick and dirty method are not suitable for handing over to managers.

This method works, but the printouts produced by it are only suitable for a SharePoint administrator to make a quick check of the data contained in a List (offline) or for handing to people who understand the ad hoc nature of the list. The main reason is that managers like to manage and will request a (in their words) "small" amendment to the list before they accept it. There is no straightforward way with this kind of list to make such "small" amendments, whether they are the addition of more fields or different headings or anything else.

The other restriction with this kind of report is that it is only possible within SharePoint to create a report from a single list. If we want to create a report that uses information from different lists, we would need to create a single list that used such techniques as Lookup fields to make data from a second list appear in the single list. Doing this just to create a poor quality report doesn't make much sense.

The following section is an overview only.

Creating a Report of a SPF 2010 List Using SQL Server Reporting Services

Using Reporting Services is perhaps the most powerful way of creating reports from SharePoint Lists, although the reports will not look any better than those produced from Access 2010.

Both SQL Server 2005 Reporting Services and SQL Server 2008 Reporting Services can be used with SharePoint systems. Setting up either application to work with Share-Point sites is complicated and is beyond the scope of this book.

By the Way

Another reason for it being beyond the scope of this book is that the Reporting Services function is only available with the full SQL Server 2005 and SQL Server 2008 products. Users of the free (in itself) SharePoint Foundation 2010 product very often—as we do here—use the free included database system and thus don't have access to a full SQL Server product.

Using either Reporting Services application is a several stage process, which is out-lined here:

1. Install Reporting Services.

2. Adjust the installation so that it can connect with a SharePoint system.

3. Create reports.

There is a need for expertise in all three areas.

Normal Reporting Services books cover items 1 and 3 of the preceding list only, so the choice is to either buy a Reporting Services book for the version (2005 or 2008) that you are using and find (on the Internet) guides for item 2 of the previous list, or to find a book that deals specifically with using Reporting Services with SharePoint. At the moment of writing, there is a single book like this that covers MOSS 2007 and SQL Server 2008 Reporting Services. Reading it can help you with SPF 2010 and SQL Server 2008 Reporting Services but no more than that.

By the Way

It is worth checking. (Try searching Amazon U.S. or my own SP 2010 Books web page at http://wssv4faq.mindsharp.com/Lists/v4FAQ/V%20Books.aspx to see if an SP 2010 version of that book has been released. SQL Server 2008 is still the current version of SQL Server and that which is most commonly likely to be used with SharePoint 2010 systems.

The following solution (using Access 2010) is both easier to set up and produces equally good-looking reports. It does however require that users have Access 2010 on their clients. This is something that you can avoid with a solution that uses Reporting Services. A Reporting Services solution is thus more scalable and more suitable for the kind of large companies that have the manpower needed to support it.

The rest of us, including the readers of this book, will find the two (single list and multiple list) solutions for reports using Access 2010 covered in this and the next hour to be perfectly good solutions for their needs.

Using Access (2010 and 2007) to Create Reports from SharePoint Lists

The third main way of creating reports from SharePoint lists is to use Access.

Both Access 2010 and Access 2007 can be used. When creating reports from a single SPF 2010 list (covered in the next main section of this hour), there is little difference between the ways the two versions work.

This book's main focus in the section of this book on combining Office products with SPF 2010 is on the use of Office 2010, so that is what will be used for the text and for screen prints that follow both in this hour and the next one (on creating reports from multiple lists). At the end of both hours there will be a short note about the differences when using Access 2007.

> Microsoft, having created a quality reporting function in Access 2007, decided that should be used for reports on SharePoint Lists. Knowing that many users were already using Excel 2003 to create such reports (and would continue to do so), Microsoft dropped the support for it in Excel 2007 (and didn't reinstate it in Excel 2010). This is one of the rare cases where an older version of a Microsoft product has more functionality than a later version or at least as in this case has some functionality removed and different functionality added.

Using Excel to Create Reports from SharePoint Lists

It is not that possible to use Excel 2007 or Excel 2010 to create reports from SharePoint lists.

It is, however, possible to do this with Excel 2003.

The only way to use Excel 2010 (and Excel 2007) for report creation from SharePoint lists would be to open a list in Datasheet View and copy across cells. Such a bulk copy of cells works only for certain—the simplest—kind of cells, so in most cases would mean that data would be lost before it arrives in Excel for tidying up and making a reasonably looking report.

I won't go into this any more in this book because the alternative of using Access 2010 (or 2007) that follows is so much better.

Creating a Simple Report from a Single SPF 2010 List

After going briefly through the alternatives, we have now reached the main topic of this hour: how to create a report from a single list.

To create a report from a list, we first need a suitable list with data so here–as we've already done this earlier in the book–is just a quick run-through of what I did to create the list that I used for the report creation here.

I've created a new site called BookSite3, using the Blank Site site template using the standard technique that you have already used (Site Actions > New Site > Specify Blank Site template).

In that site, I created (Site Actions + More Options) a new List of type Custom List, called it CompanyStaffNumbers, and then added (List Settings) four columns to it (Company; Location; Purpose; Number Of Staff). Then I made the Title field not required (and removed it from the All Items view) and removed Attachments from the List. Then I added several records to display Figure 19.1.

Company	Location	Purpose	Number of Staff
HP	Boston	Marketing	20
HP	Boston	Sales	50
HP	New York	Marketing	50
HP	New York	Production	400
HP	New York	Sales	60
IBM	Boston	Sales	30
IBM	Los Angeles	Sales	20
IBM	Seattle	Research	100
Oracle	Boston	Research	100
Oracle	Los Angeles	Production	800

FIGURE 19.1
The Company-StaffNumbers List with some records

> You can use either Single Line text or Choice (but allow the use of new texts that aren't in the list of preselected choices) for the first three columns and Number (with decimals=0) for the final column.

Did you Know?

The next step is to create an Access 2010 table from an SPF 2010 List using the technique described in Hour 18, "Sharing Access 2010 Tables with SPF 2010," "Scenario 1: Creating a Linked Access 2010 Table from a SharePoint List" section that starts from Figure 18.1. Call this database **BookDatabase19**.

At the end of this process, you should see something like Figure 19.2.

> When asked where the site is located that contains the list, remember that it is in BookSite3. In the following screen select the CompanyStaffNumbers List.

By the Way

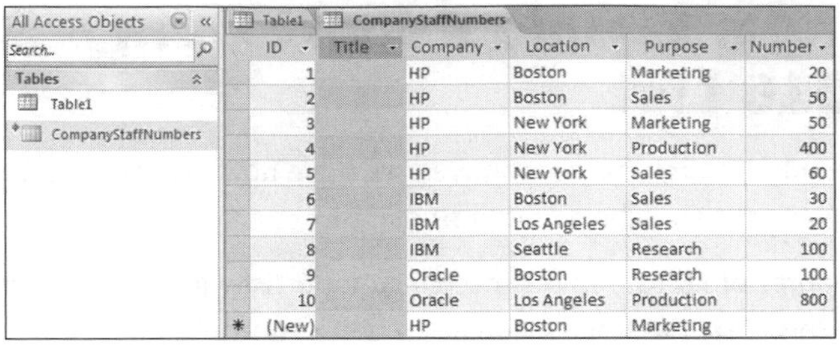

ID	Title	Company	Location	Purpose	Number
1		HP	Boston	Marketing	20
2		HP	Boston	Sales	50
3		HP	New York	Marketing	50
4		HP	New York	Production	400
5		HP	New York	Sales	60
6		IBM	Boston	Sales	30
7		IBM	Los Angeles	Sales	20
8		IBM	Seattle	Research	100
9		Oracle	Boston	Research	100
10		Oracle	Los Angeles	Production	800
(New)		HP	Boston	Marketing	

FIGURE 19.2 The Company StaffNumbers List as an Access 2010 Table

Note: Here are a few comments on what you see in Figure 19.2:

- The Title column was not deleted when the list was created. It was just marked as not required and removed from the View. Here in the database it is listed because it is a column in the List even though it has no content.
- The Company, Location, and Purpose fields were marked as required, and each had defaults (HP/Boston/Marketing, respectively). The field marked New (which doesn't exist) thus shows those default values rather than the more common spaces. They can be changed (by drop-down) when a new row is added in the table.
- Some columns have been reduced in width to make Figure 19.2 fit better on the page. The All Access Objects column has also been reduced in width slightly for the same reason.

Now that we have an SPF 2010 List in Access 2010, we can use the Access 2010 Report functions.

To create simple reports from single lists, use the Reports Wizard by following these steps:

1. Click Create in the Menu line. Figure 19.3 is an extract from the ribbon items for Create.

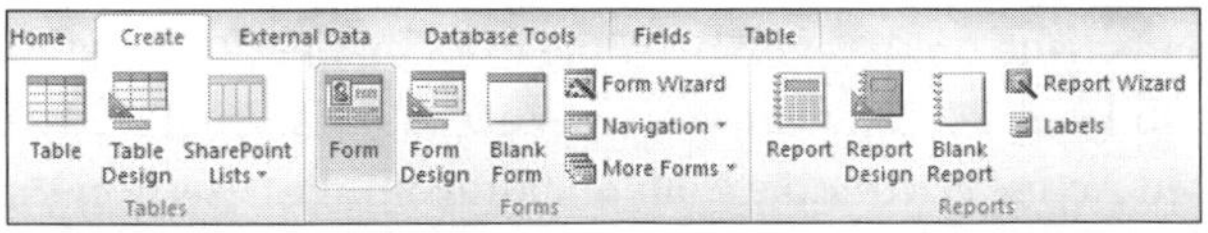

FIGURE 19.3 Part of the Create ribbon

2. Click Report Wizard.

   You may see the following Security Warning (Figure 19.4). If so just ignore it, and move on with Open.

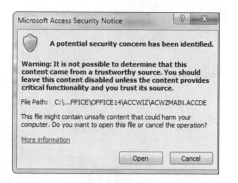

FIGURE 19.4
An Access
security warning

The Report Wizard then shows a list of Available Fields.

3. Move the Company, Purpose, Location, and Number of Staff fields from left to right to display Figure 19.5.

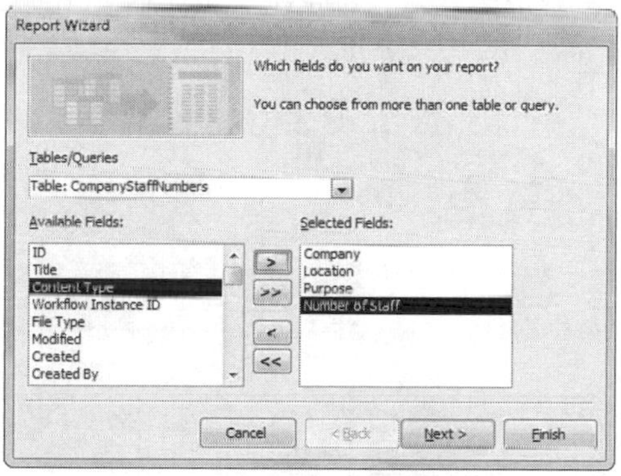

FIGURE 19.5
Selecting the
fields for the
report

4. Click Next.

Now we need to configure group levels. For this report, let's group on Company and Purpose. The basic technique used is to click the name of the field in the left column and then to click the right arrow in the center of the screen to move the field to the right column. The result, after specifying Company and Purpose groups in this way, is shown in Figure 19.6.

5. Click Next.

Now we can decide on the fields to be sorted at the detail level. Here we have two fields remaining (because we are already grouping on the other two), so it's logical to sort on the Location field (see Figure 19.7).

6. Click Summary Options.

In Figure 19.8, I have specified Sum and that the percent of the Total should be calculated for sums.

FIGURE 19.6
Grouping for a
Report

FIGURE 19.7
Specifying the
sort order

FIGURE 19.8
Specifying sum-
mary values

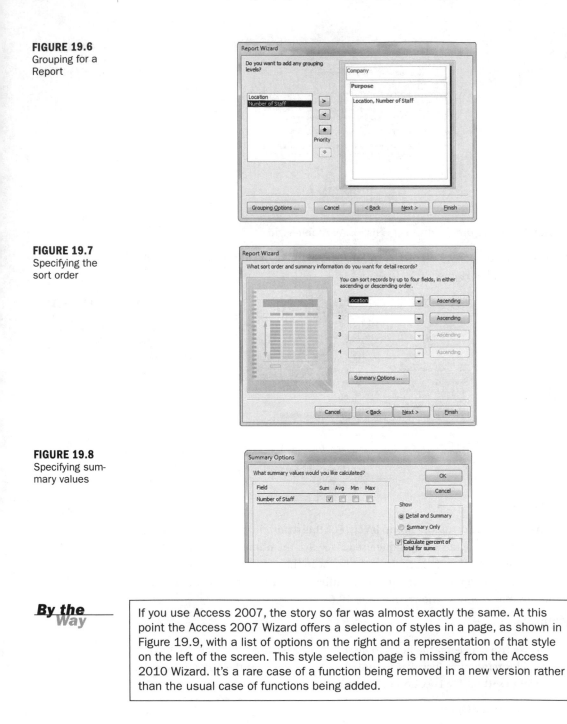

By the Way

If you use Access 2007, the story so far was almost exactly the same. At this
point the Access 2007 Wizard offers a selection of styles in a page, as shown in
Figure 19.9, with a list of options on the right and a representation of that style
on the left of the screen. This style selection page is missing from the Access
2010 Wizard. It's a rare case of a function being removed in a new version rather
than the usual case of functions being added.

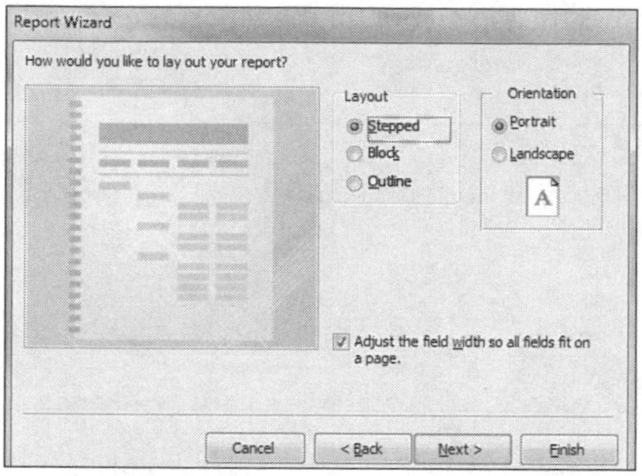

FIGURE 19.9
Selecting the
Layout Type

7. Click OK, as shown in Figure 19.8.

8. Click Next, as shown in Figure 19.7.

   The next page (Figure 19.9) lets you choose the layout from three options. The left of the page gives you a feeling for what a report using the selected layout may look like. I'm going to use the default here, Stepped, which is probably the most commonly used.

9. Click Next.

   Figure 19.10 enables us to change the name of the report, so we can just add a couple of spaces in the default name (=table name) to call it **Company Staff Numbers**.

   This screen also offers the choice of Previewing the report or Modifying it. We haven't yet seen what the report looks like, so Previewing is the best option here. That's the default value, too, so complete the process with step 10.

10. Click Finish.

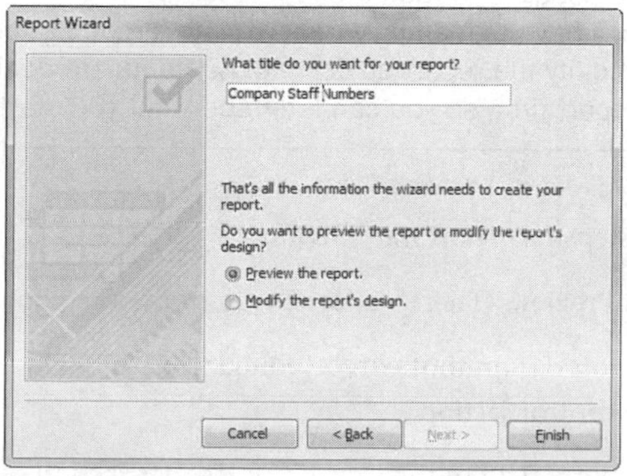

FIGURE 19.10
Changing the title
of the Report

Figure 19.11 shows the top section of the report the wizard has created.

Company Staff Numbers			
Company Purpose Location			
HP			
Marketi			
	Boston	Number of Staff	20
	New York	Number of Staff	50
	Summary for 'Purpose' = Marketing (2 detail records)		
	Sum		70
	Standard		4,29%
Producti			
	New York	Number of Staff	400

Study the whole report to see if it is good enough to present to the boss.

Several things need changing from the entire report:

▶ The company name should stand out more. Let's make it bold and underlined.

▶ No boss will be happy with "Marketi" or "Producti" in a report. We need to make the field wider. Because we have short company names, we don't need to widen the Company field this time.

▶ Including the % figure wasn't such a great idea after all because it is not a percentage within a company but a percentage of the whole list. It's more confusing than helpful, so let's get rid of this row entirely.

▶ The entire summary section at the bottom of each page is pointless. Let's get rid of a page bottom section.

> Although it would be possible to redo the report to get rid of the fourth item in the preceding list, we still have to manually deal with all the other items, so the best method here is to modify the report so that all the items are dealt with in one go. (Print the present report first, so you can later see what you started with).

There's a new set of steps for report modification:

1. Close the Print Preview. (There's a large icon at the far right of the ribbon.)

   This gives a report design that can be edited in detail. (Figure 19.12 shows the top part of the central section.)

2. Select the Company field in the Company Header section.

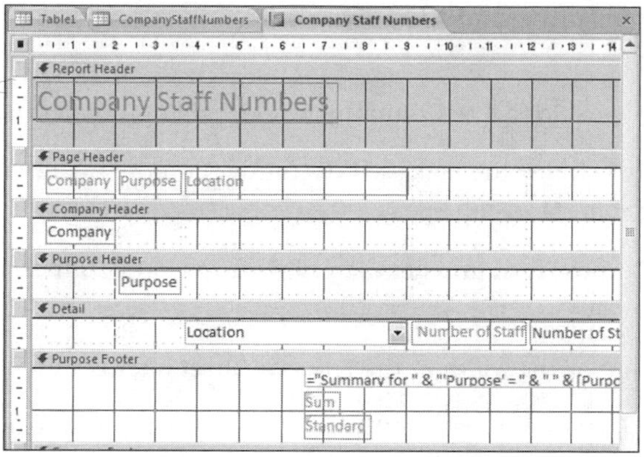
Table1
CompanyStaffNumbers
Company Staff Numbers
Report Header
Company Staff Numbers
Page Header
Company
Purpose
Location
Company Header
Company
Purpose Header
Purpose
Detail
Location
Number of Staff
Number of St
Purpose Footer
="Summary for " & "'Purpose' = " & " " & [Purpc
Sum
Standard

FIGURE 19.12
The central section of the Report Design page

When this has been done correctly, a yellow frame displays around Company and the Property Sheet on the right of the screen changes and is now full of information about the Company field (see Figure 19.13).

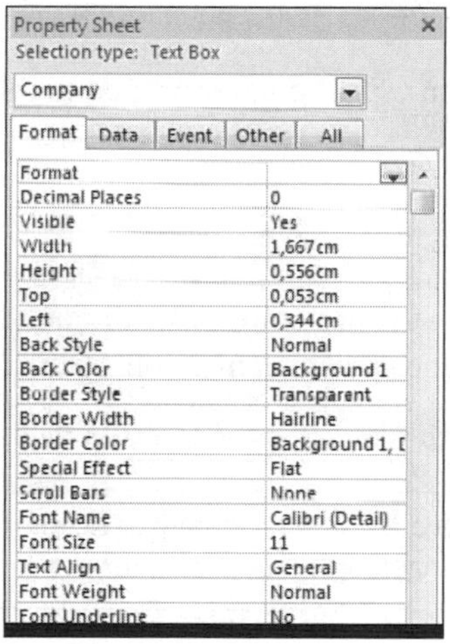
Property Sheet
Selection type: Text Box
Company
Format
Data
Event
Other
All
Format
Decimal Places 0
Visible Yes
Width 1,667cm
Height 0,556cm
Top 0,053cm
Left 0,344cm
Back Style Normal
Back Color Background 1
Border Style Transparent
Border Width Hairline
Border Color Background 1, [
Special Effect Flat
Scroll Bars None
Font Name Calibri (Detail)
Font Size 11
Text Align General
Font Weight Normal
Font Underline No

FIGURE 19.13
The Property Sheet for the Company field

> If you do not see a Property Sheet, right-click the Company field and select Properties.

By the Way

To specify bold and underline, in the Property Sheet we need to amend the values for the Font Weight and Font Underline fields.

3. Click Normal in the Font Weight line. A downward-facing arrow is visible.
4. Click the down arrow and select Bold.
5. Click No in the Font Underline line. A down arrow is visible.

6. Click the down arrow and select Yes.

This completes the first task. The Company is now bold and underlined in the report.

The second task is to widen the Purpose field (under Purpose Header) so that we see Marketing rather than Marketi:

1. Select the Purpose field and get the yellow frame around it as before with Company.

We could change the width in the Property Sheet but instead follow step 2.

2. Move the cursor on the right vertical side of the yellow frame until you see a double direction arrow symbol.

3. Without losing contact with the mouse, drag the box to the right as far as you think is necessary.

You'll notice when you do this that this action moves the header line to the right, this line to the right, and also the detail line to the right.

4. Stop the drag operation when you are satisfied the width is now suitable by letting go of the mouse.

This completes the second task.

The third task was to remove the percentage calculation. This has two parts: the word standard and a formula that can be seen by scrolling the central section to the right.

1. Select the two fields (standard and the formula field in the same row).

Did you Know?
> You can either select the two fields individually or select them both at once by clicking the left column alongside this part of the page.

2. Right-click the Standard field and select Delete.

Now the text and values are gone, but there is empty space where they were. Remove the empty space with steps 3 and 4.

3. Select the Company Footer section heading.

4. Move the cursor close to the top of that section until you get an icon with a downward-pointing arrow, a smaller upward-pointing arrow connected to it, and a horizontal line between the two. When you have this, drag the top of the Company footer section heading upward. This reclaims the space that is no longer used. This completes the third task.

The fourth task is to remove the entire Page Footer section. Here we leave it in case we change our minds but make it invisible:

1. Select the heading of the Page Footer section.

2. In the Property Sheet change (Format) Visible to No.

3. Select both formulae in this section by clicking the left border of that line; here too change the Property sheet so that Visible equals No. This completes the fourth task.

To completely get rid of the percentage calculations, these two fields also need to be removed from the Company Footer section, and if it seems appropriate, also regain the space that is no longer being used.

By the Way

Now we need to check the result by following these steps:

1. Select View at the far-left part of the ribbon.

2. Select Print Preview from the drop-down (see Figure 19.14).

Company Staff Numbers			
Company Purpose	Location		
HP			
Marketing			
	Boston	Number of Staff	20
	New York	Number of Staff	50
	Summary for 'Purpose' = Marketing (2 detail records)		
	Sum		70
Production			
	New York	Number of Staff	400

FIGURE 19.14
A revised report

It is wise to always add at least one item to a List that is linked to Access 2010 when viewing the table equivalent of the list in Access 2010. The reason for this is that until you do so none of the data in the list will be accessible to you in Access 2010 if contact between the client system running Access 2010 and the server containing the original SharePoint list is broken. So creating or amending reports on that list (or on several lists, one of which is that list) without a working network connection would not be possible.

Did you Know?

A quick check shows that all our aims have been achieved.

For a report of a single List, use the Report Wizard to create an almost correct report and then tidy it up by hand. Do not create a new report from scratch.

Did you Know?

The final thing to do is to add some more items to the original SPF 2010 list called CompanyStaffNumbers. Then reopen the Report we just created in Access 2010. The additions made in the SPF 2010 list will already be incorporated in the report that you now see.

Summary

In this hour, we first looked at several alternative methods of creating reports from SharePoint lists. We then created a table in Access 2010 that was linked to a list in one of our SPF 2010 sites and using that table created a report of the list. We showed that whenever changes are made to the list data, either in the list itself or in the table, the changes are reflected in any newly generated report.

Q&A

Q. *How do I remove a table in Access 2010 without also deleting the SharePoint list it is connected to?*

A. It's actually not a problem. In Access 2010, select the table linked to an SPF 2010 list and click Delete at the top of the page.

You'll see Figure 19.15.

FIGURE 19.15
A horrific warning

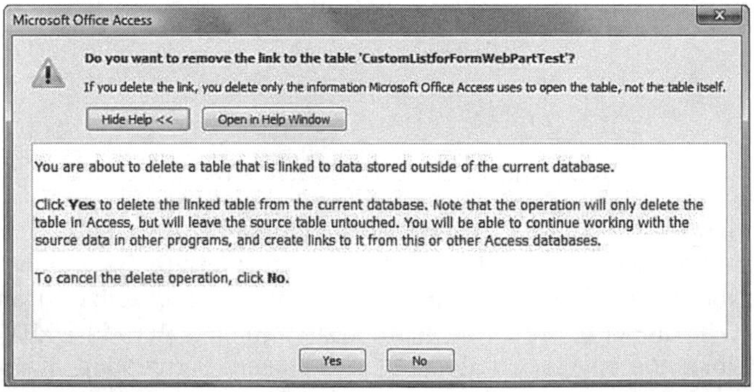

Despite appearances, this terrible looking warning is actually warning you that only the table will be deleted. Nothing else happens. The SharePoint list is preserved as before. It is just no longer linked to the Access 2010 table.

Q. *What do I lose when creating a report using Access 2007 rather than Access 2010?*

A. In the case of creating a report from a single SharePoint list that we did here in detail using Access 2010, the answer is nothing. In both cases a linked Access table is created from the list, and the Access Report Wizard is used to create a report following what essentially are the same steps. The only difference is that the Access 2007 Report Wizard enables you to specify the style of the report (see Figure 19.16), whereas this step isn't included in the Access 2010 Wizard.

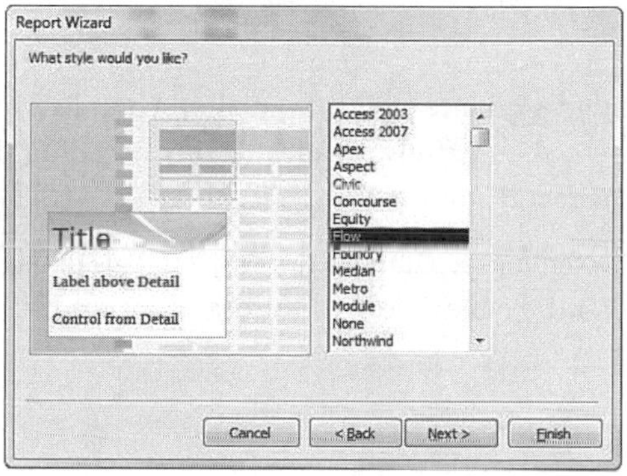

FIGURE 19.16
Access 2007
Report Wizard
offers Styles.

Q. *How does Access 2010 know what server to contact to synchronize the table with the list we started with?*

A. The address of the server is included in the properties of the tables in a database.

This is fine when using a network where the name of the server (SPF1 here) can be used to access the site throughout the network. It is not so fine when a TCP/IP address is used and when this changes—perhaps because the server is in a Virtual Machine in a portable that is sometimes connected to one network and sometimes to another.

> If you use TCP/IP addresses and are sometimes connected to one network and sometimes to another, see the "Q&A" section in the next hour where the solution is dealt with in detail.

Did you Know?

Workshop

Quiz

1. Why do we use Access 2010 to provide reports on SharePoint lists?

2. Give one reason why the details of using Reporting Services to create reports from SharePoint Lists aren't included in the book.

Answers

1. Access 2010 provides quality reports from SharePoint lists quickly. These reports when created automatically include any new data that has been added to a list since the report was run.

2. It is too complicated a procedure for the scope of this book. (It's also too expensive a solution for the typical users of the SPF 2010 product.)

HOUR 20

Creating a Report from Several Different SPF 2010 Lists

What You'll Learn in This Hour

▶ Introduction to creating a report from two or more SharePoint Lists

▶ Creating a two-lists/tables report with the assistance of the Report Wizard

▶ Creating a two-lists/tables report manually using Design View

▶ (Q&A) How to cope with an address change of the SharePoint site

After looking at creating a report from a single list in the previous hour, we now move on to creating a report from two lists. There are three main options: You can try (and fail) to create a report with a wizard; you can create a report with a wizard but only use fields from one list (and then add fields from the second list manually); or you can create a report entirely manually. The second and third options are covered in detail here.

Introduction to Creating a Report from Two or More SharePoint Lists

In this section, we create a report from two or more SharePoint lists.

Adding a Second List and Making It Available as a Table

In this hour, we create a report from two SharePoint lists that share a common field. To do this—for reasons explained in Hour 19, "Producing a Report from a Single SPF 2010 List,"—we use Access 2010.

We already have the CompanyStaffNumbers List stored as a table in BookDatabase19, so the initial task in this section is to first create a second SharePoint list and then use the same technique as for that first list to move it to BookDatabase19.

Again the technique is to create a new Custom List as we have done before. This time the Custom List will be called CompanyAddresses and will have columns, as shown in Figure 20.1. Again remove the title field from the All Items view.

FIGURE 20.1
Columns in Company-Addresses

Column (click to edit)	Type	Required
Title	Single line of text	
Company	Choice	✔
Address	Single line of text	✔
City	Single line of text	✔
State	Single line of text	
ZIP	Single line of text	
Country	Single line of text	
Web Page	Hyperlink or Picture	
Created By	Person or Group	
Modified By	Person or Group	

For this to make sense when used in connection with the existing list, you need to add a single item each for HP, IBM, and Oracle giving their company details. I'll also add the same information for Microsoft because I expect to add information for Microsoft to the CompanyStaffNumbers list some time.

Figure 20.2 displays the added data.

FIGURE 20.2
Company addresses

Company	Address	City	State	ZIP	Country	Web Page
HP	3000 Hanover St.	Palo Alto	CA	94304	USA	http://www.hp.com
IBM	1 New Oxford Road	Armonk	NY	10504-1783	USA	http://www.ibm.com
Microsoft	One Microsoft Way	Redmond	WA	98052-7329	USA	http://www.microsoft.com
Oracle	500 Oracle Parkway	Redwood Shores	CA	94065	USA	http://www.oracle.com

By the Way

The List selection screen (in Hour 18, "Sharing Access 2010 Tables with SPF 2010," Figure 18.15, where it is for a different site, so there are different Lists) will now show both Lists. CompanyStaffNumbers is already selected. Do not deselect it but also select CompanyAddresses. This will then add only CompanyAddresses to the database.

Make sure to specify that it is possible to add other values in the columns of type Choice. Note the Type of the Web Page—it uses the Hyperlink subtype.

The next steps are to create an Access 2010 table from an SPF 2010 List using the technique described in Hour 18 in the "Scenario 1: Creating a Linked Access 2010 Table from a SharePoint List" section. Start this time from step 3 there (Select External Data) after having opened BookDatabase19 in Access 2010.

It's equally valid to use a List based on the standard Contacts List for Company Addresses as to use a second Custom List. A Contacts List already has all the fields we need but many more other fields, too. There is however no difference when creating the report if we used two Custom Lists or one Custom List and one Contacts List. What is key is that only that they share at least one common column.

Now that both Lists are present in the Database as two tables (see Figure 20.3), we can use them to create a report.

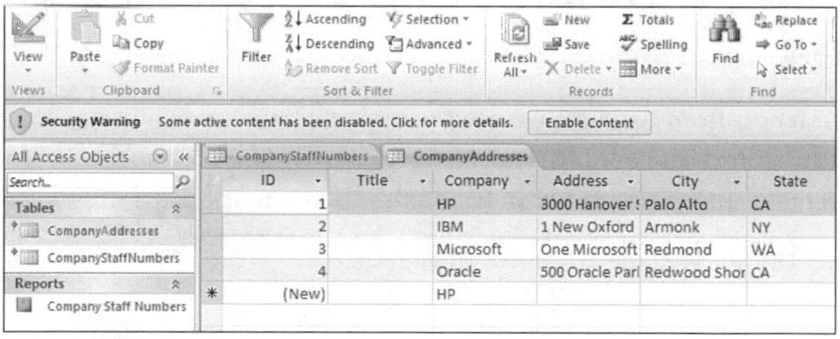

FIGURE 20.3
The starting point for report creation from two lists/tables

If you want to spend time creating this report without needing to be connected to the server, add a dummy record to each of the two Lists and then remove the dummy record. The act of adding the dummy record ensures that the data is available to Access 2010 even without a link to the original SharePoint List. Doing this once ensures that a link is not needed in future computer sessions not just this one.

Do not try at this point to run the Report Wizard thinking that you will be able in one pass of the Report Wizard to (1) specify fields from two lists/tables, (2) establish a relationship between the two tables, and (3) create a suitable report. While you can do (1) and (2), you will end up with the situation that only (2) has actually been done, after which you need to start again and consider whether to use the Report Wizard or the manual Report Design to create a report using fields for the (now connected) two lists/tables. It is far better to use the method outlined next to specify the connection between the two lists/tables.

A Description of the Report We Want to Create

The idea in this hour is to show how to add the official company address for each company to the report we created in the previous hour.

This sounds simple; we already have the report we created in the previous hour. Therefore, all we seem to need to do is to link this existing report to the new list/table and add the values from the new list/table to the existing report. Unfortunately the Access 2010 Report function doesn't enable us to add fields from a new list/table to an existing report created when the database contained only a single list/table. We therefore need to first specify that we will be using two lists/tables and then create a new report.

Creating a Connection Between the Two Tables

To create a report from two lists, we need to indicate how the two lists relate to each other. Because the SharePoint lists are stored in Access 2010 as tables, this means we need to create a connection between two tables. Here are the steps needed to do that:

1. Select Database Tools, as shown in Figure 20.4.

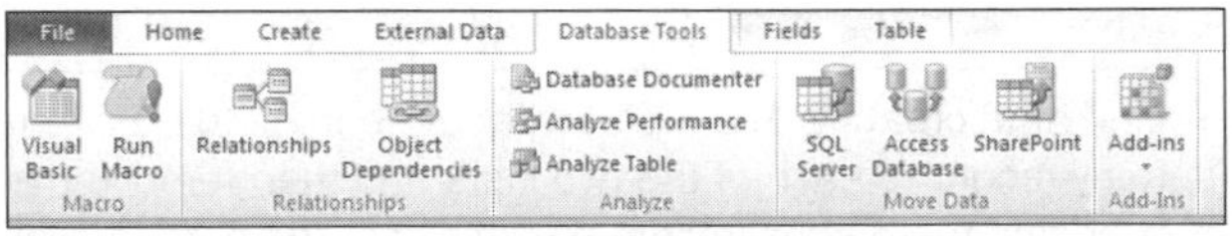

FIGURE 20.4
The External
Data ribbon

2. Select Relationships (see Figure 20.5).

3. The next step is to link the two tables via the Company address. There are two ways to do this:

   Method A is to click Company in the Company Address box in the central section of the screen (which selects this field) and then to drag the cursor across to the Company line of the Company Staff Numbers box.

Method B is to click Edit Relationships, as shown in Figure 20.5, and then click Create New in the Edit Relationships window (left part of Figure 20.6). After moving the new Create New window across and after filling in the details needed in the new window, this displays in the right part of Figure 20.6 where you confirm your selection with OK followed by Create in the Edit Relationships window.

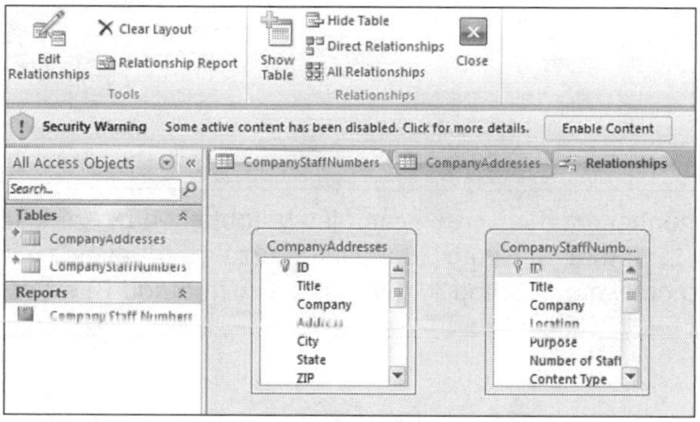

FIGURE 20.5
Listing of the only possible tables for a relationship

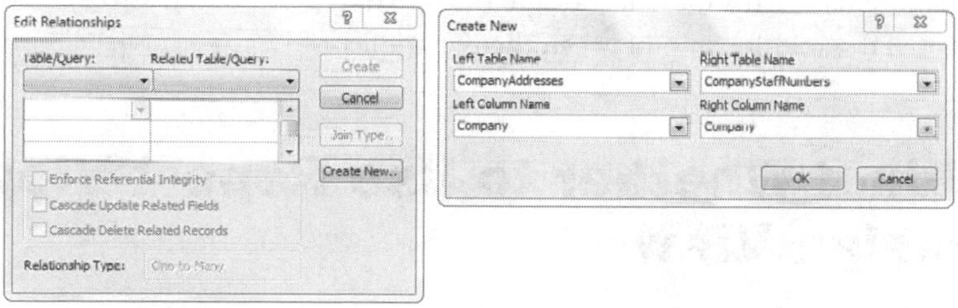

FIGURE 20.6
Specifying the relationship

It's up to you which method (A or B) you choose. For simpler relationships like this one, method A will be the best for more people (some people can't easily drag using the mouse, so they would use method B), whereas for more complicated relationships method B will probably always be more suitable.

Did you Know?

The field names could be different. You can connect two fields with different names provided the contents match.

By the Way

In both cases, what you now see in Figure 20.7 is a link between the Company field in Company Addresses and the Company field in CompanyStaffNumbers.

FIGURE 20.7
Two Company
fields connected

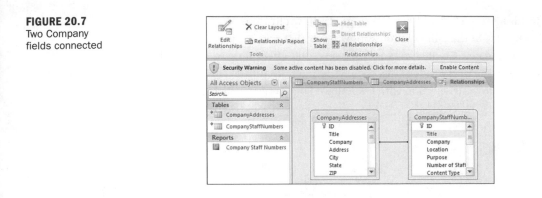

 By the Way

As previously mentioned, this screen can also be obtained by selecting Report Wizard at step 1. Getting to Figure 20.6 via Report Wizard takes 15 steps, whereas here there were (method A) three steps or (method B) six steps.

4. The final step is to close the Edit Relationships action with Close in the ribbon in Figure 20.7. This takes us back to our starting point (Figure 20.3) before we created the relationship between the two tables.

Deciding Whether to Use Report Viewer or Design View

Now we are faced with a decision:

▶ Do we use Report Wizard to create the report?

▶ Do we use Report Design to create the report?

Actually those are the wrong questions because the Report Wizard, even in the simpler case of a report from only one list/table, produced a report that we needed to edit using Design View.

So the questions should actually be

▶ Do we use Report Wizard to create a preliminary report and then use Report Design to refine it?

▶ Do we use only Report Design?

In my earlier book's hour on using Access 2007 with WSS 3.0 lists, I recommended using the Report Wizard only with single lists and never using Report Wizard with multiple lists/tables. Also with the combination of Access 2010 and SPF 2010, my tests have shown that you cannot specify the fields from two lists/tables and expect the Report Wizard to work out where you want the fields from the second table to appear.

In the present case, we have what seems to be a simple situation. We have a report where the Company is the first level of heading and where we use data from one List (CompanyStaffNumbers) in subheadings and the detail lines. The second list/table (CompanyAddresses) contains a single record for each Company. Logically therefore this is data that will occur only once per company, and we want it added to the place in the record where the Company name is.

Even in this simple case, the Report Wizard doesn't work as we want:

▶ It puts all the extra company information from CompanyAddresses in the details section.

▶ Even there, data is only visible for Country and Web Page.

Because the simple Report Wizard method won't work properly, the following sections cover the two main alternatives to that. The following section creates the report utilizing the Report Wizard followed by manual amendments in Design View, and the final section creates the report using the Design View from the start.

The conclusion is, therefore, that you should not expect to create sensible reports directly from the Report Wizard if you specify fields from two (or more) different lists/tables.

However, this doesn't mean that you should in a two-list/table never use the Report Wizard; it means that you should only use the Report Wizard to create a report using the fields from a single table.

One valid technique for creating a report using data from two or more lists/tables is therefore to first use the Report Wizard to get a report using the data from a single list/table and then to add to this basis report fields from the other list(s)/table(s).

By the Way

Creating a Two Lists/Tables Report with the Assistance of the Report Wizard

The first step in creating this report is almost identical with the report produced in Hour 19. There is one key difference between the situation now and the situation then; therefore, I repeat the steps required until we reach that point.

Here are the steps for creating a basic report on two lists/tables using Report Wizard:

1. As shown in Figure 20.3, click Create.

2. Click Report Wizard (on the ribbon).

3. Ignore the Potential Security Concern (see Figure 19.4 in the previous hour) by clicking Open. This displays Figure 20.8.

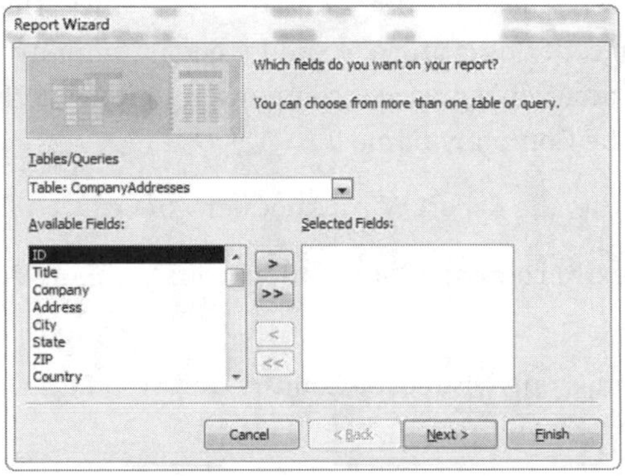

FIGURE 20.8
Starting to specify the report

By the Way

This is the key difference. When creating the report using two lists/tables, the Report Wizard gives us a list of fields in the Company-Addresses table. We need, however, to create a report that in this phase of report creation uses only fields from the CompanyStaffNumbers list/table.

4. As shown in Figure 20.8, change the table to be used to CompanyStaffNumbers.

   From now on, we follow the actions made in Hour 19, so the rest is without screenshots.

5. Move the Company, Purpose, Location, and Number of Staff fields across to the right column.

By the Way

The reason we first selected the fields from the CompanyStaffNumbers is that as far as possible we want to be adding data to a report that looks much like the report we had in Hour 19, which as you'll remember used (only) the fields from that list.

6. Click Next.

7. Group on Company and Purpose as we did in Hour 19 (see Figure 19.6).

Did you Know?

Watch out here (step 7) that you don't automatically Group on Company and Location that are the first two items in the list.

8. Click Next.
9. Specify that Sort is to be on Location.

By the Way

By Grouping on Company and Purpose, those are automatically the first and second level of sorts. Locations will actually be only the third sorting level.

10. As in Hour 19, click Summary options and complete the box that follows as was done in Figure 19.8 (by specifying Sum for the Number of Staff field).

Did you Know?

Make sure that Calculate Percent of Total for Sums is not selected this time.

11. Select OK.
12. Select Next. Now we have the same reports on offer that we had in Figure 19.9.
13. Accept the default (Stepped) with Next.
14. Change the name of the report to Company Report 2.
15. Click Finish to preview the report.

This will give you almost (% is missing) the same report as shown in Figure 19.11.

The next steps show how to add fields from the CompanyAddresses list/table so that they occur once per company in a sensible place in the report.

Here are the steps we need to create the report we want:

1. Click View > Design View (see Figure 20.9).

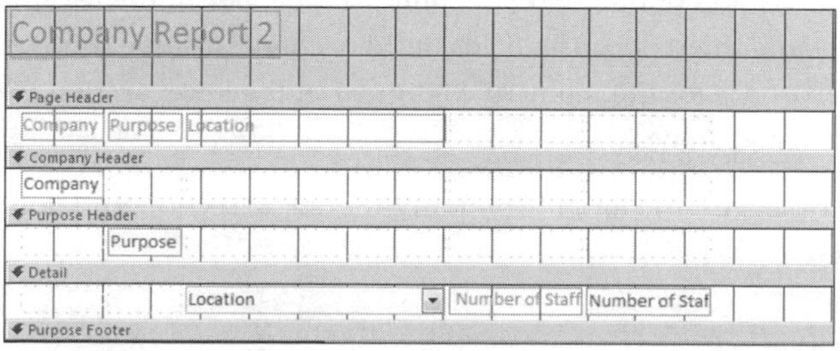

FIGURE 20.9 Design View of the initial Company Address Report

2. Expand the area available for the CompanyStaffNumbers_Company section by selecting the Purpose Header line and moving the cursor toward the top of it until you see an icon with a thick downward arrow; a thin upward arrow joined to it; and a horizontal line between the two arrows. When you have this, drag that section downward. This gives more space for the section above it.

3. Now go to the ribbon and click Add Existing Fields toward the right of the ribbon.

By the Way

If this isn't visible on the ribbon, perhaps it's because you've closed the database or the view in the meantime. You can find it again by selecting the menu item Design in the Report Design Tools section.

This opens a List of all fields in both tables that were used when creating this report (see Figure 20.10).

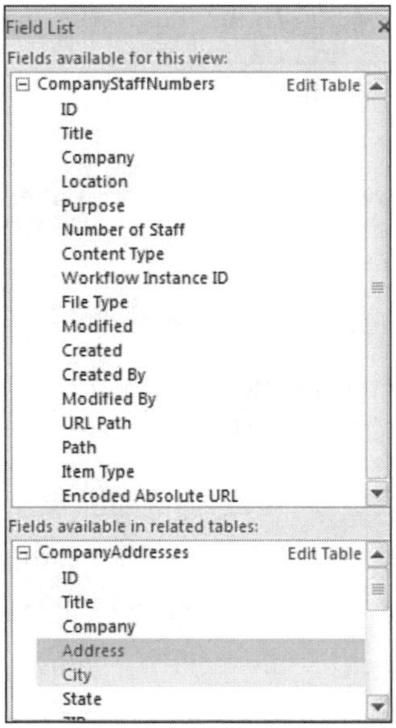

FIGURE 20.10
The field list directly after the report has been created

The upper section of the Field List contains the fields in the list/table that we used to create the report. The fields in the second list/table that we did not use in the report are for the moment contained in the lower section (Fields Available in Related Tables).

4. Open if necessary the lower (CompanyAddresses) section and double-click Address.

A dual set of Address (label) and Address (field) appear in that order somewhere in the design—probably offscreen in the Detail section that will have been increased in size, so you will have to scroll down. This is not where we want the address to be of course.

After the addition of Address there is a slight change in the Field List. The second set of fields are now included in the Fields Available in This View section where they are now placed above the Company-StaffNumbers fields.

5. Click somewhere in empty space.

   This removes the selection of *both* the label and the field.

6. Click the left Address (the label) to select it and click Delete.

7. Click the right Address (the field) to select it and then press Ctrl-X.

If you don't feel happy about this field vanishing from sight after the Ctrl-X, use Ctrl-C and then later delete the original copy of the field.

8. Click the Company field in the Company Header section.

The nice thing about doing step 8 before step 9 is that the Address field is automatically aligned directly under the Company field.

9. Click Ctrl-V.

   Now repeat the preceding steps 4 to 9 for (in turn) the City, State, Zip, Country, and Web Page fields with *one important difference*: At step 8, *always select the field you previously added.*

This is the way you should do it, and 99 times out of 100 it will work fine. My recommendation is to play it safe and switch to Report view and back to Design view after adding three fields and then again after the next three fields. Once, when I had been working for a long time on improving a report and tried to go to Report view, I was told that I hadn't enough memory to do so, and nor did I have enough memory to save my design. Removing running programs had no effect, so I just had to cancel and lose all my changes. I wouldn't like that to happen to you.

This is the way you should do it and 99 times out of a hundred it will work fine. My recommendation is to play safe and switch to report view and back to design view after adding three fields and then again after the next three fields. Once, when I had been working for a long time on improving a report and tried to go to Report View, I was told that I hadn't enough memory to do so and nor did I have enough memory to save my design. Removing running programs had no effect so I just had to cancel and I lost all my changes. I wouldn't like that to happen to you.

10. Move the Purpose Footer upward so the Detail Section is of normal height (see Figure 20.11).

FIGURE 20.11
The (almost) final Company Header section in Design view

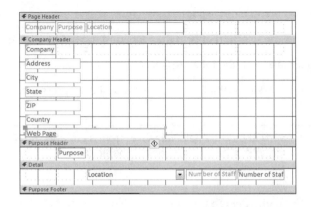

11. Before we have a look at this in Report View, it's clear that we don't want to have column headers at the top of each page saying Company, Purpose, and Location, so delete those three items in the Page Header section.

12. Although you are amending the Page Header section, try to find the Page Number function in the ribbon and specify that the page number should appear at the top of the page on the left and be centered in its field.

13. Click View > Report View (see Figure 20.12).

This almost final report is now at the stage the report in Hour 19 was before we did the final changes to it. By following the Tip after step 10 of the Report Wizard phase, we avoided the need to remove the percentage line, but we still need to widen the Purpose field, so we get Marketing and make the Company Name Bold and Under-lined. To do that, though, you can follow Hour 19—making sure your report design is saved at the end. (If you can't find how to do so, close Access. If the report design has-n't been saved, you will be asked if you want to save it.)

Here we finish with a look at creating a report from two lists/tables without the aid of the Report Wizard.

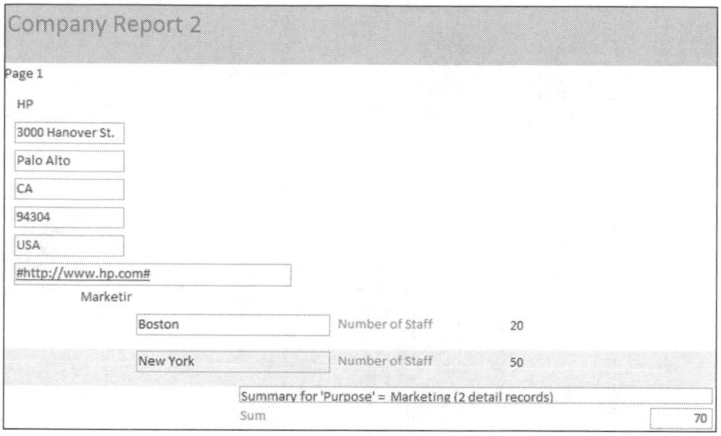

FIGURE 20.12
An almost final report

Creating a Two Lists/Tables Report Manually Using Design View

The alternative to using first the Report Wizard and then making manual changes to what that generates is to start with an empty report design sheet and add fields from the two lists to it. In the present rather simple case, this is probably a more time-consuming method than the early "wizard + amendment" method, but you need to know how to use this method anyway for cases where the initial use of the Report Wizard is more hindrance than help, so here is how to do a total report design from scratch for that same simple case.

Most of the techniques used in this section were already covered in the previous section, so we can start right away with the steps needed to create a report called Company Report 3 from the Design view:

1. Create (menu line) and Report Design (ribbon).

   This gives an empty Design View with a Page Header section, Detail section, and Page Footer section. First we need to create a Company Header section.

2. Click the Ribbon on Add Existing Fields that opens the Field List.

3. Click the + next to CompanyStaffNumbers in the Field List section.

4. Double-click Company. The Company label (left) and the Company field (right) appear in the Detail section.

5. Delete the Company label only.

6. Select the Company field and right-click (see Figure 20.13).

7. Click Group On.

FIGURE 20.13
Specifying Group-
ing for a field

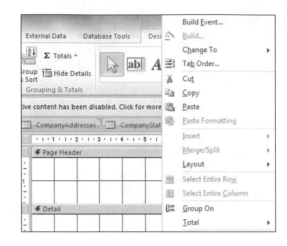

Seemingly nothing happens, but if you look again at the Design View (and upward), you'll see that a new section has been created called Company Header.

8. Drag the Company field to a suitable location (top left) in the Company Header section.

This is done by moving the cursor to the top end of the selected Company field's box until you see a small four-pointed (as in N/S/E/W directions) icon and then holding the mouse button down while moving the field.

Now that the Company Field is there, the next steps are to add the fields Address, City, State, Zip, Country, and Web Page from the CompanyAddresses part of Field List using the same method that was used previously. I start a new set of steps for this (condensed because we've seen them before):

1. Expand CompanyAddreses in Field List.

2. Double-click Address.

3. Delete the left Address (label) in the Details part of Design view.

4. Click the Address field to select it and then Ctrl-X.

5. Click the Company field in the Company Header section.

6. Click Ctrl-V.

Repeat for City, State, Zip, Country, and Web Page, not forgetting as before to always select in step 5 the field that was previously added to the Company Header section.

The following steps group on Purpose and create a couple of calculation fields in the Purpose section. Again, as the initial steps are repeats of what has been done before, they are compressed:

1. Double-click Purpose.

2. Delete the Purpose label.

3. Select the Purpose field and right-click it.

4. Click Group On.

Again, a Header section is created, this time for Purpose. This section as added later is below the Company Header section:

1. Move the Purpose field to within the Purpose section. This time align it to the right of the names in the section above it.

2. After moving it, widen the field by dragging on the right edge of the Purpose box to widen the box.

3. Drag up the Detail Header so that the Purpose section takes as little space as possible.

We've done quite a bit of work, yet we still have only a report that looks like Figure 20.14.

FIGURE 20.14
An interim hand-made report

This might be a good time to have a look at what the report we created in the previous section looked like. Having done that, we see that we are missing three rows in the Details section:

▶ Location + Number of Staff (normal fields)

▶ Location (count of)

▶ Number of Staff (sum of)

Here we can ignore the count of location and just do the first and the last item in that list and then do another review:

1. Use the usual (by now) technique to get the Location field into the Details section and move it to the top of the section positioned to the right of the end of the Purpose field in the section above.

2. Use the usual (by now) technique to get to get the Number of Staff field into the details section, but do not delete the label; move both the label and the field to the top of the section positioned to the right of the end of the Location field that was just added.

3. Reduce the size of the Details section so that it has space for just this one line.

The report now looks like (in extract) Figure 20.15.

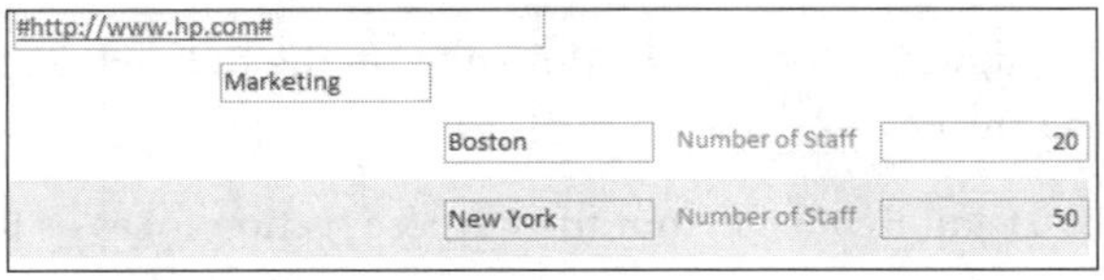

FIGURE 20.15
The Details line is now okay

#http://www.hp.com#			
Marketing			
	Boston	Number of Staff	20
	New York	Number of Staff	50

The final part of the report we cover in the book is the addition of the line giving the totals for Marketing (and all the other Purpose sections) of the number of staff. These go in the Purpose Footer section and will normally consist not only of a total, but also some text including the name of the Purpose. So Total for Marketing = 70 for instance.

Here's one way to do this:

1. Use the usual technique and add the Any field to Details.

2. Move the field to the Purpose Footer section and right-click (see Figure 20.13).

3. Click Build Events at the top of the pop-up menu.

4. Select Expression Builder from the new pop-up.

   Now to build up Total for Marketing = 70, you need to specify four different parts of this expression:

   a. A text string Total For

   b. The contents of a field (Purpose)

   c. A text string =

   d. A sum

In the Expression Builder between each of these parts, you need an ampersand (&):

a. Uses Functions/Built-in Functions (and String)

b. Uses BookDatabase19/Tables/CompanyStaffNumbers (and Purpose)

c. Uses Functions/Built-in Functions (and String)

d. Uses Functions/Built-in Functions (and Sum)

Note that the & is obtained from "Operators" and scrolling down to select "&."

This logically results in what's seen in Figure 20.16, which however might be rejected by the Expression Builder format checker.

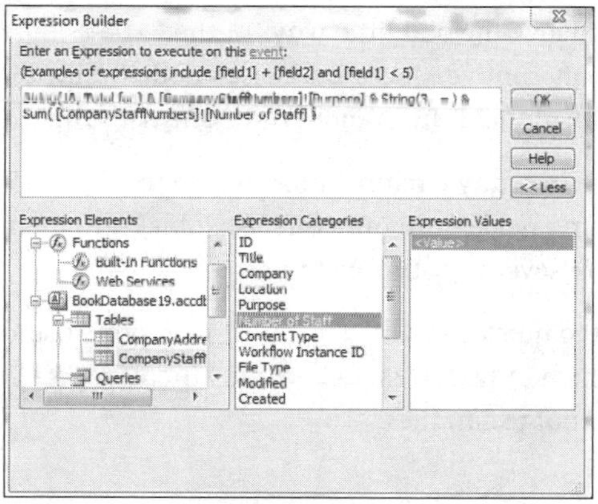

FIGURE 20.16
A seemingly good expression

This is one of the problems of the manual approach. The Expression checker routine is strict. It rejects as incorrect just about everything. It even (!) rejects some of the expressions (that work!) generated by the Report Wizard. Rather than writing a new hour about creating expressions accepted by the Expression checker routine, let us solve our problem in the simplest possible way by following these steps:

1. Click Number of Staff (field) in the Details line.

2. Right-click and select Sum.

As if by magic, this creates Sum fields just where we want them in the Purpose Footer and in the Company Footer (see Figure 20.17).

I'll leave you to tidy up the report by reducing the size of some of areas of the report. (And note that there isn't such a nice report heading as there was for the generated report—there is *no* report heading yet.)

The final section gives a few thoughts as to which approach is the most suitable.

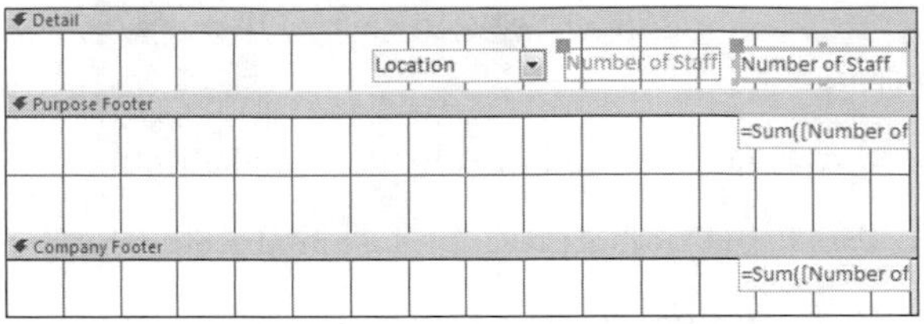

FIGURE 20.17
Sum of Number
of Staff just
where we want it

Short Comparison of the Two Methods for Report Creation from Two or More Lists/Tables

1. It is possible to create a report from scratch. You have full control, and provided you can learn to love the odd little ways of the Expression Builder checker (or how to use the alternative Macro Builder or Code Builder), you can do virtually what you want with fields from more than one list/table.

2. It is much faster in many circumstances to use the Report Wizard to create a basis report (using fields from only one list/table) and then to add fields from another (or from several) list/table to it.

3. It is also useful to quickly create a few sample reports using the Report Builder and then use them only as a model for the kind of report you want to build using only manual techniques.

Workshop

Q. *What happens if I create a link between a SharePoint List and Access 2010 using a TCP/IP address and then the TCP/IP address changes?*

A. The problem with such a change is that the TCP/IP address is built in to the Access table so that it knows where the SharePoint List is located that it needs to link to. In a situation where the TCP/IP address has changed, the link naturally doesn't work, so you need to change the link.

You do this using the same method that you would use if you had for instance moved the list to a completely different SharePoint system. Here are the steps to solve this (this does not need to be repeated for each table in the same database connected to the old TCP/IP address or server), all of which occur in Access 2010:

1. Select the table.

2. Right-click.

3. Select More Options (see Figure 20.18).

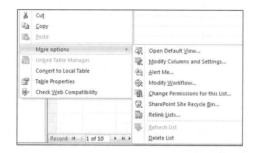

FIGURE 20.18
Preparing to
relink a table to
a List

4. Click Relink lists (see Figure 20.19).

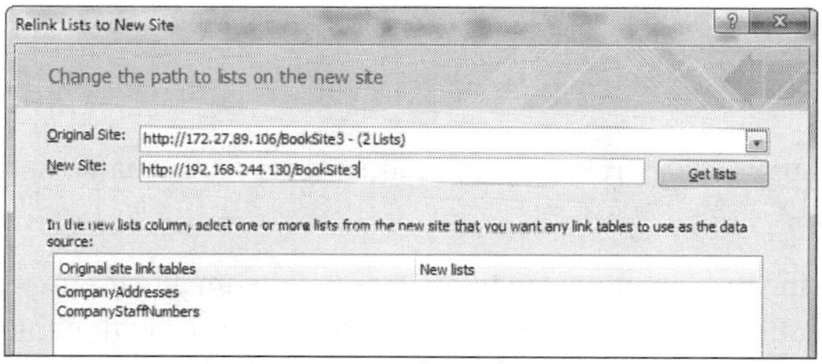

FIGURE 20.19
Relinking Lists
to a new site

Before you do this, make sure that the new TCP/IP address is listed in the Alternate Access Mappings (AAM) section of Central Administration.

By the Way

5. Click Get lists (see Figure 20.20).

Here the New Lists function automatically added the correct Lists. It was after all the same server and the same lists that were being accessed. But for cases in which perhaps the lists have different names after being moved (perhaps to a site that already had a list with the original name), there's the option of selecting the correct list.

By the Way

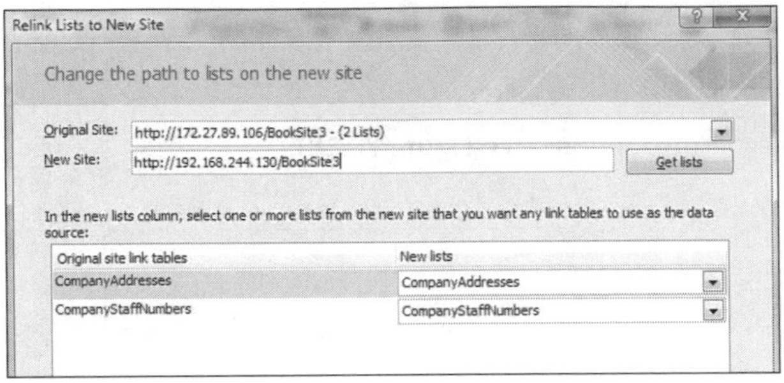

FIGURE 20.20
New Lists are
specified

6. Click OK.

This takes us back to the standard Access Page for this database; only now the both the links are operational.

By the Way

This is a good example that a right-click on one table will actually solve this problem for all the tables.

Quiz

1. Can you use the Report Wizard to produce a report that uses the fields of two or more lists?

2. When using the Report Wizard to produce an interim report that we will build on, does it matter which single list we use for the fields used in that interim report?

Answers

1. You can produce a report using Report Wizard that uses fields from two or more lists, but the chances are the report will not be of much use to you because fields from the second list will probably be used in the wrong way.

2. It depends on the lists. In this case the method we chose was the only correct one. For bonus points, you can see what would happen if a report were created using the Company Addresses list/table. It won't be as helpful as a basis for a full report as the interim report we created using the CompanyStaffNumbers list/table.

PART IV

Workflow and SPD 2010

Creating Workflows in SPF 2010

What You'll Learn in This Hour

▶ What workflow options you have as an SPF 2010 (and SPS 2010) user

▶ Creating a workflow using the three-state workflow included with SPF 2010

▶ Requirements for creating workflows for other kinds of lists than Issue Tracking and Tasks

This hour contains an overview of the various Workflow options included with the two main SharePoint 2010 products and of the Workflow options available in connection with SharePoint with the use of other products. The second half of the hour works through an example of using the single workflow option included in SPF 2010. Another way of creating workflows for a SPF 2010 site is by the use of SharePoint Designer 2007. That is covered in Hour 22, "Using SharePoint Designer 2010 to Create Workflows."

Understanding the Main Workflow Options

Workflow became one of the key functions of SharePoint when the version 3 products were released. It continues to be a key function in the v4 products with, in particular, much more functionality provided by SharePoint Designer 2010 workflows (see later in this hour and in the next hour). Workflow functionality in SharePoint products is based on the Windows Workflow Foundation (WWF).

You can use workflows in connection with SharePoint v4 products in six main ways:

▶ The single built-in workflow function included in SPF 2010

▶ The built-in workflow functions included in SPS 2010

▶ Workflows created in SharePoint Designer 2010

▶ Workflows created in InfoPath 2010

▶ Workflows created in Visual Studio 2010

▶ Workflows created using third-party products

The single built-in workflow function (the three-state workflow) in SPF 2010 is the main topic of this hour. It is covered in detail later.

Predefined SPS 2010 Workflows

The simple three-stage workflow type included in SPF 2010 is also available in an SPS 2010 installation. However, several other predefined workflow types come only with SPS 2010: Approval, Disposition Approval, Collect Feedback, Collect Signatures, and Translation Management. These workflows are preassociated with the Document content type. In other words, when you create a document library in SPS 2010, these workflows are automatically available in those document libraries.

To see the status of these (and the three-state) workflows (when in a site), go to Site Actions and click Site Workflows. This displays the status of the workflows in that site collection. SPF 2010 and SPS 2010 built-in workflows are relatively simple workflows with limited capabilities.

SharePoint Designer 2010 Workflows

You can add more complicated workflows to both SPF 2010 and SPS 2010 and still avoid programming by using SharePoint Designer 2010. This kind of workflow has been allocated an entire hour of this book (see Hour 22). Functionality of workflows is greatly improved compared to that available in SharePoint Designer 2007.

InfoPath 2010 Workflows

You don't actually create a workflow in InfoPath 20010. What you do is create InfoPath forms that display data from an existing workflow. After doing so, you can make InfoPath rules that react on changes to that data. In other words, there are no InfoPath 2010 workflows. There are standard (SPF 2010, SPS 2010, and SPD 2010) workflows (or workflows written in Visual Studio 2010) and InfoPath 2010 forms that feed off them. This sort of workflow is at second-hand—a useful technique that enables InfoPath 2010 specialists to use workflows in their forms but is not (in my opinion at least) a new workflow type.

Visual Studio 2010 Workflows

Writing workflows in Visual Studio 2010 requires the kind of developer skills needed when writing code to provide new functionality in SPF 2010 and SPS 2010. In return you get more powerful workflows than even those now available when using Share-Point Designer 2010.

Because of the developer skills required, creating workflows using Visual Studio 2010 is beyond the scope of this book. If you are interested in going further with it, look for a SharePoint developer book that dedicates considerable space to workflows. (Many don't).

Third-Party Workflow Products

Third-party products provide functionality that you could write if you had both the time and the Visual Studio-based development skills. Here are two companies that had good products for the v2 and v3 SharePoint products: the website of the first company listed does not at the moment of writing indicate whether it will be updating its product for SharePoint 2010, but it is reasonable to assume that it will. If you are interested in using either product (or products from other third-party companies) in connection with SPF 2010, ask the company if its product will work with SPF 2010 because often third-party products require the full SharePoint product (in this case SPS 2010):

- ► **OpenText (formerly Captaris)**—At the time of writing, OpenText Workflow Server (formerly Captaris Workflow 6.5) was available for MOSS 2007 (http://faxsolutions.opentext.com/workflow-server.aspx).

- ► **Nintex**—Nintex stated that it will have a product for SharePoint 2010 called Nintex Workflow 2010. (For SharePoint 3 products, the product is Nintex Workflow 2007, which was for both WSS 3.0 and MOSS 2007.) A good starter page with links to both products right at the top of the list of its products is http://www.nintex.com.

Creating a Workflow Using the Three-State Workflow Method

When reading this section, concentrate on the interchange between the two different list types during the workflow process.

For people reading this book without the advantage of working with a company network running Exchange, regard the addition of an SMTP server and the emails

By the Way

> that it should send to users in the workflow chain as a bonus. If you can't get it (the SMTP Server) to work at all, don't worry. The workflow process doesn't rely on emails being sent. You can still follow this book without a working SMTP server.
>
> Try the installation as described. If it works, that's great but if it doesn't, assume that the email arrives at the time I describe.

The three-stage workflow method is the sole workflow method built in to SPF 2010. (It is also built in to SPS 2010.) It is a simple but useful process to follow in a business environment.

The three stages are as follows:

1. Someone creates a job to be done.

2. Someone does the job.

3. Someone checks that the job has been done correctly and marks it as complete.

The principal components of the entire workflow process are

- A list based on the Issue Tracking list type

- A list based on the Tasks list type

- Outgoing email messages specified in Central Administration

- A built-in workflow service

- A working SMTP server

- A working email address (for the user)

Without these six components, workflow might work, but not properly.

Ensuring Your Users Have a Working Email Address

The sixth component is slightly different from the others: Make sure that all the people in the workflow chain can receive email. They can do this only if their correct email addresses are specified in their profiles. Check this by (as administrator) going to Site Actions > Site Settings > People and Groups. Then click the name of each user to check the email address and amend it if necessary with Edit Item. Figure 21.1 is an example of amending the default to an address at my own ISP in Finland.

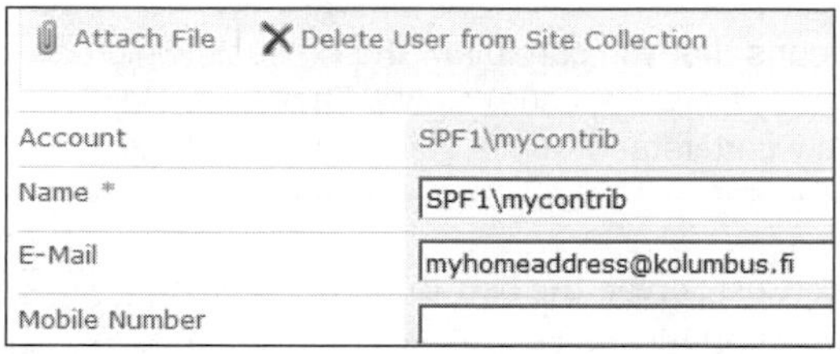

📎 Attach File	✖ Delete User from Site Collection
Account	SPF1\mycontrib
Name *	SPF1\mycontrib
E-Mail	myhomeaddress@kolumbus.fi
Mobile Number	

FIGURE 21.1
Making sure
users have good
email addresses

After checking that all the users have valid email addresses, start at the *bottom* of the principal-components list (this list is a couple of paragraphs above this section), and work upward. In this test case, make sure that the users you use for workflow—I use MyAdmin and the administrator—have valid email addresses. Also, for reasons revealed later, use one or more addresses at your local ISP unless you run Exchange in a work environment.

Ensuring You Have a Working SMTP Server

Remember from Hour 11, "Using What We've Learned So Far in a Site," you learned that to get alerts to work, you must specify your outgoing email specifications and that the difficulty is writing the correct server name. That assumed you actually had an SMTP server. In a work setting, that is likely to be the case. If you try to follow this book at home, however, that probably won't be the case (until you install one).

A free SMTP server that works and has some good options is PostCast Server. Be aware that it doesn't seem to work in the free version for Gmail and Hotmail addresses; so make sure you always use your local ISP email address for your test users.

The (nonfree) professional version should send messages to Gmail addresses. The Professional version costs $49. A free 30-day trial is available, so you can check it out at http://www.postcaseserver.com/download/.

By the Way

The website for the free version of PostCast Server is www.postcastserver.com/download/release.aspx?p=3. As when I wrote my book on WSS 3.0, the version available there is version 2.6.0. When installing it I followed the defaults.

It's a matter of choice whether you set the processing of messages to Immediately or Manually (the default). I suggest you set to Manually, and after you know everything works, switch to Immediately. While performing your first tests, however, it's easier to follow the process if you can see when a message arrives in your SMTP system.

By the Way

Using Manually means that you can follow the process (which means looking at three different places, as you will see) slowly. That said, slowly is the only way (in my opinion) to really understand what's going on behind the scenes.

Having installed PostCast Server, the best thing to do is make sure that it can send messages to your email addresses. Do this by creating a new message in the open Outbox (see Figure 21.2).

FIGURE 21.2
Confirming that the SMTP server works

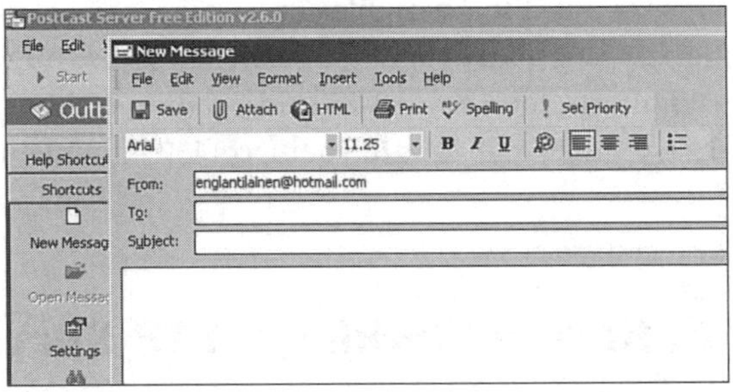

When you receive that email, you know that everything is okay. You can now check that you actually have a workflow system!

By the Way

The email message first appears in the Outbox. Then, assuming you have set the PostCast Server to Manually, you need to click the Start button at the left of the menu line that becomes available to you.

Don't worry if you get an odd small error message. Just click OK to accept it, and your real message will be sent. This seems to happen once with a new installation of PostCast Server. (Be even less worried if you don't get such a message!)

Checking for a Built-In Workflow Service

To check that you have a working workflow system, go to Site Actions > Site Settings > Workflows. (This is listed in the Site Administration section.) The Three-state workflow is listed and active (see Figure 21.3).

FIGURE 21.3
Checking that the workflow is active

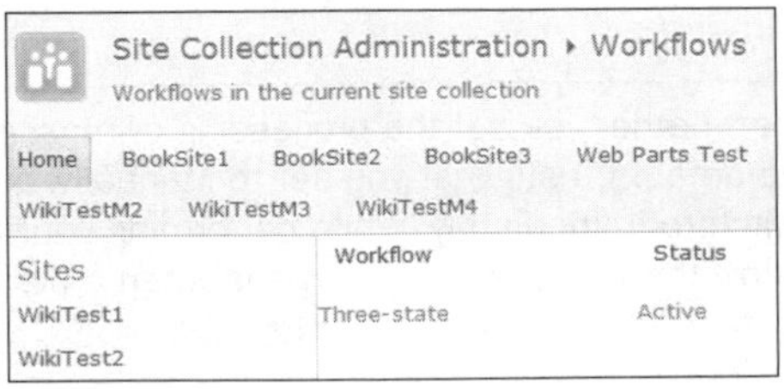

Checking That Outgoing Email Messages Are Specified

To check that you have specified working outgoing email parameters, go to Central Administration > System Settings > Configure Outgoing E-Mail Settings (see Figure 21.4). Note that this item is not listed in the Systems Settings section of the Central Administration main page; you must click System Settings to see it listed on the System Settings page.

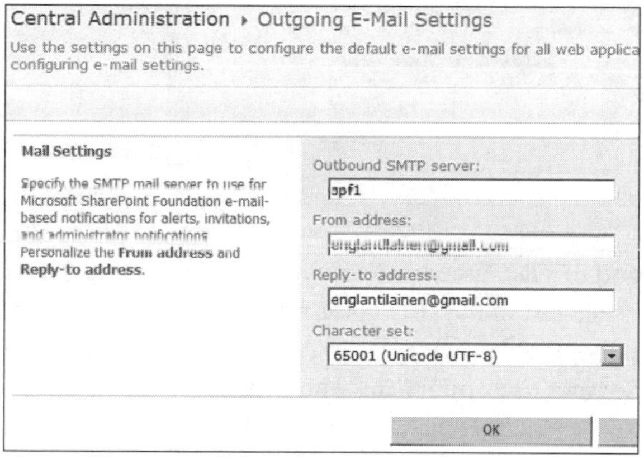

FIGURE 21.4
Specifying the outgoing email settings

You need to fill in the values in Figure 21.4 if you use the PostCast Server. If you use Exchange, they are probably already specified.

Ensuring You Have a List Based on the Tasks List Type

The next principal component is to make sure you have a list based on the Tasks list type. Here it's possible to follow the usual method of Site Actions > More Options > Tasks to create a new Tasks list, which will be used for the workflow tasks.

Instead of doing this, I strongly recommend you let the system handle this creation of a Tasks List (see the next section). When you specify the workflow settings for your Issue Tracking list, you are asked which Tasks list to use. You can ask for one to be created. In that case, the name that will be given for it is <the name of the workflow> Tasks.

The one snag with letting the system create the list (of type Tasks) is that this list will not appear in Quick Launch, which for our demonstration here is a nuisance. So you later need to enter the list and change the Quick Launch setting.

Creating a List Based on the Issue Tracking List Type

Now you create a list of type Issue Tracking. To do this, follow these steps:

1. Go to Site Actions > More Options > Issue Tracking; add the name Three-StateTest and accept the other default values (see Figure 21.5).

2. After creating this list, access the list's menu item Settings (to see this you need to have selected List in the List Tools section on the ribbon) and choose List Settings (sneakily placed as a large icon on the left, with List Permissions and Workflow Settings as normal icons and text under the Settings Tab item). Remove attachments by going to Advanced Settings and setting attachments to No. After that, you return to the same List Settings screen. You can now select Workflow Settings, after which Figure 21.6 appears.

Here it's necessary to select Add a Workflow, which leads to Figures 21.7 and 21.8.

3. Name the workflow BookWorkflow and select New Task List from the drop-down for Task list (arrowed; Figure 21.7). Also deselect the box at the top arrow point in Figure 21.8 (Allow This Workflow to be Manually Started) and activate the box at Start This Workflow When a New Item Is to Be Created. Click Next.

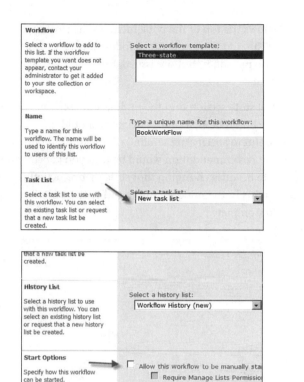

FIGURE 21.7
Amending the workflow settings (1)

FIGURE 21.8
Amending the workflow settings (2)

4. Starting at Figure 21.9, specify what happens when a workflow is started and what happens when the workflow changes to its middle state. (Changing the names of the three states is pointless—imagine changing the initial state to Complete!)

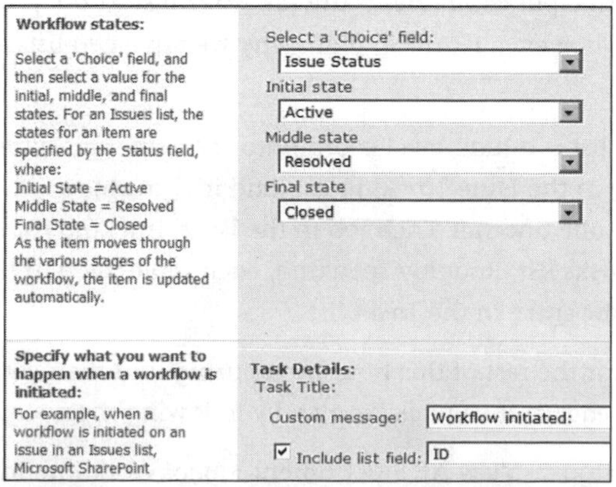

FIGURE 21.9
Specifying the details of the workflow

Figure 21.9 shows the top of the page includes the start of the settings for the initial state. (The middle state settings follow further down the page.) This lets you change the messages that are issued, but here I just leave all the standard options in place.

Both the initial state section and the middle state section enable you to specify that an email should be sent and to whom it should go. In testing this function it might be useful to specify the sending of an email in both sections, but in production my recommendation would be that you consider doing this only in the initial state because changing that state means action is needed (see Figure 21.10). Doing this in the middle state would only be confirming that an action has moved to Complete.

FIGURE 21.10
Specifying the email to be sent

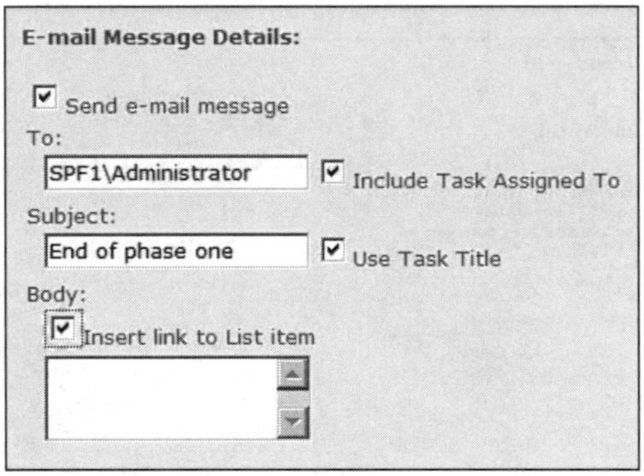

E-mail Message Details:

☑ Send e-mail message
To:
[SPF1\Administrator]   ☑ Include Task Assigned To
Subject:
[End of phase one]   ☑ Use Task Title
Body:
☑ Insert link to List item

5. Finish by clicking OK.

Creating the Workflow

Now that the six principal components are set, we can start the process of creating our workflow. First, however, let me explain why we have two lists: an Issue Tracking list and a Tasks list.

The Issue Tracking list is a high-level coordinator of numerous different jobs. Each job produces one entry in the Issue Tracking list, and it's possible in the Issue Tracking list to connect them to one another. Each job in the Issue Tracking list generates a number of jobs in the Tasks list. Roughly speaking, each major step in the progress of that Issue produces a new entry in the Tasks list.

First, let's prepare for the rest of this hour by ensuring that the new BookWorkflow Tasks tasks list appears in the Quick Launch by following these steps:

1. Go to Site Actions > View All Site Content > BookWorkflow Tasks.

2. Open BookWorkflow Tasks.

3. Go to List > Settings > List Settings > Title, Description, and Navigation.

4. Specify there that the list appears in Quick Launch and click Save.

The final preparatory step is to use two browser copies as follows:

1. Open one browser copy at the ThreeStateTest list.

2. Open the second browser copy at the BookWorkflow Tasks list.

3. Scale the browser copies to take up half the screen space; that way, you can see both.

Let's now create a new job in the Issue Tracking list.

Take this slowly. Create or change something in one of the two lists and then go to the other list (perhaps with Refresh, although this isn't necessary) to see whether the other list changed.

If you have the PostCast Server, look at the Outbox to see if a message arrived. If it has, click Start to send it on its way.

Refresh your client's mail reader to see if an email has arrived. If it has, look at its contents.

Did you Know?

1. Create a sample item in the ThreeStateTest. (The link is in Quick Launch.) Fill in the form, as shown in Figure 21.11. (MyAdmin was checked with the "head"

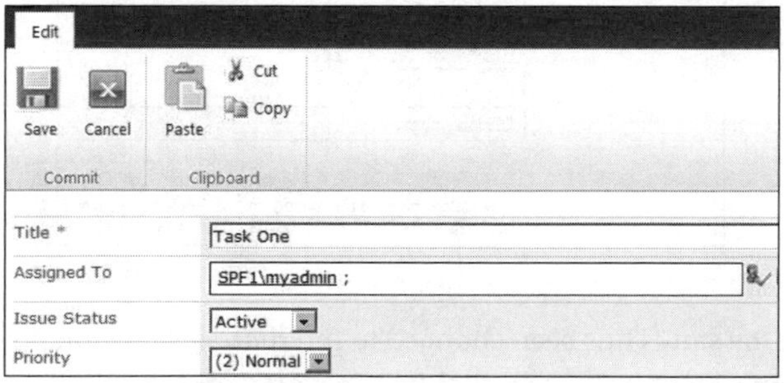

FIGURE 21.11
Adding the new job in Three-StateTest

to the right of that entry box, so it shows as spf1\myadmin—underlined with no caps).

(The rest of the form I left empty. This is enough for our test needs.)

2. Click OK to display the ThreeStateTest list containing one item (see Figure 21.12).

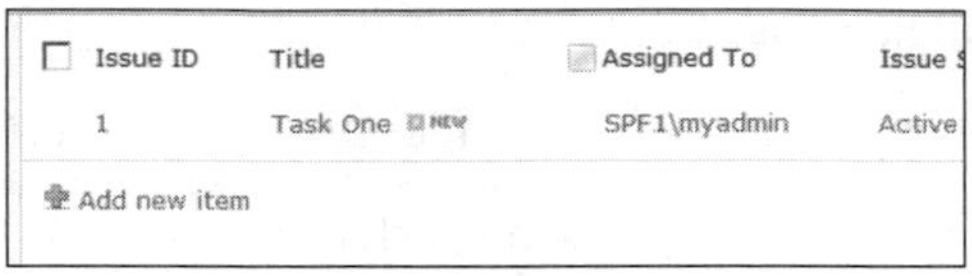

FIGURE 21.12
ThreeStateTest
list with one item

☐	Issue ID	Title	☑ Assigned To	Issue ⁚
	1	Task One ☐ NEW	SPF1\myadmin	Active
☀ Add new item				

3. At this stage, nothing has happened at the SMTP server, so we have no new email. Go to the BookWorkflow Tasks list and refresh the page, and there is a new entry (see Figure 21.13).

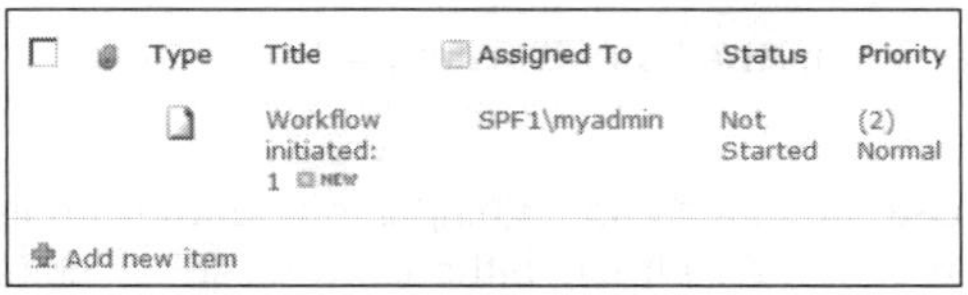

FIGURE 21.13
Tasks for Work-
flow1, with one
item

☐	⚫	Type	Title	☑ Assigned To	Status	Priority
		☐	Workflow initiated: 1 ☐ NEW	SPF1\myadmin	Not Started	(2) Normal
☀ Add new item						

Figure 21.13 shows why nothing's happened: The status shows that the job hasn't started.

4. As administrator while still at Figure 21.13, double-click the Title and then Edit Item. Change the status to In Progress (see Figure 21.14) and click Save.

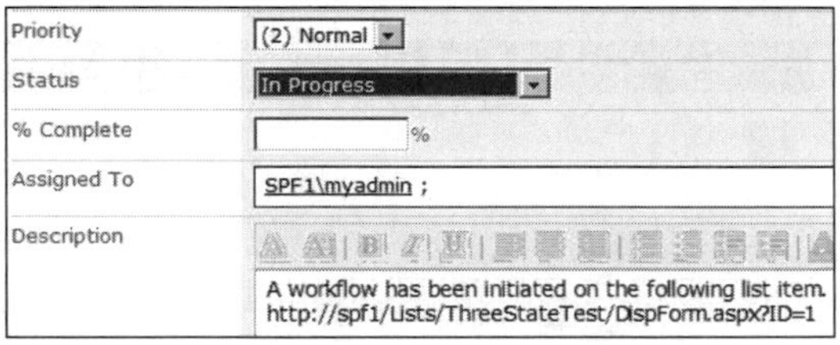

FIGURE 21.14
Telling MyAdmin
there's some-
thing for him

Priority	(2) Normal ▾
Status	In Progress ▾
% Complete	_____ %
Assigned To	SPF1\myadmin ;
Description	Ａ Ａ｜Ｂ ／ Ｕ｜▤ ▦ ▧｜☰ ☰ ☰｜Ａ
	A workflow has been initiated on the following list item. http://spf1/Lists/ThreeStateTest/DispForm.aspx?ID=1

Because the status has been changed to In Progress, an email is sent to MyAdmin so that he's aware that he can start working.

5. After the Save has been done, the status in the BookWorkflow Tasks list changes to In Progress.

Meanwhile, the ThreeStateTest list also shows the workflow in progress (see Figure 21.15).

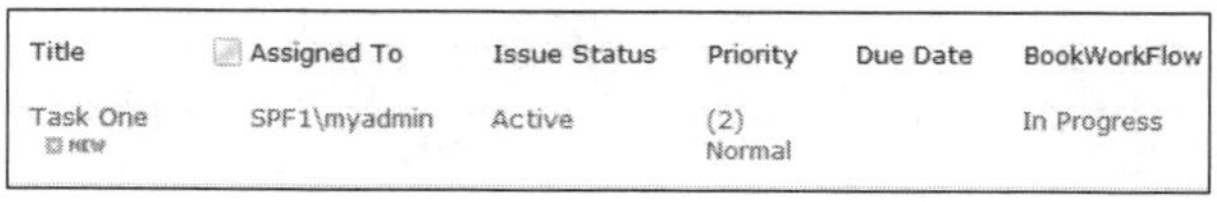

Title	☐ Assigned To	Issue Status	Priority	Due Date	BookWorkFlow
Task One ☐ NEW	SPF1\myadmin	Active	(2) Normal		In Progress

FIGURE 21.15
Issue is Active
and In Progress
in Three-
StateTest

6. Go back to the browser that is showing BookWorkflow Tasks and change the user from Administrator to MyAdmin via the drop-down when SPF1\Administrator is selected at the top-right part of the screen, and then open the Workflow Initiated: 1 item.

7. Edit the Workflow Initiated: 1 item so that the task is marked as complete and at 100 percent (see Figure 21.16). Click Save.

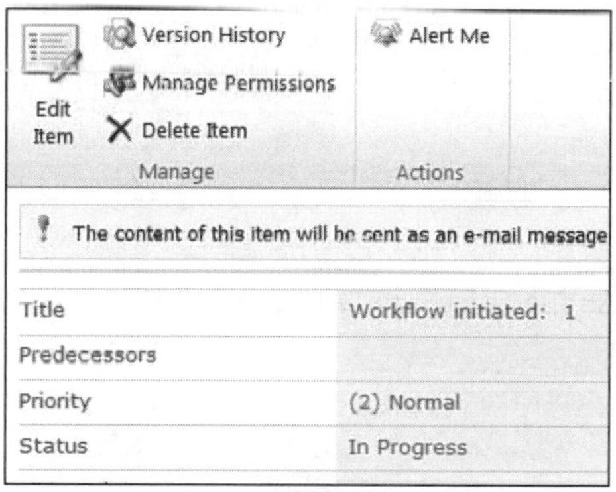

	Version History		Alert Me
	Manage Permissions		
Edit Item	X Delete Item		
	Manage		Actions

! The content of this item will be sent as an e-mail message

Title	Workflow initiated: 1
Predecessors	
Priority	(2) Normal
Status	In Progress

FIGURE 21.16
Accessing the
task when
signed in as
MyAdmin

8. Refresh the BookWorkflow Tasks page. You see a second task in the list (see Figure 21.17).

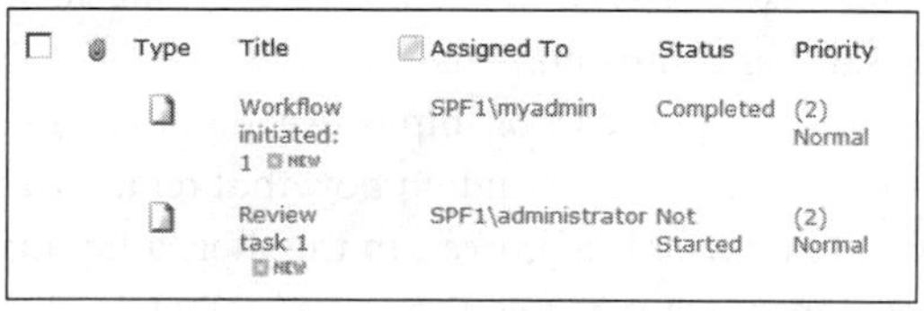

☐	⏷	Type	Title	☐ Assigned To	Status	Priority
			Workflow initiated: 1 ☐ NEW	SPF1\myadmin	Completed	(2) Normal
			Review task 1 ☐ NEW	SPF1\administrator	Not Started	(2) Normal

FIGURE 21.17
The Administrator's task is in
the task list.

Now go to the browser copy located at ThreeStateTest and refresh that page. (If you have been working with only one browser copy, make sure you change back to Administrator.)

After the refresh, that page looks like that shown in Figure 21.18.

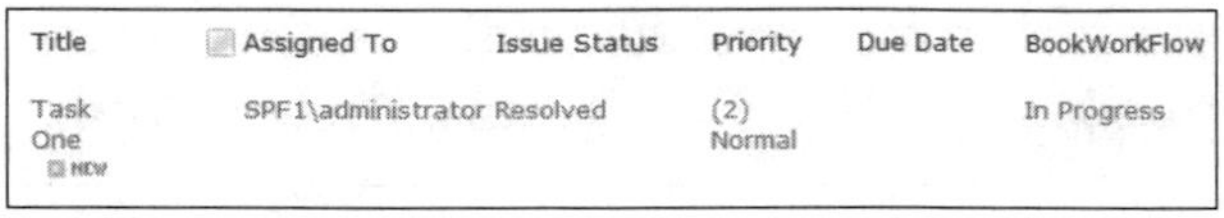

FIGURE 21.18
The state of
ThreeStateTest
after MyAdmin
has finished

Title	Assigned To	Issue Status	Priority	Due Date	BookWorkFlow
Task One □ NEW	SPF1\administrator	Resolved	(2) Normal		In Progress

The apparent contradiction of having the task resolved but still in progress is because the task has been done but has not been checked!

10. Go again to the BookWorkflow Tasks page and sign in as Administrator (if using two browser copies). Edit Review Task 1 and mark it as Completed 100%. Now BookWorkflow Tasks shows Figure 21.19.

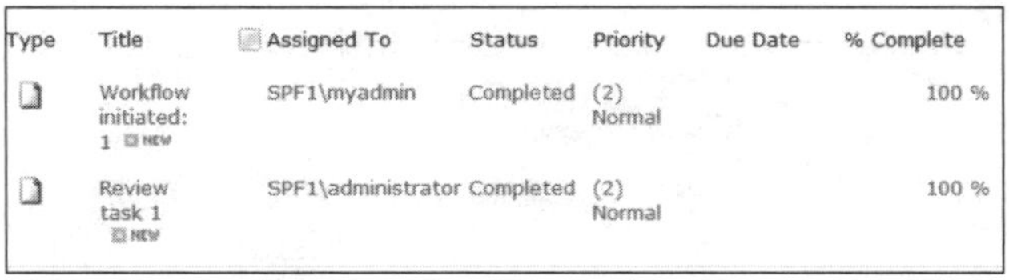

FIGURE 21.19
Two completed
tasks in Book-
Workflow Tasks

Type	Title	Assigned To	Status	Priority	Due Date	% Complete
□	Workflow initiated: 1 □ NEW	SPF1\myadmin	Completed	(2) Normal		100 %
□	Review task 1 □ NEW	SPF1\administrator	Completed	(2) Normal		100 %

11. Open and refresh the ThreeStateTest page (see Figure 21.20).

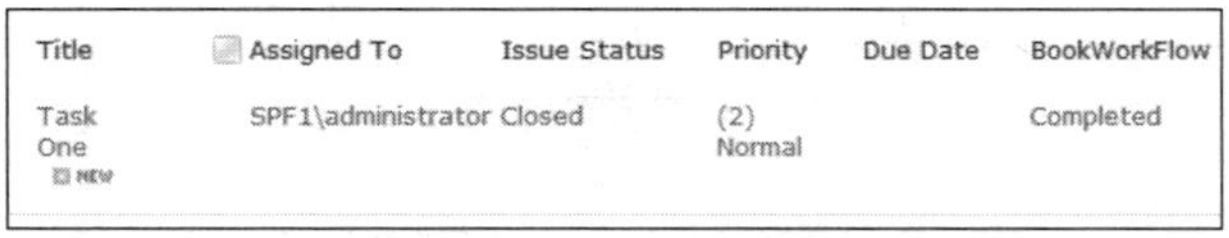

FIGURE 21.20
One completed
task in Three-
StateTest

Title	Assigned To	Issue Status	Priority	Due Date	BookWorkFlow
Task One □ NEW	SPF1\administrator	Closed	(2) Normal		Completed

With that, this workflow exercise is completed. Doing this for the first time everything probably seems rather confusing. This is no doubt because I've complicated matters by showing you the inter-relationship between the Tasks list and the Issue Tracking list. I did this because understanding how that relationship works is an integral part of understanding the entire process. In the short term adding that detail made the process seem more complicated than it actually is.

If you feel overwhelmed by this hour, do the whole thing again, and lamps will start to light up, and please take a break now and come back to it later and go through it all again—perhaps after you finish the whole book or maybe just after you work through creating workflows with SPD 2007 in the next hour.

Summary

In this hour, you learned about the different kinds of workflows that can be created using various tools for SharePoint 2010 environments. The hour continued with a detailed run-through of the three-stage workflow, which is the only workflow included in SPF 2010. The example chosen used the Issue Tracking list type, a list type specially created for the handling workflows at the overview level.

The "Q&A" section contains a question about the requirements for workflow when other types of lists (than the Issue Tracking and Tasks list types) are involved.

Q&A

Q. *A Workflow Settings option is available in most other types of lists, not just the Issue Tracking and Tasks list types. Are there any special requirements for these other list types?*

A. The main difference with using the Issue Tracking and Tasks lists is that those two list types are already set up for workflows, so they already have the necessary columns.

The main column that is needed in other list types is a Status column, which needs to be of type Choice with three options. These don't need to have the same names as the equivalent column in Issue Tracking and Tasks but must have three options to match the three-stage workflow, which is the only one available to SPF 2010.

Other useful (and usually essential) columns are a Data and Time column for the due date and a column for the name of the person/group responsible for the work at a particular stage. Both of these columns, like the Status column, are already in the Issue Tracking and Tasks list types, and it's probably a good idea to use the same names when adding these columns in the other list types.

When that is done, the process is similar to the process we've gone through in this hour. The list is opened and workflow settings specified. Just as with Issue Tracking, it's best to select New Task List (and New History List) so that just as with Issue Tracking, the detail work is done in a list of type Tasks.

Q. *How do we ensure that only certain people (rather than people with certain access rights) approve tasks?*

A. Because the process consists of a main list (Issue Tracking, document library, or whatever) and a Tasks list, it's possible to have different access rights for the two lists.

Workshop

Quiz

1. I listed six different ways to add workflows to SPF 2010. Which method isn't a way to create workflows?

2. Is it necessary to have an SMTP server available for workflows to work?

3. If I want emails to work, do I need to have an SMTP server installed on the SPF 2010 server?

Answers

1. InfoPath 2010. You can create forms that use data from workflows, but you can't create workflows in InfoPath 2010.

2. No, the workflow works fine. The difference is that no alerts or email messages can be sent if there is no SMTP server available. In other words, the people expected to react to tasks in workflows would then need to monitor the Tasks list so that they would know when to react.

3. No, you need to have an SMTP server available and specified in the Outgoing Email section. The server can be anywhere that is accessible (typical, therefore, in the domain or network) from the SPF 2010 server.

Using SharePoint Designer 2010 to Create Workflows

What You'll Learn in This Hour

▶ Background of SharePoint Designer 2010

▶ Creating workflows using SharePoint Designer 2010

Although SPF 2010 includes a functional three-stage workflow solution, it is limited to that single scenario. As discussed in the first section of the previous hour, there are other ways of creating workflows for SPF 2010. The most common method is to create workflows in SharePoint Designer 2010 (SPD 2010). One reason this is common is because SPD 2010 is free, and thus most SharePoint workflow creators have access to it. The other reason is that it does a good job, which the following sections show.

Introducing SharePoint Designer 2010

SharePoint Designer (SPD) 2010 is a follow-up product to SharePoint Designer 2007, which was a follow-up product to FrontPage 2003. SPD 2010 is a tool for customizing SharePoint 2010 websites and *only* for customizing SharePoint 2010 websites; it will not work with SharePoint 2007 websites. This is a change from the usual behavior of Office products, and it could lead to problems if you need to maintain both Share-Point 2010 and SharePoint 2007 websites.

SPD 2010 is a free download. That doesn't make it rubbish because it is a further development of SPD 2007, which until a year ago was a chargeable product. It's also a fully supported product. The theory is that if the product is free (and restricted to use with SP 2010 sites and thus theoretically better), everyone who has a SharePoint site to maintain will use it for the things it is good at. Thus, sites using SharePoint

2010 will be better, and (finally) Microsoft will sell more SharePoint licenses and CALs. It's a nice theory and certainly means that SharePoint Administrators no longer need to persuade their bosses that they need to buy it.

If you're a SharePoint site administrator, you need a copy. The problem with the product being free is that a lot of people may download it, too, so you might need to consider ways of stopping some sets of people from using SPD 2010 with your Share-Point sites.

By the Way

Throughout the recent history of SharePoint, there have been problems if products from two different Office versions (Outlook 2007 and Word 2003 say) are in use in client PCs accessing SharePoint sites. If you are wise, you will ignore Microsoft statements from the SPD 2010 team saying that to maintain both 2010 and 2007 SharePoint sites, you should install the 32-bit versions of SPD 2010 and SPD 2007 on your (single) client PC. (It is not at all possible to combine the 64-bit version of SPD 2010 with the 32-bit version of SPD 2007). Instead find a second (even old) PC and use that for maintaining your SharePoint 2007 (and 2003) sites with SPD 2007 (preferably running nothing else and certainly running no other Office product than Office 2007 products) and run only SPD 2010 on your client PC that is running other Office 2010 level applications.

This hour concentrates on creating workflows using SPD 2010. Another SPD 2010 topic is covered in Hour 23, "Using SharePoint Designer 2010 to Solve Common User Requests."

Key Facts About SPD 2010 Workflows

Following are useful things to know about SharePoint Designer 2010 workflows before you install SPD 2010:

▶ A SPD 2010 workflow, like the SPF 2010 built-in workflow we looked at in Hour 21, "Creating Workflows in SPF 2010," can be a workflow only on a single list or library.

▶ All SPD 2010 workflows are created using a wizard. This makes them powerful, but at the same time, they are initially (*) restricted to doing what the wizard makers thought you—the user—would want to do. (*) The wizard generates code, and the code can be changed by hand later.

▶ Through the wizard, SPD 2010 workflows are easy to create.

Where to Install SharePoint Designer 2010

The most common place to install SPD 2010 is on a client system (XP Pro, Vista, or Windows 7) from which you will be accessing a server system or a virtual machine (VM) running SPD 2010. This should be done only if the client system either has no Microsoft Office applications installed or only Office 2010 applications.

There is another alternative, but it's not recommended for production use: Install SPD 2010 on the server (or VM) where you run SPD 2010. This might be handy for a testing environment on a portable (especially if that portable is not running XP Pro, Vista, or Windows 7 as its own Operating System—a MacBook for instance).

> The installation process for SharePoint Designer 2010 isn't discussed here because it is a guided installation typical of Microsoft commercial (and free, formerly commercial) products.

By the Way

Starting to Use SharePoint Designer 2010

When you first opened SPD 2007, it had a clean look (see Figure 22.1), but it was a look that a Visual Studio user would feel more at home with than the typical user of Office products.

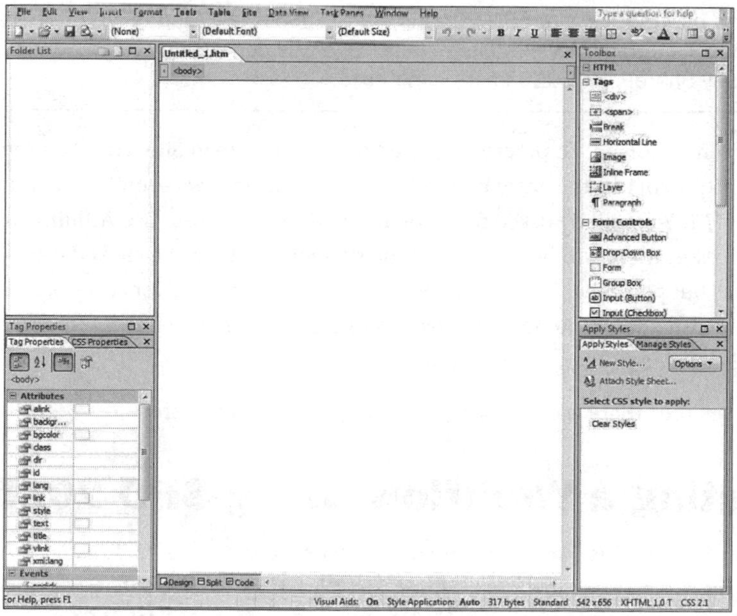

FIGURE 22.1
Opening SPD 2007 for the first time

Now look at what we get when we first open SharePoint Designer 2010 (see Figure 22.2).

FIGURE 22.2
Opening SPD
2010 for the
first time

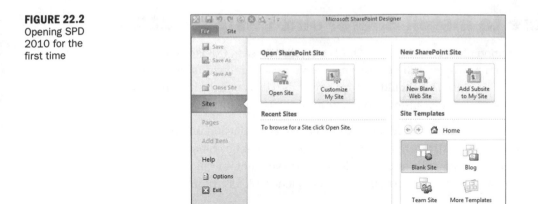

Quite a difference, isn't it? Now that's something that an Office user can feel at home with. The main problem that we now face is, "What is the difference between Open Site and Customize MySite? If we open a site in SPD 2010, we usually want to amend it in some way.

The answer for SPF 2010 users is that you can ignore the Customize MySite option entirely. MySite is a function that SPS 2010 has (which is usually written like that so you can tell it is not MySite or The Site That I Have), but which SPF 2010 does not have.

By the Way

> I find it a bit irritating that SPD 2010 is made specifically (and only) for Share-Point 2010 sites, and even so its default page still contains a link to a function that many SharePoint 2010 users don't have.

The problem is solved. To proceed we need to click the Open Site icon. You then need to write http://spf1 in the entry box in the screen that follows even if you run SPD 2010 in SPF1. You will be asked for credentials—in which case, use Administrator. In future accesses there will be an icon for the spf1 site that can be clicked after you use Open Site, but you then don't even need to use Open Site in most cases because your site will be listed in the Recent Sites section of Figure 22.2. The page you now see (Figure 22.3) is too full of information.

Did you see that there is even a link to Change Site Theme here?

Creating a Workflow Using SPD 2010

Now that SPD 2010 is open, we can create a workflow. Figure 22.3 displays two direct links to two workflow possibilities: List Workflow (where the down arrow leads to the Lists in your site) and Reusable Workflow. To see all the Workflow alternatives, select File.

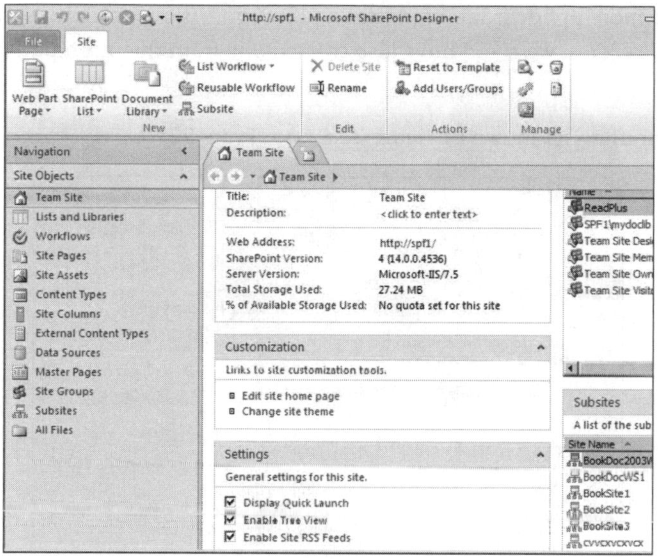

FIGURE 22.3
Opening the SPF
2010 site in
SPD 2010

Figure 22.4 shows the top of the screen. People who have already used SPD 2007 will be surprised to see that there is no longer a File Open, but instead the default is to add a web part page to the default master page.

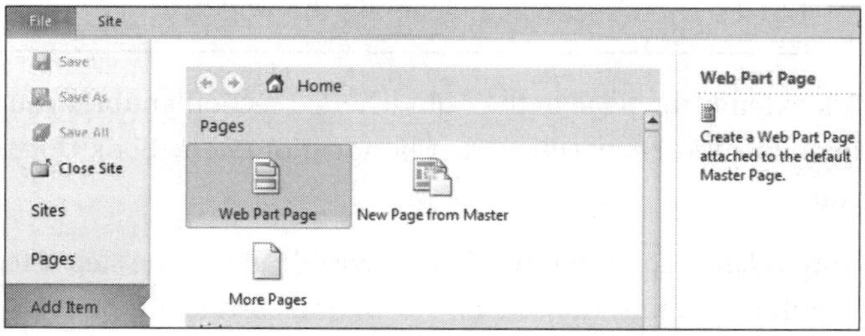

FIGURE 22.4
Selecting File,
the default option

Doing anything with the master page is not something that we are going to do just for fun. (It's a risky business that requires more knowledge than a couple of hours can give you, and typically it is safer to copy master pages and amend only the copies.) So we'll move down the page to look at the Workflow section (see Figure 22.5).

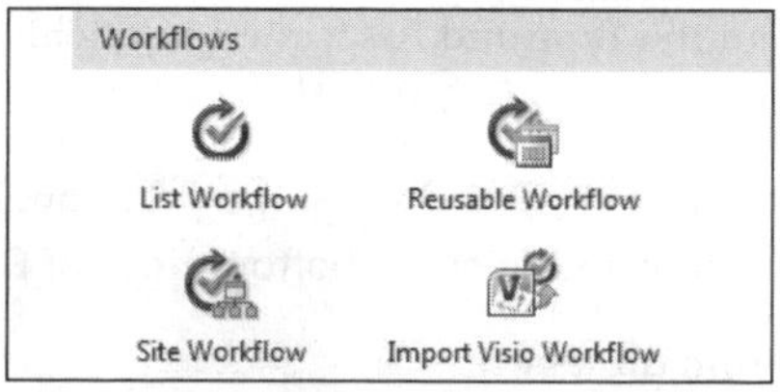

FIGURE 22.5
The Workflows
section of the
File screen

Here are two more options: Site Workflow and Import Visio Workflow. Now we create a List Workflow. (Yes, we could have also created one from the main page using the link there.).

Click List Workflow, as shown in Figure 22.5 (see Figure 22.6).

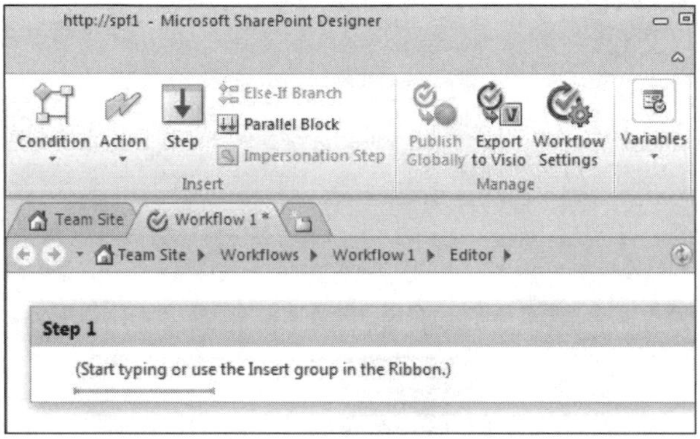

FIGURE 22.6
Defining the workflow, Step 1

Watch Out!

It is extremely important that you do not double-click List Workflow. If you do, a workflow will be generated for the Announcements List (the first List in alphabetical order), and once created, the List used cannot be changed.

By the Way

Don't worry if it takes a few seconds to generate the workflow.

The single-click extends the page to the right where a section enables you to specify the List on which this Workflow will work. Change that to The Book Documents list and click Create.

The Insert Group referred to in the step 1 box is visible above the step 1 section. There are four main options: Connection, Action, Step, and Parallel Block. Because we are just starting out with our first SPD 2010 workflow, it's not a good idea to start typing.

Before we create any steps, we need to look at Workflow Settings.

Click Workflow Settings (see Figure 22.7).

The left sections give basic information about the workflow. As you could see from the colors of the entries if this book had color images, the Name and Description fields (in blue) can be amended, but the Type and Associated List fields cannot.

The sections on the right are familiar because they are similar to the options we had in Hour 21 when we created a SPF 2010 three-stage workflow. Here are those three options (that are also partially visible at the bottom right of Figure 22.7):

▶ Manually started from an item

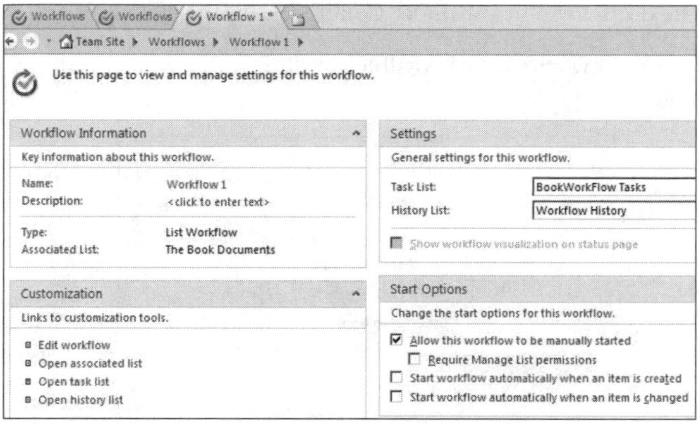

FIGURE 22.7
What does
Workflow Set-
tings tell us?

▶ Automatically started when a new item is created

▶ Automatically started when an item is changed

Here, make the same changes as in Hour 21: Specify that a New Task List should be created, deselect All This Workflow to Be Manually Started, and select Start Workflow Automatically When an Item Is Changed.

An example of this type of workflow can be something as simple as an administrator who wants to let people change the contents of documents within a document library, but he wants to stay informed about each change.

Let's see how this scenario plays out for a document in The Book Documents document library. To do this, follow these steps:

1. Change the workflow name to **SPD Workflow 1**. Click Enter to get this value to stick.

2. Have the workflow automatically started when an item is changed. We could select all three options (or any two), but let's suppose that only a changed item interests us.

> Before doing any of this, it is advisable to make sure that your update settings for the Operating System are not set to "automatically install updates." There is nothing worse than being midway through creating a workflow and finding the next day when you want to continue that an OS update has restarted your PC (and of course not bothered to save what you have done so far). Instead set upgrades to "download upgrades but do not install."

Did you Know?

3. Click Edit Workflow. This takes us back to Figure 22.6 again, only now the workflow name is SPD Workflow 1 and not Workflow 1.

4. Click the drop-down arrow under Conditions on the ribbon.

Figure 22.8 shows the list of possible conditions that you can apply to this workflow.

FIGURE 22.8
A list of conditions

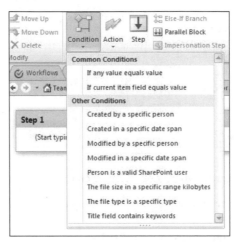

The Modified by a Specific Person option would be what our suspicious administrator is looking for.

5. Select Modified by a Specific Person.

6. Now select the drop-down button under the Action option on the ribbon.

Unlike the situation with SPD 2007, this is a long list because it shows all the items. (SPD 2007 had a short list that included an All Items option.) See Figure 22.9 for just the first items in the list.

7. Here select Create List Item (at the bottom of Figure 22.9 but not at the bottom of the drop-down on your screen).

In total, we have so far set the following:

> Condition = Modified by a Specific Person
>
> Action = Create List Item

By the Way

Send an Email is probably the more likely option if the administrator is worried. However, we had enough of sending emails in Hour 21, and what we're doing now is more interesting for what happens next. Later (in the "Q&A" section), we add a condition that sends an email.

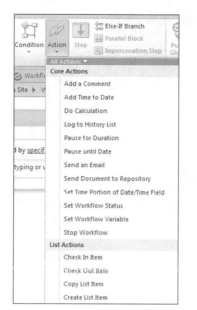

FIGURE 22.9
A image showing
some actions

Figure 22.10 shows what we now have.

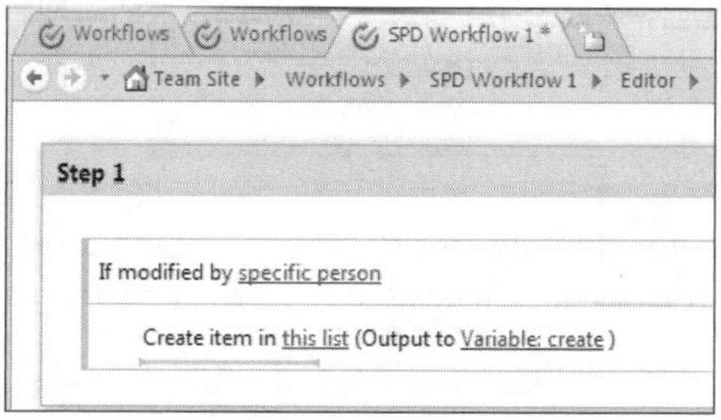

FIGURE 22.10
One condition
and one action
set

8. Click the underlined "specific person" to specify the person we want to monitor for modifying documents in the list. Click a name, and there's a useful pop-up with a list of names to choose from (see Figure 22.11).

9. Select MyContrib. (There's no point in selecting someone with only Read rights who can't modify anything.).

10. Click Add to move that name over to the Selected Users column.

11. Click OK.

12. Click "this list." (See Figure 20.9 where the user mycontrib is now specified.)

FIGURE 22.11
Choosing the
user to monitor

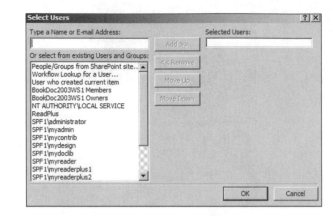

13. After a momentary panic when there is no list of Lists visible, click in the Lists section of the screen, which gives you a drop-down with a list of Lists (see Figure 22.12).

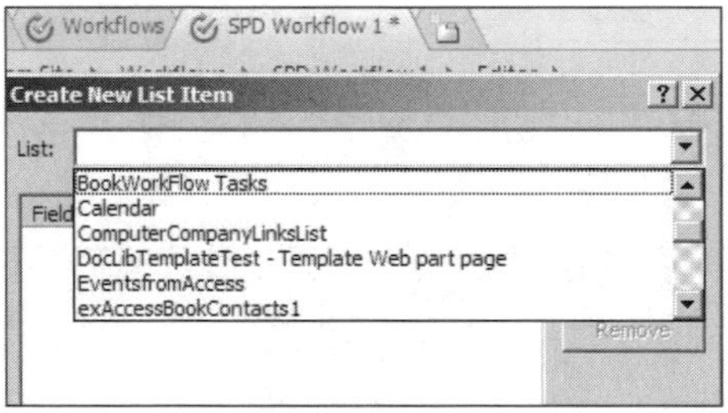

FIGURE 22.12
Selecting the
List the action
goes to

14. Select Calendar from that list (see Figure 22.13). (I'm using Calendar just to show that you can use almost any list type when creating a workflow like this.)

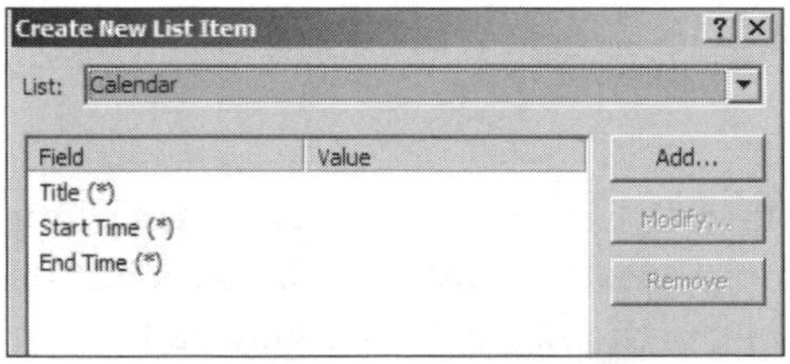

FIGURE 22.13
Completing the
information on
the calendar item

15. Double-click the Title, Start Time and End Time fields and enter the following values:

Title = Warning from Workflow

Start Time = Today

End Time = (a suitable time a few days after Today)

To specify values in the Start Time and End Time fields, click the "..." box after double-clicking the field name. Then you have the choice between "current date" (such as Today) and "specific date" where you can use a pop-up calendar to change the date from the default.

By the Way

See Figure 22.14 for a set of suitable values; this was done on February 18, so the date chosen for End Time was five days later.

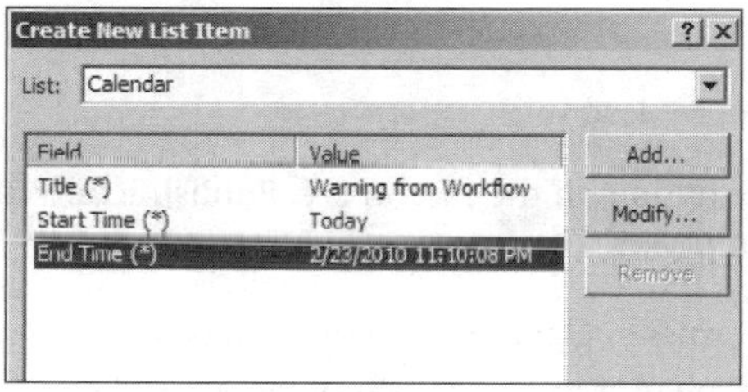

FIGURE 22.14
Appropriate values for the action

16. Click OK.

17. Click Save on the Ribbon (far left side of the ribbon).

We could at this point add another step (using Step in the ribbon, naturally) but let's decide for now this is all we need.

Creating the workflow is now finished, and after we close the workflow (which was already saved in step 16) by clicking the "x" at the top-right portion of the workflow part of the screen, you'll see Figure 22.15 where this single workflow is listed.

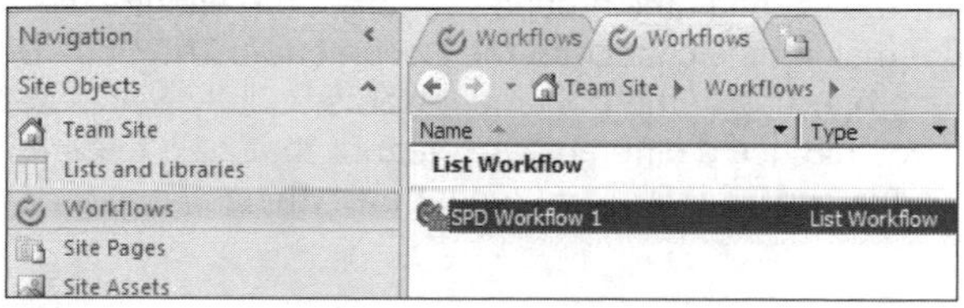

FIGURE 22.15
The list of List Workflows

We can now abandon SPD 2010 for a while (leave it open though, as you will need it again soon), because we want to determine whether the workflow we just generated actually works.

Follow these steps to see if our workflow works:

1. Go back to our browser. Open the site there. Open the My Book Documents library. Change the user to MyContrib and then open a document. Amend it and save it back to the site.

2. Look now at the Calendar, and you will not see a new entry! So what did we do wrong? While in SPD 2010 we saved the workflow. All this meant was that we had created a workflow and saved it—an action that is roughly equivalent to saving a file for later use. What we now need to ensure is that the workflow is activated.

3. Go back to SPD 2010. (It was left open, as shown in Figure 22.15.)

4. Open SPD Workflow 1 again.

5. Next to the Save option on the ribbon is a Publish icon. Click it. Now we can repeat our small test.

6. Go back to our browser. Open the site there. Open the My Book Documents library. Change the user to MyContrib (if we are not already signed in as MyContrib) and then open a document. Amend it and save it back to the site.

7. Look at the Calendar (refresh if you have left it open in a Tab), and you see a new entry (Figure 22.16).

FIGURE 22.16
A new entry in the Calendar

Calendar

2/18/2010 12:00 AM   Warning
                     from
                     Workflow
                     ☐ NEW

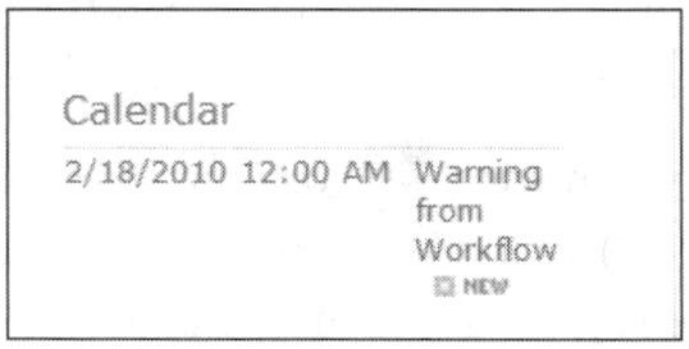

Did you Know?

If you still don't see a new entry in the Calendar, don't panic. What's probably happened is that the second time around you forgot the change the user to MyContrib before making the change to the Document in The Book Documents. (A change to the properties of the Document works equally well in setting the workflow off.) If you did use a different user, regard that as a useful test that the workflow only works for MyContrib, and repeat everything again, only this time do use MyContrib.

We've learned that using SPD 2010 to create workflows is more powerful and yet much easier to do than using the so-called "simple" three-stage workflow included in SPF 2010.

The SPD 2010 workflow wizards are powerful, relatively flexible, and will probably provide as much workflow as most people will want, so even if you are a Visual Studio expert, don't discard the SPD 2010 option for workflows, but use it when you can and use Visual Studio 2010 for your workflows only when SPD 2010 workflows aren't flexible or powerful enough for your needs.

Summary

Here we looked in general at SharePoint Designer (SPD) 2010, discussed its availability, and also considered where to install it.

SPD 2010 was used to create a workflow that enabled an administrator to be warned if a particular user did something he perhaps shouldn't.

Q&A

Q. *Once I've written a workflow in SPD 2010, can I modify it?*

A. Yes, you can. Here's how you amend the workflow we created to send a message to the Announcements list as an alternative (for a different user) to sending a message to a calendar:

1. Go back to SPD 2010 and if necessary select open the site (http://SPF1) and click Workflows. Open SPD Workflow 1 with double-click and then select Edit Workflow (see Figure 22.17).

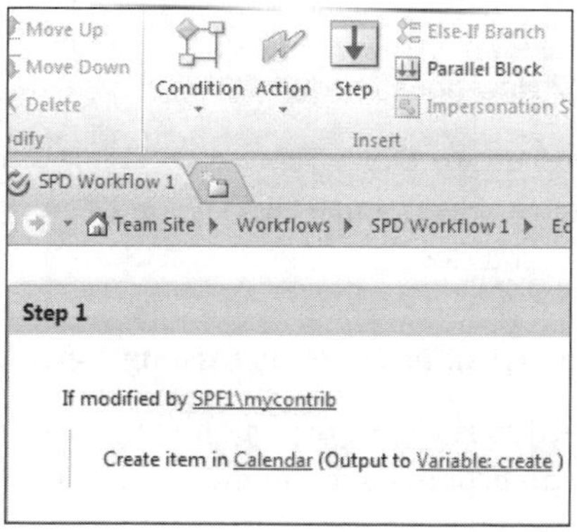

FIGURE 22.17
Starting to modify an existing workflow

2. First select Step 1; then click Step on the ribbon, and an empty Step 2 is created below Step 1.

3. Let's leave Step 1 there, but this time let's say that we want something to happen when MyAdmin amends a document. We want to change the list that the message is sent to in this case, but we still want the message to be sent when something is amended (by MyAdmin). In Step 2 we also select the Announcements list and give Title a value. We then select Add and get a list of fields from the Announcements list. We select Body from that list and write some text in it. Click OK to display Figure 22.18.

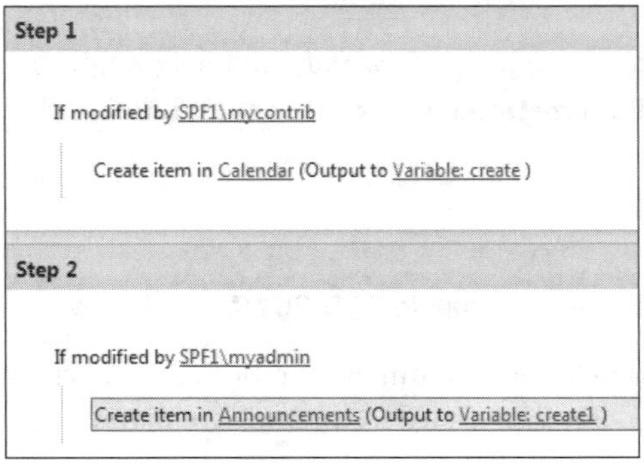

FIGURE 22.18
Adding a second condition

> **Step 1**
>
> If modified by <u>SPF1\mycontrib</u>
>
>   Create item in <u>Calendar</u> (Output to <u>Variable: create</u>)
>
> **Step 2**
>
> If modified by <u>SPF1\myadmin</u>
>
>   Create item in <u>Announcements</u> (Output to <u>Variable: create1</u>)

4. We now click Save and then Publish. An item is created in the calendar if MyContrib amends something, and a different item is created in Announcements if MyAdmin amends something. (To remove Step 1, click the drop-down that appears to the right of the If Modified By SPF1\Mycontrib Line and select Delete Condition.)

Q. *How about Else If? How does that work?*

A. Go again to the present workflow. There is an Else-If Branch option in the ribbon provided you first select (single-click) a condition or an Action. (It is not available if you select a step.)

Q. *How about just adding an action to an existing condition?*

A. To do that, you need to select the action already listed. Then select Action from the toolbar. Select an action and fill in the rest of the information. As shown in Figure 22.19, after you select email, the system needs to know who to send the email to.

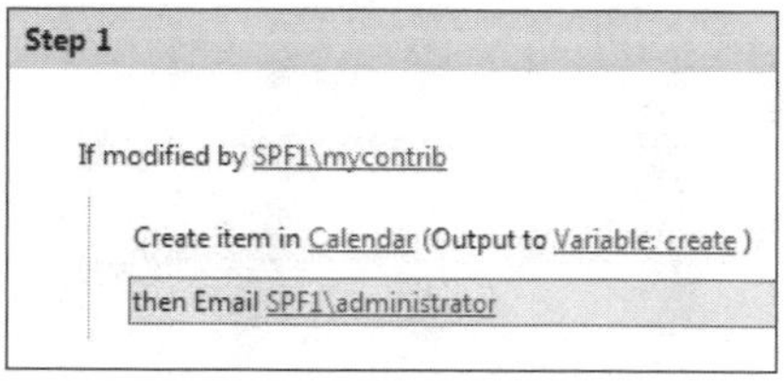

FIGURE 22.19
Adding a second
action for the
same condition

Workshop

Quiz

1. If you have a copy of Visual Studio 2010 (and development skills to match), why would you still use SPD 2010 for workflow?

2. Can you send messages to different people at the same stage in the workflow?

Answers

1. SPD 2010 can be used for prototyping or for workflows that don't require Visual Studio 2010.

2. You can add a second action to the same step of a workflow (see Figure 22.19). Two or more of the actions belonging to a condition can be emails to different accounts and people.

Using SharePoint Designer 2010 to Solve Common User Requests

What You'll Learn in This Hour

- ▶ How to make a List appear in two different sites
- ▶ How to create Data View web parts of Lists from the current site
- ▶ How to use Data View web parts to get data from outside the present site
- ▶ How to customize Data View web parts

You can do a great deal with SharePoint Designer 2010—enough to fill an entire book. So here we look in detail at something that is especially useful for SPF 2010 users because there is no easy alternative solution for non-SharePoint Server 2010 users.

This hour is about how to solve the common request of wanting to have the same data visible in two places. For SPF 2010 users the solution is to use the Data View Web Part (DVWP)—also called in some earlier SharePoint versions the Data Forms Web Part (DFWP). After we solve the main problem of showing SharePoint Lists in two places, we follow up by looking at what other kinds of data we can show in our SPF 2010 sites courtesy of DVWPs (and SPD 2010).

Avoiding Uploading the Same Document to Two Document Libraries

Some of the most common questions in the SharePoint newsgroups and forums are questions about how to upload documents to two different document libraries at the same time.

Another common question (and which is similar) is how to show the same list content in two (or more) different sites.

Uploading documents to two different document libraries at the same time could be done with a mass of special coding. When one of the standard methods for upgrading a document is used, a set of code could grab the request and ask you to specify additional destinations for the document (other than just the document library where the user was located in the browser when the upload document function was accessed).

Apart from the fact that this special coding would require quality SharePoint programming skills, it also leads to two (or more) physical copies of the same document being stored in the SharePoint database. So it requires more storage. Of course, the content of these two (or more) documents, when uploaded, could change independently over time (unless your special coding is extremely clever). So unless you actually want this, you need to look for another solution.

Creating and Using a Custom Web Part

In the previous version of SPD (SPD 2007), this problem was solved by using a Data View Web Part where you could click in a menu on a site in the same site collection and then on the List from that site that you wanted to appear in the site where you were located.

In that case there was only one copy of the List or Library (so there was no problem with duplicate sets of data), and the "list" that was created in the Data View Web Part (DVWP) was a read-only copy of that "master" List.

When you accessed (or refreshed) the page containing the DVWP, that copy always contained the latest version of the data from that list. We look at DVWPs in SPD 2010 later in this hour, but Microsoft said there were "issues" with the function described and removed it, so we need to find a new solution, which is to create a Custom Web Part of a List in one site and then use that Custom Web Part in another list. (Creating a DVWP from Lists in the same site is covered later but doesn't solve this first problem.)

Creating a Custom Web Part from a Library

The first set of steps here detail creating a custom web part of a Library located in the default website. The steps would be identical for a List apart from the List name:

1. Open the default site (http://spf1) in SPD 2010.

2. Go to the main page of the Team Site and select List and Libraries in the left column (see Figure 23.1).

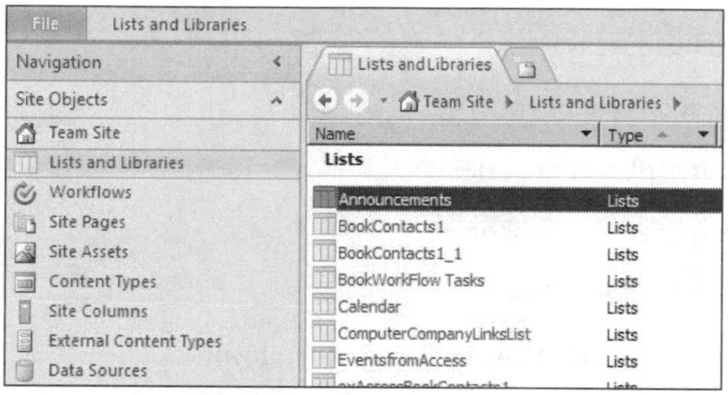

FIGURE 23.1
Selecting Lists and Libraries

3. Click The Book Documents at the end of the list. It's the final item in the Document Libraries section (see Figure 23.2).

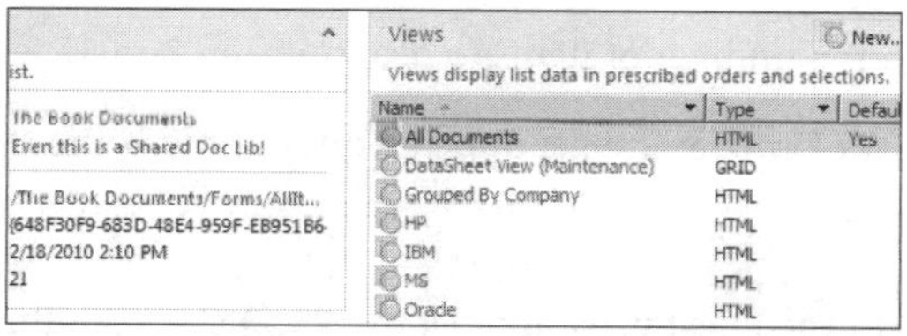

FIGURE 23.2
Selecting The Book Documents Document Library

As you can see, there is a list of all the Views available for this List. When creating a custom web part, you can specify any one of these; however, for the purposes of this test later, it would be useful if we have a View that includes all the items in the List, except for those that include Company=HP. Before we create this custom web part, we use the New link in Figure 23.2 to create a View like that.

4. Click New.

5. In the Create New List View that follows, specify the name All But HP.

6. Click OK.

Now in Figure 23.2 there will be a new item at the top of the Views section, All But HP.

It's tempting to think that we are finished with the creation of this view, but how did SPD 2010 know that All But HP as the name for a view meant that Company=HP records should be excluded? Of course it didn't, and this New function here isn't useful because all it creates is a View that isn't sorted that includes all records and many columns.

Not what we want for our test case, so it's a good idea to correct that before we move on in SPD 2010. We created Views in a browser before, so the following few action items are in shorthand with no images.

7. Open the site in a browser.

8. Open The Book Documents.

9. Click Library (ribbon menu).

10. Click Library Settings (ribbon).

11. Select the All But HP View.

12. Amend the All But HP View by doing the following:

    ▶ Unselect Modified, Modified By, and SPD Workflow1.

    ▶ Sort first by Company and then by Name (linked to Document).

    ▶ Set the Filter to Company "Is Not Equal To" HP.

    ▶ Change the number of items to display from 3 to 5.

13. Click OK. (In the browser the list appears again now without the HP rows).

    Now back to SPD 2010.

14. (In SPD 2010 at the latest version of Figure 23.2) Click All But HP (see Figure 23.3).

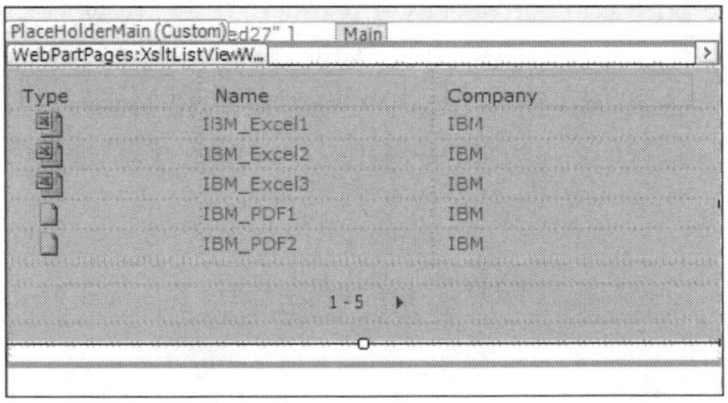

FIGURE 23.3
Opening the All But HP View in SPD 2010

Note that here, too, the list starts with the IBM items and not with the HP ones (and that there are five of them listed).

The next step is to save this as a web part.

15. Click Web Part in the List View Tools section of the ribbon (see Figure 23.4).

16. Click To Site Gallery in the Save Web Part section to the right.

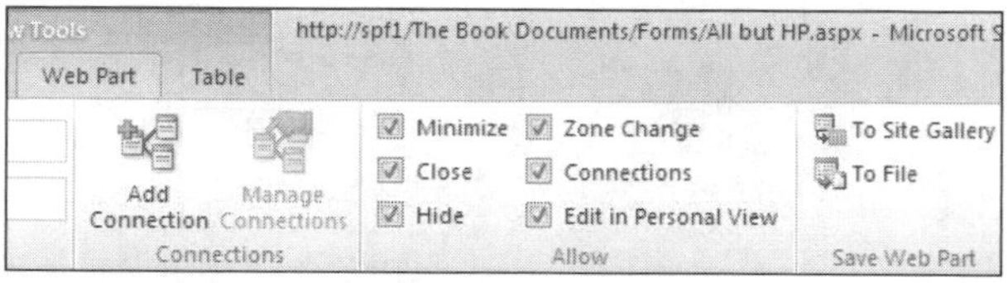

FIGURE 23.4
The List View
Tools/Web Part
ribbon

17. Click in the Save Web Part to Site Gallery window that appears. The next window is a bit trickier (see Figure 23.5).

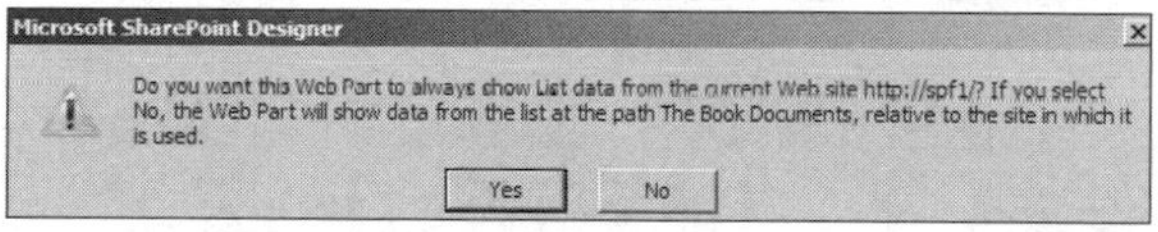

FIGURE 23.5
Selecting data
from the current
website

18. Because we want to always (no matter where we are) see data from this Document Library located in the default site http://spf1, we need to click Yes.

> Selecting No might be useful if many sites contain a List of Library with the same name. In that case you would probably make amendments to the List while in SPD 2010 before saving the web part, such as making the headings bold and in color by selecting the headings + right-click + format. Here we would only be amending a single Document Library, so we can do it later.

By the Way

Creating a New Page to Contain the Custom Web Part

Now that The Book Documents Library has been stored as a custom web part, it's time to use that web part in the subsite.

There are two parts to this. First we create a new web part page that contains several zones. Then we populate one of these zones with the custom web parts we just created.

The first set of steps creates the new web part page:

1. Access http://spf1 in SPD 2010 and select Subsites from the column at the left (see Figure 23.6).

2. Click BookSite1 (see Figure 23.7).

3. Click Web Part Page (in the ribbon at the left side), and you get a selection of layouts of possible web pages (see Figure 23.8).

FIGURE 23.6
Listing subsites
in SPD 2010

FIGURE 23.7
BookSite1 in
SPD 2010

FIGURE 23.8
Possible web
page layouts

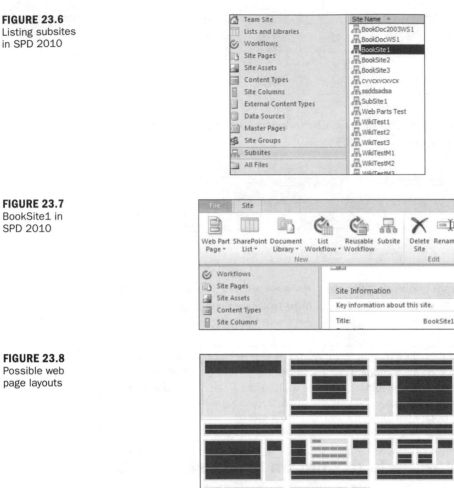

Each dark blue section and the rectangular light blue shapes are web part zones. Because we are testing, it's wise to choose a version that already has lots of zones specified. (As we see later, we put web parts into different zones.)

4. Select the version in the center of the top row. (This is Header, Footer, 3 Columns as you see if you move the cursor over it.)

5. Name the page **Page** for **Custom Web Parts**.

6. Click OK.

Adding the Custom Web Part to the New Page

Now that we have a suitable web part page, we can populate it with the custom web part we previously created. Here are the steps for that (final) phase:

1. (You are still in the Subsite BookSite1 shown in Figure 23.7.) Click Site Pages (see Figure 23.9).

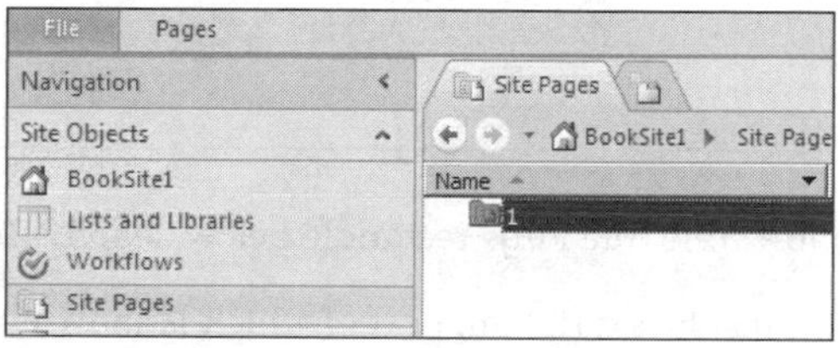

FIGURE 23.9
Site Pages list only 1

2. Double-click the 1, as shown in Figure 23.9. (A single-click enables you to edit the name, but there's not much point in doing that—just leave it as 1.)

   Figure 23.10 shows the contents of 1 that are in my site. There are two web pages because I created one earlier.

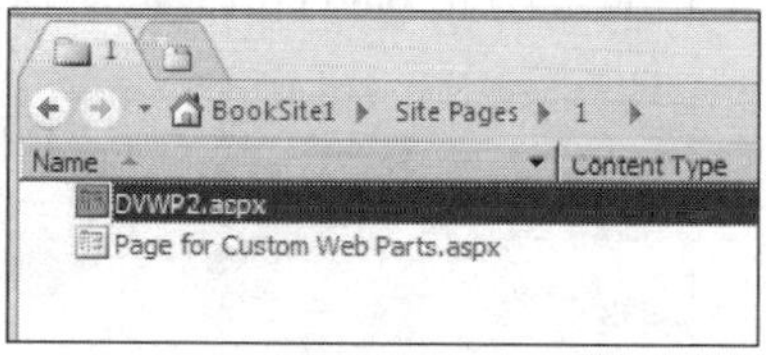

FIGURE 23.10
The real list of Site Pages

3. Click Page for Custom Web Parts.aspx.

4. Click File (see Figure 23.11).

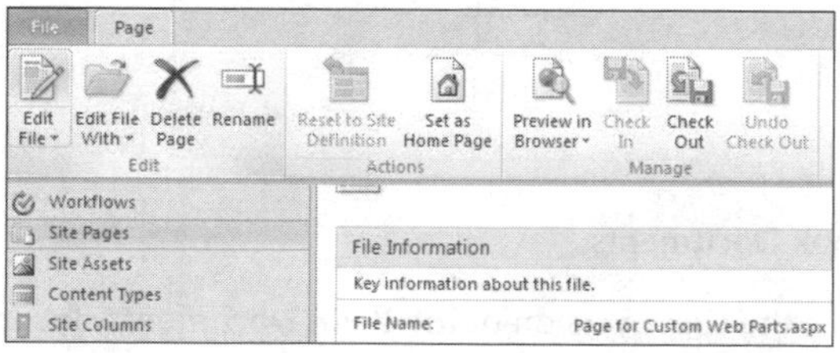

FIGURE 23.11
Options for a Site Page

5. Click Edit File.

   What you now see is the page that was just created with Headings for the site that it was created in. We can tell that it is the page we just created because we can clearly see (in Figure 23.12) the five different zones.

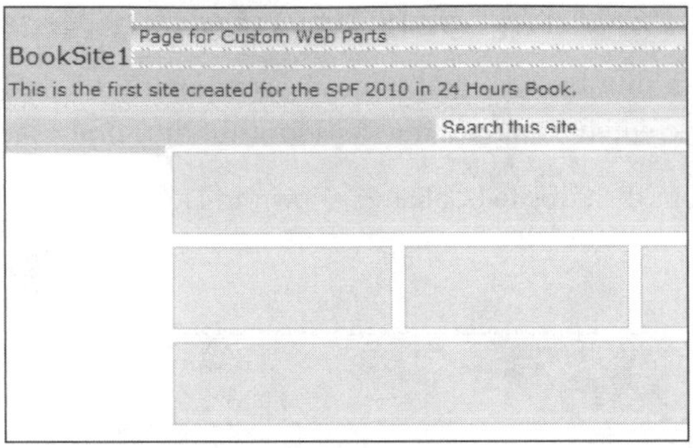

FIGURE 23.12
Starting to edit a
web part page

6. Click the top-most zone (the large rectangle below Search This Site) to select it.

7. Click Insert. This displays a ribbon, part of which is shown in Figure 23.13.

FIGURE 23.13
The Insert
Ribbon

8. Select the drop-down arrow next to Web Part (see Figure 23.14).

FIGURE 23.14
Selecting a web
part to insert

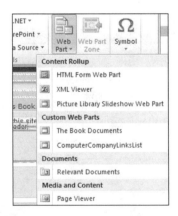

9. Click The Book Documents.

Again you see the same version of the Book Documents document library (from the top-level site, you'll remember), only now it is located in the subsite to that top-level default site.

10. Click File > Save and then the right "x" at the top-right part of the window. (Alternatively, click the right "x" and you will be asked if you want to save the page, which you do.)

At this point it would be a good idea to go in the browser to http://spf1/BookSite1/
SitePages/1/Page for Custom Web Parts.aspx to see what the page looks like. As you
can see it contains the document library from the default website.

Another useful test (which I'll leave to you) would be to open a second tab of the
browser at the default site, amend The Book Documents List in some way, and then
go again to the Page for Custom Web Parts in the first tab. Refresh it to see if the
changes you have just made in the main site appear.

Hint: They appear only if the company is not HP. (Because as you remember, the
View we used in the subsite was All but HP.)

> One of the problems when using SPD 2007's DVWP function to add a document
> library from a different site was that the hyperlink to each document file was
> incorrect (because It assumed the document was in the same site as the DVWP).
> The hyperlinks needed to be amended using a second procedure. When using
> this method in SPD 2010, the hyperlink to the document points to the site in
> which the document exists—that is here the default top-level site—and so click-
> ing the hyperlink will work with no additional effort being necessary.

By the Way

In the next section, you create a DVWP that obtains its data from a list in the same site.

Creating a Data View Web Part from a List in the Same Site

To start the process of creating a DVWP from a list, follow these steps:

1. In SPD 2010, go to the Page for Custom Webparts.aspx page previously created
   earlier in this hour. If you follow this hour without closing your server, this page
   should still be open for editing. If not, follow previous steps in this hour to open
   it for editing.

2. This time go to the zone at the bottom and select it.

3. Click Insert in the ribbon. You now see the same ribbon that was shown in
   Figure 23.13.

4. Select the down arrow to the right of Data View. Figure 23.15 displays both the
   previously added The Book Documents copy and the selected bottom zone.

   This drop-down shows the Lists and Libraries in use in that site at which we are
   now located (BookSite1).

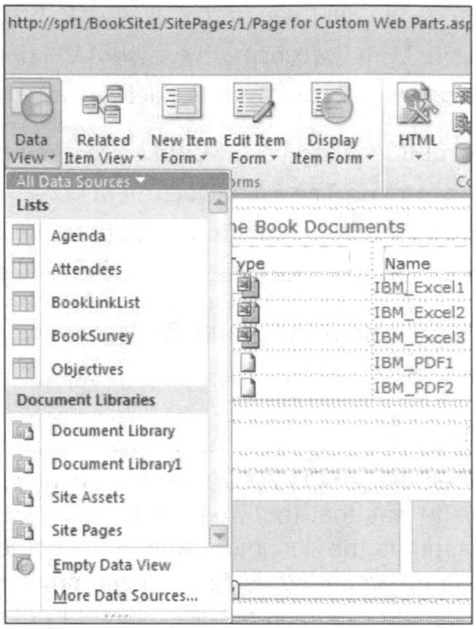

FIGURE 23.15
The Lists and more available for use in a DVWP

Clicking More Data Sources here would give us the same list shown in Figure 23.14 but with a slightly different look. We'll see in the section after this one how to create more data sources and thus have more options available when selecting More Data Sources.

5. Select BookLinkList. If you don't have this, select Document Library or any other List/Lib that has content. If none do, just add some content to a document library and use that.

For quite a long time, you see that the data view web part is being added (see Figure 23.16).

FIGURE 23.16
A long delay while the DVWP is added

Finally the DVWP has been added, and you see something like the screen shown in Figure 23.17.

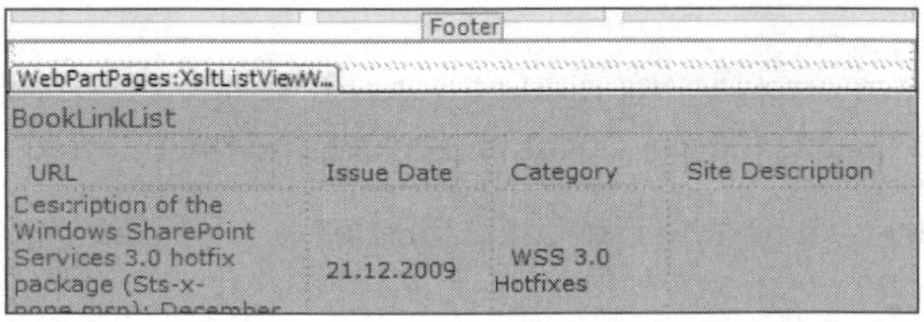

FIGURE 23.17
The DVWP has been added.

6. Save the Page (File Save).

7. Go to the browser and look at the page there. (If necessary, Refresh the page.) You should see a screen where the main section contains two sets of information. You see the first five items from The Book Documents list and the first five items from the BookLinkList List.

A question that will be looked at later in this hour is: Why do we use a DVWP to display a List from the same site? Why not just add the List itself? The answer as we see later lies in the enhanced formatting possibilities that can be done in a DVWP.

The next section deals with the creation of additional Data Sources that can be used in future DVWPs.

Creating and Using Data Sources

In this section, we create and use additional data sources.

Creating New Data Sources

In the first section of this hour, to add a top-level site's List to a subsite, we needed in SPD 2010 to first create a web part of that top-level site's List. Only when this had been done could the List be added to a subsite. The same kind of thing is necessary when creating an additional data source for a DVWP to use. Whereas SPD 2007 allowed this to be done within the DVWP creation routine, in SPD 2010 this is a completely separate action that at first seems to have nothing to do with a DVWP.

The following steps cover the creation of a new Data Source. The following section then deals with using that new Data Source in a DVWP.

1. You should still be located at the Page for Custom Web Parts.aspx; now click Data Sources in the left column.

2. Click Data Sources in the ribbon menu. The ribbon now looks like Figure 23.18.

FIGURE 23.18
The Data Sources ribbon

There are quite a few alternatives (in the New section). The most common perhaps in production use is the Database connection option, which enables you to grab data from a database and display it in a SharePoint page. The problem with that option is that accessing a particular database requires a database connection string that works only for connections to that particular database. This typically isn't straightforward, and because I don't want to spend time in this SharePoint Beginner/Intermediate guide on how to connect to databases, I'm going to take an easier example, creating an XML file connection.

3. Click XML File Connection.

I have already created an XML file called greeting.xml and stored it in the C drive on the server. Here is the simple text of that file:

```
<?xml version="1.0"?>
<!—greeting.xml —>
<greeting>
  Hello World!
</greeting>
```

4. The XML File Connection routines ask you to specify the location of the file. Use Browse to find greeting.xml and click OK.

As previously stated, this file is stored in C:\ in the server. Because I am using an SPD 2010 copy installed on the server, that is an easy place to find it. In production you would have dedicated folders for such files, and they would probably be accessible from your client PC.

Figure 23.19 shows the warning window that appears in the case of a simple XML file like this.

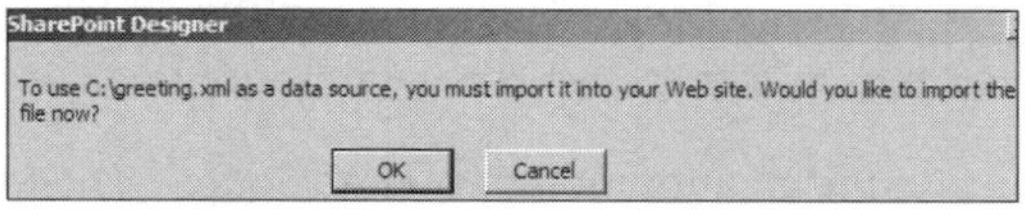

FIGURE 23.19
The warning when adding an XML file

SharePoint Designer

To use C:\greeting.xml as a data source, you must import it into your Web site. Would you like to import the file now?

OK   Cancel

5. Click OK. This displays a screen that needs to be approved, this time for the import (see Figure 23.20).

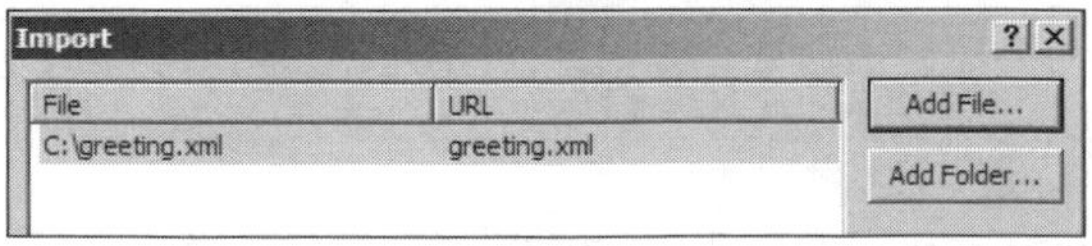

FIGURE 23.20
Importing an XML file

Import   ? X

File	URL	
C:\greeting.xml	greeting.xml	Add File...
		Add Folder...

This section is XML Files (see Figure 23.21).

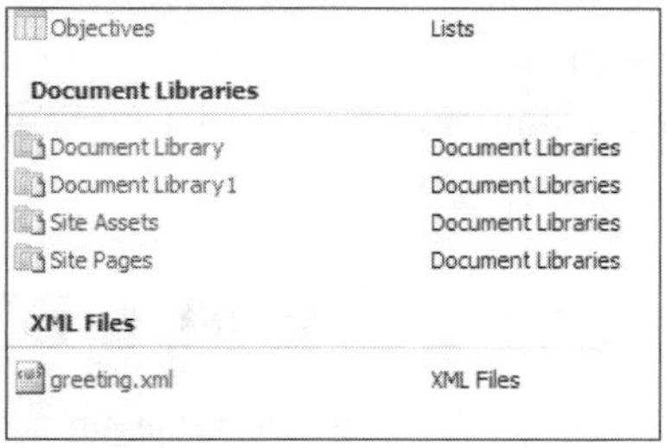

FIGURE 23.21
The revised Data
Sources page

Using the New Data Sources

Most of this section is a repeat of the "Creating a DVWP from a List on the Same Site" section. Follow the steps there in general but select one of the free zones in the center of the page until Figure 23.15 displays. Then do the following:

1. Click More Data Sources and you'll get the screen in Figure 23.22.

   Probably greeting.xml was visible in the previous screen too (just), but we've already had an image of that.

2. Click greeting.xml to select it.

3. Click OK.

4. Click File > Save to save the newest version of the page.

5. Open the page in your browser to see what it looks like. It's a heading, which can be removed by modifying the web part of greeting.xml, and a text of greeting: Hello World! (Not fantastic, but then this isn't an XML book either.)

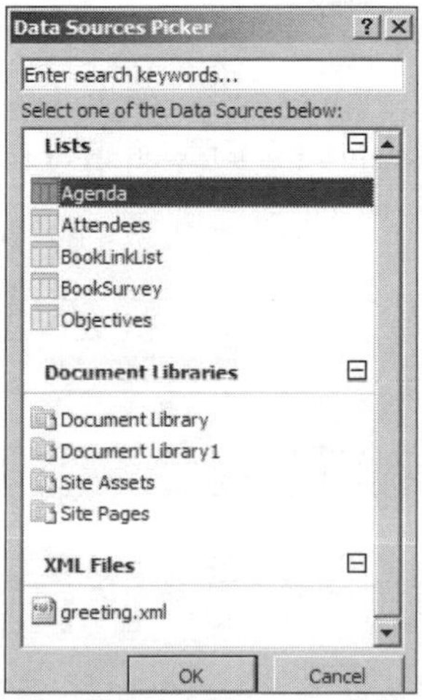

FIGURE 23.22
The More Data
Sources page

Now that we've added two completely different kinds of data view web parts, it is time for the final section of this hour, which looks briefly at the formatting and other options that a Data View Web Part (the list we added in the first section of this hour) enables us to apply to the List and so on we added as a DVWP.

Customizing the Look of a DVWP

The idea is just to indicate what options are available and to apply a couple of them.

Did you Know?

> The customization process is not as easy as it might be. Follow the steps that fol-
> low to do the customization I do there, but be prepared for considerable trial and
> error when doing anything else.

Follow these steps to customize the look:

1. Open in SPD 2010 the Page for Custom Web Parts.aspx in Edit mode.

2. Select the BookLinkList section of the page (see Figure 23.23).

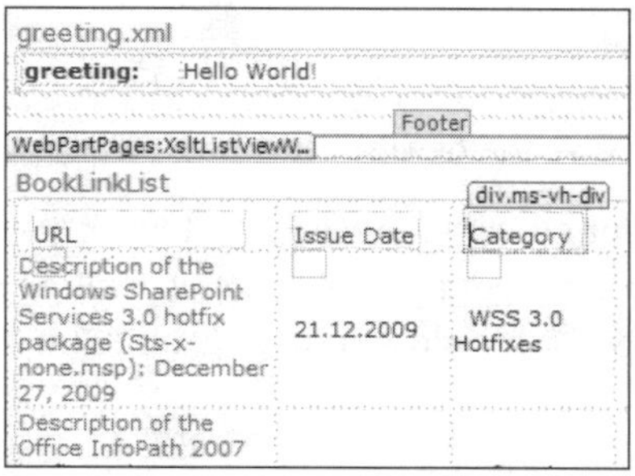

FIGURE 23.23
Selecting Book-
LinkList DVWP

I made the image slightly longer, so you can see greeting.xml on the page as well. Figure 23.24 shows what the left section of the ribbon looks like when BookLinkList has been selected.

FIGURE 23.24
The ribbon when
a DVWP has
been selected

3. Click Sort & Group in the ribbon.

4. Make the changes (add Category and Sort and Group by it) that are shown in Figure 23.25.

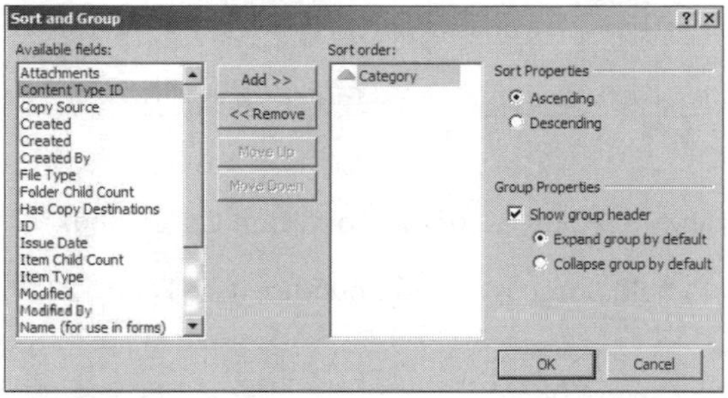

FIGURE 23.25
Sort and Group customization

5. Click OK. The DataView is updated, and you see that the DVWP is now grouped and the first group is Alerts. That screenshot will appear, but first let's use Conditional Formatting from the same ribbon (see Figure 23.24).

6. Click Conditional Formatting in the ribbon. The only valid option is Show Taskpane.

7. Click Show Taskpane.

Figure 23.26 shows a Conditional Formatting panel on the right where nothing is operable.

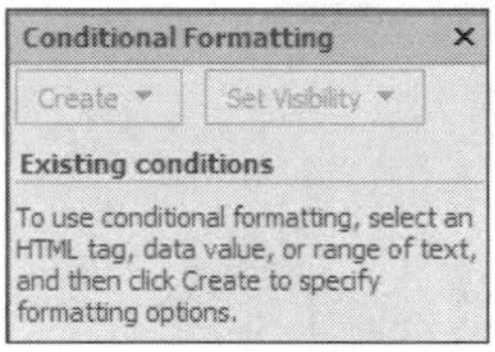

FIGURE 23.26
A Conditional Formatting pane with no valid options

8. Do what it says, which means click the Category column in the main section of the page. Click the word Category. Now Create is selectable in the Conditional Formatting pane.

9. Click Create.

10. Click Apply Formatting in the drop-down.

11. Complete the Condition Criteria box, as shown in Figure 23.27.

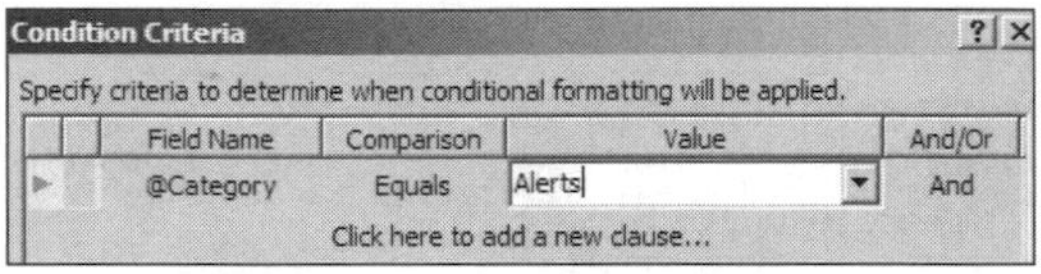

FIGURE 23.27
The Condition
Criteria box

		Field Name	Comparison	Value	And/Or
►		@Category	Equals	Alerts	And

Condition Criteria ? ✕

Specify criteria to determine when conditional formatting will be applied.

Click here to add a new clause...

12. Click Set Style (at the bottom of the Condition Criteria box).

13. Set the Font to bold, large red, and underline (see Figure 23.28).

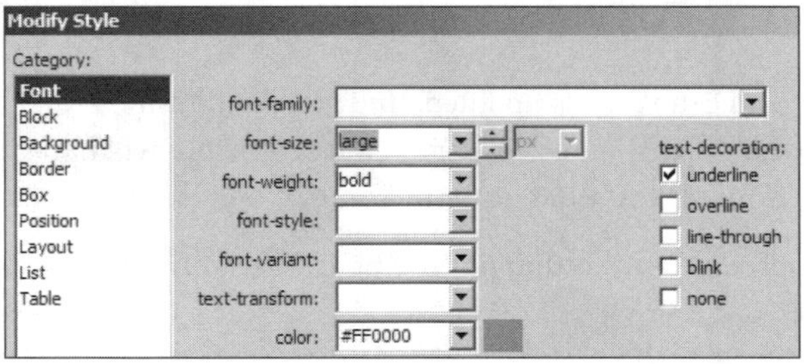

FIGURE 23.28
Setting the Style
(Font)

Modify Style

Category:

Font
Block
Background
Border
Box
Position
Layout
List
Table

font-family:
font-size: large
font-weight: bold
font-style:
font-variant:
text-transform:
color: #FF0000

text-decoration:
☑ underline
☐ overline
☐ line-through
☐ blink
☐ none

14. Click OK; you see Figure 23.29. Note the large font, bold, and the underline. You'll have to assume the color.

FIGURE 23.29
The customized
BookLinkList

WebPartPages:XsltListViewW...

BookLinkList

URL	Issue Date	Category
⊟ Category : **Alerts** (1)		
Users who have read permission do not receive alerts for drafts or for minor version documents when the Content Approval option is enabled in a Windows SharePoint Services 3.0 site	20.11.2009	**Alerts**
⊟ Category : **Configuration Wizard** (1)		
SharePoint Products and Technologies Configuration Wizard may fail to complete with error "Exception: Microsoft.SharePoint.SPExeption...	9.11.2009	Configuration Wizard

15. Complete by selecting File Save.

Again check the page in the browser.

Summary

In this hour, we added content to a site from other sites, the present site, or other locations using SPD 2010. The hour also briefly looked at customizing a DVWP.

There is an alternative to the use of the ribbon for customizing a DVWP. There are extra credits for right-clicking something in the DVWP and customizing that way.

Note too that if all you want to do is the make a column head bold (or underline), select it, as shown in Figure 23.29, and press Ctrl-B (or Ctrl-U).

Q&A

Q. *Can I use a web part connection between a standard web part and a Data View web part?*

A. Yes, provided they have a suitable matching field. You can also use the web part connection technique between two different Data View web parts based on Lists (see the first section of this hour).

Workshop

Quiz

1. Are you restricted to creating DVWPs from lists and libraries?

2. Can I customize a Data view solely by means of selection boxes?

3. Should SPD 2010 be installed on a client machine or on the server?

Answers

1. It is easier to create DVWPs from Lists or Libraries than creating them from most other things (provided the lists or libraries are in the same site). However, there are many other sources of information for DVWPs, such as databases (where it's best if these are SQL Server databases), which often are more powerful implementations and something you can't easily obtain any other way.

2. Yes, but some customization will require code.

3. In production you should install SPD 2010 on a client machine. (As stated in Hour 22, "Using SharePoint Designer 2010 to Create Workflows," if you also

maintain WSS 3.0 or MOSS 2007 sites, you should install SPD 2007 in a different client). In testing, it is sometimes useful to install SPD 2010 on the server. Testing is often done in virtual machines that have less memory and are generally slower than production servers; because SPD 2010 is not always quick to open pages, you may have annoying timeouts if using SPD 2010 on your (testing) host machine.

3. This hour was entirely written using SPD 2010 installed on the server; the previous two hours were written using a copy of SPD 2010 installed on a (Windows 7) client.

PART V

Other Available Functions and Methods

Learning to Add Even More Functionality to Your SPF 2010 System

---

What You'll Learn in This Hour

▶ How to add foreign language sites

▶ Functions that were not covered earlier

▶ Other ways of adding functionality to your SPF 2010 sites

▶ Book references that can help you go even deeper into some of those functions

This hour is somewhat different to those preceding it because apart from the first section, which is a normal learning section about how to add foreign language sites, it is not so much a learning hour as an hour that has many short sections describing functions not covered in the book and suggesting (in many cases) books that go into more detail on a particular function than a general book like this can ever hope to do.

Hour 24 is a ready-made where-do-I-go-from-here? guide. I hope you find it more useful than my spending the space in this hour on a greatly extended version of the "Adding Foreign Languages" section with one other function as filler.

Adding Foreign Languages

These days, companies work internationally. For this reason, Microsoft provides the possibility of having information and menu items in several languages. If you've ever seen a Microsoft presentation that includes languages, you've probably seen a web page that is full of useful information and where there are two or more little flag icons in the upper-right part of the page. For example, the Microsoft presenters show that when you click the German flag, a German translation of the same page appears.

This kind of functionality uses variations, which do not come with SPF 2010. It works only if the site template chosen is a Publishing template, and that is only available in SPS 2010.

That "translated" page is not translated by magic, just by clicking an icon. Instead, the variation includes the (translated by someone) German-language version of the content. SPS 2010 supplies only the menus and other things around the content (the basic interface) and these are the only things which are automatically created in German.

SPF 2010 offers completely different sites, where everything is in a different language. (SPS 2010 offers this function, too.) For example, with SPF 2010, you get the kind of German language site that you would get if you installed the German version of SPF 2010. The difference is that this German site occurs within an otherwise normal English-language installation.

This is a revised and severely cut-down (overview only) version of what I wrote in my WSS 3.0 book in the same series (*Sams Teach Yourself SharePoint 2007: Using Windows SharePoint Services 3.0*). If you want to see a more detailed list of installation steps together with images at almost every step, try to get a copy of that book. You'll need to look at Hour 23, "Enhancing Your WSS 3.0 Sites: Microsoft Official Possibilities."

Installing and Using Language Packs

Microsoft provides language packs (different ones for SPF 2010 and 2010 Office Servers (SPS 2010; Project Server 2010, or Search Server 2010 Express). If you have SPS 2010, you need to install both as free downloads. You do not need to install a language pack in the language of your SPF 2010 version. So if you are installing the French version of SPF 2010, you do not also install the French version of the SPF 2010 Language Pack. (Depending on your needs, you may however want to install the English Language Pack in that case).

The address for the SPF 2010 Language Pack is http://www.microsoft.com/downloads/details.aspx?displaylang=en&FamilyID=09567 87e-210d-4d78-9e4e-a9cdef0e8495.

The address for the Server Language Packs for various Office 2010 Server products is http://www.microsoft.com/downloads/details.aspx?displaylang=en&FamilyID=a0c7c 05d-8fca-4391-bc70-b62c9af91123.

If those URLs no longer work, go to the Microsoft Downloads site (http://www.microsoft.com/downloads) and search in that site for SharePoint 2010 Language Pack, and links to both of the preceding downloads will be listed.

There is a single SPF 2010 Language Pack download location for each IE locale, and that single location is the gateway to the individual downloads for each available language.

These downloads are then listed as separate downloads at the end of the page, each with its own Download button. You can see only the filename, but it shouldn't be too difficult to spot that "de" is the German one, and "fr" the French one, and so on. The English one ("us") is listed, too. This is to cover the situation in which you are running, for example, a Spanish ("es") version of SPF 2010 (and want to install the English language pack) but are using IE set to English.

You can install as many language packs as you like. Doing that gives you the option of creating sites in several languages (one at a time!). But only do it if you really intend to create a site in that language—it is not good practice to install these things just in case.

When the installation of the language pack (LP) is done, you must run the SharePoint Configuration Wizard. If however you are installing an LP Service Pack as well, you can wait until that too is installed before running the SharePoint Configuration Wizard.

What effect does the installation of a Language Pack have on your SPF 2010 installation? At first sight, it has absolutely no effect. Everything looks just the same as it had. You see the change only when you create a site.

The final stage of the installation following the use of the wizard opens "the site" in the browser. If you have already installed Search Server 2010 Express on top of SPF 2010 before installing the Language Packs, this opens the default page of the Search Site.

By the Way

Assuming you have already downloaded a Language Pack, installed it, and run the wizard, we can create a site and see what has changed:

(Open a new tab if necessary.) Go to http://spf1 in the browser and select Site Actions > New Sites. Fill in the name of the site and the URL and then be sure to scroll down the page.

Figure 24.1 is a combination of what you see there if English is selected (left-half of the image) or if German is selected (right-half of the image). This is an English

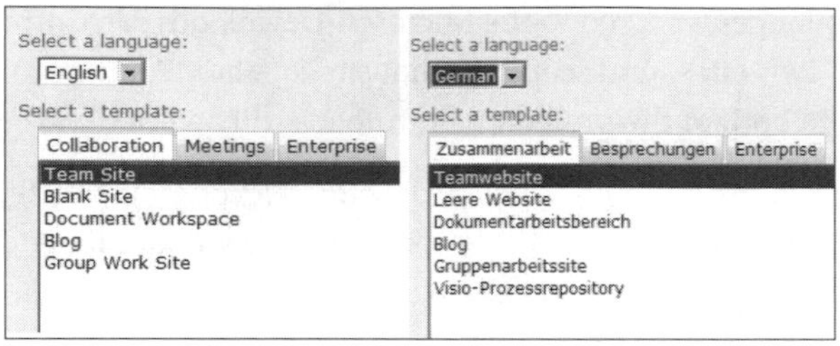

FIGURE 24.1
Comparing the English and German site options

installation of SPF 2010, so the languages in the drop-down are English (as are the fixed texts), but as you see when you select German, the options are in German.

The first five items in both options are the same and are in the same location in the list, so even if the Administrator doesn't know German, she can still find the correct kind of site to create.

The final item in the German list is something that is only available in the server SharePoint 2010 products. Whereas the English site options were created before Search Server 2010 Express was added, the German site options were created after Search Server 2010 Express was added. (It's confusing, but Search Server 2010 Express is regarded as a SharePoint Server product.)

The site that is then created is identical to an English language Team Site. Identical, that is, apart from the language used throughout the page.

Figure 24.2 displays a small extract of the default page in the German language site.

FIGURE 24.2
A small section of the German site page

Finally, as previously mentioned, you can have more than one Language Pack. In that case there are more items in the drop-down, that's all.

A Note on Application Templates

Application Templates were ready-made templates that Microsoft made available for free download to show off what you can do with SharePoint. They were not supported by Microsoft, which led to a certain amount of irritation from those users who had (incorrectly—that wasn't the idea of them) decided to install them and use them in production.

Don't make the quite common mistake of thinking that if you create both a Spanish and a German site that the Spanish site will contain the same data as the German site. All the sites, English and non-English of whatever type, are completely independent of one another. Anything added to a site is therefore added only to that site and not to another site that you have, for instance, created as a German language parallel site.

Watch
Out!

At the time of writing, these are not available for the 2010 SharePoint products, but it is expected that some 41 such Application Templates will be made available for SPF 2010 at the release of the software or shortly after. If Microsoft makes Application Templates available, it is likely that they will be in the English language. This is one reason for installing the English language version of the Language Pack because English Application Templates only work in a non-English SPF 2010 installation if the English language pack has been installed.

To see if there are any Application Templates available when you read this book, search at http://www.microsoft.com/downloads, and make sure that the items you find are for 2010 SharePoint. Hopefully, installing them is easier than the last time, but make sure that you look for installation instructions before installing the first one. Remember that if they are available, they are only intended as a source of ideas for your own sites. They are not finished and supported products suitable for production.

Third-Party Web Parts and Utilities

Another way of improving your sites is to use ready-made web parts or utilities. Web parts come mainly from commercial companies, and prices vary considerably but often are in the $100 to $500 range. No matter what the price, if you want the function offered, it is usually much cheaper than writing code and developing the functionality yourself.

Web parts are available from specialist web part maker companies such as Bamboo Solutions (www.store.bamboosolutions.com) and KWizCom (www.kwizcom.com); from SharePoint consultancy companies where they are a sideline and also from private developers who typically provide them free via a side like Codeplex (www.codeplex.com).

Utilities usually come from third-party developers via Codeplex rather than from commercial companies. Typically (and this is a general statement, so treat it as such) web parts from the specialist companies come with professional-level installation routines; web parts from consultancy companies do their jobs well and are cheaper but require a certain amount of manual effort to install; and web parts from sources such as Codeplex (free) often require a considerable amount of manual effort to install, and possibly installation instructions are incomplete and sometimes require breaking normal security requirements before you can install. In other words you pay for what you get.

There's a similar different level of support with the specialist companies in some cases providing support forums (as do Bamboo Solutions for instance) and certainly email support for registered, paid-up users, whereas at the opposite extreme there is sometimes no support at all available for free Codeplex web parts. (A requirement of Codeplex is that code is supplied for every solution, and so people with programming skills can go to the code to see the reasons for their problems or even to use the code as a base for their own solutions, which however they can't then sell.)

> Another available option is to upgrade from SPF 2010 to SPS 2010. This offers a lot of extra functionality but does mean considerable additional costs for the product and for user CALs (and for Internet connection if that is an issue). The CALs cost twice as much if Enterprise edition is used, so be careful that the functions you want are all contained in the version of SPS 2010 (Standard or Enterprise) that you choose.
>
> This option is really something that should only be considered if you require a lot of extra functionality that is in SPS 2010. Upgrading to SPS 2010 just to provide one extra function is usually not cost-effective. (There is a very brief look at some additions that come with SPS 2010 toward the end of this hour.)

> This section has been written to make you aware of the alternatives and the plusses and minuses of each of the main types of solutions.

If you are asked to provide additional functionality in your SharePoint sites, first look to see if there already is a function supplied with the product that could be used; then consider whether you can amend the standard functionality using SharePoint Designer 2010; and then look for web parts—and only finally start programming the function yourself. Far too often SharePoint user companies pay a lot of money for either in-house or external (new) programming development when the request could have been satisfied by using included functionality, by amending included functionality, or by inserting a ready-made web part.

Content Types

The previous section said that you should look to see if there was a solution already available in the product that you could use. In a book like this it's impossible to cover everything that comes in the box, so I've been forced to concentrate on what I see as the most essential.

In the early hours, we often worked with Lists and Document Libraries and needed to add a new field/column, for instance. There I described how to create a new column/field of a particular type and how (in the case of the Company field) to make it a field of the Choice type and how to add the possible values HP, IBM, MS, and Oracle to it. That field was then present only in the list in which I created it, and if I wanted a Company field in another List, I would need to create it again there (and also respecify those possible company names). If I later added a Company name, I'd need to add it to the Company fields in both Lists.

Creating a field/column in this way is a simple and universal method, which is why I use it in those hours. The use of the same field in different Lists is one of the (simpler) problems that Content Types can help you with. When you add a field to a List you could instead use a Content Type. (This choice is clearest when using SPD 2010 to add something to a list because you are offered both normal fields and content types in the drop-down.)

Content Types are ready-made fields with a prespecified name and type. (If there were one for Company, its name would be Company[Choice].) There is also a structure of content types with some content types at the highest level of the structure and others lower down in prespecified subgroups. Inheritance occurs between the levels to add another complication—another complication being that you can create your own.

In the simplest of cases, which is my Company example, you would say to yourself, "I'll look to see if there is a content type I can use," and look through the predefined names and types. Suppose you find a suitable one at the top-level of the structure; you could populate it with those names (HP, IBM, and such), and the effect of using it in the (first) List would be the same as using a normal field/column. However, when you needed to add the same data to the second (and third and so on.) List, you would use that content type again, and now the "field" would be prepopulated with HP, IBM, and such. And if you later add, for example, Citrix to the list of companies in that content type, you need to add it only once because all the Lists using that content type will pick up the change.

Content type usage can, however, be complicated—much more so than the previous example—which is why I didn't cover it in the earlier hours and am here only giving you a short introduction to it.

Instead, I recommend that if you want to use content types, you do so only when you are fully aware of all the possibilities (and dangers) of using them; therefore, I recommend that you look at a book that is about content types and nothing else.

That book is at the moment of writing only available in a version written for the v3 versions of SharePoint, but nothing important has changed in the meantime as far as content types are concerned, so it is still the best way to gain in-depth knowledge of content types and through that to utilize them correctly and fully.

The book is *Using Content Types in SharePoint 2007*, and the Amazon U.S. URL for it is http://www.amazon.com/exec/obidos/ASIN/1584506695/heme0f. Make sure you check to see if there isn't an equivalently named SharePoint 2010 book out before buying it! An interesting thing about this book is that its main focus after the initial hours is on using content types as a way of redesigning your site through the added functionality provided by content types. Another aspect of redesigning sites is covered in the next section here.

Branding Your Site

One of the problems with using a SharePoint site just as it comes out of the box is that it always looks like a SharePoint site (and thus like thousands of other sites) in its basic appearance. Doing simple things such as changing the theme used by the site does little to disguise that fact.

Many Internet sites from lots of companies look nothing like SharePoint sites but did start out as SharePoint sites. However, the look of the site was then drastically changed with a branding process. This is often done using SharePoint Designer 2010. Even though this book has three hours about using SharePoint Designer 2010, I kept well away from using that product to change the look of the site, concentrating instead on using SPD 2010 to create workflows and to add content to a site.

One of the reasons was that amending the look of a site can have consequences far beyond what a casual user of SPD 2010 might be aware of. Making certain changes to a master page, for instance, could mean that inheritance (where that master page is used as a basis for other sites for instance) can vanish, whereas other changes will mean that those sites that inherit the master page look will also automatically be affected by the change.

In other words, it was for me a question of either spending several hours on making sure that I provided enough information to make sure that nothing went disastrously wrong for you or writing this section in this hour.

To make sure that you make no terrible errors when changing the look of your sites, look for a specialist SharePoint Designer 2010 book. There are several, so look for one at the level at which you want to work. If however you want to create a site that looks nothing like a SharePoint site, go for the one specialist Branding book, *Professional SharePoint 2010 Branding and User Interface Design*, available at http://www.amazon.com/exec/obidos/tg/detail/-/0470584645/heme0f.

The majority of the writers of that 2010 volume were also involved in an equivalent 2007 book that was very good in parts but was only really good for dipping into because it lacked a really sensible chapter order. Despite continuing to have several authors, it seems from what I have been told that lessons have been learned from comments (including mine!) on that previous book, and so the 2010 version builds up knowledge in a much more ordered fashion with hours about the basics, making basic changes, making more advanced changes, and so on and thus more than justifies a recommendation here. The book covers changes to a site using the browser, but most of it is about using SPD 2010 to brand sites.

> If the 2010 book isn't released when you are reading this hour, the 2007 version will still be available at http://www.amazon.com/exec/obidos/ASIN/ 047028580X/heme0f.

Did you Know?

Reports Using Reporting Services

In the hours on using SPF 2010 with Office 2010 (and 2007/2003) products in this book, there are a couple of sections on creating reports on SharePoint Lists using Access 2010. That is a perfectly good method of creating reports and is perfect for reports that are regularly created by an administrator (or a user with suitable access rights).

Often, however, there is a demand within a company for reports-on-demand where any user in the network can go online, specify certain parameters to be applied to a report, and receive to his PC just that specific report. This kind of problem is usually solved by the use of Reporting Services. This is included in the commercial versions of SQL Server so most large- and medium-sized companies have the product available to them at no extra cost.

Setting up this product to work with SharePoint products is supported, but installation is rather complicated so that if you intend to look further at this kind of report generation, I suggest that you look for a specialist book that deals not just with SQL Server Reporting Services (there are many such books for different versions of SQL Server), but with the combination of SQL Server Reporting Services with SharePoint.

The one book at the moment that matches that requirement is *Professional Microsoft SharePoint 2007 Reporting with SQL Server 2008 Reporting Services*. As you can see, its for SharePoint 2007; however, it does use (only) SQL Server 2008 Reporting Services, which is likely to be the version of Reporting services that you will be using with SPF 2010 (and SPS 2010). You can find that book at http://www.amazon.com/exec/ obidos/tg/detail/-/0470481897/heme0f, but do look at my page with SharePoint 2010 books at http://wssv4faq.mindsharp.com/Lists/v4FAQ/V%20Books.aspx to see if they have brought out a version of it for SharePoint 2010 by the time you read this hour.

SharePoint Backup and Restore

SharePoint systems have always offered a vast array of different options for backup and restore using the product itself (various methods); using SharePoint Designer (various methods); using database software (to back up only the database); and techniques such as full-disk backup using third-party software. Some of these methods did backups of everything; some a site plus its subsites, and some just a single site.

It is also possible to use Save List as Template and Save Site as Template to do quick manual ad-hoc copies of Lists and Sites even if those techniques were designed to create models that could be reused elsewhere.

Although I had an hour on Backup and Restore in my equivalent WSS 3.0 book, I was never happy with it because I was aware that it covered only some of the options available. I also was fully aware that in my test installations for that book I used none of those techniques but made regular snapshots of the Virtual Machine in which I was running WSS 3.0 and also regularly copied the entire set of virtual machine files (including those snapshots) to offline locations (USB hard disks to be exact). As for the WSS FAQ sites that were run at hosting companies, I didn't have enough rights there to make use of backup techniques so, apart from relying to a certain extent on the hosts not to lose anything, I made irregular copies of my lists (typically after adding a lot of content) with Save List as Template.

As long as you are testing SPF 2010 to follow this book (and using your own installation of SPF 2010), those are the techniques I would recommend for you, too. Hopefully you are running in a VM because snapshots are a marvelous way of ensuring that you can go back to a particular point in time when things are messed up; however, even snapshots are lost if the disk crashes, so the occasional offline copies of the VMs can be useful, too.

But there are some of you reading this book who are about to be or already are administrators, and if not working in a large company (with dedicated backup staff), you are likely to be responsible for doing backups, too. For you I suggest reading the only book (there are two versions: one for 2007 that I have here on my bookshelf while I'm writing this, and one for 2010 that I hope is out by the time you need it) that concentrates entirely on the various alternatives that you have for SharePoint systems for doing backups so as not to lose content.

The title of the 2010 edition is rather scary: *SharePoint 2010 Disaster Recovery Guide* (I think "disaster recovery" is a bit excessive). Here's a link to it at Amazon U.S. at http://www.amazon.com/exec/obidos/tg/detail/-/1435456459/heme0f. If it is still—against expectation—not published by the time you read this, look at Amazon for a similarly named book for SharePoint 2007 from the same authors. Either book is well worth reading because they are the only books that do credit to the vast array of options you have when protecting your SharePoint sites from data loss (or "disaster").

Making Use of Visual Studio 2010

One of the mysteries for me is that companies buy SPS 2010 rather than use SPF 2010, which costs virtually nothing, and then demand that their programmers create new customer interfaces and new functionality.

Only a limited number of functions are available to programmers with SPS 2010 systems that are not available to programmers with SPF 2010 systems. So the use of Visual Studio 2010 together with SPF 2010 is a perfectly valid option that however often falls to the argument that "as SPF 2010 costs nothing, why should I pay (you) a lot of money to add functions to it?"

My theory is that this argument is the reason why all software houses that develop software for their customers' needs always say that SPS 2010 (and earlier, MOSS 2007) is a requirement. They are well aware that, having paid a lot of money for SPS 2010 licenses, the additional charges of the software house will seem (relatively) small and justified by the additional functionality.

So there *is* justification for the use of Visual Studio 2010 with SPF 2010 if you want to program additional functionality. It's not in this book because programming for SharePoint requires existing (modern) programming skills that most of the readers of this book will not possess. They are also something that I don't possess either, so having me as a guide would be rather "amusing" because modern programming requires a knowledge of what ready-made code sections are available and how to best incorporate them. And the programming job I had in the far distant past was writing assembly code for mainframes (which is more than a bit different).

If, however, you (the nonprogrammers) do have a copy of Visual Studio 2010 that you can use, do have a look at creating a workflow with it. They are supposed to be much more powerful than workflows created in SPD 2010, are straightforward to do compared to writing new functionality in code, and might well be worth checking out. Otherwise (and even for skilled programmers without SharePoint knowledge even after they have read this book to know what SharePoint is), I suggest another book. I don't often recommend Microsoft Press books, but the two SharePoint 2007 developer books that were included in most peoples' recommended list for the 2007 release of SharePoint were the two Inside books (Inside MOSS 2007 and Inside WSS 3.0).

Because the author of *Inside MOSS 2007* is regrettably no longer with us, it's an obvious suggestion to look for the SPF 2010 version of the *Inside WSS 3.0* book. It's listed here at http://www.amazon.com/exec/obidos/tg/detail/-/0735627460/heme0f. The book that has the best title by far is *SharePoint Development with Visual Studio 2010*, but it seems as if all three authors work for Microsoft, which tends in my experience to lead to books that avoid pointing out things that don't work as they should. So perhaps you should just look at the books I have listed in Group C (Development) at http://wssv4faq.mindsharp.com/Lists/v4FAQ/V%20Books.aspx and make your own choice (as indeed you always should—I can only give suggestions).

Upgrade to SPS 2010?

So you've tried doing all you can with the built-in and bought-in web parts; you've done all you can with SPD 2010; and your couple of attempts to write programs didn't make you keen to write any more—and you (or maybe more important your bosses) aren't satisfied. What's left?

At this point it's worth looking, perhaps more seriously than before, at the additional functionality offered by SPS 2010 compared with SPF 2010 (and compared with getting a software house to write it for you). Upgrading (and you can do this in-site) to SPS 2010 means that suddenly a lot of additional functionality is available to you that SPF 2010 doesn't have.

Here are just a few of those functions, and remember to be careful when making the kind of price/performance studies you make when considering buying packaged software because most of the things listed here require the Enterprise license that will double your incremental costs:

▶ **Business Data Catalog (BDC)**—Procedures to connect to enterprise systems. A certain support for BDC is available in SPF 2010, but for full support you need SPS 2010.

▶ **Excel Services**—Run large Excel spreadsheets and use them throughout the Enterprise.

▶ **Forms Services**—InfoPath 2010 forms can be used, and users don't require InfoPath 2010 on their client systems.

▶ **Visio Services**—Visio diagrams are visible to users who don't have Visio, and this browser version is automatically updated when changes are made to the original. (Microsoft loves demoing this—usually without mentioning that you need Enterprise edition.)

▶ **People Search**—Adding Search Server 2010 Express to a SPF 2010 installation adds SPS 2010-level search but doesn't include People Search.

▶ **MySite**—Personal and private individual sites for all users; access via Share-Point to your own Outlook.

The preceding are just "tasters" to give you an idea of the kinds of extra functionality available. One thing you will have noticed is that none of these introduce a completely different customer interface, which seems to be a common request in enterprises and one that often could actually be achieved without programming (by branding operations). One the other hand, especially the Enterprise (version of SPS 2010) functions in that list (the first four) are likely to be difficult and costly to achieve through add-on programming.

For books that include information on all the functionality in SPS 2010, look for the ca. 1,000-page monsters that I list in my site. One such is *Microsoft SharePoint 2010 Unleashed*. The Amazon U.S. URL is http://www.amazon.com/exec/obidos/tg/detail/-/0672333252/heme0f.

Summary

This hour discussed several ways of adding functionality to standard SPF 2010 sites. Adding foreign language sites was a working session, but the remaining sections were discussion sections that each introduced a single way of adding functionality and often suggested further reading.

Q&A

Q. *Which is better, a German language installation with an English language pack or an English installation with a German language pack?*

A. If you install the English version of SPF 2010, you are installing the version of the code that is used worldwide by the most people by far. In addition, your administration site will be in English, which means that all error messages will be in English.

If you install the German version of SPF 2010, you install a version that has nowhere near the numbers of the English version. Your administration site will be in German, so all the error messages will be in German.

If you have an error message you don't understand, search Google (or Bing) for it. If you do, you're likely to find more hits that match your search if the sentence you search for is in English than in German (and your own translation of the German text won't often be Microsoft's).

The same applies to posting questions about error messages in the SharePoint forums (http://social.technet.microsoft.com/Forums/en-US/category/sharepoint2010 is the address for the English language forums). If you post a question on an error message to an English language forum, you need to provide a translation for it, which will be probably slightly different to the English version of the error message. If you post to a German language forum, the number of eyes reading your (now 100% correct) message will be a fraction of those reading posts in the English language forum.

There are also more books in English than in German, and those books naturally always have screenshots in English.

My recommendation is therefore in such a case is to install the English language version of the software and to use language packs for the sites. However, you may well find no understanding among your bosses for that recommendation.

Workshop

Quiz

1. Are SPF 2010 foreign language sites translated copies of the English language sites?

2. What is the quickest way of taking security copies of your *test* site?

Answers

1. Yes and No. The sites are translated copies of the English language site. The content of the foreign language sites is completely independent of the content of any other site. The content will only be a translation of the content text in an English language site if efforts were made to make it so (such as by translating a document and posting the English original to a document library in the English language site and the German translation to a document library in the German language site).

2. If you are running in a Virtual Machine system, use that VM system's snapshot functionality. (If it doesn't have snapshot functionality, pay for one that does such as VM Workstation.) Remember, though, that snapshots are stored in the same location as the SPF 2010 installation, so make additional copies of the VM (including those snapshots) to an offline storage location at regular intervals.

Index

G

H

Sams **Teach Yourself**

When you only have time
for the answers

Whatever your need and whatever your time frame, there's a Sams **Teach Yourself** book for you. With a Sams **Teach Yourself** book as your guide, you can quickly get up to speed on just about any new product or technology—in the absolute shortest period of time possible. Guaranteed.

Learning how to do new things with your computer shouldn't be tedious or time-consuming. Sams **Teach Yourself** makes learning anything quick, easy, and even a little bit fun.

Visual Basic 2010 in 24 Hours

James Foxall
ISBN-13: 9780672331138

ASP.NET 4 in 24 Hours
Scott Mitchell
ISBN-13: 9780672333057

ADO.NET Entity Framework in 24 Hours
Paul Kimmel
ISBN-13: 9780672330537

Visual C# 2010 in 24 Hours
Scott Dorman
ISBN-13: 9780672331015

Windows Workflow Foundation in 24 Hours
Robert Eisenberg
ISBN-13: 9780321486998

24 Proven One-hour Lessons

Teach Yourself
SharePoint
Foundation
2010
in 24 Hours

SAMS

FREE Online
Edition

Your purchase of **Sams Teach Yourself SharePoint® Foundation 2010 in 24 Hours**
includes access to a free online edition for 45 days through the Safari Books Online
subscription service. Nearly every Sams book is available online through Safari Books
Online, along with more than 5,000 other technical books and videos from publishers
such as Addison-Wesley Professional, Cisco Press, Exam Cram, IBM Press, O'Reilly,
Prentice Hall, and Que.

SAFARI BOOKS ONLINE allows you to search for a specific answer, cut and paste
code, download chapters, and stay current with emerging technologies.

Activate your FREE Online Edition at
www.informit.com/safarifree

> **STEP 1:** Enter the coupon code: HNNNZBI.

> **STEP 2:** New Safari users, complete the brief registration form.
> Safari subscribers, just log in.

If you have difficulty registering on Safari or accessing the online edition,
please e-mail customer-service@safaribooksonline.com

Safari
Books Online